Francis Jacox

Aspects of Authorship

or book marks and book makers

Francis Jacox

Aspects of Authorship
or book marks and book makers

ISBN/EAN: 9783741191497

Manufactured in Europe, USA, Canada, Australia, Japa

Cover: Foto ©Andreas Hilbeck / pixelio.de

Manufactured and distributed by brebook publishing software (www.brebook.com)

Francis Jacox

Aspects of Authorship

ASPECTS OF AUTHORSHIP;

OR,

BOOK MARKS AND BOOK MAKERS.

Aspects of Authorship:

OR,

BOOK MARKS AND BOOK MAKERS.

By FRANCIS JACOX,

AUTHOR OF "CUES FROM ALL QUARTERS," "SECULAR ANNOTATIONS ON SCRIPTURE TEXTS," "BIBLE MUSIC," ETC.

> "All aspects of book work; its hack undertakers,
> Its heart-and-soul zealots; book marks and book makers;
> The trail of the bookworm; gold dust of gold pen,
> Common steel ware, quill-drift of quill-drivers,—what then?
> Books penn'd at a gallop, or easy jog-trot;
> Books devour'd at a meal by a reader red-hot;
> Books sold off to wrap cheese in, line trunks;—and what not?"
>
> NICIAS FOXCAR.

LONDON:
HODDER & STOUGHTON,
27, PATERNOSTER ROW, E.C.

MDCCCLXXII.

PREFACE.

ASSUMING actual purchasers of previous volumes from the same pen to be possible purchasers of the present one, and even of others yet to come, it may be due to them to say a word (which otherwise the writer, with a wholesome horror of Prefaces, would prefer to leave unsaid) on what may look like a rather too rapid rate of production.

The rate of production, however, has been anything but rapid, whatever that of publication may be. Were the volumes spread over the face of time which covers their manuscript growth, they would seem as few as far between. It is not the case of an original author inventing a new story or poem between each issue; but that of a book-maker who brings out at short intervals, and as it were in serial sections, instalments of completed work which has been the occupation of long years. In the present instance, an additional incentive to speed rather than delay, is the precarious state of the writer's health, of a kind to make him wishful to see through the press as much as he can of what is ready for it.

That his books, such as they are, find a sale, such as it is, he freely owns to be to him at once a surprise and a solace.

A surprise; because no one can well recognize more keenly the extent of their demerits in general, and the conspicuous absence in them of attractiveness for the " reading world " in particular. If any one thing more than another conciliates him towards them, it is what to censors from without is a ground of objection, that there is so little of his own in them.

A solace; because that state of health to which allusion has been made, and which enforces the exceptional (inexperience of constraint might write it exceptionable) life of a recluse, makes this mode of employment his only available resource. The plea is of course invalid, in the way of arresting judgment,

PREFACE. ix

or mitigating its sentence, on the part of those predisposed to condemn; but on his part it goes some way towards confirming him in an apparent vocation, and so far reconciling him to his lot. From the same cause, what he writes is signally deficient in that freshness and force of composition, and that breadth and depth of research, which a hale student, not confined for the most part to his own room, and limited altogether to his own bookshelves, might offer. As Goldsmith's sage connoisseur said the painter would have succeeded better had he taken more pains, so might this penman have done had he taken fewer pills. What pains he has taken, a charitable reader will perhaps give him credit for, simply on credit; the proof is hardly patent on these pages, unless it be to stamp him, in the old-fashioned phrase, a very " painful " writer.

Book-maker is the term that figures on the title-page, and, as distinguished from Author, it is by many, and often if not always rightly, considered of distinctively bad repute. Be that as it may, it is only too distinctively the designation of the present compiler. And he will merely add that his obligations to authorities are so many, that the shortest, if not the handsomest, way of expressing them, is to comprise in the avowal the entire list of literary names which pretty well make up the Index to this volume. In it the Proper Names of his creditors are properly named by a debtor of unlimited liability.

F. J.

CONTENTS.

	PAGE
PREFACE.	
I. AUTHORSHIP IN THE ACT	1
II. SELF-SEEN IN PRINT	2
III. SELF-HEARD IN SONG	40
IV. BOOKISH	51
V. BOOK MARKS: IN TALK	79
VI. BOOK MARKS: TRAIL OF THE BOOKWORM	84
VII. BOOK MARKS: MARGINAL AND MISCELLANEOUS	99
VIII. BOOK MARKS: LOCAL AND INCIDENTAL	115
IX. LITERARY SOCIETY	128
X. A HARD CRUST	160
XI. MEN OF LETTERS AND UNLETTERED WIVES	176
XII. LAPSES IN LAW	202
XIII. COMMERCIAL FAILURES	221
XIV. MERRY MASKS AND SAD FACES	235
XV. PANGS IN PRINT	244

CONTENTS.

		PAGE
XVI. READY WRITERS	. .	256
XVII. LABOR LIMÆ	. .	275
XVIII. BOOK-BUILT CASTLES IN THE AIR	. .	297
XIX. A RUN UPON A BOOK	. . . .	317
XX. ENTHRALLING BOOKS	. . .	334
XXI. UNREAD AND UNREADABLE	. . .	350
XXII. BOOKING A PLACE FOR ALL TIME	. .	368
XXIII. TRACES AND TOKENS OF TRUE FAME	. .	390
XXIV. TRANSPARENT AUTHORSHIP; OR, THE MAN BETOKENED BY THE BOOK	. . .	405
XXV. THE STYLE BESPEAKS THE MAN	. .	417
XXVI. PERSONALITY IN FICTION	. . .	428
XXVII. FICTION APPEALING TO FACTS	. . .	444
XXVIII. AUTHOR'S DEN	. .	452
XXIX. BOOK-SHELVES OF ALL DIMENSIONS	. .	459
XXX. GOOD-BYE TO ONE'S BOOKS	. .	480
INDEX	. .	487

ASPECTS OF AUTHORSHIP.

I.

Authorship in the Act.

FEW that are interested at all in the products of authorship can fail to be more or less interested in observing authorship in the act, the author at work. One likes to know that Virgil's habit was to pour forth a vast quantity of verses in the morning, which he reduced to a small number by continual elaboration and elimination. He polished and filed away at them, much after the manner, as he said himself, of a bear licking her cubs into shape. One likes to know of Erasmus, that he composed on horseback, as he pricked across the country, and committed his thoughts to paper as soon as he reached his next inn. In this way he composed his *Encomium Moriæ*, or Praise of Folly, in a journey from Italy to the land of the man to whose name that title bore punning and complimentary reference, his sterling friend and ally Sir Thomas More. It is something to know from Aubrey the manner in which Hobbes composed his "Leviathan":—he walked much, and mused as he walked, and he had in the head of his cane a pen and inkhorn, and he carried always a note-book in his pocket; and "as soon as a thought darted, he presently entered it into his book, or otherwise might have lost it. He had drawn the design of the book into chapters, etc., and he knew whereabouts it would come in." Hartley Coleridge somewhere expresses his entire conviction that it was Pope's general practice to set down in a book every line, half line, or lucky phrase that occurred to him, and either to find or make a place for them when and where he could.

As curious, if credible, a mode of composition as perhaps any on record, is that affirmed of Fuller— that he used to write the first words of every line near the margin down to the foot of the paper, and that then beginning again, he filled up the vacuities exactly, without spaces, interlineations, or contractions, and that he would so connect the ends and beginnings that the sense would appear as complete as if it had been written in a continued series, after the ordinary manner.

To Aubrey we owe this account of Prynne's method of study: "He wore a long quilt cap, which came two or three inches at least over his eyes, which served him as an umbrella to defend his eyes from the light. About every three hours his man was to bring him a roll and a pot of ale, to refocillate his wasted spirits; so he studied and drank and munched some bread; and this maintained him till night, and then he made a good supper." Refocillation is a favourite resource—whatever the word may be—with authors not a few. Addison, with his bottle of wine at each end of the long gallery at Holland House, —and Schiller, with his flask of old Rhenish, and his coffee laced with old Cognac, at three in the morning,—occur to the memory at once. Dr. Darwin wrote most of his works on scraps of paper with a pencil, as he travelled. But how did he travel? In a worn and battered "sulky," which had a skylight at top, with an awning to be drawn over it at pleasure; the front of the carriage being occupied by a receptacle for writing-paper and pencils, a knife, fork, and spoon; while on one side was a pile of books reaching from the floor to nearly the front window of the carriage; on the other, by Mrs. Schimmelpenninck's account, a hamper containing fruit and sweetmeats, cream and sugar,—to which the big, burly, keen-eyed, stammering doctor paid attention as. devoted as ever he bestowed on the pile of books.

Alexander Kisfaludy, foremost Hungarian poet of his time, wrote most of his "Himfy" on horseback, or in solitary walks; a poem, or collection of poems, that made an unprecedented sensation in Hungary, where, by the same token, Sandor Kisfaludy of that ilk became at once the Great Unknown.

Cujas, the object of Chateaubriand's special admiration, used to write lying flat on his breast, with his books spread about him.

Sir Henry Wotton is our authority for recording of Father Paul Sarpi that, when engaged in writing, his manner was to sit fenced with a castle of paper about his chair, and overhead; "for he was of our Lord of St. Albans' opinion that 'all air is predatory,' and especially hurtful when the spirits are most employed."

Rousseau tells us he never could compose pen in hand, seated at a table, and duly plied with paper and ink; it was in his *promenades*—the *promenades d'un solitaire*—amid rocks and woods; and at night, in bed, when he was lying awake, that he wrote in his brain, to use his own phrase ("j'écris dans mon cerveau"). Some of his periods he turned and re-turned half a dozen nights in bed, before he deemed them fit to be put down on paper. On moving to the Hermitage of Montmorency, he adopted the same plan as in Paris,—devoting, as always, his mornings to the penwork *de la copie*, and his afternoons to *la promenade*, blank paper book and pencil in hand; for, says he, "having never been able to write and think at my ease except in the open air, *sub dio*, I was not tempted to change my method, and I reckoned not a little on the Forest of Montmorency becoming—for it was close to my door—my *cabinet de travail.*" In another place he affirms his sheer incapacity for meditation, by day, except in the act of walking ; the moment he stopped walking, he stopped thinking too, for his head worked with, and only with, his feet. " De jour, je ne puis méditer qu'en marchant ; sitôt que je m'arrête, je ne pense plus, et ma tête ne va qu'avec mes pieds." *Solvitur ambulando*, whatever intellectual problem is solved by Jean Jacques. His strength was *not* to sit still.

His *Rêveries*, by the way, were written on scraps of paper, of all sorts and sizes, on covers of old letters, and on playing-cards—all covered with a small neat handwriting. He was as economical of *matériel* as was " paper-sparing Pope" himself. In some points Chateaubriand was intellectually, or rather sentimentally, related to Rousseau, but not in his way of using ink and paper. Chateaubriand sat at a table well supplied with methodically arranged heaps of paper, cut in sizes ; and as soon as a page was blotted over in the biggest of his big handwriting—according to M. de Marcellus, with almost as many drops of ink as words—he tossed it aside, without using pounce or blotting-paper, to blot and be blotted by its accumulating fellows. Now and then he got up from his work, to look out of window, or pace the room, as if in quest of new ideas. The chapter on hand finished, he collected all the scattered leaves, and revised them in due form,—more frequently adding to, than curtailing, their fair proportions; and paying very special attention to the punctuation of his sentences.

Johnson wrote almost all his Ramblers just as they were wanted for the press; he sent a certain portion of the copy of an essay, and wrote the remainder while the earlier part was printing. When it was wanted, and he had fairly sat down to it, he was sure, he said, it would be done. Goldsmith, in his farm-house lodgings on the Edgware Road, used to sit writing in very loose apparel,—sometimes wandering into the kitchen, without noticing any one, where he would stand musing with his back to the fire, and then hurry off again to his room, to jot down whatever thought might have struck him. It was off at a tangent with him; but then whatever he touched (*tetigit*) he adorned. Rough jottings down are seldom so smooth as his. Of Samuel Butler's miscellaneous fragments it has been remarked that they bring the author of " Hudibras" before us in the very moment of inspiration, and reveal to us the whole course and action of his poetical labour: we have in them the rough draft of his thoughts, afterwards either fitted into his great work, rejected, re-fashioned, or reserved for a future opportunity. "His custom of noting down images or ideas as they occurred to him, in the form in which they first presented themselves, is here exhibited in operation"—the same idea recurring in different shapes, expanded or condensed according to circumstances. Plotinus, among them of old time, is noted for his system—or habit rather, for there was not much system in it—of jotting down his thoughts at random, as they occurred to him.

Lessing's inherent mobility of intellect is said to have been typified in his manner of study. When in the act of composition he would walk up and down till his eye was caught by the title of some book. He would open it, his brother tells us, and be struck by some sentence which pleased him, and which he must copy out; in doing which, a train of thought would be suggested, and this must be immediately followed up,—though too often it was not.—Schiller's favourite abode during hours of composition was in the small house he built for himself, with a single chamber, on the top of an acclivity near Jena, commanding a beautiful prospect of the valley of the Saal, and the fir mountains of the neighbouring forest. On sitting down to his desk at night, says Döring, he was wont to keep some strong coffee, or wine-chocolate, but more frequently a flask of old Rhenish, or Champagne, standing by him: —often the neighbours would hear him earnestly declaiming in the silence of the night, and he might be seen walking swiftly to and fro in his chamber, then suddenly throwing himself down into his chair and writing,—drinking at intervals from the glass that stood near him. In winter he continued at his desk till four or even five o'clock in the morning; in summer, till towards three. The "pernicious expedient of stimulants" served only to waste the more speedily and surely, as Mr. Carlyle says, his already wasted fund of physical strength. In the Park at Weimar we have other glimpses of Schiller; frequently he was to be seen there wandering among the groves and remote avenues—for he loved solitary walks—with a note-book in his hand; now loitering slowly along, now moving rapidly on; "if any one appeared in sight, he would dart into another alley, that his dream might not be broken." In Joerden's Lexicon we read that whatever Schiller intended to write, he first composed in his head, before putting down a line of it on paper; and he used to call a work "ready" so soon as its existence in his spirit was complete: hence there were often reports current of his having finished such and such a work, when, in the common sense, it was not even begun. Jean Paul Richter's was a healthier organization; the early morning would lure him to take out his ink-flask, and write as he walked in the fragrant air. Such compositions as his Dream of a Madman he would set about by first seating himself at the harpsichord, and "fantasying" for a while at it, till the ideas, or "imaginings," came,—which presently they would do with a rush.

Well may the sprightly penman of Rhymes on the Road exclaim,

> "What various attitudes, and ways,
>   And tricks, we authors have in writing !
> While some write sitting, some, like Bayes,
>   Usually stand, while they're inditing.
> Poets there are who wear the floor out,
>   Measuring a line at every stride ;
> While some, like Henry Stephens, pour out
>   Rhymes by the dozen, while they ride.
> Herodotus wrote most in bed ;
>   And Richerand, a French physician,
> Declares the clockwork of the head
>   Goes best in that reclined position.
> If you consult Montaigne and Pliny on
>   The subject, 'tis their joint opinion
> That thought its richest harvest yields
>   Abroad, among the woods and fields."

Plato, on the same authority as for Herodotus,—that of M. de Valois,—is alleged to have produced "his glorious visions all in bed ;" while

> "'Twas in his carriage the sublime
> Sir Richard Blackmore used to rhyme."

But, in short, 'twere endless to recite the various modes in which men write :

> "Some wits are only in the mind
>   When beaux and belles are round them praising ;
> Some, when they dress for dinner, find
>   Their muse and valet both in waiting ;
> And manage, at the selfsame time,
>   To adjust a neckcloth and a rhyme.
>
> "Some bards there are who cannot scribble
>   Without a glove, to tear or nibble ;
> Or a small twig to whisk about—
>   As if the hidden founts of Fancy,
> Like wells of old, were thus found out
>   By mystic tricks of rhabdomancy.
> Such was the little feathery wand,
>   That, held for ever in the hand

> Of her who won and wore the crown
> Of female genius in this age,
> Seem'd the conductor that drew down
> Those words of lightning to her page."

The allusion here is to Madame de Staël, who manipulated a "little feathery wand," made of paper, twisted up like a fan or feather, in the manner and to the effect above described.

Burns usually composed while walking in the open air,—influenced, perhaps, Dr. Currie suggests, by habits formed in early life. Until he was completely master of a tune, he never could write words for it; so his way was, to consider the poetic sentiment corresponding to his idea of the musical expression; then choose his theme; begin one stanza; when that was composed, which was generally the most difficult part of the business, to walk out, sit down now and then, look out for objects in nature around him, such as harmonized with the cogitations of his fancy, —humming occasionally the air, with the verses already framed. When he felt his "muse beginning to jade," he retired to the solitary fireside of his study, and there committed his thoughts to paper; swinging at intervals on the hind leg of his elbow-chair, "by way," he says, "of calling forth my own critical strictures, as my pen goes on." Sometimes, and more than once too often, he composed, to use his own expression, "by the leeside of a bowl of punch, which had overset every mortal in company, except the hautbois and the muse." Béranger *composait toutes ses chansons dans sa tête.* "Once made, I committed them to writing in order to forget them," he said. He tells of having dreamt for ten years of a song about the taxes that weigh down the rural population. In vain he tapped his brain-pan,— nothing came of it. But one night he awoke with the air and the refrain *tout trouvés* :

> "Jacques, lève-toi ;
> Voici venir l'huissier du roi."

And in a day or two the song was a made thing.

The laborious pains bestowed by Alfieri on the process of composition may seem at first sight hard to reconcile with his impulsive character. If he approved his first sketch of a piece—after laying it by for some time, nor approaching it again until his mind was free of the subject—he submitted it to what he called "development"—writing out in prose the indicated scenes, with all the force at his command, but without stopping to analyse a thought or correct an expression. " He then proceeded to versify at his leisure the prose he had written, selecting with care the ideas he thought best, and rejecting those which he deemed" unworthy of a place. Nor did he ever yet regard his work as finished, but "incessantly polished it verse by verse, and made continual alterations," as might seem to him expedient. Hartley Coleridge so far resembled Alfieri that it was his custom to put aside what he had written for some months, till the heat and excitement of composition had effervesced, and then he thought it was in a fair condition to criticize. But *he* seldom altered. "Strike the nail on the anvil," was his advice; he never "kneaded or pounded" his thoughts, which have been described as always coming out *cap-à-pie*, like a troop in quick march. He used to brandish his pen in the act of composition, now and then beating time with his foot, and breaking out into a shout at any felicitous idea. Gray, by-the-bye, found fault with Mason for fancying he should succeed best by writing hastily in the first fervours of his imagination, and therefore never waiting for epithets if they did not occur at the time readily, but leaving spaces for them, and putting them in afterwards. This enervated his poetry, said Gray, and he says the same thing of the same method by whomsoever adopted, for nothing is done so well as at the first concoction.—One of Shelley's biographers came upon the poet in a pine forest, writing verses on a guitar, and, picking up a fragment, saw a "frightful scrawl," all smear and smudge and disorder—such a dashed-off daub as conceited artists are apt to mistake for genius. Shelley said, "When my brain gets heated with thought, it soon boils, and throws off images and words faster than I can skim them off. In the morning, when cooled down, out of that rude sketch, as you justly call it, I shall attempt a drawing."

Christopher North describes himself as writing "by

screeds"—the fit coming on about ten in the morning, which he encouraged by a caulker, ("a mere nutshell, which my dear friend the English Opium-eater would toss off in laudanum;") and as soon as he felt there was no danger of a relapse, that his demon would be with him the whole day, he ordered dinner at nine, shut himself up within triple doors, and set manfully to work. "No desk! an inclined plane—except in bed—is my abhorrence. All glorious articles must be written on a dead flat." His friend the Ettrick Shepherd used a slate.

Washington Irving wrote most of "The Stout Gentleman" while mounted on a stile, or seated on a stone, in his excursion with Leslie the painter round about Stratford-upon-Avon,—the latter taking sketches in the meantime. The artist says his companion wrote with the greatest rapidity, often laughing to himself, and from time to time reading the manuscript aloud.

It was in a bookseller's back-shop, M. Nisard tells us, on a desk to which was fastened a great Newfoundland dog,* that Armand Carrel, one moment absorbed in English memoirs and papers, another moment in caressing his four-footed friend, conceived and wrote his History of the Counter-Revolution in England.—Mr. Walker, in this as in other respects

---

* Who, by-the-bye, one day banged through the window of an upper room, desk and all, to join his master in the street below.

"The Original," adopted a mode of composition which, says he, "I apprehend to be very different from what could be supposed, and from the usual mode. I write in a bedroom at an hotel, sitting upon a cane chair, in the same dress I go out in, and with no books to refer to but the New Testament, Shakspeare, and a pocket dictionary." Now and then, when much pressed for time, and without premeditation, and with his eye on the clock, he wrote some of his shorter essays at the Athenæum Club, at the same table where other members were writing notes and letters.— Douglas Jerrold worked at a desk without a speck upon it, using an inkstand in a marble shell clear of all litter, his little dog at his feet. If a comedy was in progress, he would now and then walk rapidly up and down the room, talking wildly to himself. "If it be *Punch* copy, you shall hear him laugh presently as he hits upon a droll bit." And then, abruptly, the pen would be put down, and the author would pass out into the garden, and pluck a hawthorn leaf, and go nibbling it, and thinking, down the side walks; then "in again, and vehemently to work," unrolling the thought that had come to him along little blue slips of paper, in letters smaller than the type in which they were presently to be set.—Dr. Channing had the same habit of taking a turn in the garden, during which he was a study for the calm concentration of his look, and the deliberateness of his step: "Calmer, brighter, in a few moments he is seated again at his table, and his rapidly flying pen shows how full is the current of his thoughts."—Jane Taylor, who commenced authorship as a very little girl indeed, and who used at that early stage to compose tales and dramas while whipping a top,—committing them to paper at the close of that exercise,—was in the habit, her brother Isaac tells us, of rambling for half an hour after breakfast, "to seek that pitch of excitement without which she never took up the pen." Charlotte Brontë had to choose her favourable days for writing—sometimes weeks or even months elapsing before she felt that she had anything to add to that portion of her story which was already written; then some morning she would wake up, and the progress of her tale lay clear and bright before her, says Mrs. Gaskell, in distinct vision; and she set to work to write out what was more present to her mind at such times than her actual life was. She wrote on little scraps of paper, in a minute hand, holding each against a piece of board, such as is used in binding books, for a desk—a plan found to be necessary for one so short-sighted—and this sometimes as she sat near the fire, by twilight.

Many of the more energetic descriptions in "Marmion," and particularly that of the battle of Flodden, were struck off, by Mr. Skene's account, while Scott was out with his cavalry, in the autumn of 1807. In the intervals of drilling, we are told, Scott used to delight in walking his powerful black steed up and

down by himself upon the Portobello sands, within the
beating of the surge; and now and then you would
see him plunge in his spurs, and go off as if at the
charge, with the spray dashing about him. "As we
rode back to Musselburgh, he often came and placed
himself beside me, to repeat the verses that he had
been composing during these pauses of our exercise."
In after-years, Mr. Cadell, then a guest at Abbotsford,
observing how his host was harassed by lion-hunters,
and what a number of hours he spent daily in the
company of his work-people, expressed his wonder
that Scott should ever be able to work at all while in
the country; "Oh," said Sir Walter, "I lie *simmering*
over things for an hour or so before I get up—and
there's the time I'm dressing to overhaul my half-
sleeping, half-waking *projet de chapitre*—and when I
get the paper before me, it commonly runs off pretty
easily. Besides, I often take a dose in the plantations, and while Tom [Purdie] marks out a dyke or a
drain as I have directed, one's fancy may be running
its ain rigs in some other world." By far the greater
portion of *The Bride of Lammermoor*, the whole of the
Legend of Montrose, and almost the whole of *Ivanhoe*,
were dictated by him to his faithful amanuenses,
William Laidlaw and John Ballantyne, while he lay
prostrate and exhausted by acute suffering. Laidlaw
would often beseech him affectionately to stop dictating, when his audible suffering filled every pause.
But Scott would bid him only see that the doors were

AUTHORSHIP IN THE ACT.

fast, for he would fain keep all the cry as well as all the wool to themselves; but as to giving over work, that could only be when he should be in woollen. John Ballantyne, after the first day, took care to have always a dozen of pens made before he seated himself opposite the sofa on which Scott lay,—the sufferer usually continuing the sentence in the same breath, though he often turned himself on his pillow with a groan of anguish. "But when dialogue of peculiar animation was in progress, spirit seemed to triumph altogether over matter—he arose from his couch and walked up and down the room, raising and lowering his voice, and as it were acting the parts." In this last particular we are reminded of the celebrated Russian author Gogol, whose practice it is said to have been, in composing a dialogue, to recite all the different speeches in character before committing them to paper, to assure himself of their being in complete consonance with what the character and situation required.

It is amusing to read Sir Walter's candid avowal, when commencing the third volume of *Woodstock*, that he had not the slightest idea how the story was to be wound up to a catastrophe. He declares he never could lay down a plan—or that, if he laid one down, he never could stick to it. "I only tried to make that which I was writing diverting and interesting, leaving the rest to fate. . . . This *hab-nab at a venture* is a perilous style, I grant, but I cannot help it."

Coleridge told Hazlitt that he liked to compose in walking over uneven ground, or breaking through the straggling branches of a copsewood; whereas Wordsworth always (if he could) wrote walking up and down a straight gravel-walk, or in some spot where the continuity of his verse met with no collateral interruption. And Hazlitt seems to accept this fact as representative of their respective styles; Coleridge's manner being more full, animated, and varied; and Wordsworth's more equable, sustained, and "subjective;" the former more dramatic, the latter more lyrical.— Schiller could never leave off talking about his poetical projects, and thus he discussed with Goethe all his best pieces, scene after scene. On the other hand, it was contrary to Goethe's nature, as he told Eckermann, to talk over his poetic plans with anybody—even with Schiller. He carried everything about with him in silence, and usually nothing was known to any one till the whole was completed.— Tradition, as we get it through the historian of the Clapham Sect, informs us that Wilberforce wrote his "Practical View" under the roof of two of his best friends, in so fragmentary and irregular a manner, that one of them, when at length the volume lay complete on the table, professed, on the strength of this experience, to have become a convert to the opinion that a fortuitous concourse of atoms might, by some felicitous chance, combine themselves into the most perfect of forms,—a moss-rose, or a bird of paradise.

AUTHORSHIP IN THE ACT. 19

A separate and rather long chapter of instances might be penned, on the ways and means of musical composers; such as Gluck's habit of betaking himself with his harpsichord, on a fine day, into some grassy field, where the ideas came to him as fast again as within doors. Handel, on the contrary, claims to have been inspired for his grandest compositions by the murmurous din of mighty London—far from mighty as the London of George the Second may seem to those with whom the nineteenth century is waning. Sarti composed best in the sombre shadows of a dimly-lighted room. The Monsieur Le Maître commemorated in Rousseau's autobiography, typified a numerous section in his constant recourse, *en travaillant dans son cabinet*, to a bottle, which was replenished as often as emptied, and that was too often by a great deal. His servant, in preparing the room for him, would no more have thought of omitting *son pot et son verre*, than his ruled paper, ink, pens, and violoncello; and one serving did for these,—not so for the drink.—Charles Dibdin's method of composition, or rather the absence of it, is illustrated in the story of his lamenting his lack of a new subject, while under the hairdresser's hand, in a cloud of powder, in his rooms in the Strand, preparing for his night's "entertainment." The friend that was with him suggested various topics—but all of a sudden the jar of a ladder sounded against the lamp-iron, and Dibdin exclaimed, "The lamplighter! a good notion,"—and at once began humming and fingering on his knee. As soon as his head was dressed, he stepped to the piano, finished off both music and words, and that very night sang "Jolly Dick, the Lamplighter" at the theatre, nor could he, we are assured, on critical authority, have well made a greater hit if the song had been the deliberate work of two authors—one for the words, another for the air—and had taken weeks to finish it, and been elaborated in studious leisure, instead of the distraction of dressing-room din.

It is an exceptional *physique* that enables an author to write at his ease amid interruptions and distractions, lets and hindrances, of a domestic kind. Heloise gave this singular reason for her constant refusal to become Abelard's wife—that no mind devoted to the meditations of philosophy could endure the cries of children, the chatter of nurses, and the babble and coming and going in and out of serving men and women. Of Abelard himself, however, we are told that he had a rare power of abstracting himself from all outward concerns; that no one knew better how to be alone, though surrounded by others; and that, in fact, his senses took no note of outward things. —When Cumberland was composing any work, he never shut himself up in his study, but always wrote in the room where his family sat, and did not feel in the least disturbed by the noise of his children at play beside him. The literary habits of Lord Hailes, as

Mr. Robert Chambers remarks, were hardly such as would have been expected from his extreme nicety of diction: it was in no secluded sanctum, or "den," that he composed, but by the "parlour fireside," with wife and bairns within very present sight and sound. Cowper describes himself at Weston (1791) as working in a study exposed to all manner of inroads, and no way disconcerted by the coming and going of servants, or other incidental and inevitable impediments. A year or two later he writes from the same spot, "amidst a chaos of interruptions," including Hayley spouting Greek, and Mrs. Unwin talking sometimes to them, sometimes to herself. Francis Horner relates a visit he and a friend paid to Jeremy Bentham at Ford Abbey, one spacious room in which, a tapestried chamber, the utilitarian philosopher had utilized into what he called his "scibbling shop"—two or three tables being set out, covered with white napkins, on which were placed music desks with manuscripts; and here the visitors were allowed to be "present at the mysteries, for he went on as if we had not been with him." The fourth of Dr. Chalmers's Astronomical Discourses was penned in a small pocket-book, in a strange apartment, where he was liable every moment to interruption; for it was at the manse of Balmerino disappointed in not finding the minister at home, and having a couple of hours to spare—and in a drawing-room at the manse of Kilmany, with all the excitement of meeting for the first time, after a year's absence, many of his former friends and parishioners—that he penned paragraph after paragraph of a composition which, as his son-in-law and biographer, Dr. Hanna, says, bears upon it so much the aspect of high and continuous elaboration. His friend and sometime associate in pastoral work, Edward Irving, on the other hand, could not write a sermon if any one was in the room with him. Chalmers appears to have been specially endowed with that faculty of concentrated attention which is commonly regarded as one of the surest marks of the highest class of intellect, and which Alison so much admires in Wellington—as, for instance, on the day when he lay at San Christoval, in front of the French army, hourly expecting a battle, and wrote out in the field a long and minute memorial on the establishment of a bank at Lisbon on the principles of the English ones.

We read of Ercilla, whose epic poem the *Araucana* has admirers out of Spain, that he wrote it amidst the incessant toils and dangers of a campaign against barbarians, without shelter, and with nothing to write on but small scraps of waste paper, and often only leather; struggling at once against enemies and surrounding circumstances. Some evenly-balanced natures can write at their ease amid any environment of lets and hindrances. Louis de Cormontaigne, the distinguished French engineer, composed his treatise on fortification from notes written in the trenches and on the breaches, even under the fire of the enemy.

Delambre was in Paris when it was taken by the allies in 1814, and is said to have worked at his problems with perfect tranquillity from eight in the morning till midnight, in the continued hearing of the cannonade. "Such self-possession for study under that tremendous attack, and such absence of interest in the result of the great struggle, to say nothing of indifference to personal danger," is what one of his biographers confesses himself unable to understand. Small sympathy would the philosopher have had with the temperament of such a man, say, as Thomas Hood, who always wrote most at night, when all was quiet and the children were asleep. "I have a room to myself," exclaims Hood triumphantly, in a letter describing a change of lodgings, "which will be worth £20 a year to me,—for a little disconcerts my nerves." Mrs. Hood brought up the children, we learn from one of them, in a sort of Spartan style of education, on her husband's account, teaching them the virtues of silence and low voices. Washington Irving was of a less morbid *physique*; and his genial nature could put up with obstacles and obstructions neither few nor small; but even in his Diary we meet with such entries as this at Bordeaux, in 1825: "Harassed by noises in the house, till I had to go out in despair, and write in Mr. Guestier's library." It was upon the Essay on American Scenery that he was then engaged.

Unlike Maturin, who used to compose with a wafer

pasted on his forehead, which was the signal that if any of his family entered the *sanctum* they must not speak to him,—Scott allowed his children (like their mute playmates, Camp and the greyhounds) free access to his study, never considered their tattle as any disturbance, let them come and go as pleased their fancy, was always ready to answer their questions; and when they, unconscious how he was engaged, (writes the husband of one of them,) entreated him to lay down his pen and tell them a story, he would take them on his knee, repeat a ballad or a legend, kiss them, and set them down again to their marbles or ninepins, and resume his labour as if refreshed by the interruption. There was nothing in that manly, sound, robust constitution akin to the morbid irritability of Philip in the poem :

> " When Philip wrote, he never seemed so well—
> Was startled even if a cinder fell,
> And quickly worried."

Biographers of Mistress Aphra Behn make it noteworthy of that too facile penwoman, that she could write away in company, and maintain the while her share in the talk. Madame Roland managed to get through her Memoirs with a semblance at least of unbroken serenity, though so often interrupted in the composition of them by the cries of victims in the adjoining cells, whom the executioners were dragging thence to the guillotine. Madame de Staël, "even in her most inspired compositions," according to Madame Necker de Saussure, "had pleasure in being interrupted by those she loved." She was not, observes Lord Lytton, of the tribe of those who labour to be inspired; who darken the room, and lock the door, and entreat you not to disturb them. Rather she came of the same stock as George Sand's Olympe, who "se mit à écrire sur un coin de la table, entre le bouteille de bière et le sucrier, au bruit des verres et de la conversation, aussi tranquillement que si elle eût été dans la solitude. Cette puissance de concentration était une de ses facultés les plus remarquables." The artist temperament, as a rule, is more accurately represented in the inability ascribed to the late William Collins, when engaged in painting, either to speak himself, or attend to what was spoken by others; the presence of any one, even a member of his family, by the testimony of his elder son, perplexed and interrupted him. That Lord Castlereagh was able to write his despatches at the common table in the common room of a country house, is not unjustly among the admiring Reminiscences of a Septuagenarian (Countess Brownlow): once only we find the talking and laughter were too much for his power of abstraction, and then he went off into his own room, saying next morning at breakfast, "You fairly beat me last night; I was writing what I may call the metaphysics of politics." Celebrated in the *Noctes Ambrosianæ* is the Glasgow poet, Sandy Rogers, not less for his lyrics, one at least of which

is pronounced by Christopher North to be "equal to
anything of the kind in Burns," than for the fact that
his verses—some of them, too, of a serious character
—were thought out amidst the bustle and turmoil of
factory labour, the din of the clanking steam-engine,
and the deafening rattle of machinery, while the work
of committing them to paper was generally performed
amidst the squalling and clamour of children around
the hearth, now in the noise of fractious contention,
and anon exuberant with fun and frolic. Tannahill,
too, composed while plying the shuttle,—humming
over the airs to which he meant to adapt new words;
and, as the words occurred to him, jotting them down
at a rude desk which he had attached to his loom,
and which he could use without rising from his seat.
But no more note-worthy example of the pursuit
of authorship under difficulties—the difficulties of
a narrow home, *res angusta domi*,—is probably on
record, in its simple, homely way, than that of Jean
Paul, as Döring pictures him, sitting in a corner of
the room in which the household work was being
carried on—he at his plain writing-desk, with few or
no books about him, but merely with a drawer or two
containing excerpts and manuscripts; the jingle and
clatter that arose from the simultaneous operations at
stove and dresser, no more seeming to disturb him
than did the cooing of the pigeons which fluttered to
and fro in the chamber, at their own sweet will.

II.

Self-seen in Print.

MADELON, one of Molière's *Précieuses ridicules*, can easily fancy how great must be the pleasure of seeing oneself in print: "Je m'imagine que le plaisir est grand de se voir imprimé"—a notion to which *Mascarille*, playing the marquis, assents, with a complacent but becomingly nonchalant *Sans doute*. *Alceste*, the misanthrope, on the other hand, upbraids a real marquis with sheer folly in letting his verses get into print. Even if one could pardon the publishing a sorry book, still, who but poor wretches who have to live by it would compose? Well, the author's heart knoweth its own exultancy, as well as its own bitterness.

> "None but an author knows an author's cares,
> Or Fancy's fondness for the child she bears.
> Committed once into the public arms,
> The baby seems to smile with added charms."

It is not every one, nor nearly every one, that can or will incline to say with Shaftesbury, even if *he* meant it, "And thus am I nowise more an author for being in print"—he professing himself conscious of no additional virtue, from having at any time lain under the weight of that alphabetic engine called the press. Gibbon gives the subject another turn, in his panegyric on the art of printing, where he says of a single manuscript imported from Greece which is thus revived in ten thousand copies, that each copy is fairer than the original, and that in this form Homer and Plato would peruse with more satisfaction their own writings. But the fact of publication is the thing; and with many the character of the type goes for little. Indeed, in one sense, the commoner and meaner the better, as that bespeaks popularity. In a letter to Crabbe, Bernard Barton mentions his having written some verses, long years before, in a Child's Annual, to accompany a print of Doddridge's mother teaching him Bible History from the Dutch tiles round the fireplace; which verses, as well as the print, he had clean forgotten—for even a versemaker's mind has its statute of limitations,—when some one sent him a child's penny cotton handkerchief, on which he found a transcript of that identical print, with four of his stanzas printed under it. And greatly he exulted thereat, as proof positive of true fame. Far more lively seems to have been his satisfaction than that ascribed by Cowper to the polite author who

"sees the name of idol self,
Stamped on the well-bound quarto, grace the shelf."

It stands to reason that the authors who profess themselves indifferent, or even reluctant, to see themselves in print, should be in a decided minority. Such as Schleiermacher, when he declares in one of his letters, "It is disagreeable to me to see myself in print. I could hardly bear it even in the case of these few detached thoughts, which scarcely fill a sheet." But even him we find saying within two months of this avowal, "Among the sweetest of my dreamings yesterday, was that of sending the discourses to Wedike. What a delight it will be to me to do so as soon as they have been endowed with a corporeal existence!" So that Schleiermacher liked well enough to be seen in print, whatever might be the truth as regards seeing himself there. To Goethe his English biographer assigns a virtue, perhaps of all virtues the rarest in youthful writers—a reluctance to appear in print. Interpreting this reluctance by his own experience, Mr. Lewes takes the explanation of it to be, that Goethe's delight in composition was rather the pure delight of intellectual activity than a delight in the result : not in the work, but in the working ; his interest in a composition ceasing as soon as it was composed. Still, there are not wanting in Goethe's correspondence such passages as this : " I was pleased to see my dramatic sketch in clean proof sheets; it looked really better than I myself expected." But there was nothing about him in common with the *sot* scarified by Boileau—

> "Et, toujours amoureux de ce qu'il vient d'écrire,
> Ravi d'étonnement, en soi-même il s'admire."

Poor Haydon has left a vivid record of the "fluster of elation" with which he greeted the result of his dropping a letter into the letter-box of the *Examiner*. "Never shall I forget that Sunday morning. In came the paper, wet, uncut; up went the breakfast knife— cut, cut, cut. Affecting not to be interested, I turned the pages open to dry, and to my certain immortality saw, with a delight not to be expressed, the first sentence of my letter. I put down the paper, walked about the room, looked at Macbeth [his picture], made the tea, buttered the toast, put in the sugar, with that inexpressible suppressed chuckle of delight that always attends a condescending relinquishment of an anticipated rapture till one is perfectly ready. Who has not felt this? who has not done this?" For of course the sensation is not limited to authorship's first flight.

At the age of fourteen Charles Mathews the elder tells us he "commenced author," by translating the Princess of Cleves, which appeared in monthly instalments in the *Ladies' Magazine*; and he describes the delight with which he gazed on his first proof as boundless. He thought the eyes of Europe were upon him, and that the ladies who took in the work would unite in calling upon the editor to insist upon "C. M." declaring himself.—Douglas Jerrold was a youthful compositor at the printing offices of Mr. Bigg, in Lombard Street, when *he* "commenced author" by dropping a criticism on Der Freyschütze, for "*Arliss's*

Magazine, into Mr. Bigg's letter-box ; and an anxious night he is said to have passed, and a bright morrow it was when the editor handed him his own composition to (technically speaking) compose, together with an address to the anonymous contributor, asking for further contributions. His sisters are said to remember the boisterous delight with which he would occasionally afterwards bound into the house, with a little publication in his hand, shouting, "It's in ! it's in !"—Leigh Hunt's first prose endeavours were a series of papers in the *Traveller* (afterwards incorporated with the *Globe*), which he offered with fear and trembling to the editor, Mr. Quin, and was astonished at the gaiety with which he accepted them. What astonished him more, by his own account, was a perquisite of five or six copies of the paper, which he enjoyed every Saturday when his essays appeared, and with which he used to reissue from Bolt Court in a state of transport ; nor could he behold the long columns of type, written by himself, in a public paper, without thinking there must be some merit in them, besides that of being a stop-gap, or, as the phrase now goes,—padding.

Bolt Court must have been as venerated a spot to him as to the sometime denizen of Bolt Court had been St. John's Gate, the place where the *Gentleman's Magazine* was originally printed, and which on that account Johnson "beheld with reverence." Boswell surmises that every young author has had the same kind of feeling for the magazine or periodical publication which has first entertained him, and in which he has first had an opportunity of seeing himself in print, without the risk of exposing his name. "I myself recollect such impressions from the *Scots Magazine*. . . . I cannot yet help thinking of it with an affectionate regard."—The first time that a youthful poet sees himself in print, O'Keeffe declares to be assuredly an epoch unparalleled. He duly records his own sensations, after writing some verses on Summer, and sending them with his initials to a Dublin journal, at being hailed next day by an attorney's clerk, his particular friend, with the rapturous intelligence, "Jack, your song is in the paper!" His fellow-countryman, Moore, opens a paragraph of his autobiography with the impressively worded announcement: "It was in this year, 1793, that for the first time I enjoyed the honour and glory (for such it truly was to me) of seeing verses of my own in print." Said verses were headed "To Zelia," and subscribed "Romeo"—the name Romeo being an anagram of Moore. The magazine which accepted them was the *Anthologia Hibernica;* and Romeo assures us that his pride on seeing his own name in the first list of subscribers to it,—"Master Thomas Moore," in full,—was only surpassed by that of finding himself one of its "esteemed contributors." A more distinguished compatriot of Moore's and O'Keeffe's, Dean Swift, had long before depicted the pleasurable experiences of young authorship, from the time of forwarding a fair copy in neatest manuscript to Lintot, and his acceptance of it for immediate publication:

> "And how agreeably surprised
> Are you to see it advertised;"

to say nothing of the flush of delight when

> "The hawker shows you one in print,
> As fresh as farthings from the mint."

The third great George our king one day got Fanny Burney into a corner, and kept her there till he got a straightforward answer from her as to what prompted her to write and to publish "Evelina." Coming close up to her, he said, "But what?—what?—how was it?" "Sir?" cried she, not well understanding him. "How came you—how happened it—what?—what?" "I—I only wrote, sir, for my own amusement—only in some odd, idle hours." "But your publishing—your printing—how was that?" "That was only, sir,—only because——" She hesitated, by her own account, "most abominably," and grew terribly confused; but the *What!* was iterated and reiterated, with so earnest a look that, forced to say something, she stammeringly answered, "I thought, sir—it would look very well in print!" Madame d'Arblay, in her Diary, flatters herself that this was really the silliest speech she ever made. The king laughed heartily, and walked away to enjoy it, crying out, however, as he did so, "Very fair, indeed! that's being fair and honest."—Gibbon lays due stress in his Memoirs, on what, retrospectively reviewing it, he calls the petty circumstances and period of its first publication, "a memorable æra in the life of a student." Is there, indeed, Hartley Coleridge asks, any anxiety greater than that of a young author on the eve of appearing in print, when his darling effusions are to throw off their nursery-attire of manuscript, in which they were only producible at family parties, or, at most, to a few friends, and appear in type before the expectant public? Lord Melbourne, whose practical pursuit of the law as a profession was limited, Mr. Hayward tells us, to a single attendance at the Lancashire Sessions, in company with the late Lord Abinger, through whose recommendation he received a guinea brief, used to say that the first sight of his name upon this document gave him the highest feeling of triumph he ever experienced, very far transcending that which he enjoyed on being appointed Prime Minister. So is it with the young author and his first proof. No triumph of mature authorship can match his exultant pride in that previous production. Mr. Pendennis was thoroughly *blasé* when Colonel Newcome, who had never been in the rooms of a literary man before, inquired with eagerness as he glanced around him, "Excuse me, is that—that paper really a proof-sheet?" And Arthur handed over to him that curiosity, smiling at the enthusiasm of the honest gentleman who could admire what was to *him* as unpalatable as a tart to a pastrycook. Mr.

Dickens has made the public his confidant in respect of the emotion that overcame him on first seeing himself in print. His first "effusion" was dropped stealthily one evening at twilight, with fear and trembling, into a dark letter-box, in a dark office, up a dark court in Fleet Street ; and when it appeared in all the glory of print, he walked down to Westminster Hall, he tells us, and turned into it for half an hour, "because my eyes were so dimmed with joy and pride, that they could not bear the' street, and were not fit to be seen there." A popular writer of his school, drawing apparently upon personal reminiscence, gives a rather elaborate sketch in one of his fictions of a young author luxuriating in the scrutiny of himself in print —the mere smell of the wet ink and paper affording him unmixed satisfaction for some time—after which he betook himself to cutting the pages slowly, and regarding each page separately as a mere artistic effect of light and shade ; and next tried various devices of folding and opening, and looked at the paper, as a whole, from various points of view—at arm's length, with his eyes half closed, with his head nearly upside-down ; all before he could bring himself to settle to the literature of the work, reserved as a *bonne bouche*, to be seriously read, marked, and inwardly digested, line upon line, paragraph upon paragraph.

Longfellow's Baron of Hohenfels, in *Hyperion*, considers the sight of a proof-sheet quite as delightful as a walk in the Prater of Vienna. To gaze on the metamorphosis of his manuscript into print, is a rapture to which confessedly he gives himself up without reserve. "This melancholy pleasure, which would have furnished the departed Voss with worthy matter for more than one blessed Idyl—the more so," adds the sentimental baron, "as on such occasions I am generally arrayed in a morning gown, though I am sorry to say, not a calamanco one, with great flowers—this melancholy pleasure has already grown here in Halle to a sweet pedantic habit. Since I began my hermit's life here, I have been printing; and so long as I remain here, I shall keep on printing. In all probability, I shall die with a proof-sheet in my hand." *Qualis vita, finis ita.*

Samuel Rogers would expatiate on the "to all agreeable, to many intoxicating," impression of first seeing himself in print, in the *Gentleman's Magazine* of 1781. The amorous, fond delay with which young authorship lingers over an inspection of its printed handiwork, is of a piece with the zest of Carrio's contemplation of the blue-coloured board, on which, in letters of gold, that worthy Roman freedman, in a modern tale of Rome, had written his patron's proclamation to all whom it might concern. Carrio could not prevail upon himself to pass by the work of his own ingenuity without examining its magnificence anew; and for some time we see him stand looking at it with the same expression of lofty and complacent approbation which illumines a linen-draper's face, as he surveys from the pavement his morning's arrangement of the shop window. Dr. Wynter somewhere hints at an almost equal satisfaction brightening up the visage of the poor shrinking girl who is obliged to advertise for a place, when, after anxiously searching the wet page of the advertisement column next day, it wellnigh takes her breath away when she lights on herself in print—she, the timid little thing, thus to speak out as boldly as the best of them.—In some authors, the interest excited by a proof-sheet hardly wears away to the last. In Southey it did not. "If you have as much pleasure in reading a proof-sheet as I have, I may wish you enjoyment of your employment," he writes, as quite an old man, to Mrs. Bray of Tavistock. And about the same time he tells his old schoolfellow, Charles Wynn, "The greatest pleasure I have with a book of my own, is in cutting open the leaves when it first comes." Even at one's last gasp, says one of Mrs. Gore's heroes, one is never sorry to see oneself in print: the hero says this as a military hero, in reference to his being mentioned with honour in the despatches from Waterloo; but the saying admits of a very general application. Of David Gray, who died at twenty-three, we are told that the thought of the publication of that poem he could get no one to print, haunted his perturbed spirit—" it troubles me like an ever-present demon;" and that when at length, chiefly by Mr. Sydney Dobell's unwearying exertions, it was printed, and a specimen page was sent to him, " David, with the shadow of death then dark upon him, gazed long and lingeringly on the printed page. All the mysterious past—the boyish yearnings, the flash of anticipated fame, the black surroundings of the great city—flitted across his vision like a dream. It was 'good news,' he said." That was on the second day of December, 1861 ; and on the third, David was dead and gone.

Scott's Antiquary was stricken in years when he yearned so wistfully to appear in print, ("like many other men," observes Sir Walter, "who spend their lives in obscure literary research ;") but then he never had so appeared, and the sensation was an untried one. Miss Braddon declares that "she can never again feel the exquisite emotion aroused by the *first* proof-sheet" of her first story "as it was presented to her—very badly printed on very bad paper, and embellished with an oblong smudge which demanded no small effort of imagination on the part of the beholder to accept as an illustration." A self-styled Commonplace Philosopher who hails from the north, whose volumes are numerous, and to whom, though the freshness is somewhat gone, "it is still a curious feeling to see one's thoughts in print,"—the publication of every fresh volume being a little epoch in a quiet life,—supposes that the editor of a daily newspaper, seeing himself in print every day of his life, must cease, in a few years, to feel any special attraction to the columns that have come from his own pen. But our philosopher frankly owns to an abiding zest in the "set up" aspect of his copy. In another of his works he welcomes the arrival of the postman who brings him "the daily pages of pleasing type, in which things look so different from what they look in the cramped magazine printing" (in which his essays had originally appeared). Great he declares to be the enjoyment which an advancing volume by one's self affords to a simple mind. Southey's example we have already cited ; and A. K. H. B. cites him as a man who, after writing probably more in quantity than any English author of the present century, with but two or three exceptions, retained to the last the keen interest of a quite fresh writer in his own articles—chafing and fretting if a new *Quarterly* were a day late in reaching him ; and no doubt reading his own paper the first. Southey was the wight, if ever wight there were, to appreciate to the full what his nephew Hartley (Job, as Uncle Robert loved to call him, for his *im*patience) candidly confessed in a copy of verses:

"I own I like to see my works in print ;
The page looks knowing, though there's nothing in't."

III.

Self-heard in Song.

TO the pleasure of seeing one's self in print, closely akin in kind, if not even keener in degree, seems to be the pleasure the song-writer has in listening to his songs from other lips. Cowper's charming stanzas to Catharina will at once occur to the mind. She came, she was gone, they had met—to meet, perhaps, never again; Catharina had fled like a dream, but had left with the poet the pleasantest of winsome memories behind. On the eve of her flitting, together had they listened to the nightingale warbling nigh, in their twilight rambles; and to Catharina there was rapture in the comparative novelty of the strain, for she was town-bred, though country-loving; but to Cowper the sweetness was less marked than usual, for he had listened to sweeter singing that day from the gentle warbler now beside him. She had sung the songs he had written, and dearer were the songs for such singing and for such a singer.

> " My numbers that day she had sung,
> And gave them a grace so divine

> As only her musical tongue
> Could infuse into numbers of mine.
> The longer I heard, I esteemed
> The work of my fancy the more,
> And e'en to myself never seemed
> So tuneful a poet before."

It was better still than being effectively quoted by Charles James Fox in the House of Commons,[*] even had Cowper been there to hear[†] him.

Bishop Ken deemed it would be an addition to his happiness in a happier world than this, if he should know that his devotional poems were answering on earth the purpose for which he had piously composed them :

> " And should the well-meant songs I leave behind,
> With Jesus' lovers an acceptance find,
> 'Twill heighten ev'n the joys of heaven to know
> That in my verse the saints hymn God below."

And fain would he bow down his ear to listen, if haply the strain might be borne so far, as it was ever aimed so high.

---

[*] The lines quoted by Fox were those on the Bastille, in the fifth book of *The Task*. Hayley came to Weston with a newspaper containing the speech. Mrs. Unwin was demonstratively delighted; Cowper smiled expressively, and held his peace.

[†] Sir T. F. Buxton, after listening with delight in the House of Commons, in 1835, to the late Earl of Derby, then Mr. Stanley, enforcing from the Treasury Bench, with a splendour of eloquence all his own, the very facts and arguments against the slave trade which Sir Thomas, with Dr. Lushington, had for years been endeavouring to impress upon the House, quoted with gusto Cowper's lines to Mrs. Courtenay, so far as they expressed the listener's delight at the grace infused into his statements by that musical tongue, and his the more and more esteeming the worth of them, the longer he listened.

Dryden was overdoing his flattery, as in prefaces and dedications he was apt to do, when he assured his honoured friend, Sir Robert Howard, on his superlative versification, that

"Singing no more can your soft numbers grace,
Than paint adds charms unto a beauteous face."

Had it been some vocal dame that Glorious John was bent on flattering, he would have reversed his affirmation, changed his figure, and eaten his words with a vengeance.

Sir Walter Scott declares the sweetest sounds which mortal ears can drink in, to be the reading aloud of a youthful poet's verses by the lips which are dearest to him. He indulges his Francis Osbaldistone with this luxury, in the instance of Diana Vernon. So too Mr. Disraeli puts his young duke into a rapture of delight at overhearing Miss Dacre read his composition to her father. "He starts—his eye sparkles with strange delight—a flush comes over his panting features, half of modesty, half of triumph. . . . She is reading to her father with melodious energy. . . . The intonations of the voice indicate the deep sympathy of the reader." Hannah More is pleased to call it "the most ridiculous circumstance in the world," but for all that, she is delighed beyond measure with what she has to record, during one of her sojourns with the Garricks, in 1776, of David's reading aloud her last poem, and with what effect. "After dinner, Garrick . . . . read *Sir Eldred* with all his pathos and all his graces. I think I never was so ashamed in my life; but he read it so superlatively, that I cried like a child. Only think what a scandalous thing, to cry at the reading of one's own poetry!" But the beauty of the jest she declares to have lain in this—that Mrs. Garrick "twinkled," as well as herself, and made as many apologies for crying at her husband's reading, as Hannah did for crying at her own verses. "*She* got out of the scrape by pretending she was touched at the story, and *I*, by saying the same thing of the reading."—At the first audience the old poet Ducis had of his restored king and ever-beloved master, Lewis the Eighteenth, that monarch had the good-nature to recite to him some of his own verses. In an esctasy of delight Ducis exclaimed, "I am more fortunate than Boileau or Racine: they recited their verses to Lewis the Fourteenth, but my king recites my verses to me!" Mr. Leigh Hunt, in his autobiography, expressly states that the wife he won, or rather that won him, completed her conquest by reading verses better than he had ever heard before, "and she reads verses better than ever to this day, especially some that shall be namelcss." The same author had, many years previously, in *The Seer*, put on record this testimony of his gratification on hearing words of his sung by perhaps the finest singer of her day, to her father's setting. He had not thought it possible, he said, for any words of his own to give him so much pleasure in the repetition, as

when he "heard her father's composition sung by the
pure and most tuneful voice of Miss Clara Novello
(Clara is she well named)." Mr. Vincent Novello, by
the way, mentions having seen the composer Winter,
when the first performance of his beautiful opera on
the story of Proserpine was over, "stoop down (he
was a very tall man) and kiss Mrs. Billington's hand
for her singing in the character of Ceres."*

Dr. Walker's *Life of Burns* relates the author's once
calling for the ploughman poet at the house of a
friend [Mr. Cruikshank], and finding him seated by
the harpischord of the young lady of the house, listening with the keenest interest to his own verses,
which she sung and accompanied. "In this occupation he was so totally absorbed, that it was difficult to
draw his attention from it for a moment." Fond of
French poetry, if not also sometimes a little Frenchi-
fied in his compliments, Robert Burns might have
addressed the fair warbler in the style of Molière's
glozing, gloating hero :

"C'est sans doute, madame, une douceur extrême
Que d'entendre ces mots d'une bouche qu'on aime ;
Leur miel dans tous mes sens fait couler à longs traits
Une suavité qu'on ne goûta jamais."

Another of his biographers tells us that when Burns
dwelt at Ellisland, it was his custom, after writing a

---

* "I wonder he did not take Grassini in his arms," is Leigh Hunt's
tribute to that great contralto's execution of the music for *Proserpina*
herself. "She must have had a fine soul, and would have known
how to pardon him. But perhaps he did."—*Autobiography*, chap. vi.

song, to pay a visit to *Kirsty*, or Christian Fitzpatrick, whose fine voice and good ear could do justice to the songs of Scotland ; and he would set her to sing it at once, trying what old tune would suit it best. Professor Gillespie speaks of having, when a schoolboy, seen Burns's horse tied by the bridle to the *sneck* of a cottage door near Thornhill, and of lingering for some time to overhear the songs to which, seated in an arm chair by the fireside, Robert the Rhymer was eagerly listening. The poet's wife was no unaccomplished or unattractive songstress either,—her voice being as good as her acquaintance with Scotch airs was extensive. But Dr. Chambers tells us that as Burns had never felt the full measure of the beauty of his poems till he heard Mr. Aikin read them, so neither did he find out to the full the charm of his songs until he heard George Lockhart, of Glasgow, sing them. On hearing him sing several of them for the first time, the poet's exclamation, frank and fervent, was, " I'll be hanged if I ever knew half their merit till now ! " Otherwise the lips of a lassie were instrumentally his preference. He could have sympathized with every line of Owen Meredith's *Good-night in the Porch :*

" And oft, you know, when eves were cool,
In summer-time, and through the trees young gnats began to be about,
With some old book upon your knees, 'twas here you watch'd the stars
   come out,
While oft, to please me, you sang through some foolish song I made for
   you."

Goethe's ablest biographer describes him lingering

about Lili's house after dark, satisfied if he could catch a glimpse of her shadow on the blind, as she moved about the room; and tells how the poet's pulses throbbed when, one night, in the song she was singing at the piano, he distinguished a *lied* of his own. "I cannot," says James Hogg, the Ettrick Shepherd, "express what my feelings were on first hearing a song of mine sung by a beautiful young lady in Ettrick, to her harpsichord" accompaniment. One of his following proclaims,

> "There's one reward doth all eclipse,
> And this shall be my prize—
> To see my thoughts move ruby lips,
> Enlighten glorious eyes;
> To hear a silver-sounding voice
> Sweetly my words prolong:
> Say, what reward can more rejoice
> The bard who writes a song?"

It was "To a Lady Singing a Song of his Composing" that the delighted Waller indited the stanzas beginning,

> "Chloris! yourself you so excel,
> When you vouchsafe to breathe my thought,
> That, like a spirit, with this spell
> Of my own teaching, I am caught.
>
> That eagle's fate and mine are one,
> Which, on the shaft that made him die,
> Espied a feather of his own,
> Wherewith he wont to soar so high."

Paulo minora canamus. The strain we next hear is in a lower mood. And yet, perhaps, otherwise in reality. Bernard Barton ends a letter descriptive of an endearing girl's village funeral with telling how the clergyman, at the close of the service, stated that, by her wish, a little hymn, which was a great favourite with her, would be sung beside her open grave by the school-children—some five-and-twenty little things, whose eyes and cheeks were red with crying. "I thought they could never have found tongues, poor things; but once set off, they sang like a little band of cherubs. What added to the effect of it, to me, was that it was a little almost forgotten hymn of my own, written years ago, which no one present, but myself, was at all aware of."

We have all read how Goldsmith, in his college career, would write street ballads to save himself from actual starving, sell them at the Rein-deer depository in Mountrath Court, for five shillings apiece, and steal out of college at night to hear them sung. "Happy night, to him worth all the dreary days!" exclaims Mr. Forster. "Hidden by some dusky wall, or creeping within darkling shadows of the ill-lighted streets, this poor neglected sizar watched, waited, lingered there, for the only effort of his life which had not wholly failed. Few and dull perhaps the beggar's audience at first, but more thronging, eager, and delighted, as he shouted forth his newly-gotten ware. Cracked enough, I doubt not, were those ballad-singing tones: very harsh, extremely discordant, and passing from loud to low without meaning or melody;

but not the less did the sweetest music which this earth affords fall with them on the ear of Goldsmith." It is related of Robert Tannahill, the Paisley poet, that during a solitary walk he once overheard a country girl in an adjoining field singing by herself a song of his, "We'll meet beside the dusky glen, on yon burnside," and that no tribute to his popularity was ever so welcome to him as this. Caressed by every order of society during his long residence in Rome, then a musical city, Grétry found nothing so gratifying as to hear his airs sung in the streets.* It must have been a disappointment to Cowper that the songs or ballads he wrote on the slave trade, for the express purpose of being sung in the streets, and by that means widely circulated among the people, came to nothing. " If you hear ballads sung in the streets on the hardships of the negroes in the islands," he writes to Mr. Rose, " they are probably mine." But Mr. Rose heard them not, nor was the song writer ever to have that satisfaction himself. Great was the glee of Professor Aytoun at hearing his verses chanted by street singers in Auld Reekie. This was a kind of popularity to which he was no stranger, Mr. Theodore Martin tells us; many an election squib and ballad of his finding favour with " those unshaven and raucous gentlemen

---

* A story is told in Rome of Canova's putting on a monk's dress and cowl, and in this disguise mingling with the crowd, to hear the criticisms that were made when his model of the monument of Clement XIII. (in St. Peter's) was first exposed to public view.

to whose canorous mercies," in his own diction, "we are wont, in times of political excitement, to entrust our own personal and patriotic ditties."* His ballad of *The Elder's Warning*, which struck a deeper note, and appealed to a wider sentiment than usual, was of exceptional interest to him when first he heard it sung to an admiring crowd. " Seldom," he wrote in *Blackwood*, with ample use of the orthodox "we" of reviewers, here as uncomfortable as it is uncompromising, "seldom have we experienced a keener sense of our true greatness as a poet than when we encountered, on one occasion, a peripatetic minstrel deafening the Canongate with the notes of our particular music, and surrounded by an eager crowd demanding the halfpenny broadsheet." No doubt he could have found it in his heart to treat that raucous vocalist to a beaker of whisky as cordially as Landor's Tasso bestows a luscious slice of water-melon on the boy that sang his Aminta.† Mrs. Broderip reports of her father's pleasure in the immense popularity of his Song of the Shirt, that what delighted and yet touched him most deeply, was that

---

* The Caxtonian creator of John Durley, bard, journalist, pamphleteer, and bookseller's hack, describes him as very fond of scribbling off penny ballads, and then standing in the streets to hear them sung.

† " Where is the boy who sang my Aminta ? Serve him first ; give him largely. Cut deeper," he bids Cornelia ; " the knife is too short : deeper ; mia brava Corneliolina ! quite through all the red, and into the middle of the seeds. Well done !"—*Imaginary Conversations: Tasso and Cornelia.*

the poor creatures to whose sorrows and sufferings he,
Thomas Hood, had given such eloquent voice, seemed
to adopt its words as their own, by singing them
about the streets to a rude air of their own adaptation. Perhaps he might have heard it in Genoa, and
Paris, and Berlin; for it was translated into Italian,
French, and German. *Not* into Persian, like the
ditties of Thomas Moore, on Henry Luttrell's showing or surmising :

> "I'm told, dear Moore, your lays are sung,
> (Can it be true, you lucky man?)
> By moonlight, in the Persian tongue,
> Along the streets of Ispahan."

IV.

𝔅ookish.

SIR THOMAS BROWNE, in his characteristic diction, calls it "an unjust way of compute, to magnify a weak head for some Latin abilities; and to undervalue a solid judgment, because he knows not the genealogy of Hector." They do most by books, he says, who could do much without them; and he that chiefly owes himself unto himself, is the substantial mart.* An ounce of mother-wit is, proverbially, worth a pound of clergy. How vain, says the Greek adage, is learning, unless good sense be united with it: ὡς οὐδὲν ἡ μάθησις ἂν μὴ νοῦς παρῇ. So Pope, in his homage to

"Good sense, which only is the gift of Heaven,
And though no science, worth the other seven."

In more than one page of his treatise Locke recog-

---

* "Value the judicious, and let not mere acquests in minor parts of learning gain the pre-estimation.... Natural parts and good judgments rule the world. States are not governed by ergotisms (which is good Brunonian for conclusions deduced according to the forms of logic: ergo)... Where natural logic prevails not, artificial too often faileth."
—*Christian Morals,* sect. iv.

nizes the aptitude of a man unskilful in syllogism, to perceive at first hearing the weakness and inconclusiveness of a long, artificial, and plausible discourse, wherewith others better skilled in syllogism have been misled. "I am apt to think that he who shall employ all the force of his reason only in brandishing of syllogisms, will discover very little of that mass of knowledge which lies yet concealed in the secret recesses of nature; and which, I am apt to think, native rustic reason (as it formerly has done) is likelier to open a way to, and add to the common stock of mankind, rather than any scholastic proceedings by the strict rules of mode and figure." So Hazlitt writes up "the common people" against pedants and bookmen,—ascribes to the former eloquence to express their passions, and wit at will to express their contempt and provoke laughter,—says of their natural use of speech that it is not hung up in monumental mockery, in an obsolete language, nor is their sense of what is ludicrous, or readiness at finding out allusions to indicate it, buried in collections of *Ana;* and then adds: "You will hear more good things on the outside of a stage-coach from London to Oxford, than if you were to pass a twelvemonth with the undergraduates, or heads of colleges, of that famous university." Sir T. Fowell Buxton bore witness of Abraham Plastow, his father's gamekeeper, and confessedly his own "guide, philosopher, and friend," who could neither read nor write, but whose memory was stored with varied rustic knowledge, that he had more of natural good sense and mother-wit than almost any person his young master ever met with since; a knack which he had of putting everything into new and singular lights, making him a most entertaining and even intellectual companion. "Such was my first instructor, and, I must add, my best; for I think I have profited more by the recollection of his remarks and admonition, than by the more learned and elaborate discourses of all my other tutors." Hosea Biglow's avowal is—

> "An' yit I love th' unhighschooled way
> Ol' farmers hed when I wuz younger;
> Their talk wuz meatier, an' 'ould stay,
> While book-froth seems to whet your hunger."

Lessing is as shrewdly sensible as sententious in his remark that the wealth of foreign or extraneous experience acquired from books is learning (*Gelehrsamkeit*), one's own experience is wisdom (*Weisheit*), and that the smallest stock-in-trade of the latter is worth more than millions of the former. The discourses of Epictetus are full of sharp sarcasms against people who read books, or practise their reasoning powers, or study philosophy, for show or mere amusement; and pitiless, as one of his expositors remarks, is the ridicule he lavishes on the man who had read Chrysippus through, and declared that he understood him, and could pass an examination in his books: " As if I should say to a wrestler, Show me your muscles, and he should say, See my dumb-bells. Your dumb-bells are your own affair; I want to see the effect of them." Charron loved to differentiate the *sage* from the *savant:* "Qui est fort savant n'est guère sage, et qui est sage n'est pas savant. Il y a bien quelques exceptions en ceci, mais elles sont bien rares. Ce sont des grandes âmes, riches, heureuses. Il y en a en l'Antiquité, mais il ne s'en trouve presque plus."

Books are said to be less often made use of as spectacles to look at nature with, than as blinds to keep out its strong light and shifting scenery from weak eyes and indolent dispositions. "The bookworm wraps himself up in his web of verbal generalities, and sees only the glimmering shadows of things reflected from the minds of others. Nature puts him out." To expect the mere learned reader to throw down his book and think for himself, is called as unreasonable as to ask the paralytic to leap from his chair and throw away his crutch, or, without a miracle, to take up his bed and walk. The bookman clings to his book for his intellectual support, and his dread of being left to himself is compared to the horror of a vacuum. "He can only breathe a learned atmosphere, as other men breathe common air. He is a borrower of sense. He has no ideas of his own, and must live on those of other people." The habit of supplying our ideas from foreign sources, says Hazlitt, in his essay on the Ignorance of the Learned, "enfeebles all internal strength of thought," as a course of dram-drinking destroys the tone of the stomach. The faculties of the mind, when not exerted, or when cramped by custom and authority, become listless, torpid, and unfit for the purposes of thought or action.* A mere scholar, who knows nothing but books, is affirmed to be necessarily ignorant of them. "Books do not teach the use of books." The learned pedant is conversant with books only as they are made of other books, and those again of others, without end: he parrots those who have parroted others.; he can translate the same word into ten different languages, but he knows nothing of the thing which it means in any

---

* "The description of persons who have the fewest ideas of all others, are mere authors and readers. It is better to be able neither to read nor write, than to be able to do nothing else. A lounger who is ordinarily seen with a book in his hand, is (we may be almost sure) equally without the power or inclination to attend either to what passes around him, or in his own mind. Such a one may be said to carry his understanding about with him in his pocket, or to leave it at home on his library shelves." The essayist goes on to describe this typical bookman as afraid of venturing on any train of reasoning, or of striking out any observation that is not mechanically suggested to him by passing his eyes over certain legible characters; as shrinking from the fatigue of thought, which, for want of practice, becomes insupportable to him; and sitting down contented with an endless wearisome succession of words and half-formed images, which fill the void of the mind, and continually efface one another. "The learned are mere literary drudges. If you set them upon original composition, their heads turn; they don't know where they are." And the indefatigable readers of books are likened to the everlasting copiers of pictures, who, when they attempt to do anything of their own, find they want an eye quick enough, a hand steady enough, and colours bright enough to trace the living forms of nature.—See Hazlitt on *The Ignorance of the Learned*.

one of them. "He stuffs his head with authorities built on authorities, with quotations quoted from quotations, while he locks up his senses, his understanding, and his heart." Says Shakspeare's Biron,

> "Small have continual plodders ever won,
> Save base authority from others' books."

And later on he iterates the charge:

> "Why, universal plodding prisons up
> The nimble spirits in the arteries."

Biron's doctrine is, that learning is but an adjunct to ourself, and where we are, our learning likewise is. Biron's namesake, a good hater, declares that

> "One hates an author, that's *all author*, fellows
> In foolscap uniforms turn'd up with ink,
> So very anxious, clever, fine, and jealous,
> One don't know what to say to them, or think,
> Unless to puff them with a pair of bellows;
> Of coxcombry's worst coxcombs e'en the pink
> Are preferable to these shreds of paper,
> These unquench'd snuffings of the midnight taper."

Addison classifies pedants into species; but of all these, he pronounces the book-pedant to be the most insupportable—the worst type being such as are naturally endowed with a very small share of common sense, and have read a great number of books without taste or distinction. The truth of it is, he says, that learning, like travelling, and all other methods of improvement, as it finishes good sense, so it makes a silly man ten thousand times more insufferable, by supplying variety of matter to his impertinence, and giving him an opportunity of abounding in absurdities.

> "Yes, you despise the man to books confined,
> Who from his study rails at human kind ;
> Though what he learns he speaks, and may advance
> Some general maxims, or be right by chance,"

just as "the coxcomb bird" may be, so talkative and grave, that from his cage cries dunce, or fool, or knave ; though many a passenger he rightly call, you hold him no philosopher at all. The elder Caxton had too great a reverence for scholarship not to wish his son to become a scholar if possible ; but he more than once said to him, somewhat sadly, "Master books, but do not let them master you. Read to live, not live to read. One slave of the lamp is enough for a household ; my servitude must not be a hereditary bondage." Pisistratus himself applies to his sire what Robert Hall said of Dr. Kippis, "He had laid so many books on the top of his head, that the brains could not move." And the day comes when, affrayed with the prospect of college life, with three years of book upon book, a great Dead Sea before him, three years long, and all the apples that grow on the shore full of the ashes of pica and primer,— the younger Caxton, shrinking from a mere booklife, seeks counsel of the sage Trevanion how he may by any means " escape these eternal books, and this mental clockwork and corporeal lethargy."

Some persons, as Edward Clayton says, are like Pharaoh's lean kine; they swallow book upon book, but remain as lean as ever. These are they with whom reading is only a form of mental indolence, by which they escape the labour of thinking for themselves. "The books that have influenced the world the longest, the widest, and deepest, have been written by men who attended to things more than to books." A Chinese proverb runs, that a single conversation across the table with a wise man, is better than ten years mere study of books. The ambition of a man of parts, says Sydney Smith, should be not to know books, but things; not to show other men that he has read Locke, and Montesquieu, and Beccaria, and Dumont, but to show them that he knows the subjects on which Locke and Beccaria and Dumont have written. He need no more remember the different books which have made him wise, than the different breakfasts and dinners which have made him healthy. "Let us see the result of good food in a strong body, and the result of great reading in a full and powerful mind." Butler's Satire upon the Abuse of Human Learning tells us—

> "The pedants are a mongrel breed, that sojourn
> Among the ancient writers and the modern;
> And, while their studies are between the one
> And th' other spent, have nothing of their own. . . .
> For squandering of their wits and time upon
> Too many things has made them fit for none;
> Their constant overstraining of the mind
> Distorts the brain, as horses break their wind;

> Or rude confusions of the things they read
> Get up, like noxious vapours, in the head,
> Until they have their constant wanes, and fulls,
> And changes in the inside of their skulls :
> Or venturing beyond the reach of wit
> Has rendered them for all things else unfit ;
> They never bring the world and books together,
> And therefore never rightly judge of either ;
> Whence multitudes of reverend men and critics
> Have got a kind of intellectual rickets,
> And by th' immoderate excess of study
> Have found the sickly head t' outgrow the body."

Mr. Thackeray's comparison or contrast of his Warrington and Paley, in their chambers in the Temple, after having been competitors for university honours in former days, and running each other hard, is typically suggestive. Everybody said now that the former was wasting his time and energies, whilst all people praised Paley for his industry. But their author submits a doubt as to which was using his time best ; for at any rate the one could afford time to think, and the other never could ; the one could have sympathies and do kindnesses, and the other must needs be always selfish. "He could not cultivate a friendship, or do a charity, or admire a work of genius, or kindle at the sight of beauty or the sound of a sweet song—he had no time, and no eyes for anything but his law-books. All was dark outside his reading-lamp. Love, and Nature, and Art (which is the expression of our praise and sense of the beautiful world of God), were shut out from him." Applaudingly Horace Walpole quotes his friend Gray's pet paradox, that learning never should be encouraged, as it only draws fools out of their obscurity; "and you know," Horace reminds Bentley, "I have always thought a running footman as meritorious a being as a learned man. Why is there more merit in having travelled one's eyes over so many reams of paper, than in having carried one's legs over so many acres of ground?" What Young calls

> "Voracious learning, often over-fed,
> Digests not into sense her motley meal.
> This bookcase, with dark booty almost burst,
> This forager on others' wisdom, leaves
> Her native farm, her reason, quite untill'd."

The man whose knowledge all comes from reading, observes Mr. Charles Reade, accumulates a great number of what? facts? no, of the shadows of facts, "shadows often so thin, indistinct, and featureless, that when one of the facts themselves runs against him in real life, he does not know his old friend, round about which he has written a smart leader in a journal, and a ponderous trifle in the Polysyllabic Review." This comes of what the laureate calls "with blinded eyesight poring over miserable books." Argemone, in *Yeast*, differs from a commendatory notice of a certain rising statesman, so far as to confess, "To me, he seems to want life, originality, depth, everything that makes a great man. He knows nothing but what he has picked up ready-made from books." A French author has said of *le peu de souveraine sagesse* vouchsafed to men, that "le livre le plus savant n'en dira jamais autant que la rêverie au bord de la mer, dans la forêt ténébreuse, sous la vigne qui rit et qui chante." That which some would call idleness, Owen Feltham called the sweetest part of his life,—meditation ; and entirely to his mind was the saying of "a monk of an honester age, who on being asked how he could endure such a life, without the pleasure of books, answered, that the works of creation were his library, wherein, when he pleased, he could muse upon God's deep oracles." Diodati, in one of his Greek epistles to Milton (Θεόδοτος Μίλτωνι χαίρειν), while regretting a lack of society in his rustic seclusion, expresses his delight in scenery blooming with flowers and teeming with leaves, and then, turning on his correspondent, puts the question home, "But you, wondrous youth, why do you despise the gifts of Nature? why do you persist in tying yourself night and day to your books?" In Hawthorne's mystical fantasy-piece of the New Adam and Eve, the world's one lady would fain see her husband toss aside his book and lay aside his abstracted mien : "My dear Adam," she cries, " you look pensive and dismal ! Do fling down that stupid thing ; for even if it should speak, it would not be worth attending to. Let us talk with one another, and with the sky, and the green earth, and its trees and flowers. They will teach us better knowledge than we can find here." And those familiar with this spiritually suggestive author, America's most original genius, of the cultured class, may recall a passage in the imaginative vision named *Earth's Holocaust*, where a bookworm, a heavy-looking gentleman, in green spectacles, "one of those men who are born to gnaw dead thoughts," whose clothes are palpably covered with the dust of libraries, and who has no inward fountain of ideas, is thus addressed by the narrator: "My dear sir, is not Nature better than a book?—is not the human heart deeper than any system of philosophy? —is not life replete with more instruction than past observers have found it possible to write down in maxims? Be of good cheer,"—that is, in reference to the destruction of his books in the holocaust,—" the great book of Time is still spread wide open before us, and, if we read it aright, it will be to us a volume of eternal Truth." ."Oh, my books, my precious, printed books!" reiterates the forlorn bookworm. "My only reality was a bound volume; and now they will not leave me even a shadowy pamphlet!" Montaigne breaks out against the "snivelling, weak-eyed, slovenly fellow," who may be seen turning out of his study after midnight, and who has been tumbling over books, not to learn how to become a better man, wiser and more contented; "no such matter, but to teach posterity the metre of Plautus's verses, and the true orthography of some Latin word." A late essayist described ours as an age of books; and books, he said, with all their merits, do not promote originality: the ideas we get from them are seldom our own, for it requires "as much genius to appropriate an idea as to conceive one." We now seek in books for knowledge, whereas little knowledge is really to be gained, except from life and observation. "A man would not be very vigorous, if, instead of eating and drinking, he took a fancy to support himself by injecting ready-made chyle into his vessels." Mr. Slick is clear that "books spile the mind." He wouldn't "swap ideas" with any man. He professes to make his own opinions, as he used to make his own clocks, and finds them truer than other men's.* *La science!* exclaims Rivarol,—" un homme qui pense en sait toujours plus long qu'un homme qui apprend ; un homme qui agit vaut mille fois mieux qu'un homme qui pense." As for books, meditates Marcus Antoninus, "never be over-eager about them : such a fondness for reading will be apt to perplex your mind." Chaucer would add,

"And I say his opinion was good.
Why shulde man studie and make himselven wood,
Upon a book in cloistre alway to pore?"

---

* Speaking of the Turks as so ·plaguy heavy, they have people to dance for them, our spry Yankee adds, "The English are wuss, for they hire people to think for 'em. Never read a book, squire ; always think for yourself."—*The Attaché*, chap. xv.

In an earlier work he had harped on the same string. "Book-larned men seldom know nothin' but books, and there is one never was printed yet worth all they got on their shelves, which they never read, nor even so much as cut the leaves of, for they don't understand the handwritin', and that is—human natur'."—*The Clockmaker*, Third Series, chap. ix.

So Churchill with his fling at those who plod in college trammels to degrees,

> "Beneath the weight of solemn toys who groan,
> Sleep over books, and leave mankind unknown."

The genealogy of Experience, as traced by Mr. Disraeli, is brief; for Experience, he takes it, is the child of Thought, and Thought is the child of Action. We cannot, he urges, learn men from books, nor can we form, from written descriptions, a more accurate idea of the movements of the human heart, than we can of the movements of nature. Just as a man may read all his life, and form no conception of the rush of a mountain torrent, or the waving of a forest of pines in a storm; so a man may study in his closet the heart of his fellow-creatures for ever, and have no idea of the power of ambition, or the strength of revenge. Lord Macaulay is out of all patience with Johnson for declaring the "boasted Athenians" to be barbarians, as the mass of every people (the doctor assured Mrs. Thrale) must be barbarous where there is no printing. Seeing that a Londoner who could not read was a very stupid and brutal fellow, and seeing that great refinement of taste and activity of intellect were rarely found in a Londoner who had not read much, and because he saw it to be by books that people acquired almost all their knowledge in the society with which he was acquainted, Johnson concluded, as Macaulay explains the deductive process,—and concluded in defiance of the strongest and clearest evidence,—that the human mind can be cultivated by means of books alone. The doctor ignored the Athenian's other, and in 'some respects superior, inlets of knowledge,—a chat with Socrates, a speech from Pericles, a play by one of the great triad, etc., etc. An Athenian who did not improve his mind by reading "was, in Johnson's opinion, much such a person as a Cockney who made his mark, much such a person as Black Frank before he went to school, and far inferior to a parish clerk or a printer's devil." Dr. Holmes comments on the way the world has got into of thinking what it calls an "intellectual man " to be made up of nine-tenths, or thereabouts, of book-learning, and one-tenth himself; but adds, that even if the man is actually so compounded, he need not read much ; for society is a strong solution of books, drawing the virtue out of what is best worth reading, as hot water draws the strength of tea-leaves. The world's great men, he remarks in another place, have not commonly been great scholars, nor its great scholars great men. "The Hebrew patriarchs had small libraries, I think, if any; yet they represent to our imaginations a very complete idea of manhood." The passion for reading in many young people, however excellent in reason, has been called in many cases a blind and paralysing instinct, a mere bondage to type which cuts them off from half the important influences of their age: the eye fastening on a printed page, the mind helplessly pursues whatever comes to it under this guise, and eye and ear are dead and impervious to every other call; for there is such bondage to a habit, in some persons' reading, as implies a mind not so much anxious for knowledge, or even amusement, as set against all knowledge and amusement that does not come to it in the received method—that calls for independent effort and the employment of unpractised faculties. These are they who *will* only learn through books, and who would "rather open any page than look into intelligent eyes," and to whom cheerful voices and animated discussion are a simple interruption to the preoccupied attention. Naturally they come to think literature more instructive than life. It was of Sir James Mackintosh that Hazlitt said, "He might like to read an account of India; but India itself, with its burning, shining face, was a mere blank, an endless waste to him." And the caustic critic adds, in his rather splenetic style, that persons of this class have no more to say to a plain matter of fact staring them in the face, than they have to a hippopotamus. The mildest of critics must recognize, however, the existence of a whole class of minds which prefer the literary delineation of objects to the actual eyesight of them. To some, as Mr. Bagehot puts it, life is difficult: an insensible nature, like a rough hide, resists the breath of passing things; an unobserving retina in vain depicts whatever a quicker eye does not explain. "But any one can understand a book; the work is done, the facts are observed, the formulæ suggested, the subjects classified." Not but that labour is needed, and to some extent a "following fancy," to peruse the long lucubrations and descriptions of others; but a fine detective sensibility is not needed ;." type is plain, an earnest attention will follow it and know it." We are all taught books too much, and things too little,* says Mr. Caldwell Roscoe; the notion being still common that the most important part of knowledge consists in knowing what other men have said about things; to be familiar, not with what is, but what is printed. Sainte-Beuve has a sigh and a smile in one for those "qui ne sauraient rien que par les livres, par les auteurs, et qui ne communiqueraient avec les choses réelles que par de belles citations littéraires." Professor Masson can very well conceive that literature and culture, "and all that," formed but a small part of the general system of things in Shakspeare's daily thoughts, and that he would have been absolutely ashamed of himself if, when anything else, from the state of the weather to the quality of the wine, was within the circle of colloquial topics, he had said a word about his own plays. He "led so full and

---

* When Adam Bede, in the story, deferentially says to Mr. Donnithorne, "But where's the use o' me talking to you, sir? You know better than I do,"—"I'm not so sure of that, Adam," answers the young squire; "I think your life has been a better school to you than college has been to me." "Why, sir," Adam rejoins, "you seem to think o' college something like Bartle Massey does. He says college mostly makes people like bladders—just good for nothing but t' hold the stuff as is poured into 'eth."—*Adam Bede*, chap. xvi.

keen a life, and was drawn forth on so many sides by nature, society, and the unseen, that Literature, out of the actual moments in which he was engaged in it, must have seemed to him a mere bagatelle, a mere fantastic echo of not a tithe of life." No play, we are assured, could have seemed to the greatest of playwriters (it is otherwise with mere playwrights) worth a day of the contemporary actions of men, no description worth a single glance at the Thames, or at the deer feeding in the forest, no sonnet worth the tear it was made to embalm.

Dr. Hamilton used to compare the quitting one's book-den for the garden or the public road, to the collier coming up from his mine. He would have held with the old French master in Mrs. Gaskell's sketch, that above all it was a shame to coop young creatures up in a room, when every other young animal was frolicking in the air and sunshine. A pronounced lover of books has said that books are but one inlet of knowledge ; and the pores of the mind, like those of the body, should be left open to all impressions.

"Up ! up ! my friend, and quit your books,
Or surely you'll grow double,"

is Wordsworth's expostulating appeal.

"Books ! 'tis a dull and endless strife :
Come, hear the woodland linnet,
How sweet his music ! on my life,
There's more of wisdom in it."

That is the poetical side of an appeal of which Hogarth's is the prosaic one, in the impromptu he is said to have penned to Mr. Tighe, who was perversely intent on some Greek book when dinner was ready:

> "Then come to dinner,* do, my honest Tighe,
> And leave thy Greek, and η β τ.
>   eat a bit o' pie."

Systematically bookish boys developing into bookish men "can never make the use they ought of their acquirements by talking well, and so improving and enriching the general tone of thought." As with a contemporary poet's genesis and progress of a man of science,—

> "Deep, then, we plunge into Acrogens, Ætheogams, Amphigams, still:
> I hope to get on by degrees into Exogens, Endogens: meantime
> Moons wax and wane; summers fleet; from the student, as patient he crams still
> Dry leaves under the tin lids, steals sighing the glad and the green time."

Maximin's answer, in Landor's *Fra Rupert*, to his sister Agatha's statement that reading and needle-

---

* From the Greek is adapted Hood's epigrammatic address to Minerva, in which the overtasked student complains that his temples throb, his pulses boil, he's sick of song, and ode, and ballad, and so he takes the midnight oil, and pours it on a lobster salad.

> "My brain is dull, my sense is foul,
> I cannot write a verse, or read—
> Then, Pallas, take away thine Owl,
> And let us have a Lark instead."

work with her employ the day, is a sighing remonstrance:

> "Ah! our good mother little knew what pests
> Those needles and those books are; to bright eyes;
> Rivals should recommend them, mothers no."

Halbert Glendinning tells his brother Edward in their young days, when the elder is for joining the Laird of Colmslie at the head of the glen with his hounds, and the younger expresses indifference to the chase, and is for sticking to his books, that he will labour at the monk's lessons till he turns monk himself. True, a word from Mary Avenel makes Halbert fling aside his bonnet, and with a smile and a sigh take up the primer, and turn student himself; but he cannot for long endure the constraint, and starting up, dashes his book from him as he exclaims, "To the fiend I bequeath all books, and the dreamers that make them!—I would a score of Southrons would come up the glen, and we should learn how little all this muttering and scribbling is worth."* Many books, wise men have said, and Milton after them, or with them, as one of them,—

> "are wearisome; who reads
> Incessantly, and to his reading brings not
> A spirit and judgment equal or superior,
> (And what he brings what needs he elsewhere seek?)

---

* "Yes, Mary, I wish a score of Southrons came up the glen this very day, and you should see one good hand and one good sword do more to protect you than all the books that were ever opened, and all the pens that ever grew on a goose's wing."—*The Monastery*, chap. xi.

> Uncertain and unsettled still remains,
> Deep versed in books, and shallow in himself,
> Crude or intoxicate, collecting toys
> And trifles for choice matters, worth a sponge;
> As children gathering pebbles on the shore."

Breaking in upon his son in the study, "I thought I should find thee here, lad," Squire Hamley tells studious Roger, in Mrs. Gaskell's last story: "it smells musty enough, and yet I see it's the place for thee. I want thee to go with me round the five-acre. I'm thinking of laying it down in grass. It's time for you to be getting into the fresh air; you look quite wobegone over books, books, books; there never was a thing like 'em for stealing a man's health out of him." So, and yet not altogether so, with Beryl stirring up George Geith, she from without, on the garden terrace, appealing through an open window to him at his books (not of belles lettres, by-the-bye), and entreating him to cease writing before he grew into a machine, and exclaiming "How you can go on, on, hour after hour; ... how you can live out of the sunshine, away from the flowers, puzzles me." Later in the book, Beryl's more peremptory younger sister protests, to the same purpose, that she cannot imagine what flowers, and fields, and trees were given to people for, if they never look at them.

The poetess of the *Deserted Garden* records how oft she read within her nook such minstrel stories! till the breeze made sounds poetic in the trees—and then she shut the book. *That* is just what a mere bookish being would not have done. Rogers and Charles Fox were one day expatiating, as the story goes, on the delight of lying in summer time deep in sunny grass and flowers, and looking up at the white clouds toppling past overhead. "Delightful—with a book," exclaimed Rogers. "But why with a book?" said Fox. Wordsworth* would have backed Fox.

> "One impulse from a vernal wood
> May teach you more of man,
> Of moral evil and of good
> Than all the sages can."

But speaking of impulse, one remembers Goethe's Wagner, true type of the bookish man; how he tells Faust,

> "But impulse such as this I ne'er have known;
> Nor woods, nor fields, our thoughts can long engage,
> Their wings I envy not the feather'd kind;
> Far otherwise the pleasures of the mind
> Bear us from book to book, from page to page!
> Then winter nights grow cheerful; keen delight
> Warms every limb; and ah! when we unroll
> Some old and precious parchment, at the sight
> All heaven itself descends upon the soul."

Not he the man to respond to Gresset's summons: *Venez, de la docte poussière osez franchir les tourbillons.* Not on ethical but purely on intellectual ground would he have taken his stand against Chesterfield's counsel: "An hour at Versailles, Compiegne, or St.

---

* In his stanzas *To my Sister* he bids her put on with speed her woodland dress, "And bring no book: for this one day we'll give to idleness."

Cloud, is now worth more to you than three hours in your closet, with the best books that ever were written." No sympathy have the Wagners with a Cowper singling out a woodland recess, and saying of it,

> "Meditation here
> May think the hours to moments. Here the heart
> May give a useful lesson to the head,
> And learning wiser grow without his books."

For, on Cowper's showing, knowledge and wisdom, far from being one, have ofttimes no connexion: knowledge dwells in heads replete with thoughts of other men, wisdom in minds attentive to their own. The erudition which remains extraneous to the mind, as Mrs. Browning puts it, in her eloquent dissertation on the *Greek Christian Poets*, is and must be in some degree an obstruction and deformity. "How many are there, from Psellus to Bayle, bound hand and foot intellectually with the rolls of their own papyrus— men whose erudition has grown stronger than their souls." Not that knowledge is bad, but that wisdom is better, and that it is "better and wiser in the sight of the angels of knowledge to think out one true thought with a thrush's song and a green light for all lexicon," than to mummy our benumbed souls with the circumvolutions of twenty thousand books.

> "For hark! how blithe the throstle sings!
> He, too, is no mean preacher:
> Come forth into the light of things,
> Let Nature be your teacher."

There, in Wordsworth as in Mrs. Browning, we have

in conjunction the thrush and the light. Sweetness and light, one might call it, in Mr. Matthew Arnold's phrase.

When the scholar or the writer, says Emerson, has pumped his brain for thoughts and verses,* and then comes abroad into Nature, " has he never found that there is a better poetry hinted in the piping of a sparrow, than in all his literary results ?" A frank young countrywoman of his owns that books to her are just like dry hay—very good when there isn't any fresh grass to be had. She would rather be out of doors and eat what's growing. Nature never bores her, but almost every book she ever saw does. Lucy Aiken tells us of Joanna Baillie that of all the readers she had ever known, that poetess of the passions spoke the least of books: it was not from them, but from real life, and from the aspects of rural nature, that her imagination drew the materials in which it worked, and it had been the penance of her youth to be drawn away from these to her letterpress studies.

It is not a pleasant picture one of Pope's biographers has painted of the sickly stunted young poet shut up in his room at Binfield, building himself up with books, reading till the stars twinkle in upon him unheeded, reading while the wonders of the sun-setting

---

* Moore in his Diary notes his breaking off from penwork to some purpose : " Walked four hours ; the day exquisite. Felt bursts of devotion while I walked and looked at the glorious world about me, which did me more good than whole volumes of theology."—(Diary, Jan. 12, 1819.)

and sun-rising pass by unknown. "He is ignorant how the little birds answer each other among the trees, and how the wood-pigeons coo. The mavis and the merle are never singing among the branches, nor is it a 'good greenwood' to the boy-poet." He has nothing to do with the beauty outside; the dews fall not, the balm breathes not, for him. Windsor Forest was the scene, its glades and recesses the surroundings; but in a "curious mental workshop," as one critic expresses it, the lad lived and laboured, "with his windows shut, we may be sure," and the fever of toil on his worn face: it was a juvenile manufactory, where verse was already turned and re-turned, and where a correct couplet was reckoned the highest product of earth and heaven. Thus at least modern criticism rates him, and rates his work. And this, if true, is about as bad, or worse, than the insensibility to impulses from Nature, pure and simple, attributed by Elia to didactic dominies, who must needs, *ex officio*, seize every occasion (the season of the year, a passing cloud, a rainbow, a waggon of hay) to inculcate something useful; who can receive no pleasure from a casual glimpse of Nature, but must catch at it as an object of instruction, and must interpret beauty into the picturesque; for to them nothing comes that is not spoiled by the "sophisticating medium of moral uses." When Guy Darrell asks Lionel Haughton if he is fond of reading, and the young man answers that he thinks so, but is not sure,

"You mean perhaps," surmises the former, "that you like reading, if you may choose your own books." Or rather, is Lionel's amendment, if he may choose his own time to read them, and that would not be on bright summer days. Guy Darrell suggests that without sacrificing bright summer days, one finds one has made little progress when the long winter nights come. Agreed. But, urges Lionel, must the sacrifice be paid in books? He fancies he learned as much in the playground as he did in the schoolroom, and if he can boast of any progress at all in afterlife, the books (to his thinking) have the smaller share in it. The Autocrat of the Breakfast-table professes to have always believed in life rather than in books. He supposes every day of earth, with its hundred thousand deaths and something more of births,—with its loves and hates, its triumphs and defeats, its pangs and blisses, has more of humanity in it than all the books that were ever written, put together; just as he believes the flowers growing at this moment send up more fragrance to heaven than was ever exhaled from all the essences ever distilled. How would Pliny the elder have endured this autocracy? he who rebuked Pliny the younger for taking a walk: "You might have managed," he said, "not to lose the hours," for he considered all time lost* which

---

* So Bayle: "Je ne perds pas une heure," was his bookish boast. A later critic accounts it his shame. "O philosophie aveugle! qui ne connaît pas les joies contemplatives du temps perdu."

was not given to study. It was for the Apostle of Muscular Christianity to preach as gospel truth that whatever ministers to the *corpus sanum* will minister also to the *mens sana ;* that a walk along Durdham Downs shall send a man home wiser and happier than poring over many wise volumes or hearing many wise lectures. "How often," exclaims the canonical author or authority here referred to, "is a worthy fellow spending his leisure honourably in hard reading, when he had much better have been scrambling over hedge and ditch, without a thought in his head save what was put there by the grass and the butterflies, and the green trees, and the blue sky!" Mr. Ruskin expatiates on the beauty of the types presented by trees, of the truths most essential to mankind to know, truths uttered in "lovely language," "not in frightful black letters, nor in dull sentences, but in fair green and shadowy shapes of waving words, and blossomed brightness of odoriferous wit, and sweet whispers of unintrusive wisdom, and playful morality." Perhaps the most keenly appreciative and subtilely sympathetic, as well as eloquent,. of all Wordsworth's admirers, says of him, from daily and intimate personal observation, that even the few books which his peculiar mind had made indispensable to him, were not in such a sense indispensable, as they would have been to a man of more sedentary habits; for he lived in the open air, and the enormity of pleasure which he drew from the common appearances of nature and their everlasting variety, was to him in the stead of many libraries. Applying to him his own lines, "One impulse from a vernal wood could teach him more of man," etc., Mr. de Quincey goes on to say of him that, able as he was to draw "even from the meanest flower that blows, thoughts that do often lie too deep for tears,"—to find pleasures in the mere daisy, the pansy, the primrose,—not the puerile pleasures which his most puerile and worldly insulters imagined, but pleasures drawn from depths of reverie and meditative tenderness far beyond all power of *their* hearts to conceive,—" that man would hardly need any large variety of books." The one vernal impulse taught him more of Man, of moral evil and of good, than all the sages and budge doctors of stoic or any other fur, combined, could avail to teach him.

V.

Book Sparks: In Talk.

GIBBON's great conversational defect, says M. Guizot, was a studied arrangement of his words, which never allowed him to utter one not worth hearing. He talked "like a prent book." This precision, when conjoined with fluent ease, has its charm, as in the instance of M. de Tocqueville, who, though always perfectly simple, preserved, in the most intimate and familiar conversations, the purity of expression and admirable choice of words which M. Ampère calls a part of his nature. "While sitting on the rocks around Sorrento," writes the latter, "I might have written down (and why did I not?) all that escaped his lips in those moments of friendly intercourse." But, taken generally, the expressive phrase that a man talks like a book, is well said to exactly hit off the person who retails the sort of information we generally look for in books, and puts it in the same way in which it is ordinarily put in print. This is pretty unanimously voted priggish; and the prig is condemned as a bore when he gets on a big subject, because we feel that his opinions are second-hand, however right they may be. Chesterfield, in one of his letters, describes himself as tired, jaded, nay tormented by the recent company of a most worthy, sensible, and learned man, a near kinsman too, who, "far from talking without book, as is commonly said of people who talk sillily, only talks by book; which, in general conversation, is ten times worse. .... He is acquainted with books, and an absolute stranger to men." Hazlitt cautions a close student not to be surprised, when he goes out into the world, to find men talk exceedingly well on different subjects, who do not derive their information immediately from books; for common sense is not a monopoly, and experience and observation are sources of information open to the man of the world as well as to the retired scholar. "It is the vice of scholars to suppose that there is no knowledge in the world but that of books." Moore rather congratulates himself, in his autobiography, on his early association with two such unbookish sparks as Beresford Burston and Bond Hall. Had he been at all inclined to pedantic display in conversation, the society of this pair would, it seems, have most effectually cured him of it, as the slightest allusion to literature or science in their presence was at once put down. Indeed, such influence have early impressions and habits upon all our after-lives that Moore expresses his conviction that the common and ordinary level of his own habitual conversation—which, while it disappointed, no doubt, Blues and *savans*, enabled him to get on so well as he claims to have done, with "most hearty and simple-minded persons"—arose a good deal from having lived chiefly, in his young days, with such sprightly fellows as Bond Hall, instead of, as he puts it, "consorting with your young men of high college reputation, almost all of whom that I have ever known were inclined to be pedants and bores." Bolingbroke, in the first of his celebrated letters on the study of history, speaks of bookish people who have the disadvantage of becoming a nuisance very often to society, in proportion to the progress they make in their studies; for they are apt to grow in impertinence as they increase in learning. "The persons I mean are those who read to talk, to shine in conversation, and to impose in company; who, having few ideas to vend of their own growth, store their minds with crude unruminated facts and sentences; and hope to supply by bare memory the want of imagination and judgment." During their tour to the Hebrides, Johnson said to Boswell one day, "They call me a scholar, and yet how very little literature there is in my conversation." "That, sir, must be according to your company," Boswell replied; "you would not give literature to those who cannot taste it. Stay till we meet Lord Elibank." Some weeks later we find the doctor observing again to Boswell how common it was for people to talk from books—to retail the sentiments of others, and not their own; in short, to con-

verse without any originality of thinking. He was
pleased to say, "You and I do not talk from books,"
as Boswell is pleased to record.

Madame d'Arblay describes the learned Mrs.
Carter's talk as very unaffected and good-humoured,
"though all upon books (for life and manners she is
as ignorant of as a nun)." Elsewhere Madame, as yet
Fanny Burney, journalizes a large party at home,
where "Mr. Pepys led the conversation, and it was all
upon criticism and poetry. . . . The conversation grew
so very bookish, I was ashamed of being one in it, and
not without reason, as everybody, out of that party,
told me afterwards, 'they had been afraid of approaching me, I was so well engaged.'" Who cannot, asks
Hartley Coleridge, distinguish a man, or a book, that
is talking by rote? there being in all such talkers, and
all such books, an air of studied facility that instantly
betrays them. What is called a fluent man, who talks
"like a prent book," is, he bids us depend upon it,
always a shallow man (if at least the faculty of easy
speaking is natural to him, for the deepest intellects
may acquire it by practice). Formerly, women and
mechanics were the best company to be found, when
everything they said was original, the product of
their own thoughts and feelings. But now, in an age
when the so-called universality of education has a
tendency to stifle all originality, the sex and the class
in question are "crammed with just enough knowledge
to display the magnitude of their ignorance." Now-

adays, whatever they say, complained old-fashioned Hartley, is something out of a book. "Now I hate to hear people talk out of books. I can read myself," says he.

The dislike of pure bookworms notoriously begins very early in life, and the same popular disrespect besets them when they go up from school to the university; while, as regards after-life, a man of letters must, in order to be appreciated by his generation, be a man of letters and something more. The world, which despises a bookworm, appreciates doubly the cleverness of a man who has a distinct social turn. Genius and action are declared to be inseparable companions; and the bookworm, "paradoxical as it may seem, is a compound of laboriousness and inaction." Libraries, as an essay-writer on the bookworm puts it, are only worth anything to the world so far as they serve as a means of inspiration; and the bookworm is not always inspired. As the bookworm does nothing openly for the world, and shuns all intercourse with it, naturally it conceives of him as a misanthrope, whose "books are to him what men, women, and horses are to less retired and refined human beings." But having thus got on the trail of the bookworm, let us assign him a section all for himself.

VI.

Book Hacks: Trail of the Bookworm.

AS Peter *Comestor* is commemorated by Disraeli the elder as receiving his nickname from his amazing voracity for food he could never digest, so is Magliabechi as the *Helluo* or Glutton of Literature. Mag., as Mr. de Quincey loved to call him, had all his rooms crammed with books; they were piled in heaps on the floor, and you had to sidle along a narrow space between the heaps to walk from one room to another; the staircases were lined with them, and the very beds in the bedrooms groaned beneath their weight. Mag. read them day and night, and never lost sight of any: "he ate on his books, he slept on his books, and quitted them as rarely as possible,"—only twice in his life going a league or two from Florence. His interest in anything printed was beyond that pleasantly asserted of himself by the Spectator, who professes to have so much of the Mussulman about him that he cannot forbear looking into every printed paper that comes in his way, under whatsoever despicable circumstances it may appear.*

Perhaps for no other particular is that William King who figures in Johnson's *Lives of the Poets* so likely to be had in remembrance as for this one, that during his university course at Christ Church he is said to have prosecuted his studies with so much intenseness and activity, that before he was of eight years' standing, he had read over, and made remarks upon, twenty-two thousand odd hundred books and manuscripts. With Johnson, we must need draw the obvious inference that the books were certainly not very long, the manuscripts not very difficult, and the remarks not very ample; for a calculator will find that King the poet despatched seven a day for every day of his eight years, with a remainder more than large enough to satisfy most other students. The Christopher Clutterbuck of fiction is fiction founded upon fact—the absorbed, abstracted student, never seen out of the precincts of his college "rooms," except in obedience to the stated calls of lectures, hall, and chapel, when his stooping form is to be marked, as he crosses the quadrangle with a hurried step, rude in garb, and saturnine of aspect, though eagerness speaks from his wan cheek and emaciated frame, as he scuffles

---

* "This my inquisitive temper . . . gives me a good deal of employment when I enter any house in the country; for I cannot for my heart leave a room, before I have thoroughly studied the walls of it, and examined the several printed papers which are usually pasted upon them," etc.—*Spectator*, No. 85.

back, after every such legitimate interruption, to his enjoyment of the crabbed characters and wormeaten volumes, which contain for him all the seductions of pleasure and all the temptations of youth.

> " For him was lever have at his beddes heed
> Twenty bookes, clothed in blak and reed,
> Of Aristotil, and of his philosophie,
> Than robus riche, or fithul, or sawtrie.
> But al though he were a philosophre,
> Yet hadde he but litul gold in cofre ;
> But al that he might of his frendes hente,
> On bookes and his lernyng he it spente."

All history, observes Bolingbroke, in his letters on the study of it, is not an object of curiosity for any man; and he who improperly, wantonly, and absurdly makes it so, indulges a sort of canine appetite ; the curiosity of the one, like the hunger of the other, devours ravenously, and without distinction, whatever falls in its way, but neither of them digests : they heap crudity upon crudity, and nourish and improve nothing, but their distemper. Accomplished St. John draws upon his memory for a picture of such a *helluo librorum*—one who, having read almost constantly twelve or fourteen hours a day, for five-and-twenty or thirty years, had heaped together as much learning as could be crowded into a single brain-pan. The noble lord consulted his too, too learned friend once or twice,—not oftener ; for he found this mass of learning of as little use to the applicant as to the owner. The man was communicative enough, it seems; but nothing was distinct in his mind. How could it be otherwise? he had never spared time to think; all was employed in reading. His reason had not, to his candid friend's mind, the merit even of common mechanism; for, at any rate, when you press a watch or pull a clock, they answer your question with precision, repeating exactly the hour of the day, and telling you neither more nor less than you desire to know. But when you asked this man a question, he overwhelmed you by pouring forth all that the several terms or words of your question recalled to his memory; and if he omitted anything, it was that very thing to which the sense of the whole question should have led him and confined him. "To ask him a question, was to wind up a spring in his memory, that rattled on with vast rapidity and confused noise till the force of it was spent; and you went away with all the noise in your ears, stunned and uninformed." Bolingbroke never left him without feeling disposed to say to him, "Dieu vous fasse la grace de devenir moins savant!" a wish that La Mothe le Vayer mentions upon some occasion or other, and which it is well said he would have well done to have applied to himself upon many.

Non cuivis contingit to escape congestion of the brain, and collapse of its motive power, as Gibbon did, who overlays it as Gibbon seemed to do with perilous stuff enough to weigh upon it with a dead weight as of death itself. Right early the trick of study began, and robust indeed must have been the constitution that sustained such excesses, first and last. As we hear of the boy Chatterton sitting alone for hours in his garret, amid all kinds of out-of-the-way lumber, devouring whatever he had pounced upon for his solitary meals, whether the Bible, or theological treatises, or old magazines, or odd volumes of history and verse, or whatever else in the shape of a printed book might come in his way; so from Gibbon himself we hear how to the "kind lessons" of his aunt Porten he owed, or at least ascribes, that "early and invincible love of reading which," in mature age, he "would not exchange for the treasures of India." His indiscriminate appetite subsided by degrees in the historic line—which result he traces to his assiduous perusal of the *Universal History*, as the octavo volumes successively appeared. All the Greek and Roman historians to which he could gain access;—" All that I could find were greedily devoured, from Littlebury's lame Herodotus, and Spelman's valuable Xenophon, to the pompous folios of Gordon's Tacitus, and a ragged Procopius of the beginning of the last century." From the ancients he leaped to the modern world; many crude lumps of Speed, Rapin, Mezeray, Davila, Machiavel, Father Paul, Bower, etc., he devoured like so many novels; and he swallowed, as he phrases it, with the same voracious appetite the descriptions of India and China, of Mexico and Peru. Mahomet and the Saracens anon fixed his attention. Simon Ockley, "an original in every sense," first opened his eyes, and he was led from one book to another, till he had ranged round the circle of oriental history. Before he was halfway through his teens, Edward Gibbon had exhausted all that could be learned in English of the Arabs and Persians, the Tartars and Turks; and the same ardour, he tells us, urged him to guess at the French of D'Herbelot, and to construe the barbarous Latin of Pocock's Abulfaragius. He concedes that reading so vague and multifarious could not teach him to think, or write, or act; and the only principle that darted, as he intimates, a ray of light into the undigested chaos, was an early and rational application to the order of time and place. Accordingly, the maps of Cellarius and Wells imprinted in his mind the picture of ancient geography; from Strauchius he learned the elements of chronology; while the tables of Helvicus and Anderson, the Annals of Ussher and Prideaux, familiarized him with the connection of events, and with the multitude of names and dates in a clear and (to him) indelible series. In fine, he "arrived at Oxford with a stock of erudition that might have puzzled a doctor," but, also, on his own showing, with "a degree of ignorance of which a schoolboy would have been ashamed." Writing in middle life, he allows himself to observe that he had never consciously bought a book from a motive of ostentation, and that every volume, before he deposited it on the shelf, was either read or sufficiently examined. And at what a rate he bought books, and with what zest he exchanged gold for paper,—not the tissue paper of bank-notes, but the bookseller's own particular,—his Memoirs show. Witness the record of never-to-be-forgotten joy with which, on the receipt of his first quarter's allowance, he appropriated twenty pounds to the purchase of the twenty volumes of Memoirs of the Academy of Inscriptions. And for evidence of the love's labour he never counted lost on literature, witness his record of the solution of a passage in Livy, that involved him in the dry and dark treatises of Greaves, Arbuthnot, Hooper, Bernard, Eisenschmidt, Gronovius, La Barré, Freret, etc. By degrees his chosen library came to comprise from six to seven thousand volumes. " My seraglio was ample, my choice was free, my appetite was keen. After a full repast on Homer and Aristophanes, I involved myself in the philosophic maze of the writings of Plato." Like the speaker in *The Elder Brother*, his cue was,

> "Give me leave
> To enjoy myself: that place that does contain
> My books, the best companions, is to me
> A glorious court, where hourly I converse
> With the old sages and philosophers."

Very near the end of his autobiography comes Gibbon's complacent avowal: "The love of study, a passion which derives fresh vigour from enjoyment, supplies each day, each hour, with a perpetual source of independent and rational pleasure; and I am not sensible of any decay of the mental faculties," any more than of appetite for the food that kept them going, in more than one sense. Even May-day might have been to him no exception, as in Chaucer's case it was, to the rule, otherwise in the old poet's instance universal, of bookish predilections all the world over, and all the year round :

> "On bokes for to rede I me delyte,
> And to hem geve I feyth and ful credence,
> And in myn herte have hem in reverence
> So hertely, that ther is game noon,
> That fro my bokes maketh me to goon."

Mark the raptures of Anthony à Wood over Dugdale's *Antiquities of Warwickshire:* "My pen cannot enough describe how A. Wood's tender affections, and insatiable desire of knowledg, were ravished and melted downe by the reading of that book," at Oxford, in the summer of 1656. "What by musick and rare books that he found in the public library, his life, at this time and after, was a perfect Elysium." Years later we come upon him perusing the registers of abbeys and priories, and "it was an exceeding pleasure to him, and he took very great delight to be poring on such books, and collecting matter from them." Next year he is almost pathetic in describing his "esurient genie in antiquities," and his supreme delight in being entrusted by Dr. John Wallis, the keeper of the university registers, with the keys of the school-tower, containing the said registers,—all to aid the progress of his laborious work, *Hist. et Antiqu. Univ. Oxon.* " He [Anthony] was so exceedingly delighted with the place and the choice records therein, and did take so much paynes for carrying on the work, least the keys should be taken away from him, that a great alteration was made in him. About 2 months after his entrance into the said tower, his acquaintance took notice of the falling away of his cheeks, the chang of the redness in them to white, etc." Our human and humane bookworm was seemingly the prey of such a worm as Viola idealizes— letting concealment, like a worm i' the bud, feed on his damask cheek. " Yet he was very cheerfull, contented and healthfull, and nothing troubled him more than the intermission of his labours by eating, drinking, sleeping, and sometimes by company which he could not avoid." Once more, an entry from the Diary in 1666. " About that time [Feb. 16] A. W. began to peruse the MSS. in the public library, and took great paynes in plucking downe every book." None to be passed by ; no, not one. A modern bibliophile avows his love for an ancient author the more when himself a lover of books ; for whereas the idea of an ancient library perplexes one's sympathy by its map-like volumes, rolled upon cylinders, and one's imagination cannot take kindly to a yard of wit, or to thirty inches of moral observation, rolled out like linen in a draper's shop, yet we conceive of Plato as of a lover of books ; of Aristotle, certainly; of Horace, Plutarch, Pliny, and Marcus Antoninus. "Virgil too must have been one, and, after a fashion, Martial. May I confess," writes our self-styled Literary Examiner, "that the passage which I recollect with the greatest pleasure in Cicero, is where he says that books delight us at home, and are no impediment abroad (*non impediunt foris*), travel with us, ruralize with us." He takes our four, great English poets to have been all fond of reading: Milton and Chaucer proclaim themselves for hard sitters at books; Spenser's reading is evident by his learning; and if there were nothing else to show for it in Shakspeare, his retiring to his native town, long before old age, is submitted as proof positive of it— since it is held to be impossible for a man to live in solitude without such assistance, unless he is a metaphysician or mathematician, or the dullest of mankind; and any country town would be solitude to Shakspeare, after the bustle of theatre-life in the great city. Prior, again, is noticed by Leigh Hunt for his bookish propensities: he first attracted Dorset's attention by his study of Horace, as a boy, sitting in his uncle's tavern. Fenton is cited as a martyr to contented scholarship (including a sirloin and a bottle of wine): he died, among his books, of inactivity. Gray was a book man: his express, and expressed, and expressive wish, was, to be ever lying on the sofa, reading ever new and new novels of Crébillon and Marivaux. Among the older writers are not to be forgotten Cowley, whose boyish love of books stuck to him to the last; and Izaak Walton, and Selden, that "walking library of our nation," and Dr. Donne, and Ben Jonson, whose reading was, in one sense, the making of his plays, some think the spoiling of them; and Drayton, who was "addicted to all the luxuries of scholarship;" and Chapman, who is pictured sitting among his books like an astrologer among his spheres.

Few writers of any note have been more fervid and frequent in their avowals of a passion for books than Leigh Hunt. The passion was strong and lusty even in his school-days. He tells us how he doted on the little sixpenny numbers of Cooke's British Poets, as they came out in that cheap serial—doted on their size, doted on their type, on their ornaments, on their wrappers containing lists of other poets; how, when the masters tormented him, he would comfort himself with thinking of the sixpence in his pocket, with which to sally out anon to Paternoster Row, and buy another number of an English poet. "My books were a never-failing consolation to me, and such they have ever continued." Later on he mentions his "delighted perusal of the whole set of classics (for I have ever been a 'glutton of books')." When in prison he bought the collection of poetry called the *Parnasso Italiano*, in fifty-six duodecimo volumes, and thought it cheap at thirty pounds, considering himself, though a poor man all his life, repaid a mil-

lion times over in the pleasure he received from it.*
And towards the end of his days he describes himself
as reading everything that was readable, old and new,
particularly fiction, and philosophy, and natural history—always however returning to something Italian,
or in Spenser, or in the themes of the East; losing
no particle of Dickens or Thackeray, of Mrs. Gaskell
or Mrs. Gore; hailing even every fresh publication
of the then inexhaustible G. P. R. James, though
knowing all about what it would be beforehand;
relishing every paragraph in *Punch*, and a devoted
subscriber to and literally a peruser of a weekly penny
journal.

To George Dyer, his friend, and emphatically
Lamb's, books "were a real world, both pure and
good," as Talfourd applies the line; among which he
passed, unconscious of time, from youth to extreme
age, vegetating on their dates and forms, and "trivial
fond records," in the learned air of great libraries,
or the dusty confusion of his own, but all this with
the least possible apprehension of any human interest vital in their pages, or of any spirit of wit or
fancy gleaming across them. Herein a vivid contrast is drawn between him and his fast friend Elia,
in their several relations to the literature they both
loved; George devoted with assiduity to its externals,

---

* "In prison it was truly a lump of sunshine on my shelves; and I
have never since been without it. I even took it with me to its native
land."—*Autobiography of Leigh Hunt*, chap. xxiii.

while Charles divined its inmost essences, plucked out the heart of its mysteries, and shed light on its dimmest recesses.

Coleridge, by his own account, was from eight to fourteen a *helluo librorum*; and his appetite was indulged by an odd incident: a stranger who was struck by his conversation, made the bluecoat boy free of a circulating library in King Street, Cheapside. Here he professes to have read through all that was in the catalogue, folios and all, whether he understood them or did not understand them, running all risks in skulking out to get the two volumes which he was entitled to have daily. "Conceive what I must have been at fourteen;* I was in a continual low fever. My whole being was, with eyes closed to every object of present sense, to crumple myself up in a sunny corner and read, read, read." The common friend of all the authors we have recently named, Henry Crabb Robinson, was another voracious devourer of books. He read before he got up, Dr. Sadler tells us, and after he went to bed, and while walking, and while travelling by coach. In a Christmas visit to Rydal,

---

* Speaking of himself at about the same age, Polevoy, the Russian (or rather *the* Siberian) author, says, "I had read about a thousand volumes of all kinds, and remembered all that I read from the verses of Karamzin, and the articles of the [Russian] *Courier of Europe*, to the Chronological Tables and the Bible, from which I could repeat whole chapters by heart. I was known in Irkutzk as 'the wonderful boy,' with whom the director of the grammar school used to dispute as with a learned man." Yet he never, apparently, received any schooling.

for a month or five weeks, he would read a score of such works as those of Arnold, Whately, and Isaac Taylor. "Nor was he one of those who think they have read a work when they have only skimmed through it, and made themselves acquainted with its general contents." He would make a digest as he went on; and himself digest a very heavy meal of book-matter he could, and did. But, as M. de Sacy has remarked, "Ne lit pas et n'étudie pas qui le veut. Il y faut une disposition particulière, non seulement de l'esprit, mais du corps et de la santé." Shenstone was constitutionally a predisposed and so a predestinated reader, from those days of infancy when he was always calling for fresh entertainment, and expected that, when any of the family went to market, a new book should be brought him, which, when it came, was in fondness carried by him to bed; and the story goes of his once, when the purchase had been neglected, being pacified for the night by a piece of wood, its form and counterfeit.

Heeren relates the acquaintance young Heyne made in the Brühl Library with Johann Winkelmann, then a wholly unknown man, whose visits could not be specially desirable for the librarians, such endless labour did he cost them. For he seemed insatiable in reading; and so many were the books he called for, that his reception there grew rather of the coolest.

The late Dr. James Hamilton was avowedly a confirmed glutton of books. He declared that no miser can ever have gloated over gold as he revelled over them. He tells his publisher of his almost untellable sensations on receiving a monster parcel—how his temples throbbed with incipient fever; how the fruition of the contents made him as "a cow among clover;" and how altogether the endless tomes and tomelets supplied him with "the most satisfying banquet that was ever furnished to a morbid appetite for printed paper, a *monomania librorum*." Jefferson in old age expatiated on his "canine appetite for reading," which he confessedly indulged because he saw in it, and, alas! only in it, a relief against the *tædium senectutis*,—a lamp to lighten his path through the dreary wilderness of time before him, whose bourne he knew not.

VII.

Book Marks: Marginal and Miscellaneous.

A SATURDAY Reviewer has said of Coleridge, whose *Literary Remains* he accounts one of the most instructive books it is possible to mention, that if he had forced himself to think with more continuity, and had shown a greater degree of mental continence, he would have earned greater fame for himself, but he would also have taught less to his contemporaries. The depth, the weight, the originality, and variety of criticisms written on the margins of books by S. T. C., without the fear of scandalizing weak brothers, are declared to be "full of every kind of excellence. They are unsystematic; they may, for aught we know, be inconsistent; but they would be ill exchanged for the most symmetrical composition of almost any other hand." The heart of Elia would have warmed to the penman of this praise. Lamb's copy of Donne contains many marginal notes by Coleridge,[*]

---

[*] In the Diary of their common friend, the late H. C. Robinson, we read, some two years after the death of Coleridge: "I rose early, and copied some curious marginal notes by Coleridge in Lightfoot's works.

with this memorandum: "I shall die soon, my dear Charles Lamb, and then you will not be vexed that I have bescribbled your book.—S. T. C., 2nd May, 1811." In the same essay which taxes Coleridge with inveterate book-borrowing, Elia credits him with unique gifts of almost priceless marginal annotation. To lose a volume to *him* carried some sense and meaning in it. But oftener he returned the volume (often before the time appointed) with usury; enriched with annotations that tripled their value. "Many are these precious MSS. of his—(in *matter* oftentimes, and almost in *quantity* not unfrequently, vying with the originals) in no very clerkly hand—legible in my Daniel; in old Burton; in Sir Thomas Browne; and those abstruser cogitations of the Greville, now, alas! wandering in Pagan lands." Hence Elia prompts his reader, if he lend books at all, to lend them to such as Coleridge. "I counsel thee, shut not thy heart, nor thy library, against S. T. C." On the fly-leaf of the fourth volume of Anderson's British Poets, Hartley Coleridge indited this characteristic notice, to all whom it might concern: "Where-

They are pious and reverential in thought, though sometimes almost comic in expression. He regrets that Lightfoot should *paw* the sacred mysteries,—an admirable expression, and one that came from Coleridge's heart, and might well continue to be employed."—*Diary of Henry Crabb Robinson*, vol. iii., p. 97.

Mr. Robinson was an eager student of manuscript marginalia. Elsewhere he refers with admiring interest to a copy of Chaucer, containing notes written in it by Horne Tooke when in the Tower, and other books, with annotations by the same Eminent Hand.

as this volume doth contain certain notes and observations, written by the late Samuel Taylor Coleridge, of blessed memory, with his own hand, as I, Hartley Coleridge, am ready to make affirmation: This is to give Notice, That any person or persons presuming to exscind, cut out, purloin, or abstract the said notes or observations, or any thereof, or any line, word, or syllable, or letters thereof, shall be prosecuted with the utmost severity of the law." And thereunto annexed are the precautionary, prohibitory lines, Hudibrastic-looking, but Hartley's very own,—

> "Ye autograph-secreting thieves,
> Keep scissors from these precious leaves,
> And likewise thumbs, profane and greasy,
> From pages hallowed by S. T. C."

The penmen of marginalia comprise oddly assorted names and natures. A glance at some of the more notable ones will here suffice. Pellisson's four years of captivity, consequent upon the disgrace of Fouquet, in whose behalf he composed three memoirs while in the Bastile, were made extra irksome by the prohibition of the use of ink and paper; in default of which he wrote on the margin of his books with the lead of the casements. Archbishop Leighton enriched his copy of George Herbert's Poems with abundant notes—that saintly man seeming, as Tytler says, (who rejoiced as one that findeth great spoil, at meeting with the volume in the library at Dumblane,) to have delighted in writing short pious apophthegms of his own, as well as sentences from the Fathers, in his books. Augustine's *Confessions*, in the same library, he similarly marginalized; also, Burnet's *Life of God in the Soul of Man*, and Pascal's *Pensées*, and the *Essais* of Montaigne, and the Homilies of St. Chrysostom, the *Theologia Mystica*, the *Thesaurus Biblicus*, Howe's *Blessedness of the Righteous*, and not only à Kempis, but Virgil, Horace, Lucian, and Seneca, who are all marked throughout.

Swift's Advice to the Grub Street Verse-writers of 1726 tends to this conclusion:

> "Get all your verses printed fair,
> Then let them well be dried;
> And Curll must have a special care
> To leave the margin wide.
>
> Lend these to paper-sparing Pope;*
> And when he sits to write,
> No letter with an envelope
> Could give him more delight.
>
> When Pope has fill'd the margins round,
> Why then recall your loan;
> Sell them to Curll for fifty pound,
> And swear they are your own."

* *Paper-sparing Pope* is a title that has stuck to the poet. Swift loved to harp on that string, without malice however, unless in the French sense. In some stanzas addressed to Pope while engaged on *The Dunciad*, we meet with this renewed mention of the practice, in a picture of Pope as he "walks and courts the Muse," the Dean meanwhile plodding on a book, and both of them in sociable silence:

> "Now backs of letters, though designed
> For those who more will need 'em,
> Are fill'd with hints, and interlined,
> Himself can hardly read 'em.

This the Dean proposed as a trick to make the ragged poetasters thrive, a very quaint device, to revive their still-born poems, and save them from the else sure and speedy doom of wrapping up groceries

> Each atom by some other struck,
> All turns and motions tries;
> Until, in lump together stuck,
> Behold a poem rise."

In his *Letter to a Young Clergyman*, Swift censures the trick "many clergymen have . . . from a habit of saving time and paper" of writing in illegibly small hand, and being lavish of blots, etc. "Let me entreat you, therefore, to add one half-crown a year to the article of paper." One of his (and Pope's, conjoined,) *Thoughts* is that a man acquires the character of covetousness more generally through some petty parsimony than in expenses of any consequence: "A very few pounds a year would ease that man of the scandal of avarice." It is mark-worthy that Swift himself, on his own showing, was weakly addicted to the perversity of paper-sparing. He gives this counsel to Dr. Sheridan: "I say again, keep very regular accounts, in large books, and a fair hand; not like me, who to save paper confuse everything." One of the most salient traits of character has been said to be the tendency of each individual to practise some economy of his own; everybody has got his or her saving point, and clings to it in the oddest way. "The object is not to save the money, for the same people will spend needlessly in two minutes all that their little pet economy could treasure up for them in the year; but they practise their economy as birds take gravel, to administer a gentle alterative to their usual habits, and to assure themselves that their mind has its healthy side." To people whose own economy lies in a different direction, the instances of this accidental economy they see in their neighbours are very amusing, and almost incomprehensible. "There are ladies who love to entertain their friends, who provide abundant and handsome meals, who wear the most ravishing silks and the newest gloves, and who yet are as chary of their stationery as if they were in the depths of poverty. They will cross their letters so as to make them illegible, rather than use a new sheet—they will weigh their correspondence up to the exact limit of the penny stamp, as if they were making up the nicest and most scientific medicine—and they will collect the envelopes that are sent

or lining trunks. How copiously Swift himself could and would annotate when the humour took him, may be seen in his marginalia on Dr. Gibbs's *Lyric Version of the Psalms*. Bishop Warburton, who professed to

them, and fold them so as to use the inside for their reply." Mr. Harness tells us of Miss Mitford's MSS., by him to be edited, that the handwriting was often so small as to be scarcely legible by the unassisted eye, and that many of the more interesting letters were written on unfolded envelopes, fly-leaves of books, or any odd scraps of paper that came readiest to hand, of which several were sent off under one cover, as parts of the same epistle.

Chateaubriand devotes a graphic section of his Memoirs to Madame de Coislin, whom he depicts in her boudoir, with its incongruous adornments. "Scattered around her on the quilt lay in all directions covers of letters, separated from the letters themselves; and upon these covers the Marchioness de Coislin wrote down her thoughts in all sorts of ways. She never bought paper—it was the post which supplied her with it."

Not only did William Hazlitt turn to author's uses every scrap of paper that came to hand—backs of letters being specially in request,—but he got into disfavour with some of the landladies of his too numerous lodgings by writing out heads of projected essays, over the mantelpiece, in lead-pencillings.

Turner's biographer speaks of that artist's notes of Alpine study (in 1809) as being on tinted paper, "which is often used on both sides, with an economy worthy of Pope." Niebuhr is described by a contributor to *Blackwood*, to whom he offered letters of introduction to Frederick Thiersch and Hermann, as writing them on a very narrow strip from a folio sheet, which he cut off with a large pair of scissors, "with an economy of paper that would have done credit to Alexander Pope." Mr. Savage's Dean, in *Reuben Medlicott*, who is meant for somebody, and perhaps another over, chalks out a whole course of reading for his grandson, "all upon a loose scrap of paper, in the Dean's usual rough and hasty way of committing even his best considered views to writing." Mrs. Medlicott is more hurt than she will confess at the slovenly, informal way in which her father thus communicates his ideas to her son, upon a loose, fragmentary, and not over-nice scrap of paper.

have read Clarendon's History at least a dozen times, filled every leaf of his copy with manuscript observations. Other books of his the omnivorous bishop (with, in Bentley's words, the monstrous appetite and the very bad digestion) enriched or defaced, as the case might be, or his critics please to call it, with a like abundance of marginal comments.

Rousseau never ceased to regret that he did not preserve in his own keeping that prized copy of the works of Rohault which had been copiously annotated with manuscript marginalia by his grandfather, the minister Bernard: "les marges étaient pleines d'excellentes scholies qui me firent aimer les mathématiques." The editors of Voltaire's *Œuvres complètes*, a few years since, made much of a secured copy of Daniel's Critical Observations on the History of France, full of marginal annotations in the handwriting of the philosopher of Ferney. Father Daniel corrected by Voltaire is, a British critic remarks, amusing enough, but only fancy Thomas à Kempis with autograph comments by Jean Jacques Rousseau!—an enthusiastic description of which literary curiosity may be found in the *Mémoires d'un Bibliophile* (Dentu). A Variorum edition of à Kempis, with the marginalia miscellanea of his readers of all sorts and sizes, would make up many volumes, and curious ones. Rousseau would read strange between, say, Bishop Andrews and Bishop Burgess, which latter prelate, shortly before his death, took down from a bookshelf a copy of

Payne's Kempis, and pointed out with emotion to his biographer (Dr. J. S. Harford) its numerous marginal annotations, as indicating his state of mind while residing at Winston, and as no less expressive of his latest convictions.* Mrs. Piozzi (Thrale) was very fond of writing marginal notes; and after annotating one copy of a book, would take up another and do the same.† Biographers of Porson preserve the name of that "excellent writing-master," Mr. Summers, of whom young Richard learnt the beautiful handwriting which in after-years enriched both his own books and those of his friends with "characteristic annotations, which added to the value of every book that passed through his hands." One scholarly critic mentions having looked through the editions of Greek books that belonged to him, now in the hands of different individuals or in public libraries, not one of which books does not bear marginal traces of his careful and scrutinizing perusal. But it takes a scholar to appreciate Porson's calligraphy, in the full range of its meaning. Given a competent inquirer, and his enjoyment is of the kind Pisistratus Caxton records when turning over volume after

---

* His Nelson on *True Devotion* is said to be replete with similar annotations; as also are his copies of Bishop Wilson's *Sacra Privata*, Doddridge's *Rise and Progress*, Law's *Serious Call*, Baxter's *Saints' Rest*, and other devotional books.

† A copy of Boswell's Life of Johnson, annotated by her like Dr. Wellesley's, is referred to by Mr. Hayward, as in the possession of Mr. Bohn (1861).

volume of Sir Percival Tracey's, rich and rare with marginal annotations. "I was greatly struck with the variety and minuteness of the knowledge in many departments, whether of art, scholarship, or philosophy, which these annotations displayed, and the exquisite critical discrimination and taste by which the knowledge was vivified and adorned." Wanting this competency, on the reader's part, the curiosity to scan such marginal meanderings is as bootless as that of Vivien to master Merlin's book:

> " *You* read the book, my pretty Vivien !
> O ay, it is but twenty pages long,
> But every page having an ample marge,
> And every marge enclosing in the midst
> A square of text that looks a little blot,
> The text no larger than the limbs of fleas ;
> And every square of text an awful charm,
> Writ in a language that has long gone by.
> . . . . . *You* read the book !
> And every margin scribbled, cross'd, and cramm'd
> With comment, densest condensation, hard
> To mind and eye."

When Mr. Hawthorne dwelt in the old manse he has made famous, he found in one of its venerable garrets a part of his predecessor's library, heirloom volumes, transmitted through a series of consecrated hands, from the days of the mighty Puritan divines ; and there were marginal observations, or interpolated pages closely covered with manuscript, in illegible shorthand, perhaps concealing matter of profound truth and wisdom, but for which the world will never be the better. No one has the wistful query to set up in regard of these, that De Quincey made concerning the *ubi gentium*, the where in the world, or whither away, of that set of huge quartos once presented by him to Coleridge, of Law's English version of Jacob Boehmen—one volume at least of which the donor saw, some months afterwards, overflowing with the commentaries and corollaries of Coleridge. " Whither has this work, and so many others swathed about with Coleridge's MS. notes, vanished from the world ?" Whither, oh whither *?* as shepherd's son and shepherdesses sing in the *Winter's Tale.*

Sir Philip Francis was a great marginal note-maker; he criticized all that came under his eye, Mr. Herman Merivale says,* and especially what related to political events, even to his latest hour.

Leigh Hunt lends Dr. Southwood Smith his beloved Chinese novel, *In-Kioo-Li,* (beloved by him as a work of genius, curious for its pictures of national manners, and exhibiting in passages the most exquisite refinement of heart,) and in doing so is careful to call his attention to the marginal notes marked T. C., which "are by Carlyle, to whom I lent it once, and who read it with delight." Southey devotes a chapter in *The Doctor* to a recondite Spanish authoress, and to

---

* Singularly enough, however, yet in accordance with much that we know of him, and with all that we must suppose, if Junius he was,—his books of the Junian period were scantily noted, as if to avoid keeping up, in this way, his connection with the time in which "his sinister anonymous fame was achieved."—H. Merivale's *Historical Studies,* p. 188.

an account of the manner in which he obtained her works from Madrid, and of the pleasure and advantages which he derived from Dr. Dove's landmarks in the books perused by him: "That precious copy is now in my possession; my friend has noted in it, as was his custom, every passage that seemed worthy of observation, with the initial of his own name—a small capital, neatly written in red ink. Such of his books as I have been able to collect are full of these marks, showing how carefully he had read them. These notations have been of much use to me in my perusal, leading me to pause where he had paused, to observe what he had noted, and to consider what to him seemed worthy of consideration."

A reviewer of Capgrave's *Chronicle*, as printed from the Parker MS., expresses a hope that it was not that Protestant Archbishop himself who, wherever Becket was styled "St. Thomas," ran a pen through the words, and substituted "a knave." Too much in the spirit and style of the "empty pragmatical fellow, in the country," commemorated by Addison, who upon reading over *The Whole Duty of Man*, had written the names of several persons in the village at the side of every sin which is mentioned by that excellent author; so that he had converted what the Spectator esteems one of the best books in the world into a libel against the squire, churchwardens, overseers of the poor, and all other the most considerable persons in the parish. It is one characteristic of *le rat* of French *salons de lecture* to inscribe on the margins of papers and books such notes of admiration, exclamation, expostulation, and reprobation as these: "!!!" "Bah," "Poof," and their correlatives or congeners. Lord Macaulay has his side-glance and side-thrust at those "profound and interesting annotations* which are pencilled by sempstresses and apothecaries' boys† on the dog-eared margins of novels borrowed from circulating libraries: 'How beautiful!' 'I don't like Sir Reginald Malcolm at all.' 'I think Pelham is a sad dandy.'"—But let us turn from this degraded type to marginalia conceived and carried out in a more proper sense and style. And yet not quite proper. We read in the *Maloniana*‡

---

* A pleasant essayist on the subject of long voyages, and their dreary monotony, says of the particular copy of the convalescent passenger's favourite poet, to be had on shipboard, that it—of course it is Mr. Tennyson—is so certain to be adorned with the pencil comments of previous readers as to furnish too many interruptions to placid enjoyment. It is highly vexatious, the essayist submits, when you are feebly kindling over *Locksley Hall*, to find rude uncritical annotations scrawled on all available margins, while a vigorous caricature of the captain of the ship is an unpleasing diversion to the reader of *Ulysses*.

† Mr. Spedding thus accounts for the marginal allusions to Shakspeare in the copy he recently edited of Bacon's *Conference of Pleasure*: "At the present time, if the waste-leaf on which a law-stationer's apprentice tries his pens were examined, I should expect to find on it the name of the poet, novelist, dramatic author, or actor of the day, mixed with snatches of the last new song, and scribblings of 'My dear sir,' and 'Yours sincerely,' and 'This Indenture witnesseth,' and this is exactly the sort of thing which we have here."—See the Editor's Introduction to *A Conference of Pleasure*, composed 1592, published 1870.

‡ Malone had an open eye for marginalia. Visiting Waller's house, he takes note of the poet's name written in many of the books, and

that on examining the library of Parson Cole, Walpole's correspondent, his books were found to contain a great many sarcastic remarks against intimate friends of his in general, and against Horace of Strawberry Hill in particular. Johnson's comment on the discovery was, that if Mr. Cole had scribbled in the margin of his books merely to give vent to his thoughts, it was a very harmless amusement; but then he ought to have ordered them to be burnt at his death; that if, however, it arose from malignity, it argued a very base disposition, especially in the case of Walpole, with whom he kept up a friendly correspondence to the last. But if a man finds he cannot restrain his ill-humour within bounds, it would be much the shortest and fairest way, suggested the doctor, with a smile, "to keep one fair paper-book, for the purpose of abusing all his acquaintance."

Burns tells Miss Williams of the way he has, whenever he reads a book, if at least a poetic one, and his own property, of taking a pencil and marking at the ends of verses, or noting on margins and odd paper, little criticisms of approbation or disapprobation, as he goes along. Complimenting Dr. Moore on his *Zeluco*, he adds: "I have quite disfigured my copy of the book with my annotations. I never take it up without at the same time taking my pencil, and mark-

---

" As he is said to have formed his versification on Fairfax's *Tasso*, I was curious to examine it. But it contained not a single remark in the margin."

ing with asterisms, parentheses, etc., wherever I meet with an original thought, a nervous remark on life and manners, a remarkably well-turned period, or a character sketched with uncommon precision." In the following year he again tells the doctor, " I have just read over, once more of many times, your Zeluco. I marked with my pencil, as I went along, every passage that pleased me particularly," etc.; and the pleased author, in his reply, is solicitous to have a sight of these marginal comments, and prays Burns to transcribe them for him, and not to suppress one in which he censures the sentiment or expression. " Trust me, it will break no squares between us—I am not akin to the Bishop of Granada." Years after we find the poet asking Mrs. Dunlop to tell him how she likes his marks and notes through the aforesaid copy of *Zeluco*. " I would not give a farthing for a book," he protests, " unless I were at liberty to blot it with my criticisms." He was as ready with them almost as Mrs. Schimmelpenninck, who, in so remarkable a degree, to her biographer's thinking, was willing to bestow her mental riches on all who asked for them," without herself giving a thought to the value of the gift. Many a manuscript it seems, as well as printed volume, "did she in this manner adorn and enrich with the graces of her mind, which was forgotten as soon as done." William Blake was another copious contributor of marginalia to books all and sundry that came in his way,[*]

---

[*] Byron could marginalize with similar fertility and facility, when

or at least that, in another sense, were in his way. Hartley Coleridge, again, inherited his father's addiction to the practice, and knack for improving it. His brother signalizes his copy of (Haddington) John Brown's *Dictionary of the Bible* as especially enriched in this manner—a double and even treble series of annotations crowding the pages; and indeed, from the care with which these notes appear to have been written, and in some instances corrected, they would seem to have been designed as studies, of which he intended to make systematically some after use. Considering what the boy Hartley had been, and what the man Hartley became, and that the man never quite outgrew the boy, one feels to be applicable to him in particular what has been said of the old school-books of boys in general, that they are a strangely touching link between the past and the future: an old school-book will often, with its characteristic marginal embellishments, reproduce vividly, as nothing else can, the boyhood of a man who has left on the world which he has quitted the abiding mark of his maturity. And perhaps to few men that have never outgrown or discarded most of the feelings and some of the tricks of school-boyishness, would be more applicable than to

---

the fit, or the book, took him. Vastly prized by Lord Blessington was the copy he lent Byron of John Galt's story of *The Entail*, and which was returned with a liberal supply of the poet's cursory comments. Thrice was this book read through, its admirers are apt to remind us, not only by Byron, but by Sir Walter Scott.

him, all allowances made, the lines in Mr. Browning's *Fra Lippo Lippi*, in waggish mood, and, as Corporal Nym would say, in the humour on't,—

> "I had a store of such remarks, be sure,
> Which, after I found leisure, turned to use:
> I drew men's faces on my copy-books,
> Scrawled them within the antiphonary's marge, . :
> And made a string of pictures of the world
> Betwixt the ins and outs of verb and noun."

VIII.

Book Marks: Local and Incidental.

IT was at Rome, on the 15th of October, 1764, that Gibbon, as he sat musing amidst the ruins of the Capitol, while the bare-footed friars were singing vespers in the temple of Jupiter, first conceived the idea of writing the history of the Decline and Fall. It was on the night of the 27th of June, 1787, between the hours of ten and twelve, that he wrote the last line of the last page, in a summer-house in his garden at Lausanne; and every reader must remember how the writer describes his laying down his pen, and taking several turns in a *berceau*, or covered walk of acacias, which commanded a prospect of the country, the lake, and the mountains; how all nature was silent as he paced that leafy aisle —the air temperate, the sky serene, the silver orb of the moon reflected from the waters; and how his first emotion was of joy on the recovery of his freedom, and, perhaps, the establishment of his fame,—an emotion all too soon exchanged for a sober melan-

choly at taking an everlasting leave of an old and
agreeable companion, and at the conviction that
whatever might be the date of his history, the life of
the historian must be short and precarious. Authorship naturally delights in these local reminiscences.
Leibnitz lovingly recalls the spot where, early in his
teens, he deliberated on the tenableness of "substantial forms" as an article of his metaphysical
creed. It was in a grove near Leipzig, called
Rosendale: there he walked in solitary meditation,
much musing on the great *quæstio vexanda*. It was
during a Sunday afternoon walk on Glasgow Green,
when just about half-way between the Herd's House
and Arn's Well, that the idea flashed upon the mind
of James Watt which was the germ of all his im-
provements of the steam-engine; and dear was the
remembrance to him of that exact locality. Cumberland wrote his *West Indian* at a friend's country-seat
in Ireland; and entirely he approved the good taste
of his host in ever afterwards holding in great veneration a spot in the garden where he studied: the
owner, in respect to his memory, would never suffer
the summer-house to be removed or altered. Robert
Burns, while he lived in Dumfries, had one favourite
walk, secluded, and commanding a view of the distant
hills, and the romantic towers of Lincluden, and affording soft greensward banks to rest upon, within
sight and sound of the river Nith; and here he composed many of his finest songs, which he loved to

identify with autumn* days and the Martingdon ford. Wilberforce cherished a remembrance of that spot at the root of an old tree at Holwood, just above the steep descent in the vale of Keston, where, after an earnest conversation with Pitt on the slave-trade, he resolved to bring that subject before the House of Commons. Vividly remembered by Warren Hastings tothe last day of his long life was that spot where, at seven years old, he lay on the brink of a little rivulet in the Daylesford estate, and first formed the resolution to regain his family possessions.

Simson, of Euclidian fame, used ever after to show with pride the stump of an old tree by the side of which the solution flashed upon his mind of that great problem, the riddle of centuries, What is a porism? (Now commonly recognized as "an indeterminate case of a generally determinate problem.") Whitefield loved to commemorate the place where, with the time when, and the manner how, of a memorable spiritual experience : " I remember once, in Gloucester, I know the room—I look up to the window when I am there, and walk along the street," etc. Luther, in his table-talk, dwells on the remembrance that " Here, under this very pear-tree, I have over and over again argued with Dr. Staupitz, as to whether it was my vocation to preach." Equally tenacious in its way was Rousseau's memory of the tree

---

* " Autumn is my propitious season. I make more verses in it than all the year else."—*Burns to Mr. Thomson, Aug.* 1793.

on the road to Vincennes, under which *une inspiration subite* impelled him to write on the question of the Academy of Dijon. "O monsieur!" is his exclamation, if pen can be made to exclaim, to Malesherbes,—" si j'avais jamais pu écrire le quart de ce que j'ai vu et senti sous cet arbre. . . ." A later genius of the *genus* Jean Jacques is at pains to record not only how often Robespierre visited Rousseau's hut in the forest of Montmorency, but that "in this house and in this garden" he indited his "report" against atheism; "under those very trees where his master had so magnificently written of God," as Lamartine phrases it.

At least one modern painter has commemorated in water-colours the "view from Heaven's Gate, Longleat, Wilts, where Bishop Ken composed the Morning and Evening Hymns." Petrarch was making inquiries for a retired spot, wherein he might take refuge as in a secure harbour, when he chanced upon that "little secluded valley, named Vaucluse," in which the Sorgue takes its rise, that "queen of all other springs," and of which he says, "Here it was that I composed my poems in the vulgar tongue—poems in which I described my youthful sorrows." Beethoven writes to Frau von Streicher, at Baden: "When you visit the ancient ruins, do not forget that Beethoven has often lingered there; when you stray through the silent pine forest, do not forget that Beethoven often wrote poems there, or, as it is termed, composed."

Telling how, on the return from the Emigration,

there was not a single French exile, however poor, but decorated his ten feet of recovered ground with the winding walks of an English garden, Chateaubriand adds, "Did I not myself plant the Vallée-aux-Loups? Did I not there commence these memoirs? Did I not contrive to write them in the Parc de Montboissier? .. Have I not lengthened them out in the Parc de Maintenon," etc. What he calls the Park of Kensington was at least equally prominent in his literary associations. In Kensington Gardens he meditated his *Historical Essay;* there too he devised *Atala;* and "it is also in this park that, after having wandered in distant countries, beneath the arctic sky, golden-hued and as it were penetrated with the polar light, I traced in pencil the first sketches of the passions of *René.*" Leigh Hunt lingers lovingly in the telling how sometimes in Kensington Gardens, sometimes in the quondam Nightingale Lane of Holland House, he "had the pleasure of composing *The Palfrey,* the scenes of which are partly laid in the place." Walter Savage Landor relates in a footnote how he wrote a poem on Godiva, "sitting, I remember, by the *square pool* at Rugby,"—the italics are his, and significantly his. Pleasantly piqued was Thomas Moore by a letter "from Lees, of the county of Wicklow," begging him to decide a question which was producing "a sort of civil war" in the neighbourhood, whether he wrote his song of the Meeting of the Waters under Castle Howard, at the meeting of the Avon and Avoca, or at the meeting of the rivers, four miles lower down, under Ballyarthur House.* Washington Irving was heard to say, in his old age, that he gave the finishing touch to his *Stout Gentleman* as he sat on a gravestone in Lillington churchyard, near Leamington, while his genial companion Leslie, R.A., was sketching a view of Warwick Castle. Etty liked to tell of his *Judith* as "first conceived" in York Minster, while the solemn tones of the organ were pealing through the aisles; and of his *Joan of Arc* as "first thought of in Westminster Abbey," in Henry the Seventh's Chapel, under the chivalric banners that hang there. Hearing the anthem sung, and looking towards the grand portal, he seemed to see her, he said, in imagination, riding into the gates of Orleans. If minsters and abbeys were mainly associated with his conceptions and projects, even the theatre has served a like purpose with minds of another cast. Dr. Andrew Combe, for instance, writes: "I recollect, one evening, sketching out an improved system of medicine, very much to my satisfaction, in the theatre,—a place, by the way, where many of my good thoughts and resolutions first came in force into my mind, although it is not generally looked upon as the source of much good."

The closing paragraph of *The Last Days of Pompeii*

---

* "William Parnell wrote to me on the same subject two or three years since. The fact is I *wrote* the song at neither place, though I believe the scene under Castle Howard was the one that suggested it to me."—*Diary of Thos. Moore*, Nov. 9, 1818.

records how a stranger, from that remote and barbarian isle which the imperial Roman shivered when he named, paused amidst the delights of the soft Campania, and, on the spot, "composed this history." Nathaniel Hawthorne describes himself in his Notebook for 1840, sitting in that old accustomed room in Salem where he had written so many tales,—a room that claimed to be a haunted chamber, for thousands upon thousands of visions had appeared to hive in it, and some of them had become visible to the world: "If ever I should have a biographer, he ought to make great mention of this chamber in my memoirs, because . . . here my mind and character were formed. . . . And here I sat a long, long time, waiting patiently for the world to know me, and sometimes wondering why it did not know me sooner, or whether it would ever know me at all,—at least, till I were in my grave." He may be taken to have been drawing again on his own experience when, in another of his books, he makes another narrator declare how many recollections throng upon him, as he turns over the leaves of his old manuscript; and how one scene in particular came into his fancy as he walked along a hilly road, on a starlight October evening; when, in the pure and bracing air, he became all soul, and felt as if he could climb the sky, and run a race along the Milky Way.

Of interest to readers at large, and not merely to

authors as such, are the incidental records that authors have left us of the impression made on their minds by a first perusal of some markworthy book. Scott, for example, making acquaintance with Bishop Percy's *Reliques of Ancient Poetry.* " I remember well the spot where I read these volumes for the first time. It was beneath a huge platanus tree, in the ruins of what had been intended for an old-fashioned arbour. . . . The summer day sped onward so fast, that notwithstanding the sharp appetite of thirteen, I forgot the hour of dinner, was sought for with anxiety, and was still found entranced in my intellectual banquet." The first time Walter could scrape a few shillings together, he bought for himself a copy of these beloved volumes, and no other book did he ever, by his own account, read half so frequently or with half the enthusiasm.* Perhaps one of the best known passages among Hazlitt's multitudinous essays is that in which he pictures himself sitting up half the night to read *Paul and Virginia,* which he picked up at an inn at Bridgwater, after being drenched in the rain all day; and at the same place getting through two volumes of Madame

---

* Mr. Lockhart describes his visit to Kelso in 1820, in company with his father-in-law,—how they walked together (John Ballantyne of the party) over that pretty town, lounged away an hour among the rivers of the abbey, and closed their perambulation with " the *garden,* where Scott had spent some of the happiest of his early summers, and where he pointed out with sorrowful eyes the site of the platanus under which he first read Percy's Reliques."—Lockhart's *Life of Scott,* chap. I.

d'Arblay's *Camilla;* and then comes: "It was on the 10th of April, 1798, that I sat down to a volume of the New Eloise, at the inn at Llangollen, over a bottle of sherry and a cold chicken." It was his birthday, and he had brought the book with him as a *bonne bouche* to crown the evening with, for the sake of dwelling on St. Preux' description of his feelings as he first caught a glimpse from the heights of the Jura of the Pays de Vaud.* The late Lord Cockburn, in probably the most feeling paragraph of his *Memorials,* expatiating on the delights of his paradise at Bonaly, in the parish of Colinton, close by the northern base of the Pentland Hills,—where the glories of the prospects, and the luxury of the wild retirement, made him only too happy,—cites Warburton's saying that there was not a bush in his garden whereon he had not hung a speculation, for the sake of capping that *mot* with the assertion that there was not a recess in the valleys of the Pentlands, nor an eminence on their summits, but was familiar to his, Harry Cockburn's, solitude. "One summer I read every word of Tacitus

---

* Hazlitt was fond, somehow, of associating his reading sensations with culinary ones. In another essay he narrates his going to market, providing himself with sausages and potatoes, to be duly mashed, and, while these were getting ready, and he could hear the former hissing in the pan, his reading a volume of *Gil Blas,* "containing the account of the fair Aurora. This was in the days of my youth. Gentle reader, do not smile! Neither Monsieur de Very, nor Louis XVIII. over an oyster-paté, nor Apicius himself, ever understood the meaning of the word *luxury* better than I did at that moment."—Hazlitt's Essay *On the Want of Money.* Also that *On Going a Journey.*

in the sheltered crevice of a rock (called 'My Seat') about 800 feet above the level of the sea, with the most magnificent of scenes stretched out before me." Cowper tells one of his correspondents that he can boast of, not indeed a good memory in general, but a good local memory; for which reason his plan is, in summer, to localize his outdoor reading: "What I read at my fireside I forget, but what I read under a hedge, or at the side of a pond, that pond and that hedge will always bring to my remembrance; and this is a sort of memoria technica which I would recommend," etc. It was the casual citation of a passage from Spinoza which made Goethe's youth restless, and to his old age he remembered distinctly the local surroundings of the page, as well as the very aspect of the paper and type.

Mr. Carlyle is using the periodical We, for periodical uses, when he writes: "We ourselves can remember reading in Lord Clarendon, with feelings perhaps somehow accidentally opened to it,—certainly with a depth of impression strange to us then and now,—that insignificant looking passage where Charles, after the battle of Worcester, glides down with Squire Careless, at nightfall, being hungry," etc.* Which of us, he elsewhere asks, in reference to what he calls the *Johnsoniad* of Boswell, but remembers, as one of the sunny spots in his existence, the day when

---

* Clarendon, *History of the Rebellion*, iii., 625.

he opened these airy volumes, fascinating him by a true natural magic! * Mr. Keightley says that the reading of *Paradise Lost* for the first time forms, or should form, an era in the life of every one possessed of taste and poetic feeling; and that to his own mind that time is ever present. "It was just as I was emerging from boyhood; the season was summer; the scene a residence amid wood and water, at the foot of mountains, over which I beheld each morning the sun rising, invested with all his glories." Hoole's tame version of the *Jerusalem Delivered* was in reading at the same time; and the two poems combined to hold the reader in an ecstasy of delight. "Alas, that such happy days can never return, not even in imagination!"

It was while reading one day in Hutcheson a passage on man's asserted capacity for disinterested affection, that there suddenly burst on the mind of William Ellery Channing that view of the dignity of human nature of which he became so tenacious for ever after. "He was, at the time, walking as he read beneath a clump of willows, yet standing in the meadow a little to the north of Judge Dana's. This was his favourite retreat for study, being then quite undisturbed and private, and offering a most serene

---

* It was as if the curtains of the past were drawn aside, and we looked mysteriously into a kindred country, where dwelt our fathers; inexpressibly dear to us, but which had seemed for ever hidden from our eyes."
—Carlyle's *Critical and Miscellaneous Essays*, iii. 11, 33. (3rd edit.)

and cheerful prospect across green meadows and the glistening river to the Brookline hills." The place and the hour were always sacred in his memory, and he frequently, his biographer says, referred to them with grateful awe.[*]

Margaret Fuller tells how "at Chicago I read *Philip van Artevelde*, and certain passages in it will always be in my mind associated with the deep sound of the lake, as heard in the night." She used to read at night, and now and then look out on the moon that shone full on the lake, thinking how well the calm breath, pure light, and deep voice harmonized with the ideal of the Flemish hero. In a pencil memorandum, half effaced, of Washington Irving's, found among his papers after his death, we have a sketch of him at the Hoffmans' rural retreat on the Hudson, stealing forth to read an eagerly borrowed first copy of *The Lady of the Lake*, before the American publisher had put it to press (1810)—and often was he heard in his old age to descant upon the delight of this stealthy perusal, and the surprise with which he started to his feet at the unexpected *dénouement*,

---

[*] Charles Wesley, at Oxford, having frequently observed George Whitefield walking by himself, and heard something of his character, invited him to breakfast; and here is what came of the interview, as *Leucouomos* himself words it: "He put a book into my hands called the *Life of God in the Soul of Man*, whereby God showed me that I must be born again, or damned. I know the place; it may be superstitious perhaps, but whenever I go to Oxford, I cannot help running to that place where Jesus Christ first revealed Himself to me, and gave me the new birth!"

"And Snowdon's knight is Scotland's king." Here he is at his solitary session: "August 12, 1810.—Seated, leaning against a rock, with a wild cherry tree over my head, reading Scott's Lady of the Lake. The busy ant hurrying over the page—crickets skipping into my bosom—wind rustling among the top branches of the trees. Broad masses of shade darken the Hudson, and cast the opposite shore in black." His biographer is reminded, by this picture, of his expressive invitation to a friend, at a later day, to make him a visit at Sunnyside. "Come and see me, and I'll give you a book and a tree." The devout and accomplished author of *Select Memoirs of Port Royal* loved to refer in afterlife to a favourite haunt in the scenery of Barr, by an old saw-pit, where, on logs of wood, many a time that gentle student sat and read Virgil's first Eclogue, listening to the wild bees and the woodlark's song. John Foster somewhere journalizes his conviction of the advantage of connecting, if we can, some striking association with every idea, as well as every scene, (the one aiding and abetting the other,) which we desire to remember with abiding interest. He compares it to framing and glazing the mental picture; the best means of preserving it for an indefinite length of time.

IX.

Literary Society.

AGAIN and again, in his voluminous writings, does Mr. de Quincey enlarge on the flat and unprofitable character of merely "literary society"—by which society he means all such as, having no strong distinction in powers of thinking or in native force of character, are yet raised into circles of pretension and mark, by the fact of having written a book, or of holding a notorious connexion with some department or other of the periodical press. No society, he explicitly affirms, after long and varied experience, is so vapid and uninteresting in its natural quality, none so cheerless and petrific in its influence upon others. Ordinary people, in such company, are in general, he observes, repressed from uttering with cordiality the natural expression of their own minds or temperaments, under a vague feeling of some peculiar homage due, or at least customarily paid, to these lions: such people are no longer at their ease, or masters of their own natural motions in their own natural freedom; whilst indemnification of any sort is least of all to be looked for from the literary dons who have diffused this unpleasant atmosphere of constraint. They disable others, and yet do nothing themselves to fill up the void they have created. One and all—unless by accident people of unusual originality, power, and also nerve, so as to be able without trepidation to face the expectations of men—the literary class labour under two opposite disqualifications for a good tone of conversation: they are either spoiled by vices of reserve, and of over-consciousness directed upon themselves— this is one extreme; or, where manliness of mind has prevented this, beyond others of equal or inferior power, they are apt to be desperately commonplace. "Another mode of reserve arises with some literary men, who believe themselves to be in possession of novel ideas. Cordiality of communication, or ardour of dispute, might betray them into a revelation of those golden thoughts, sometimes into a necessity of revealing them, since, without such aid, it might be impossible to maintain theirs in the discussion. On this principle it was—a principle of deliberate unsocial reserve—that Adam Smith is said to have governed his conversation: he professed to put a bridle on his words, lest by accident a pearl should drop out of his lips amongst the vigilant bystanders."

It is not, however, by reserve, whether of affectation or of Smithian jealousy, that De Quincey pronounces the majority of literary people to offend—at least not by the latter; for, so far, he says, from having much novelty to protect against pirates, the most general effect of literary pursuits is to tame down all points of originality to one standard of insipid monotony. On the other hand, he takes a body of illiterate rustics. He bids us listen to the talk of a few scandalous village dames collected at a tea-table; and contends that, vulgar as the spirit may be which possesses them, and not seldom malicious, still, "how full of animation and of keen perception it will generally be found, and of a learned spirit of connoisseurship in human character, by comparison with the *fade* generalities and barren recollections of mere literati!" Recalling one of his own earliest experiences in literary society— that, namely, which he mixed with in Liverpool circles, and which comprised Roscoe, and Dr. Currie, and Mr. Shepherd of Gatacre (author of a Life of Poggio Bracciolini), and others, of similar calibre,—the Opium-eater mentions it as a striking illustration of the impotence of mere literature against natural power and mother-wit, that the only man who was considered indispensable in these parties, for giving life and impulse to their vivacity, was a tailor; and this tailor, not a capitalist who employed sartorial craftsmen, himself sublimely remote from goose and shears, but one who drew his own honest daily bread from his own honest needle, except when he laid it aside for the benefit of drooping literati, who needed to be watered with his wit.

Elsewhere again, with characteristic emphasis of

rhetoric, De Quincey thus paraphrases the warning proverb, "Put not your trust in princes," which has been the farewell moral, winding up and pointing the experience of so many dying statesmen: "Not less truly it might be said—'Put not your trust in the intellectual princes of your age:' form no connexions too close with any who live only in the atmosphere of admiration and praise. The love or friendship of such people rarely contracts itself into the narrow circle of individuals. You, if you are brilliant like themselves, they will hate; you, if you are dull, they will despise. Gaze, therefore, on the splendour of such idols as a passing stranger. Look for a moment as one sharing in the idolatry; but pass on before the splendour has been sullied by human frailty, or before your own generous homage has been confounded with offerings of weeds." The bitterness of disenchantment is painfully manifest in every line of this monition.

To only one other parallel passage from the same author will we refer in passing—to that in which, describing his London intercourse with Edward Irving, he records the entire agreement that celebrated orator expressed with our author's dislike of common literary society, by comparison with that of people less pretending, left more to the impulses of their natural unchecked feelings, and entertaining opinions less modelled upon what they read.

Most persons of an unsophisticated mind, with any dash of vigour or originality in it, must share in the preference here avowed. A purer type of the literary man than Southey can hardly, perhaps, be named; but to him, too, literary society was altogether offensive. When he first made acquaintance with Charlotte Smith, in 1801, Southey rejoiced in finding her " more humanized, more akin to common feelings, than most literary women,"—and bore witness of her, that, although she had done more and done better than other women writers, writing had not been her whole employment—"she is not looking out for admiration, and talking to show off. I see in her none of the nasty little envies and jealousies common enough among the cattle." His aversion to the cattle did not, however, keep Southey from anticipating with some zest, as the same letter shows, the prospect of dining with Longman on Wednesday, " to meet a few literary friends." They would probably be new to him, he said, and might furnish some amusement—at any rate, he loved to see all odd people.

Possibly his thoughts carried him to the odd people, in the style of a few literary friends, whom Matthew Bramble and his nephew met at Dr. Smollett's, rather than of those assembled at Dick Ivy's, who seemed afraid and jealous of each other, and sat in a state of mutual repulsion, like so many particles of vapour, each surrounded by its own electrified atmosphere. Of these gentlemen Squire Bramble remarked, that there is seldom anything extraordinary in the appearance and address of a good writer; whereas a dull author generally distinguishes himself by some oddity or extravagance; for which reason the Squire fancies that an assembly of grubs must be very diverting. The reunion at Smollett's amply confirms his impression. There are eight or ten "unfortunate brothers of the quill" gathered round the doctor's board, where they are treated (once a week, and all the year round) to beef, pudding, potatoes, port, punch, and Calvert's entire butt beer; and Jerry Melford questions if the whole kingdom could produce such another assemblage of originals; what strikes him being oddities produced in the first instance by affectation, and afterwards inveterately established by habit. Odd people of this extravagant type, we may assume to be the only class of literary professionals in whose company Robert the Rhymer could sit with patience. In Smollett's set, it is observable, that there was nothing pedantic in their discourse; that they carefully avoided all learned disquisitions, and endeavoured to be facetious; nor did their endeavours always miscarry; some droll repartee passed, and much laughter was excited; and if any individual lost his temper so far as to transgress the bounds of decorum, he was effectually checked by the master of the feast, who exerted a sort of paternal authority over this irritable tribe.

A letter of Southey's to a distinguished literary friend commences: "I am so completely removed from what is called literary society (which is at this time about the worst society in the world)," etc. In another, he congratulates himself on meeting Joanna Baillie at Rogers's, in 1831, with no other guest than Sister Agnes, and his own daughter Bertha,—" for, as to literary parties, they are my abomination." One of the latest entries in Byron's journal runs thus: "In general, I do not draw well with literary men; not that I dislike them, but I never know what to say to them after I have praised their last publication." He makes several exceptions, to be sure; but these have either been men of the world, such as Scott and Moore, or visionaries out of it, such as Shelley: "But your literary every-day man and I never went well in company, especially your foreigner, whom I never could abide; except Giordani, and—and—and—(I really can't name any other)." One of Byron's biographers lays it down as a general rule that it is wise to avoid writers whose works amuse or delight you, for when you see them they will delight you no more. Shelley he distinguishes as a grand exception to this rule.

Madame de Sévigné thinks her adored child a great deal too innocently good-natured when she talks of being afraid of literate wits in company. "Vous êtes bonne encore quand vous dîtes que vous avez peur des beaux-esprits : hélas ! si vous saviez qu'ils sont petits de près, et combien ils sont quelquefois empêchés de leurs personnes, vous les remettriez bientôt à hauteur d'appui." Rousseau complains bitterly of the *cabales des gens de lettres* he encountered in Paris—of their *honteuses querelles*, the want of good faith in their books, their *airs tranchants dans le monde*, and the general offensiveness of their social bearing,—which he, at least, professes to have found intolerable. Gibbon, who was familiar with literary Paris of Rousseau's time, and who mixed freely with D'Alembert, and Helvetius, and D'Holbach, and Diderot, and Barthelemy, and Raynal, and Suard, and ever so many more, reports, that alone and in a morning visit, he found the artists and authors of Paris less vain, and more reasonable, than in the circles of their equals, with whom they mingled in the houses of the rich. Alexandre Vinet, by the way, in treating of Fontenelle and his circle, asserts that dignity of manners is much more common among men of science than of literature, because their passions do not furnish the materials for their works. Literary men, he says, live in the world of mankind; scientific, in the world of God. The solitude of the literary man is not a real solitude: among his books he lives with the dead and the living; especially he lives with himself, and often this is not too good company. Compare the lives of sixty-nine literary men with those of sixty-nine men of science, and the chances are, according to M. Vinet, that with the latter you will be pleased, with the former disgusted and annoyed.

In one of Schiller's letters from Leipzig, written in his six-and-twentieth year, we find him describing the alluring invitations to Berlin and Dresden that come to him from various quarters, and which it will be difficult for him to withstand. It is quite a peculiar case, he tells his correspondent, half-complainingly, half-complacently, to have a literary name. "The few men of worth and consideration who offer you their intimacy on that score, and whose regard is really worth coveting, are too disagreeably counterweighed by the baleful swarm of creatures who keep humming round you, like so many flesh-flies; gape at you as if you were a monster, and condescend moreover, on the strength of one or two blotted sheets, to present themselves as colleagues." Berlin, like most other cities, Mr. Carlyle has observed, prides itself in being somewhat of a modern Athens; and Hoffmann, the wonder of the day, was invited with the warmest blandishments to share in its musical and literary *tea*. "But in these polished circles Hoffmann prospered ill; he was sharp-tempered; vain, indeed, but transcendently vain; he required the wittiest talk or the most attentive audience; and had a heart-hatred to inanity, however gentle and refined." Accordingly we are told that when his company grew tiresome, he "made the most terrific faces;" would answer the languishing raptures of some perfumed critic by an observation on the weather; would transfix half a dozen harmless dilettanti through the vitals, each on his several bolt; nay, in the end, would give vent to his spleen by talking like a sheer maniac; in short, never cease till, one way or other, the hapless circle was reduced to utter desolation.

We have the attestation of Samuel Taylor Coleridge, when describing an evening spent among the more intelligent tradesmen of Birmingham, that nowhere is more unaffected good sense exhibited, and particularly nowhere more elasticity and *freshness* of mind, than in the conversation of the reading men in manufacturing towns. Thomas de Quincey bears witness that in Kendal, especially, in Bridgwater, and in Manchester, he has been present at more interesting conversations, marked by as much information, and more natural eloquence in conveying it, than usually in literary circles, or in places professedly learned. One reason for this assigned by him is, that in trading towns the time is more happily distributed; the day given to business and active duties—the evening to relaxation; on which account, books, conversation, and literary leisure are more cordially enjoyed: the same satiation never can take place, which too frequently deadens the genial enjoyment of those who have a surfeit of books and a monotony of leisure. Another reason assigned by him is, that more simplicity of manner may be expected, and more natural picturesqueness of conversation, more open expression of character, in places where people have no previous name to support: men in trading towns are not afraid to open their lips, for fear they should disappoint your expectations, nor do they strain for showy sentiments* that they may meet them. "But elsewhere many are the men who stand in awe of their own reputation: not a word which is unstudied, not a movement in the spirit of natural freedom dare they give way to; because it might happen on review something would be seen to retract or to qualify—something not properly planed and chiselled, to build into the general architecture of an artificial reputation."

The young scholar, it has been said, fancies it happiness enough to live with people who can give an inside to the world; without reflecting that they too are prisoners of their own thought, and cannot apply themselves to yours. The conditions of literary success are, in Mr. Emerson's judgment, almost destructive of the best social power, as they do not leave that frolic liberty which only can encounter a companion on the best terms. It is probable, says he, "you left some obscure comrade at a tavern, or in the farms, with right mother-wit, and equality to life, when you [as Emerson himself did] crossed sea and land to play bo-peep with celebrated scribes."

It is one of Christopher North's Recreations to classify dinner-parties of all sorts and sizes, and among

---

* When M. le Comte de Marcellus started with Chateaubriand for London, Madame de Montcalm, *cette aimable sœur* of the Duc de Richelieu, warned the young nobleman against exaggerated expectations of the people he would meet. "Chez ces génies qui expriment si bien le sentiment, le sentiment réside peu. Leur estime, leur confiance même, ne mène pas à l'affection."—*Marcellus, Chateaubriand et son Temps*, p. 214.

them a Literary Dinner stands out in capitals, backed by a note of admiration. On each side of the lord of the mansion he places a philosopher—on each side of the lady, a poet—somewhere or other about the board, a theatrical star—a foreign fiddler—an outlandish traveller—and a continental refugee.

And all the air a solemn stillness holds.

All lips are hermetically sealed. The author of the five-guinea quarto on the drawing-room table is sound asleep, with round unmeaning face, breathing tranquillity. The author of a profound treatise on the Sinking Fund sits beside him, with eyes fixed on the ceiling. The illustrious traveller, whose conversational prowess has been the talk of Europe, has been stroking his chin for the last half-hour, and nothing more. You might not only hear a pin drop—a mouse stir—but either event would rouse the whole company like a peal of thunder. A prandial parallel, in short, to Wordsworth's tea-bibbing "party in a parlour"—all silent, and all—something else, in the least quotable of monosyllables. So, again, in the *Noctes*, the Shepherd interrupts a remark of Mr. North's, on all great poets being great talkers, with the conditional assent, "Tiresome often to a degree—though sometimes . . . they are a sulky set, and as gruffly and grimly silent as if they had the toothache, or something the matter wi' their inside."

Sir Walter Scott could never "willingly endure,"

his son-in-law records, either in London or in Edinburgh, the "little exclusive circles of literary society," much less their occasional fastidiousness and petty partialities. He often complained of the real dulness of parties where each guest arrived under the implied and tacit obligation of exhibiting some extraordinary powers of talk or wit. "If," he said, "I encounter men of the world, men of business, odd or striking characters of professional excellence in any department, I am in my element, for they cannot lionise me without my returning the compliment and learning something from them."—But as for a table-full of essayists and reviewers, or an evening with bards and blues, give him a crack with Tom Purdie in preference to that, a thousand times over.

Leigh Hunt makes the hero of his seventeenth-century historical fiction record, after dining with Dryden and the wits, first at a ducal table, and afterwards in their own sphere, that at great tables they never appeared at advantage: either the host did not know how to treat them; or they were too anxious to shine; or they affected an indifference to their value, and wished to be confounded with fine gentlemen; or they were too many of them together, and so were afraid to speak, lest another should excel; or one of the lowest of their fraternity was present, who was most welcome on that account, and gave himself airs; or something else was sure to occur, which made them uneasy, and showed them to a disadvantage, both as wits and gentlemen. Happy, and rare the happiness of, a host like Mrs. Gore's Bernard Forbes, the circle of whose "literary friends," so far from meriting the stigma of "cold, solemn, and formal," assigned by the narrow experience of the coteries, was no less cheerful than intellectual; no one among them pretending to wisdom, because the pretension would have been ridiculous where the claim was so well established. "No one talked for conquest, as when two men of superior information find themselves matched against each other in an arena, in presence of a crowd of dunces. In Bernard Forbes's house there was still a republic of letters. Every citizen furnished his quota, without pomp or parsimony."*

The unpleasantness of a literary party, gathered together mainly as such, is a by-word in satirical fictions founded upon fact. Theodore Hook describes one which, from its miscellaneous character, promised a great treat, the sequel of which was, however, "most disappointing"—every one of the guests being celebrated for something, and each of them jealous of his neighbour. Mr. Peacock makes out the under-

---

* In another of her books this shrewdly observant writer comments on a feeling that is apt to render the society of public or literary men a constraint in private life—the feeling of John Watts, in *Diamond and Pearl*, who is impatient of the monopoly of fashionable fribbles in talk, to the exclusion of all rational or profitable conversation. Incessant attention to the lofty questions which impel the currents of the world's wide atmosphere, as she puts it, removes their sympathies too high above the petty interests of the day; and abstracted, or impatient, they become obstacles to the social pleasures of commonplace people.

standing of literary people to be so exalted, less however by the love of truth and virtue, than by arrogance and self-sufficiency, that "there is perhaps less disinterestedness, less liberality, less general benevolence, and more envy, hatred, and uncharitableness among them, than among any other description of men." What is it that makes you literary persons so stupid? asks Mr. Thackeray's Fitzboodle of Oliver Yorke, Esquire. "I have met various individuals in society who I was told were writers of books, and that sort of thing, and, expecting rather to be amused by their conversation, have invariably found them dull to a degree, and as for information, without a particle of it."

So again the same author's George Warrington impatiently exclaims, "A fiddlestick about men of genius!" when Pen, his protégé, is glorifying that august race. "The talk of professional critics and writers," Mr. George is pleased to add, after considerable experience, "is not a whit more brilliant, or profound, or amusing, than that of any other society of educated people." And after his younger associate has had *his* first experience of the same community, the disenchanted authorling comes to a not dissimilar conclusion. Pen was forced to confess, a subsequent chapter tells us, that the literary personages with whom he had become acquainted had not said much, in the course of the night's conversation, that was worthy to be remembered or quoted;—in fact, not one word about literature had been said during the whole course of that night at Mr. Bungay's, the eminent publisher; and Mr. Thackeray does not mind whispering to those uninitiated people who are anxious to know the habits and make the acquaintance of men of letters, that there are no sort of people who talk about books, or, perhaps, who read books, so little as literary men.

But, sir, once said Boswell to Johnson, when the doctor was bepraising a life of rustic seclusion—but, sir, is it not a sad thing to be at a distance from all our literary friends? "Sir," was Johnson's reply, "you will by-and-by have enough of this conversation which now delights you so much."

Leigh Hunt, in his essay on Amiableness as superior to Intellect, refers assentingly to a remark of Hazlitt's, that the being accustomed to the society of men of genius renders the conversation of others tiresome, as consisting of a parcel of things that have been heard a thousand times, and from which no stimulus is to be obtained. But a common complaint by men of genius themselves is, as we have seen and shall see, rather the other way.

Converse with a mind that is grandly simple, says Emerson, and literature looks like word-catching. "The mere author, in such society, is like a pickpocket among gentlemen, who has come in to steal a gold button or a pin."

Chesterfield, from quite another point of view, warns his son that a company wholly composed of men of learning, though greatly to be valued and respected, is not "good company"—"they cannot have the easy manners and *tournure* of the world, as they do not live in it." So pray let young Mr. Stanhope beware of being engrossed by such company; for, if he is, he will be "only considered as one of the *literati* by profession, which is not the way either to shine or rise in the world."

Horace Walpole shared notably in these precautionary principles and practice. Consistent enough, and rather too demonstrative, was his avowed aversion to literary society, as such. He writes of young Mr. Burke, in 1761, that although a sensible man, he "has not worn off his authorism yet, and thinks there is nothing so charming as writers, and to be one. He will know better one of these days." Of Rousseau he writes from Paris, some five years later, "But, however I admire his parts, neither he nor any *genius* I have known has had common sense enough to balance the impertinence of their pretensions. They hate priests, but love dearly to have an altar at their feet; for which reason it is much pleasanter to read them than to know them." Seven years later we have Horace trying to decline the acquaintance of Mr. Gough, and telling a correspondent, "Besides, you know I shun authors, and would never have been one myself, if it obliged me to keep such bad company." They are always in earnest, he complains, and think their profession serious, and dwell upon trifles, and reverence learning; while *he* laughs at all those things, and writes only to laugh at them, and divert himself. This was one of Walpole's most cherished and most transparent affectations.—And once more, we find him recording the avowal of a fellow-feeling by one of Fanny Burney's favourite friends. " Mr. Cambridge has been with me, and asked me if I knew the famous Beaumarchais, who has been in England. I said, ' No, sir, nor ever intend it.' ' Well, now,' said he, ' that is exactly my way: I made a resolution early never to be acquainted with authors, they are so vain and so troublesome.'" For all which, Horace is persuaded that this protesting friend has already got acquainted with Beaumarchais.

Bayle says in one of his letters—which, after the earlier ones, are notably free from *la superstition littéraire pour les illustres*—that when once you have come to know personally a good number of persons celebrated for their writings, you find out that it is no such great matter after all to have composed a book, and that a good one. " Tous ces gens-là," writes Madame de Charrière, " sont sujets non-seulement à préférer leur gloire à leurs amis, mais à ne voir dans leurs amis, dans la nature, dans les événements, que des récits, des tableaux, des réflexions à faire et a publier." On the other hand, Miss Mitford's *young* experience affirmed " most writers" to be mere "good-humoured chatterers," neither very wise nor very witty, but nine times out of ten unaffected and pleasant, and quite removing by their conversation any awe that may have been excited by their works. Nearly forty years later we find her assuring a correspondent that authors, as a general rule, are the most disappointing people in the world ; and she quotes her old bookseller, George Whittaker, on the subject, who used to say that "booksellers, next to authors, were the most stupid and ignorant persons under the sun." In a yet later letter, referring, in her illness, to the many kind friends she had, some of them persons of note in literature, Miss Mitford was fain to own her preference of those who loved letters without actually following the trade of authorship,—of the intelligent audience to the actors on the stage.

Montaigne duly records his sire's enthusiasm—with more zeal than knowledge—in imitating the king's[*] new-born ardour for literature and for the company of literary men. "Moy," adds Michel the malicious, "je les aime bien, mais je ne les adore pas." The point of the *adoration* consists in what Montaigne had said just before—that his father kept the doors of his house for ever open *aux hommes doctes*, whom he as reverently as eagerly welcomed under his roof *comme personnes saintes.*

When pleasure and business combined first brought Francis Jeffrey to London, in 1804, his account of the great metropolis, in its social aspects, includes this avowal : "The literary men, I acknowledge, excite my reverence the least." One of Charlotte Brontë's letters,

[*] Francis I.

which is almost entirely occupied with the works and ways of Mr. G. H. Lewes, has this passage to the purpose: " He gives no charming picture of London literary society, and especially the female part of it ; but all coteries, whether they be literary, scientific, political, or religious, must, it seems to me, have a tendency to change truth into affectation. When people belong to a clique, they must, I suppose, in some measure, write, talk, think, and live for that clique ; a harassing and narrowing necessity." Long before Currer Bell's time had Washington Irving's "poor devil author" put on record his experiences to a like effect—how he determined to cultivate the society of the literary, and to enrol himself in the fraternity of authorship—how he found no difficulty in making a circle of literary acquaintances, not having the sin of success lying at his door ("indeed, the failure of my poem was a kind of recommendation to their favour") ; —and how soon he discovered his want of *esprit de corps* to turn these literary fellowships to any account : he could not bring himself to enlist in any particular sect : he saw something to like in them all, but found that would never do, for that the tacit condition on which a man enters into one of these sects is, that he abuses all the rest.

" I perceived," says honest Dribble, of Green Arbour Court, "that there were little knots of authors, who lived with, and for, and by one another. They considered themselves the salt of the earth. They fostered and kept up a conversational vein of thinking, and talking, and joking on all subjects; and they cried each other up to the skies." *Orna me* is apt to be a *bien entendu*, all round, for a good understanding in such circles.

Goldsmith's citizen of the world had visited many countries, and been in cities without number, yet never a town had he entered which could not produce ten or a dozen little great men, all fancying themselves known to the rest of the world, and complimenting each other upon their extensive reputation, and promising each other an assured immortality. He found it amusing enough when two of these Little Pedlington prodigies mounted the stage of ceremony, and gave and took praise *inter se*. "I have been present when a German doctor, for having pronounced a panegyric upon a certain monk, was thought the most ingenious man in the world; till the monk soon after divided this reputation, by returning the compliment; by which means they both marched off with universal applause." Highly typical quadrupeds are La Fontaine's *deux ânes qui, prenant tour à tour l'encensoir, se louaient tour à tour, comme c'est la manière.**

---

* Later in the fable, the line
"Ces ânes, non contents de s'être ainsi *grattés*,"
recalls a passage in Marot's *Epîtres:*
" Ce Huet et Sagon se jouent ;
Par écrit l'un l'autre se louent,
Et semblent (tant ils s'entre-flattent)
Deux vieux ânes qui s'entre-*grattent.*"

> "Thus we dispose of all poetic merit,
> Yours Milton's genius, and mine Homer's spirit.
> Call Tibbald Shakspeare, and he'll swear the Nine,
> Dear Cibber! never matched one Ode of thine."

Honest was Scott when he declared in his diary that no man who ever wrote a line despised the *pap* of praise as heartily as he did: there was nothing he scorned more, except those who thought the ordinary sort of praise or censure a matter of the least consequence. He held it to be the purpose of such folks as take the trouble to praise you, to be, in general, to get you to puff away in return. To him their rank praises no more made amends for their bad poetry, than—his own the unsavoury simile—tainted butter would pass off stale fish. There is nothing, says Horace Walpole, more foolish than the hyperboles of contemporaries on one another, who, like the nominal Dukes of Aquitaine and Normandy at a coronation, have place given to them above all peers, and the next day shrink to simple knights. As to authors, exclaims Sir John Ellesmere, they are generally in ecstasies (honest ecstasies) when talking to one another of each other's performances. "Have I not seen a number of serpents in a cage as civil to each other as possible, upreared upon the penultimate parts of their tails, and bowing affably to one another,—in process of time to become quite fond and fondling?" Like the two professors of music in Mr. Thackeray's story of *The Ravenswing*, who used to meet with such delightful cordiality on both sides: "Mein lieber Herr," Thrum would say, "your sonata in X flat is sublime." "Chevalier," would Baroski reply, "dat andante movement of yours in W is worthy of Beethoven. I gif you my sacred honour," and so forth. During the penultimate decade of the last century, the most high-flown encomiums on each other were constantly being penned by Hayley and Miss Anna Seward; of whom Malone remarked, at the time, that some of the old Italian writers would have condemned them to lash each other from morning till night with nettles, for their folly and vanity. But a wit of the day inflicted on them a milder punishment in the form of a

"*Dialogue between Miss Seward and Mr. Hayley.*

'Tuneful poet! Britain's glory,
  Mr. Hayley, that is you——'
'Ma'am, you carry all before you,
  Trust me, Lichfield Swan, you do——'
'Ode, didactick, epick, sonnet,
  Mr. Hayley, you're divine——'
'Ma'am, I'll take my oath upon it,
  You alone are all the Nine!'"

Boswell tells, with a spice of gleeful malice, how a foreign minister of no very high talents, who had been in Johnson's company for a considerable time quite overlooked, happened luckily to mention that he had read some of the *Rambler* in Italian, and admired it much. This pleased the doctor so greatly, that henceforth he was all attention to the minister, and on the first remark which he made, however simple, exclaimed, "The Ambassador says well;—his Excellency observes—," and then he expanded and enriched the little that had been said into something of apparent consequence; insomuch that for after-years, "The Ambassador says well," became to those who were present a laughable term of applause, when no mighty matter had been expressed. Wordsworth relates an incident in a debate he once had with a local poet, in the cottage at Townend, on the merits and demerits of the versification of Pope, of whom the visitor was an enthusiastic admirer, and whom he defended with a warmth that indicated much irritation: nevertheless he of Rydal would not abandon his point, and said, "In compass and variety of sound your own versification surpasses his." Never did or could Wordsworth forget the change in his visitor's countenance and tone of voice: "The storm was laid in a moment; he no longer disputed my judgment, and I passed immediately in his mind, no doubt, for as great a critic as ever lived." Cowper says of the self-enamoured author, who, Pygmalion-like, dotes on his own workmanship, that

> " If some mere driveller suck the sugared fib,
> One that still needs his leading-string and bib,
> And praise his genius, he is soon repaid
> In praise applied to the same part—his head;
> For 'tis a rule that holds for ever true,
> Grant me discernment, and I grant it you."

Vadius and Trissotin ring the changes of panegyric on each other, with more ingenuity and effusion than the great little originals of Molière's satire, Ménage and Cotin, could themselves have done, at their best, or their worst.

> *Tr.* Vos vers ont des beautés que n'ont point tous les autres.
> *Vad.* Les Grâces et Vénus règnent dans tous les votres.
> *Tr.* Vous avez le tour libre et le beau choix des mots.
> *Vad.* On voit partout chez vous l'*ithos* et le *pathos*.
> *Tr.* Nous avons vu de vous des églogues d'un style
> Qui passe en doux attraits Théocrite et Virgile.
> *Vad.* Vos odes ont un air noble, galant, et doux,
> Qui laisse de bien loin votre Horace après vous.
> *Tr.* Est-il rien d'amoureux comme vos chansonnettes?
> *Vad.* Peut-on rien voir d'égal aux sonnets que vous faites?
> *Tr.* Rien qui soit plus charmants que vos petits rondeaux?
> *Vad.* Rien de si plein d'esprit que tous vos madrigaux?
> *Tr.* Aux ballades surtout vous êtes admirable.
> *Vad.* Et dans les bouts-rimés je vous trouve adorable.
> *Tr.* Si la France pouvait connaître votre prix,
> *Vad.* Si le siècle rendait justice aux beaux esprits,
> *Tr.* En carosse doré vous iriez par les rues,
> *Vad.* On verrait le public vous dresser des statues."

It is like Menas and Enobarbus in Shakspeare, unlike though Vadius and Trissotin be to Menas and Enobarbus. "You have done well by water," quoth the latter. "And you by land," quoth the former. "I will praise any man that will praise me," rejoins Enobarbus, "though it cannot be denied what I have done by land." "Nor what I have done by water," Menas is in hot haste to reply. Dryden defied the "blast of common censure" when he penned a prologue of panegyric for Lee's *Alexander*, mindful of the like services Lee had done for him:

> "For 'twill be thought, and with some colour too,
> I pay the bribe I first received from you;

> That mutual vouchers for our fame we stand,
> And play the game into each other's hand;
> And as cheap pen'orths to ourselves afford;
> As Bessus and his brothers of the sword."

Lady Mary Wortley Montagu compared the confederacy of Bolingbroke with Swift and Pope to that of the aforesaid Bessus and his sword-men, in *King and No King*, who endeavour to support themselves by giving certificates of each other's merit. "Pope has triumphantly declared that they may do and say whatever silly things they please, they will still be the greatest geniuses nature ever exhibited." Readers of Fielding, if there are such folks nowadays, may remember a discourse between poet and player in *Joseph Andrews*, at one turn of which the former adroitly mollifies the latter by this pat of butter: "No, sir, if we had six such actors as you, we should soon rival the Bettertons and Sandfords of former times; for without a compliment to you, I think it impossible for any one to have excelled you in most of your parts." Nay, Mr. Poet affirms it as a solemn truth, and he has heard many, and all of them great judges, express as much; and Mr. Player must pardon him if he tells him that, at every fresh performance, he has constantly acquired some new excellence, like a snowball; thus deceiving Mr. Poet in his estimate of perfection, and outdoing what *he* thought inimitable. Whereupon Mr. Player at once invokes summary doom upon himself if there are not many strokes, aye whole scenes, in Mr. Poet's last tragedy, which at least equal Shakspeare. Whether Mr. Player be Garrick or not, Goldsmith pictures Garrick by name as a mere glutton of praise, who swallowed all that he came across, and mistook for absolute renown the puff of a dunce ; and then again,

> "If dunces applauded, he paid them in kind.
> Ye Kenricks, ye Kellys, and Woodfalls so grave,
> What a commerce was yours, while you got and you gave!
> How did Grub Street re-echo the shouts that you raised,
> While he was be-Rosciused and you were bepraised!"

As an essay writer on the ever-green subject of laurels has said, some people seem to think that praise is such a wholesome, pleasant thing that it is not easy to have too much of it: they like the praise market to be brisk and open, and delight in large and liberal transactions on that Exchange. With the least hint from you that you are disposed to accept a reciprocity treaty on this subject, they will consign to you any amount of eulogy that you are ever likely to require; but they do like reciprocity, or an approach to it. "If you will only praise their dexterity in carving a leg of mutton, they will cover you with encomiums for your surpassing skill in carving a sirloin of beef."* Many a mutual admiration society

---

* An equally shrewd essayist of the same school,—possibly, both of them being anonymous, the selfsame writer,—ventures wholly to dissent, however, in an essay on "Friends' Judgments," from the popular notion that the judgments of literary friends are, as such, to be at once cast aside; though he agrees that the popular notion, like most popular notions, has an element of truth in it. In most cases the favourable judgment, he contends, is older than the friendship, and is, in fact, the

(*not* limited as regards their stock in trade, of admiration) may be typically set forth in Le Sage's triad of Count, Licentiate, and Wit, in *Le Diable Boiteux*, who always go about in company, a threefold cord that is not easily broken; paying visits together, and together bepraising one another with one consent, and on one uniform system. The Count, indeed, is mainly, if not exclusively, taken up with praising himself; his brother, the ecclesiastic, praises him, without forgetting himself; while the wit is charged with the triple duty of praising both brothers, and of mingling his praises with theirs. The poor *bel-esprit* comes off badly in this joint-stock undertaking. Such a wit as Voiture would have scouted his share in it— he who, in Victor Cousin's words, "voudrait occuper de lui et à tout moment la terre entière," and who had *éloges* for none but those who could or would eulogize him; and Voiture was capable of discovering wit in a

---

groundwork of the friendship. "A and B become acquainted with each other's writings or discourses, they are mutually struck by their merits, and they naturally wish to improve an acquaintance of this sort into actual personal friendship. It is rather hard if a friendship of this kind is held to disqualify a man from ever after speaking well of his new-made friend. It is strange if his judgment, which, till their intimate acquaintance began, would be allowed to be of some value, is held to be of no value precisely from the moment when nearer acquaintance begins to afford better means of forming it." Now this is affirmed to be really the most common history of friendship between author and critic, or between author and author,—each wishing to know more of a man of whom he had already learned to think well. It is surely hard, the essayist argues, if both are to be tongue-tied from the moment when they cease to be strangers.

Costar, if Costar would but devote himself to glorify Voiture. Mr. de Quincey takes an amused note of Pope one morning, in some of his own verses, lodging a compliment to the Duke of Buckingham (not either of *the* Dukes) as a poet and a critic; and how immediately " the Duke was down upon him with an answering salute of twenty-one guns, and ever afterwards they were friends,"—although, in Pope's own judgment, nine out of ten who found their way into the *Dunciad* had not by half so well established their right of entrance as his Grace.

When Bussy-Rabutin found his name hoisted into a line of Boileau's, " Despréaux," he wrote, " est un garçon d'esprit et de mérite, que j'aime fort." When Johnson published his first critical attempt on *Macbeth*, he commended the critical talents of Warburton; and Warburton repaid the kindness in kind, in the preface to his edition of Shakspeare, where he distinguishes Johnson as " a man of parts and genius." The tone soon changed on both sides, and changed with a vengeance. So with Voltaire and Frederick the Great in their correspondence, and the final issue of it all. Mr. Carlyle describes the correspondence between them, once kindled, as going on apace, and soon bursting forth, finding nourishment all round, into a shining little household fire, pleasant to the hands and hearts of both parties: the mutual admiration, which was high, by no means deficient in emphasis of statement; superlatives, tempered by art, passing and repassing. "Friedrich, reading Voltaire's immortal manuscripts, confesses, with a blush, before long, that he himself is a poor apprentice that way. Voltaire, at sight of the princely productions, is full of admiration, of encouragement." On his side the style is, "Oh what a Crown Prince, ripening forward to be the delight of human nature, and realize the dream of sages, Philosophy upon the Throne!" And on Frederick's: "Oh what a Phœbus Apollo, mounting the eastern sky, chasing the nightmares—sowing the earth with orient pearl, to begin with!" We must go to the Baviad and the Mæviad to learn what Mrs. Robinson thought and said of Dr. Tasker, and what he of her. Of him she says, for instance, that "the learned and ingenious Dr. Tasker . . . has pronounced some of Mrs. Robinson's poems superior to those of Milton on the same subject, particularly her address to the nightingale. The praise of so competent and disinterested a judge stamps celebrity that neither time nor envy can obliterate." So she. Now he:

> "In ancient Greece by two fair forms were seen
> Wisdom's stern goddess, and Love's smiling queen;
> Pallas presided over arms and arts,
> And Venus over gentle virgins' hearts:
> But now both powers in one fair form combine,
> And in fair Robinson united shine."

John Foster rather scandalized the cautious editor of the *Eclectic* by the vigour with which he reviewed the correspondence of Dr. Beattie and Sir William Forbes, "habitually larding one another with flattery from head to foot." Dr. Parr had only to magnify an obscure but reverend Mr. Stewart, "an Irish poet," by levelling him up to Byron, Crabbe, Campbell, and Moore, to be hailed by him in return as an infallible critic. "Mrs. Parr," the doctor had said to his wife when the said clerical "Irish poet" was filling a chair at their fireside, "you have seen Moore in this spot some time ago, you now see Mr. Stewart. The race of true poets is now nearly extinct. There is you," turning to Mr. Stewart, "and Moore, and Byron, and Crabbe, and Campbell,—I hardly know of another. You, Stewart, are a man of genius, of real genius, and of science too, as well as genius. I tell you so." No wonder Mr. Stewart prefaces his delectable narrative of this interview with the affirmation, "Dr. Parr's taste was exquisite, his judgment infallible." It is a suggestive sequence in the Table-talk of Samuel Rogers, that next to a paragraph telling how, when that poet first came forward as one, he was emphatically praised by Hayley, should occur another which begins: "If Hayley was formerly overrated, he is now undervalued. He was a most accomplished person," etc. Southey's reviewer in his own *Quarterly* declares the monstrous extravagance of the compliments exchanged between him and the two or three bards with whom he was really cordial, to be a matter of sheer astonishment to prosaic minds. It is a little too much, in this critic's judgment, to be told that Mr. Landor's Latin verses are of "the best kind"—

(Virgil being elsewhere styled " a bad poet.") that his *Gebir* "contains the finest poetry in the language,"— and that Mrs. Brooks's *Zophiel* is "by far the most original poem that this generation has produced." These and similar eulogies are cited in evidence of the reviewer's assertion that there certainly does not seem to have ever lived a man whose judgments of others depended more on their expressed opinions of him. But be the allegation ever so true, it can go a very little way towards depreciating Robert Southey, in the esteem of any one at least who, familiarly knowing, cannot but love a man so lovable, so pure-hearted, sound-hearted, manly, tender, and true.

X.

A Hard Crust.

EXCEPT for the absolutely incompetent, of whom there will ever be plenty, and the utterly unappreciated, who must be just as few, the author's craft, as a means of winning his daily bread, can no longer be said to bear the ill name it once bore, and that not long since. The loaf of daily bread thus won is no longer all, and such very, hard crust. Pudding as well as praise, the practised penman is pretty safe to see smoking on his board—from plain suet, or batter, to richest plum pudding, that seems all plums.

Goldsmith makes his Chinese philosopher recount the names of some on the long roll of indigent genius. Homer he cites as the first poet and beggar among the ancients—a blind man, who sang his ballads about the streets, and whose mouth was more frequently filled with verses than with bread. If Plautus, the comic poet, was better off, it was because he had two trades,—being a poet for his diversion, and helping to turn a mill for his livelihood. Was not Terence a slave, and did not Boethius die in a jail? Tasso was "often obliged to borrow a crown from some friend, to pay for a month's subsistence,"—and his pretty sonnet is had in remembrance, addressed to his cat, and begging the light of her eyes to write by, he being too poor to afford a candle. Has not Spain her story of a Cervantes dying of hunger, and Portugal hers of a Camoens ending his days in a hospital? France tells of her Vaugelas, surnamed The Owl, because venturing out only by night, through fear of his creditors. But the sufferings of poets and authors in other countries, according to Lien-Chi Altangi, is nothing when compared to their distresses in the British isles: "The names of Spenser and Otway, Butler and Dryden, are every day mentioned as a national reproach; some of them having lived in a state of precarious indigence, and others literally died of hunger." Mr. Carlyle glances grimly at the Heynes dining on boiled peascods, the Jean Pauls on water, the Johnsons bedded and boarded on fourpence-halfpenny a day. So does Longfellow at Johnson and Savage rambling about the streets of London at midnight, without a place to sleep in; at Otway, starved like a dog; at Goldsmith, penniless in Green Arbour Court. "Next to the Newgate Calendar, the Biography of Authors is the most sickening chapter in the history of man." Says Dryden, in one of his prologues,—

> "The unhappy man who once has trailed a pen,
> Lives not to please himself, but other men;
> Is always drudging, wastes his life and blood,
> Yet only eats and drinks what you think good.

> What praise soe'er the poetry deserve,
> Yet every fool can bid the poet starve."

The miseries of a poet's life had long before been one of the favourite topics of *The Return from Parnassus*, where they are treated as by one who had "felt them knowingly." It is the theme of Lloyd's octosyllabics:

> "O glorious trade! for wit's a trade
> Where men are ruined more than made.
> Let crazy Lee, neglected Gay,
> The shabby Otway, Dryden gray, . . .
> Repeat their lives, their works, their fame,
> And teach the world some useful shame."

It was to a young man of mark that Southey, in 1813, wrote his conviction that no young man could support himself by literary exertions, however great his talents and his industry. "Woe be to the youthful poet who sets out upon his pilgrimage to the temple of fame with nothing but hope for his viaticum! There is the Slough of Despond, and the Hill of Difficulty, and the Valley of the Shadow of Death upon the way." Shenstone pictures a "hapless hypocrite" who, with seeming ease and laboured peace, indites a care-defying sonnet, which implies his debts discharged, and himself in full possession, with uncontested right and property, of half-a-crown: does any beholder admire this wight? let him be

> "Forewarned, be frugal, or with prudent rage
> His pen demolish; choose the trustier flail,
> And bless those labours which the choice inspired."

Mr. Thackeray had not yet found the pursuits of literature a paying concern, when he bade all parents and guardians pray that their darlings might not be born with literary tastes. How much money had all the literature of England in the Three Per Cents? he asked in 1843. Was there a single penman by profession who had laid by five thousand pounds of his own earnings? Lawyers, doctors, and all other learned persons, save money, said he; "the Jew-boy who sells oranges at the coach-door, the burnt-umber Malay who sweeps crossings, save money: there is but Vates in the world who does not seem to know the art of growing rich, and, as a rule, leaves the world with as little coin about him as he had when he entered it." We shall see, further on, however, how clear the author of *Pendennis* and *The Newcomes* was from the cant of maudlin pity for impecunious authorship, as such.

The second Calender in the *Arabian Nights* is asked by the tailor if he has learnt anything whereby he may get a livelihood, and not be burdensome to any man; and he replies that he understands the laws both human and divine, and that he is both grammarian and poet. The tailor tells him that by all this he will not be able, in that age and country, to purchase himself one bit of bread. It is perhaps meant as a moral for all time.

Coleridge addresses "an affectionate exhortation" to youthful literati at large, grounded on his own ex-

perience, and it is this: "Never pursue literature as
a trade." With the exception of one extraordinary
man, he professes to have never known a man of
genius healthy or happy without a profession,—that
is, some regular employment which does not depend
on the will of the moment, and which can be carried
on so far mechanically that an average quantum
only of health, spirits, and intellectual exertion is
requisite to the faithful discharge of it. Three hours
of leisure, unannoyed by any alien anxiety, and
looked forward to with delight as a change and recreation, will, he promises, suffice to realize in literature a larger product of what is truly genial, than
weeks of compulsion.* Talfourd hails, as most
wholesome for every youth who hesitates whether he
shall abandon the certain reward of plodding industry
for the "splendid miseries of authorship," the letter
in which Charles Lamb remonstrates with Bernard
Barton (Quaker, poet, and banker's clerk) on his
project (too literally) of "throwing himself on the
world," without any rational plan of support, beyond
what the chance employ of booksellers may afford
him. Let him, by Lamb's advice, throw himself rather
from the Tarpeian rock, slap-dash headlong upon
iron spikes. If he has but five consolatory minutes

---

* "Money and immediate reputation form only an arbitrary and accidental end of literary labour. The hope of increasing them by any
given exertion will often prove a stimulant to industry; but the necessity
of acquiring them will in all works of genius convert the stimulant into
a narcotic."—*Biographia Literaria*, chap. xi.

between the business desk and bed, let him make much of them, and live a century in them, rather than turn slave to the booksellers. "I have known many authors want for bread, some repining, others envying the blessed security of a counting-house, all agreeing they had rather have been tailors, weavers— what not? than the things they were. . . . Oh, you know not, may you never know, the miseries of subsisting by authorship. 'Tis a pretty appendage to a situation like yours or mine; but a slavery, worse than all slavery, to be a bookseller's dependant." So, let him keep to the bank, and the bank will keep him. Let him beware of trusting to the public: he may hang, starve, drown himself, for anything that worthy "personage" cares. And Elia, who so often had banned his office desk, and the drudgery of its details, now blesses it altogether—retracts all his fond complaints of mercantile employment, and looks upon them as lovers' quarrels. "Welcome dead timber of a desk, that makes me live."* A laureate of the last

---

* Lamb would have applauded to the echo the resolve of that more intimate friend of his, Henry Crabb Robinson, after producing a translation of the German *Amatonda* of Antou Wall, and of excerpts from Jean Paul, (which, by the way, Lamb pronounced the finest things he had ever seen from the German language,)—a book which, so far as the translator knew, was never reviewed, and for which he obtained no credit. "Perhaps *happily*," he surmises in his Reminiscences, "for it was the failure of my attempt to gain distinction by writing that made me willing to devote myself honestly to the Law, and so saved me from the mortification that follows a *little* literary success, by which many men of inferior faculties, like myself, have been betrayed into an unwise adoption of literature as a profession, which after this year (1811) I

century enforces the monition, in what he calls *A Charge to the Poets*,—

"If nature prompts you, or if friends persuade,
Why write, but ne'er pursue it as a trade."

One of Lord Lytton's successful men of letters avowedly owes his success to his three rules (equally applicable, however, to all professions), of never trusting to genius for what can be obtained by labour, never professing to teach what he had not studied to understand, and never engaging his word to what he did not strive his uttermost to execute. With these rules, he tells a literary aspirant, literature—provided a man does not mistake his vocation for it, and will, under good advice, go through the preliminary discipline of natural powers, which all vocations require —"is as good a calling as any other. Without them, a shoeblack's is infinitely better." * In Juvenal's style, better to vend, in a poor salesman's post, 'mid squabbling crowds, to him who bids the most, old casks, shelves, chests, cracked stools, and rusty pots :

"Et vendas potius, commissa quod auctio vendit
Stantibus, œnophorum, tripodes, armaria, cistas."

Not less wholesome for ink-shedders in general than was Charles Lamb's counsel to Bernard Barton in particular, are all the protests uttered first and last

---

never once thought of."—*Diary and Reminiscences of H. C. Robinson*, vol. i., p. 360.

* Lord L'Estrange hints the objection that nevertheless there have been great writers who observed none of these rules. "Great writers, probably, but very unenviable men," is Henry Norreys's reply.

by Mr. Thackeray against the pleas and practices of impecunious authorship. A literary man, as he says, has often to work for his bread against time, or against his will, or in spite of his health, or of his indolence, or of his repugnance to the subject on which he is called to exert himself, just like any other daily toiler. When you want to make money of Pegasus (as he must, perhaps, who has no other saleable property), farewell poetry and aerial flights: Pegasus only rises now like Mr. Green's balloon at periods advertised beforehand, and when the spectator's money has been paid. Pegasus trots in harness over the stony pavement, and pulls a cart or a cab behind him. Often Pegasus does his work with panting sides and trembling knees, and not seldom gets a cut of the whip from his driver. "Do not let us, however, be too prodigal of our pity upon Pegasus. There is no reason why this animal should be exempt from labour, or illness, or decay, any more than any of the other creatures of God's world." If he gets the whip, Mr. Thackeray is sure that Pegasus very often deserves it, and he for one is quite ready to protest with his friend George Warrington against the doctrine which some poetical sympathisers are inclined to put forward, viz., that men of letters, and what is called genius, are to be exempt from the prose duties of this daily-bread-wanting, tax-paying life, and are not to be made to work and pay like their neighbours. That is the sort of answer he would make to querimonious queries dating from the Castle of Indolence:

> "Is there no patron to protect the muse? . . .
> To every labour its reward accrues,
> And they are sure of bread who swink and moil,"

whereas the Aonian hive is none too sure of honey. In a later work the author of *The Virginians* commented on the disproportionate stress laid by the brotherhood of the pen on their poverty, hardships, and disappointments; and the failure to take due count of some "advantages belonging to our trade,"—including present independence of "patrons," and the requiring scarce any capital "wherewith to exercise our trade." What other learned profession, he asked, is equally fortunate in that respect? A doctor, for instance, must set up an establishment, and perhaps have to humour hypochondriacs, and wheedle dowagers, and practise a score of little subsidiary arts in order to make that of healing profitable. And as to the barrister, the question occurs, how many hundreds of pounds he has to sink upon his stock in trade before his returns are available,—the costly charges of university education, of chambers in the inn of court, of clerk and his maintenance, circuit travel, etc., etc. And yet in the case of a highly educated man of letters, in the true sense, some of these costliest preliminary charges are to be equally presumed; and the outgoings have been large and prolonged, in the process of qualification, before ever any incomings begin to tell on the balance-sheet.

Malheur à qui attend tout de sa plume, was Mdme. de Tencin's warning to Marmontel: *Rien de plus casuel;* for whereas the man who makes or mends shoes is sure of his wages, the man who makes a book or a play is never sure of anything. Well may an author impress his brains upon prepared rags, with a pen of a foolish bird that is driven with a rag, exclaims the Richard Savage of fiction (matter-of-fact fiction), when he bewails his ever having taken to the author-business, and wishes he were fit to carry burdens, —a chairman grunting under half a dowager, or a porter with an impregnable scull. An author can't, observes Mr. Slick, "live upon nothin' but air, like a chameleon,* though he can change colour as often as that little critter does." In the preface to his *Calamities of Authors*, the elder Disraeli—perhaps with a keen remembrance of his own "antecedents"—assumes that no affectionate parent would consent to see his son devote himself to his pen as a profession; and asserts that the most successful author can obtain no equivalent for the labours of his life. Most authors, on this showing, "close their lives in apathy or despair, and too many live by means which few of them would not blush to describe." To become an "Author by Profession" is to have no other means of subsistence

---

* Praise, said Nat Lee, in *his* time, "is the greatest encouragement we chameleons can pretend to, or rather the manna that keeps soul and body together; we devour it as if it were angels' food, and vainly think we grow immortal."

than such as are extracted from the quill; and, no one, it is affirmed on the first page of the *Calamities*, believes these to be so precarious as they really are, until disappointed, distressed, and thrown out of every pursuit which can maintain independence, the noblest mind is cast into the lot of a doomed labour. In this minor key the strain of the whole book is pitched. The picture of the man of letters in it is drearier still than that painted of him by Cervantes, as a man always wretched, and sometimes persecuted, and very often lacking the necessaries of life. Spenser is brought in by Oldham dissuading that author from the study of poetry, in terms like these:

> "Had I the choice of flesh and blood again,
> To act once more in life's tumultuous scene,
> I'd be a porter, or a scavenger,
> A groom, or anything but poet here."

Béranger's advice was emphatically given: write if you will, versify if you must, sing away, if the singing mood is an imperative mood, but on no account give up your other occupation, "mais ne quittez jamais le travail;" let your authorship be a pastime, not a trade; let it be your avocation, not your vocation; depending upon it, you will be dependent indeed, with a debtors' prison looming in the background.*

---

* "A moins d'un concours extraordinaire de circonstances, on ne gagne aux lettres qu'une sotte réputation, qui vous mène à Bicêtre, appuyé sur le bras de la misère."

To an artisan who had turned poet, or poetaster, Béranger wrote in the very style of Lamb to his Quaker correspondent: "Mon cher poëte,

To Madame de Staël's lament that Campbell was so poor, poverty unsettling his mind so that he could not write, the reply of Samuel Rogers was, why did he not take the situation of a clerk? he could then compose verses during his leisure hours. This answer was reckoned very cruel both by Madame de Staël and by Sir James Mackintosh; but the banker-bard used to maintain the real kindness as well as truth of it. When literature is the sole business of life, he would say, it becomes a drudgery; when we are able to resort to it only at certain hours, it is a charming relaxation. And Rogers would recall, in his table-talk, the early years when, as a banker's clerk, he had to be at the desk every day from ten till five o'clock; never could he forget the delight with which, on returning home, he used to read and write during the evening.

Even Robert Southey, while declaring his choice of literature for a profession to have been that to which he owed the happiness of his life, the esteem in which he was held, and that in which he confidently believed he should be held hereafter, speaks of it in a letter to Mr. Wynn, as late as 1835, as "the one great imprudence" of his life; nay, more, as "the greatest which any man can commit." *A fortiori*, any woman, some women would be prompt to assert. Miss Mitford is an emphatic witness, as taken in her busiest, liveliest,

---

je ne vous conçois guère ; vous avez un emploi, et vous le quittez ! Rêvez-vous ?" etc.—*Mémoire sur Béranger*, par Lapointe, p. 243.

most productive epoch. "But I would rather serve in a shop—rather scour floors—rather nurse children, than undergo these tremendous and interminable disputes, and this unwomanly publicity. . . . I am now chained to a desk, eight, ten, twelve hours a day, at mere drudgery. All my thoughts of writing are for hard money." This was in 1823, when theatrical managers and speculating publishers were worrying the life out of her. If she could but get the assurance of earning for her parents a humble competence, (but then a spendthrift father is scarcely content with *that*,) she should be, she protests, the happiest creature in the world. "But for these dear ties I should never write another line, but go out in some situation, as other destitute women do." Again; "Since I have become a professed authoress, woe is me! A washerwoman hath a better trade." To another correspondent she says, a year later: "I write merely for remuneration; and I would rather scrub floors if I could get as much by that healthier, more respectable, and more feminine employment." Half a dozen years after that, the strain is still the same: "I myself hate all my own doings [in literature], and consider the being forced to this drudgery as the greatest misery that life can afford. But it is my wretched fate, and must be undergone—so long, at least, as my father is spared to me. If I should have the misfortune to lose him, I shall go quietly to the workhouse, and never write another line—a far preferable destiny." Nearly half a dozen later still, we come upon this exceeding bitter cry: "No woman's constitution can stand the wear and tear of all this anxiety. It killed poor Mrs. Hemans, and will, if not averted, kill me."

Washington Irving wrote in 1824 to his nephew Pierre, expressing a hope that his literary vein had been a transient one, and that he was preparing to establish his fortune and reputation on a better basis than literary success. It was the successful Geoffrey Crayon's earnest wish that none of those whose interests and happiness were dear to him should be induced to follow his footsteps, and wander into what he calls "the seductive but treacherous paths of literature." There is, he assures his aspiring kinsman, no life more precarious in its profits and fallacious in its enjoyments than that of an author. He speaks from an experience which might be considered a favourable and prosperous one; and he would earnestly dissuade all those with whom his voice has any effect, from trusting their fortunes to the pen. "For my part, I look forward with impatience to the time when a moderate competency will place me above the necessity of writing for the press. I have long since discovered that it is indeed 'vanity and vexation of spirit.'" Yet long after the modest competency was won, even to the end of his days, literary composition was Washington Irving's delight; a fact which, however, makes none the less noteworthy his repeated testimony to its vexation as well as vanity, while still writing for bread. He declares that many and many a time had he regretted that at his early outset in life he was not imperiously bound down to some regular and useful employment, and thoroughly inured to habits of business; and a thousand times deplored bitterly his ever having been led away by his imagination. "Believe me, the man who earns his bread by the sweat of his brow, eats oftener a sweeter morsel, however coarse, than he who procures it by the labour of his brains."* Ellesmere, of *Friends in Council*, pronounces authorship to be the last trade he should think of taking up. Sooner would he elect to be one of those men who carry advertising boards, like tabards, behind and before them; and whose only duty is to perambulate crowded thoroughfares in long line. "This would be very superior to making a living by literature. . . . If any ideas came into my head during the long walk of the day, I could put them down in the evening and publish them, if I liked, but I should not expect to live or thrive by so doing." And the more moderate Milverton, of the same goodly fellowship, gives this as the sum and substance

---

* In a subsequent letter to his nephew he iterates the appeal to his own case, as showing how insensibly a young man gets beguiled away by the imagination, and wanders from the safe beaten path of life, to lose himself in the mazes of literature. "Scarcely any author ever sets forth with the intention or surmise of becoming such; he becomes so by degrees; and I have seen enough of literary life to warn all those who are dear to me, should I see any danger of their straying into it."—(Letters of Dec. 7, 1824, and March 29, 1825.)

of all that he has to say upon the subject : that literature does not hold out any safe reward ; and that if he were advising any person whose heart was set upon such things as reward, he should perhaps agree with Ellesmere in recommending a tabard-bearer's life, as likely to be more advantageous than a literary one. For himself, he should prefer sweeping a crossing ; but that is mere matter of taste.

XI.

Men of Letters and Unlettered Wives.

THE wives of poets, according to Hazlitt, are, for the most part, mere pieces of furniture in the room. "If you speak to them of their husbands' talents or reputation in the world, it is as if you made mention of some office that they held." In another of his books he refers to a certain poet's wife, on canvas, as handsomer than falls to the lot of most poets, who are generally, he says, more intent upon the idea in their own minds than on the image before them, and are glad to take up with Dulcineas of their own creating. We men are so exacting, Parson Dale tells Riccabocca; we expect to find ideal nymphs and goddesses when we condescend to marry a mortal; and if we did, our chickens would be boiled to rags, and our mutton come up as cold as a stone.* It is

---

* This is said in answer to the Italian Philosopher's disparaging estimate of his good but rather goodly little wife: "so good, I allow, but you must own that she and I cannot have much in common." Parson Dale will own nothing of the sort. He tells him they twain, in the dual unity of wedlock, have their house and interests, their happiness and their lives, in common. Anon the parson becomes confidential, by

quite another sort of Country Parson who muses on the extent to which men of an imaginative turn have to "come down," when they get married : not that he supposes anything about the clever man's wife but what is very good ; but surely she is not always the sympathetic, admiring companion of his early visions ? For instance, we are put in mind of the poet who, walking in the summer fields, said to his wife, as together they gazed on the frisking lambs, that he wondered not at the lamb being taken, in all ages, as the emblem of happiness and innocence; and of the revulsion in his mind produced by the thoughtful lady's answer, after a little reflection, "Yes, lamb *is*

way of clinching his argument. "There's my dear Mrs. Dale, the best woman in the world, . . . but I too might say that 'she and I have not much in common,' if I were only to compare mind to mind, and when my poor Carry says something less profound than Madame de Staël might have said, smile on her in contempt from the elevation of logic and Latin." Yet when Parson Dale remembers all the little sorrows and joys that he and his Carry have shared together, and feels how solitary he would have been without her—he at once recognizes a something in common between them infinitely closer and better than if the same course of study had given them the same equality of ideas, and he had been forced to brace himself for a combat of intellect, as when falling in with the redoubtable Riccabocca. In no unlike spirit Dr. Holmes's Clement Lindsay communes with himself on the subject of his betrothed, simple Susie—a poor, innocent, trusting creature, utterly incapable of coming into any true relation with his aspiring mind, his large and strong emotions. Was this pretty idol for a weak, and kindly, and easily satisfied worshipper, to be enthroned as the queen of *his* affections, to be adopted as the companion of his labours ? But no ; he would never leave her so long as her heart clung to him. He had been rash in engaging himself, but she should not pay the forfeit. "And if I may think of myself, my life need not be wretched because

very nice,—at any rate with mint sauce." Some poets, or poetasters, however, have urgent need of such wives, and are a sore trial to their patience after all. The Harold Skimpole type is, in Yankee style, a caution. There is a story of one of the tribe whose wife had laid by fourpence (their whole remaining stock) to pay for the baking of a shoulder of mutton and potatoes, which they had in the house, and on her return home from some errand, she found he had expended it in purchasing a new string for a guitar. The purchase suggested the Miltonian aspiration, "And ever against *eating* cares, Wrap me in soft Lydian airs." The exasperated Mammoth in one of

---

she cannot share all my being with me. The common human qualities are more than all exceptional gifts." At the same time he cannot but brood on the difference there might have been in his coming career, had it pleased God to mate him with one more equal in other ways, who could share his thoughts, and kindle his inspirations, and who had wings to rise into the air with him as well as feet to creep by his side upon the earth.

Walter Warton, in the *Waterdale Neighbours*, is pictured as a man of letters who finds himself bound for life to an innocent, overgrown child,—an animated wax doll, with a tender heart and no brains. For a time he honestly tries hard to love his wife still. But only for a time. "Often in society he saw women who were in one sense crowns to their husbands; who understood politics, shared man's ambition; . . . who could advise and stimulate and guide; who could plan and scheme and conquer; and sometimes Warton felt that Providence had been unkind to him." Captain Marryat somewhere observes that however much the public may appreciate the works of a man of genius, whether they be written to instruct or to amuse, certain it is that a literary man requires in his wife either a mind congenial to his own, or that pride in her husband's talents which induces her to sacrifice much of her own domestic enjoyment to the satisfaction of having his name extolled abroad.

Jerrold's forgotten comedies, declares that the wives of geniuses live only in the kitchen of imagination.

Jean Paul Richter has typified in Lenette the unappreciative wife of an exacting, or at least expectant, man of genius; and blessed is he that expecteth nothing, in such cases, for only he shall not be disappointed. Lenette is the wife of Siebenkäs, Advocate of the Poor, in that story among the *Blumen-Frucht-und-Dornenstücke* collection which is recognized as not only one of the most remarkable, but most personal, of all Jean Paul's writings. Lenette, an alleged portrait of his mother, in her salient characteristics, is representative of a nature essentially of sterling worth and even nobility, but hampered by the limitations of her state of life; cabined, cribbed, confined by circumstances; uncultivated, and correspondingly unsympathetic. Nothing, it has been said, can be more true, and of more universal application, than Richter's view in *Siebenkäs* of the unhappiness of an ill-assorted union, when there is neither vice nor crime, only an unequal standard of mind, and a deficiency of culture in one of the pair. Lenette is "incapable of understanding her gifted husband," who, full of tenderness and fine qualities, has married her for her innocence and simplicity, but is at length worn out by her narrowness, obtuseness, and want of sympathy.

To have a common past is well said to be the first secret of happy association; a past common

in ideas, sentiments, and growth, if not common in
external incidents. One reason why a cultivated man
is wretched with a vapid woman, is that she "has not
travelled over a yard of that ground of knowledge
and feeling which has in truth made his nature what
it is." Untended nature, as in the case of an unlettered wife, is notoriously more likely to produce
weeds than choice fruits; and the chances in such
cases are declared to be beyond calculation in favour
of the lettered husband having got a weed—in other
words, having wedded himself to a life of wrangling,
gloom, and swift deterioration of character. Dr. Johnson would expatiate on the importance to a man of
sense and education, of meeting a suitable companion
in a wife. It is a miserable thing, he said, when the
conversation can only be such as, whether the mutton
shall be roasted or boiled, and probably a dispute
about that. Bitterly Mr. Shandy curses his luck, for
being master of one of the finest chains of reasoning
in nature, and having a wife, at the same time, with
such a headpiece that he cannot hang up a single inference within-side of it, though 'twere to save his
life. Writing long since in behalf of what he called
the Enfranchisement of Women, Mr. Stuart Mill was
free and fain to own that, not indeed from anything
in the feminine faculties themselves, but from the
petty subjects and interests on which alone they are,
or then were, exercised, the companionship of women
often results in a "dissolvent influence on high

faculties and aspirations in men." If one of the two, he observed, has no knowledge and no care about the great ideas and purposes which dignify life, or about any of its practical concerns save personal interests and personal vanities, her conscious, and still more her unconscious influence, will, except in rare cases, reduce to a secondary place in his mind, if not entirely extinguish, those interests which she cannot or does not share. "As to mental progress, except those vulgarer attainments by which vanity or ambition are [? is] promoted, there is generally an end to it in a man who marries a woman mentally his inferior; unless, indeed, he is unhappy in marriage, or becomes indifferent." A total want of ideas in a companion, or of the power to receive them, is indeed, says Leigh Hunt, to be avoided by men who require intellectual excitement; but he deems it a great mistake to suppose that the most discerning men demand intellect above everything else in their most habitual associates. "A un homme d'esprit il ne faut qu'une femme de sens : c'est trop de deux esprits dans une maison," says M. de Bonald. Among the *Sit mihi* aspirations of Martial, is this expressive one,

"—— sit non doctissima conjux."

If one's intimate in love or friendship cannot or does not share all one's intellectual tastes or pursuits, that, rules the Autocrat of the Breakfast-table, is a small matter : intellectual companions can be found easily in men and books.

A sagacious reviewer of one of Mrs. Ellis's *Chapters on Wives*, which represents the frivolity of a young lady married to a scientific doctor, and invites us to observe how much better it would have been had she qualified herself to talk with her husband by having made herself a proficient in botany, chemistry, and geology,—professes to hardly know what to say to this. He submits that men who are engaged in some study or occupation or business do not want to be talking of nothing else in their leisure moments: they want recreation, rest, and change: it would be a most dreary thing if men always talked shop to their wives. Besides, allowing for a few rare exceptions, the wife would after all be incapable, in such a case, of really discussing the subjects in which her husband is interested. "Supposing she does her best to get up a little geology before she is married, how can she be scientifically the equal of a man who has given eight hours a day for a dozen years to this branch of science?" The reviewer says it would be as wise to encourage a girl to suppose that, if she did but learn the Eton Latin Grammar, she would share with her husband the delight of reading Virgil and Lucretius. He allows the value of education in a wife—and even of a slightly scientific education—to be very great; not, however, because she will be able to talk science with her husband, but because of her general intelligence being raised. "Men like so far to share their labours with their daily companions, that they are pleased when these companions can understand great general results stated in simple language. This is what a wife can oblige her husband by understanding and taking an interest in." And our critic regards it as exceedingly desirable that these results should be communicated, for the wife's sake as well as the husband's. Although he takes it to be foolish and pedantic to attempt to raise the tone of conjugal conversation above the domestic level,* yet as the occasional introduction of larger and more serious subjects increases self-respect and ennobles life, he allows it to be true, in a sense, that learning chemistry and geology will make a wife more acceptable to a scientific husband; though not true in the sense intended by Mrs. Ellis.

A man who has taken up a great subject, remarks an Essayist on Social Subjects, is apt to be so engrossed by it that he does not much trouble himself about his neighbours, and their opinions of him. "He

---

* Rousseau records his regrets at not having taken more pains (though elsewhere he speaks of all such pains as purely thrown away) in trying to instruct and educate his Thérèse, "pour l'orner de talents et de connaissances qui, nous tenant plus rapprochés dans notre retraite, auraient agréablement rempli son temps et le mien, sans jamais nous laisse sentir la longueur du tête-à-tête. Ce n'était pas que l'entretien tarît entre nous, et qu'elle parût s'ennuyer dans nos promenades; mais enfin nous n'avions pas assez d'idées communes pour nous faire un grand magasin. ... Les objets qui se présentaient m'inspiraient des réflexions qui n'étaient pas à sa portée. ... C'est surtout dans la solitude qu'on sent l'avantage de vivre avec quelqu'un qui sait penser."—*Les Confessions*, livre ix.

is aware, perhaps, that the excellent grocer of the place who officiates as churchwarden, thinks him odd and dangerous." But the Essayist is satisfied that a man who spends ten hours a day in thinking whether knowing and being are the same, whether there is or is not a science of history, or whether it was colder sixty millions of years before or sixty millions of years after the primary glacial epoch, gets to be hardened as to the opinions of churchwardens in particular, as well as of neighbours in general. "He is more likely to suffer through his wife than directly in person; for she has to bear the odium of his dangerousness, without the absorption of mind which makes him impervious to the criticism of the vicinity. There is no doubt that this may be a trial to her, and that he may be very sorry to see her so tried." It may be, too, that the wife is incapable of tasting high pleasures of any kind, but is always whining and boring him about the social disadvantages he causes her;* or she may be an obstinate person, with scruples and opinions and conscientious objections. In which case, "the philosopher has married the wrong sort of woman; but when the deed is done, he has no other resource than to work himself

---

* "But then very few wives have any notion of shrinking from fighting the battles of their husbands, and if they lose the pleasure of being well received by society, they gain the pleasure of sticking closely to a dear friend in distress, and perhaps the latter is the keener pleasure of the two."—Essay on *Great Subjects*.

up to such an intense pitch of absorption in knowing and being, and the science of history, and the glacial epoch, that the words of his wife are to him as the words of the churchwarden."

There is an ordinance of nature, says Mr. Walter Bagehot, at which men of genius are perpetually fretting, but which to his thinking does more good than many laws of the universe which they praise: it is, that ordinary women ordinarily prefer ordinary men. "Genius," as Hazlitt would have said, "puts them out;" the common female mind prefers usual tastes, settled manners, customary conversation, defined and practical pursuits. And it is maintained to be a great good that it should be so. "Nature has no wiser instinct. The average woman suits the average man; good health, easy cheerfulness, common charms, suffice." Of Shelley's first wife it is reasonably submitted that she was capable of making many people happy, though not of making Shelley happy. "Suppose your favourite Clive is an eagle, Arthur," says Mrs. Pendennis," don't you think he had better have an eagle for a mate? If he were to marry little Rosey, I dare say he would be very good to her; but I think neither he nor she would be very happy.* My dear,

---

* Henrietta Temple, in Mr. Disraeli's story of that name, meets Miss Grandison's demur to a match with Ferdinand (on the ground of conviction that the match would not be a happy one) with the demand, "But why should you not be happy?" "Because we are not suited to each other. Ferdinand must marry some one whom he looks up to, some-

she does not care for his pursuits; she does not understand him when he talks." Galileo's wife, in M. Ponsard's play, cannot understand why he cannot enjoy his meals,* and leave the planets to themselves.

Rousseau, in his *Confessions*,† has passed a very contemptuous judgment on Diderot's Annette, to whom he vastly prefers his own illiterate and unpolished Thérèse. Without deciding on the comparative merits or demerits of the two, M. Sainte-Beuve allows that, *bonne femme au fond*, Madame Diderot was

---

body brilliant like himself, some one who can sympathize with all his fancies. I am too calm and quiet for him."—(Book vi., chap. xii.)

The narrator of Mrs. Gaskell's *Cousin Phillis* is "rather sorry for cousin Holman; for do what she would, she was completely unable even to understand the pleasure her husband and daughter took in intellectual pursuits, much less to care in the least herself for the pursuits themselves, and was thus unavoidably thrown out of some of their interests."—(Part ii.) Once or twice the narrator had thought her a little jealous of her own child, Phillis, as a fitter companion for her husband than she was herself; and the husband seemed not unaware of this feeling, for there was observable in that good "minister" an occasional sudden change of subject, and a tenderness of appeal in his voice as he spoke to her, which always made her look contented and peaceful again.

* There is a pronounced smack of Lenette about Mrs. Churchill in Longfellow's *Kavanagh*; as where she is described as having something of Martha in her, as well as of Mary, and leaving the room and her guests when the conversation took a literary turn, and coming back to announce that dinner was ready.

† Where he writes of his Thérèse, "Je ne rougis point d'avouer qu'elle n'a jamais bien su lire. . . . Elle n'a jamais pu suivre l'ordre des douze mois de l'année, et ne connaît pas un seul chiffre, malgré tous les soins que j'ai pris pour les lui montrer. Elle ne sait ni compter l'argent ni le prix d'aucune chose. Le mot qui lui vient en parlant est souvent l'opposé de ce qu'elle veut dire. . . . Mais cette personne si bornée, et, si l'on veut, si stupide, est d'un conseil excellent dans les occasions difficiles." (Livre vii.)

commonplace in mind, vulgar in education, and incapable of comprehending her husband.* Buffon was happier in a wife who anxiously watched all his steps on the road to fame, and rejoiced with him at the honours showered upon him by crowned heads and learned societies. Daudin the ornithologist, again, was happy in a wife who actively assisted in the composition and prepared the illustrations of his works. Such a wife, too, had William Blake. It is amusing to read of Jasmin, the popular poet of Gascony, that his wife in particular, as well as his kinsfolk in general, discouraged him when he began to write; but afterwards, when the sale of his poems had afforded him the means of buying the house in which he still followed his trade of barber and hairdresser, she would pick out for him the best pen and the smoothest paper (*not* curl-paper), and say, "Every verse you write, Jacques, puts a new tile on the roof."

Lady, then Mrs. Walter Scott, being spoken of

---

* To Clayton's sententious dissertation on great men as the road-makers for the rest of the world,—quarry-masters, that quarry out marble enough for a generation to work up, Nina Gordon replies, in maiden meditation, fancy free, "Well, I shouldn't want to be a quarry-master's wife. I should be afraid that some of his blocks would fall on me." A companion asks if she would not like it were the quarry-master wholly her slave? it would be like having the genius of the lamp at her feet. "Ah!" sighs Nina, "if I could keep him my slave; but I'm afraid he would outwit me at last. Such a man would soon put *me* upon the shelf for a book read through. I've seen some great men,—I mean great for our times,—and they didn't seem to care half as much for their wives as they did for a newspaper."—*Dred*, chap. xxix.

disparagingly at a dinner party in 1812, at which Wordsworth, and Sir Humphry Davy, and H. Crabb Robinson "assisted," Joanna Baillie gave her this good word, that there was a great deal to like in her, that she seemed to admire and look up to her husband, and that the children were well-bred, and the house in excellent order. "And she had some smart roses in her cap, and I did not like her the less for that."

George Dyer, perhaps better known as the friend of Charles Lamb than as the biographer of Robert Robinson of Cambridge—albeit that biography was declared by Wordsworth to be one of the best in the language—married his laundress, described as a very worthy woman by one of his acquaintance, to whom he once said, "Mrs. Dyer is a woman of excellent natural sense, but she is not literate." That is, the narrator explains, she could neither read nor write.

The wife of Heinrich Heine was a Frenchwoman, very fond of her husband, but utterly incapable of understanding him. This Siebenkäs would say, laughing, of his Lenette, that she had never read a line of his poems.*

---

* Which of the Tatlers does Mrs. Steele prefer? accomplished St. John asks that lady in *Esmond*. "I never read but one, and I think it all a pack of rubbish, sir," is the reply. "Such stuff about Dickerstaffe, and Distaff, and Quarterstaff, as it all is." "A fig, Dick, for your Mr. Addison!" cries the lady in another place, where Captain Steele is exalting his great friend and fellow-workman.

Be it here remarked, however, with regard to Heine, that the series of letters he addressed to his wife during his absences in Germany, although (as treating of domestic affairs, and written to a lady who made no pre-

De Quincey describes Mrs. Coleridge as wanting all cordial admiration, or indeed comprehension, of her husband's intellectual powers, and wanting also the original basis for affectionate patience and candour; for, hearing from everybody that Coleridge was a man of most extraordinary endowments, and attaching little weight, perhaps, to the distinction between popular talents and such as by their very nature are doomed to a slower progress in the public esteem, she naturally looked to see, at least, an ordinary measure of worldly consequence attend upon the exercise of them. And thus was laid a sure ground of "discontent and fretfulness in any woman's mind, not unusually indulgent or unusually magnanimous." Another critic, who speaks of two things only as wanting to S. T. C.,—a will, and a wife,—a will of his own, and a wife of his own,—or say even one thing only wanting, a wife who could have become a will to him, and who could have led him to labour, regularity, and virtuous living,—pronounces his "pensive Sara" to have failed, without any positive fault on her side, but from "mere non-adaptation," in managing her gifted lord. If Miss Westbrook had, as one of Shelley's critics suggests, married an everyday person—"a gentleman, suppose, in the tallow line"—she would

---

tensions to intellectual culture) they cannot be expected to be brilliant, are yet, on high critical authority, estimated as something better, for yet speak the language of sincere affection, and show that Heine *could* be amiable and considerate.

have been happy, and have made him happy; her
mind could have understood his life, and her society
would have been a gentle relief from "unodoriferous
pursuits," (though the epithet seems scarcely applicable
to the heavy-laden atmosphere of candle-making)—
but with Shelley she had nothing in common, whose
mind was full of eager thoughts, wild dreams, and
singular aspirations. If some eccentric men of genius
have, indeed, felt, in the habitual tact and "serene
nothingness" of ordinary women, a kind of trust and
calm,—admiring an instinct of the world which themselves possessed not, a repose of mind they could not
share,—this, Mr. Bagehot contends, is commonly in
later years—the years that bring the philosophic
mind.

Explain it how you may, your very clever man, on
the showing of the Caxtónian philosopher, never seems
to care so much as your less gifted mortals for
cleverness in his helpmate; your scholars, and poets,
and ministers of state are more often than not found
assorted with exceedingly humdrum, good sort of
women, and apparently liking them all the better for
their deficiencies. We are asked to note how happily
the author of *Athalie* lived with his wife, and what an
angel he thought her, though she had never read his
plays. "Certainly Goethe never troubled the lady
who called him 'Mr. Privy-Councillor' with whims
about 'monads,' and speculations on colour, or those

stiff metaphysical problems on which one breaks one's shins in the Second Part of the Faust." The probable explanation ironically suggested is, that such great geniuses—knowing that, as compared with themselves, there is little difference between your clever woman and your humdrum woman—merge at once all minor distinctions, relinquish all attempts at sympathy in hard intellectual pursuits, and are quite satisfied to establish that tie which, after all, best resists wear and tear,—the tough household bond between one human heart and another.

It is out of their own imagination of what is excellent, and their power to adorn what they love, that men of genius, according to the *Seer* essayist, will be enamoured, in their youth, of women neither intelligent nor amiable nor handsome. "They make them all three with their fancy; and are sometimes too apt, in after-life, to resent what is nobody's fault but their own."* The wise espouse the foolish, says the consul in Landor's *Siege of Ancona*, and the fool bears off from the top branch the guerdon of the wise: those who are clear-sighted in all other things

---

* "Are you surprised that our friend Matthew has married such a woman? and surprised, too, because he is a man of genius? That is the very reason of his doing it. To be sure she came to him without a shift to her back: but his genius is rich enough to deck her out in purple and fine linen. So long as these last, all will go on comfortably. But when they are worn out, and the stock exhausted, alas poor wife! shall I say? or alas poor Matthew!"—*Guesses at Truth*, First Series.

> "Cast down their eyes, and follow their own will,
> Taking the hand of idiots. They well know
> They shall repent, but find the road so pleasant
> That leads into repentance."

Love is made of contraries, quoth a sententious satirist; who cites the fair woman preferring the dark man, the tall man the little woman, and the wisest of mankind seeking in the weakest of womankind a pleasing relaxation from the austerer occupations of their life.* An anonymous essayist calls it rather hard lines that so many celebrated men have dowdy wives; artists, poets, self-made men of all kinds often failing in this special article; so that while they themselves have caught the tone of the circle to which they have risen, and "pay their shot" by manner as well as by repute, their wives lag behind among the ashes of the past, like Cinderella before the advent of the fairy godmother. It is, however, Mr. Disraeli's dictum that few great men have flourished, who, were they candid, would not acknowledge the vast advantages they have experienced in the earlier years of their career from the spirit and sympathy of woman.

---

* As the poet tells his Chloe, for her he leaves whate'er the world thinks wise or grave:

> "Ambition, business, friendship, news,
> My useful books, and serious Muse . . .
> And choose to sit and talk with thee
> (As thy great orders may decree)
> Of cocks and bulls, and flutes and fiddles,
> Of idle tales, and foolish riddles."
> *Prior.*

A female friend, amiable, clever, and devoted, he declares to be a possession beyond price, and without which as few men can succeed in life, so are none content. Hannah More's Miss Sparkes characteristically observes, that the meanest understanding and most vulgar education are competent to form such a wife as the generality of men prefer; and that a man of talents, dreading a rival, always takes care to secure himself by marrying a fool. " Clever men," observes the Lady Selina of a later novelist, "do, as a general rule, choose the oddest wives. The cleverer a man is, the more easily, I do believe, a woman can take him in." A well-known apophthegm of this author is, that poets need repose when they love—a condition seemingly incompatible with any equality of intellectual intercourse; and although his fictions abound with "clever women to flirt with," and to lead the hero through the necessary vicissitudes of feeling, to rack his sensibilities, and teach him experience, he never, it has been broadly asserted, lets any one he cares for marry a woman of superior intellect: he would not do him such an ill turn. He settles him down, says a critic, after the turmoil of passion, with some gentle creature who does not, it is true, understand one word in ten that he utters, but who looks up to him all the more with docile, undoubting worship. Even this limited intelligence, it is averred, he derives second-hand through the affections, and he does not shrink from the comparison with the inferior animals; for twice he likens a favourite heroine to a dog.*

No one, as we are reminded in the Caxton Essays, is all poet, author, artist; every demigod of genius has also his side as man; and as man, though not as poet, author, artist, he may reasonably yearn for sympathy.† Such a sympathy, so restricted, will probably, the Essayist surmises, not be denied to him. "It has been said that the wife of Racine had so little participation in the artistic life of her spouse, that she had never even read his plays. But as Racine was tenderly attached to her, and of a nature too sensitive not to have needed some sort of sympathy in those to whom he attached himself, and as, by all accounts, his marriage was a very happy one, so it is fair to presume that the sympathy withheld from his artistic life was maintained in the familiar domestic everyday relationship of his positive existence, and that he did not ask the heart of Madame Racine to beat in unison with his own over the growing beauties of those children whom she was not needed to bring into the world." Why, it is added, ask her to shed a mother's tears over the fate of *Britannicus*, or recoil

---

* "She understood little or nothing till she had found an inspirer in that affection which inspires both beast and man, which makes the dog (in his natural state one of the meanest of the savage race) a companion, a guardian, a protector, and raises instinct half-way to the height of reason."—*Ernest Maltravers*, ii. 93.

† This refers to Goethe's assertion that to desire the sympathy of others is a very great folly, and that *he* never desired any such thing.

with a mother's horror from the guilt of *Phèdre?*—
they were no offspring of hers.* Molière's Martine
is pert and pertinent, piqued and piquante, on the
main topic:

> "L'esprit n'est point du tout ce qu'il faut en ménage;
> Les livres cadrent mal avec le mariage;"

but then, to be sure, it is of the husband's scholarship, not the wife's, she is thinking; and her avowed design, if ever she marry at all, is, to take *un mari qui n'ait point d'autre livre que moi.* We have all seen such cases, to cite the Professor at the Breakfast-table, as that of a brilliant woman marrying a plain, manly fellow, with a simple intellectual mechanism; at which the world often stares a good deal and wonders; for might she not have taken that other, with a far more complex mental machinery? Might she not have had a watch with the philosophical compensation-balance, with the metaphysical index which can split a second into tenths, with the musical chime which can turn every quarter of an hour into melody? How came she to choose a plain one, that keeps good time, and that is all? "Let her alone. She knows what she is about. Genius has an infinitely deeper reverence for character than character can have for genius." You talk of the fire of genius, he goes on to say. "Many a blessed woman, who dies unsung and unremembered, has given out more of the real vital heat

---

* Caxtoniana: The Sympathetic Temperament.

that keeps life in human souls, without a spark flitting through her humble chimney to tell the world about it, than would set a dozen theories smoking, or a hundred odes simmering, in the brains of so many men of genius." Such latent caloric as warms the wistful wife in stanzas many a heart has warmed to, husband's as well as wife's,—

> "Her life is lone, she sits apart,
> He loves her yet, she will not weep,
> Though rapt in matters dark and deep
> He seems to slight her simple heart.
>
> He thrids the labyrinth of the mind,
> He reads the secret of the star,
> He seems so near and yet so far,
> He looks so cold : she thinks him kind.
>
> For him she plays, to him she sings
> Of early faith and plighted vows ;
> She knows but matters of the house,
> And he, he knows a thousand things."

M. de Tocqueville says in one of his letters, descriptive of harassed nerves amid the pains and perplexities of authorship : "I could not go on with my task if it were not for the refreshing calm of Marie's companionship. It would be impossible to find a disposition forming a happier contrast to my own. In my perpetual irritability of body and mind, she is a providential resource." In another letter he affirms that, however frivolous they may be, women soon discover the remarkable qualities of their husbands, and are generally willing to recognize a superiority in which they may almost be said to have a personal interest.* Bernard Barton, in the course of a letter the key-note of which, struck at starting, and vibrating throughout, is, that it is impossible for a man to write long together with any interest, if no one is interested in his compositions,—confides to his correspondent the fact that no one, not even his wife, in and around the home circle, seems to comprehend his literary aspirations; not even his wife, "for to say the truth of her, she has not that average leaven of vanity which, without authorizing you to call a character vain, makes her sympathise with the cravings after sympathy in others."

The Countess Brownlow describes the wife of Talleyrand as very handsome, but also very silly, so silly that Napoleon asked the Prince how he could marry her; to which he replied, "Ma foi, sire, je n'ai pu trouver une plus bête." With her his mind was in complete repose. The apparent aim of George I., in his liaisons, to shun with the greatest care the overpowering dissertations of a learned lady, reminds Earl Stanhope of the sort of feeling well expressed in the pretended memoirs of Madame de Barry. "J'aimais à les voir," she says of two blockheads;

---

* "Still I own that there are in the world some cold, silly, female fools over whom one can have no influence, and who very likely would speak of their husbands as Madame —— did to me of Bonaparte, whom she saw frequently before his Italian campaigns: 'I never knew such a tiresome man with his eternal politics; so I always ran away when I saw him coming in.' But these are exceptions."—*Letters of M. de Tocqueville*, I., 338; II., 46.

"leur entretien me reposait l'imagination." Never, in the counsel of one of Barry Cornwall's dramatic fragments,

> "Never, boy, wed a wit. Man does not marry
> To poise his reason 'gainst a quarrelling tongue;
> But for sweet idleness."

When Harley l'Estrange says of the brilliant Violante that if she is not to be some prince's bride, she should be some young poet's, Leonard Fairfield interposes a prompt negative: Poets need repose where *they* love, he asserts. Harley is struck by the answer, and muses over it in silence. He all at once perceives that what is needed by the man whose whole life is one strain after glory—whose soul sinks, in fatigue, to the companionship of earth—is not the love of a nature like his own. It is repose. Just as, to apply a figure of Dr. Oliver Holmes's, the eye seeks to refresh itself by resting on neutral tints after looking at brilliant colours, the mind turns from the glare of intellectual brilliancy to the solace of gentle dulness; the tranquillizing green of the sweet human qualities which do not make us shade our eyes like the spangles of conversational gymnastics and figurantes. *Mais une femme habile est un mauvais présage*, quoth Molière's Arnulphe;

> " Et je sais ce qu'il coûte à de certaines gens
> Pour avoir pris les leurs avec trop de talents."

Not he the man to accept the hand any more than the argument of the Lady in *Hudibras:*

> "Quoth she, 'What does a match imply,
> But likeness and equality?
> I know you cannot think me fit
> To be th' yoke-fellow of your wit;
> Nor take one of so mean deserts
> To be the partner of your parts.'"

She would be too clever by half for him, who confessedly "aimerait mieux une laide bien sotte, qu'une femme fort belle avec beaucoup d'esprit."* Clever Men's Wives is the subject of an essay by one of our best essayists, who agrees that when a refined and sentimental friend, full of generous schemes and airy aspirations, marries a woman who proves "a good wife to him,"—in other words, who looks carefully after his children and his shirt-buttons,—it is reasonable to sigh over his unworthy fate; as also over that of the man who, taking an eager interest and an active part in public affairs, has a wife like the "cold, silly female fool" mentioned by De Tocqueville, who ran out of the room whenever Bonaparte came in, "because he was always talking his tiresome politics." Yet it is submitted that our pity for these and the like seemingly ill-mated couples may, after all, be wholly unnecessary. If history tells us of illustrious men who found bliss in wives of their own mental stature, does it not also of as many others who "got on

---

* "Je veux . . . .
En un mot, qu'elle soit d'une ignorance extrême ;
Et c'est assez pour elle, à vous en bien parler,
De savoir prier Dieu, m'aimer, coudre, et filer."
L'Ecole des Femmes, I., 1.

admirably well with fools"? Of the four varieties of
wives, some one out of which a clever man, like anybody else, may choose for himself,—a clever woman,
a sensible woman, a fool, and an echo,—the last is
unquestionably, on the essayist's contention, the least
to be coveted—for the man who marries her awakes
to find himself married to his shadow, a mere echo
of himself, who from being a stimulant has degenerated
into a sheer absorbent; so that he has only doubled
himself. If once she might have been to him, in Mr.
Tennyson's words, "as water is to wine," the result of
the combination bears a natural resemblance to their
"detestable compound"—as the essayist accounts it
—negus. The fact is, he argues, that "a clever man,
more than all others, requires a slightly acidulous
element in his companion"—all clever men being
more or less infected with vanity; which vanity may
be blatant and offensive, or excessive indeed, yet not
unamusing, or again showing itself just as a bare
flavour, but is never entirely absent, and needs to be
counteracted by something more potent than a hot
and sugary intellectual negus. "A clever husband, like
the good despot, will be all the better for a little
constitutional opposition." For although it is con-
ceded that the height of domestic felicity would not
probably be attained by a man whose wife could set
him right in a Greek quotation, or oppose his views
about Hebrew points, or thwart him in his theory
of the origin of evil; still less is it to be looked for

where he is never treated to an occasional dose of wholesome and vigorous dissent, and is allowed to make assertions and advance opinions without fear of criticism or chance of opposition.*

---

* "Solitude tends to make a man think a great deal too highly of himself, but this half-solitude is still worse, where he only sees his own mental shadow, and hears his own mental echo."—*Modern Characteristics*, xlii.

XII.

Lapses in Law, and Commercial Failures.

I. LAPSES IN LAW.

A CHAPTER OF INSTANCES.

NEXT in esteem and authority to Sir Roger de Coverley in the Spectator's club, is "another bachelor, who is a member of the Inner Temple," who has chosen his place of residence "rather to obey the direction of an old humorsome father, than in pursuit of his own inclinations. He was placed there to study the laws of the land, and is the most learned of any of the house in those of the stage. Aristotle and Longinus are much better understood by him than Littleton or Coke." Pope's couplet comprehends a multitudinous company, in its presentation, a representative one, of

> "A clerk foredoom'd his father's soul to cross,
> Who pens a stanza when he should engross."

That fathers have flinty hearts, is almost as trite and threadbare a truism of sentimental complaint on the part of reluctant law-students as on that of recalcitrant lovers.

Ovid was put to study for the bar by a father who snubbed his poetic aspirations. In this chapter of instances we shall constantly be coming upon cases virtually identical with that of Charles Nodier, of whom Sainte-Beuve tells us that "son père l'avait voulu avocat;* il suivit le droit à Besançon, mais inexactement et sans fruit. A cette époque il en était déjà aux romans, soit à les pratiquer, soit à les écrire." Ovid senior, in Ben Jonson's *Poetaster*, is loud in his laments over the perverseness and perversion of his

---

* When Basil, in Mr. Wilkie Collins's story, decides on the bar for a profession, his father appears to be a little astonished at the choice; not suspecting the real motive, which is, that Basil, having an ambition to make a name in literature, chooses the bar as that profession which offers him the greatest facilities for pursuing his project. Secure of an independent fortune, "I might practise my profession or not, just as I pleased. I could devote myself wholly and unreservedly to literature," etc. But a love of literary pursuits is a dangerous reputation for a young barrister, as Mr. Theodore Martin says of Professor Aytoun, whose magazine proclivities "did him no good with the solicitors." Between desire to comply with the wishes of his father, whom he loved deeply, and his own aversion to this profession, the author of *Bothwell* and *Norman Sinclair* is said to have undergone a severe struggle at the outset of his career. "Mere disinclination to the legal profession he could overcome from a sense of duty, and overcome it he did in the end; but he felt that he had not the special qualities of mind which are required to ensure success or distinction in that profession." But further on we read: "The truth is, he never conquered his dislike to the profession; nor do I think he ever applied himself in earnest to rise to distinction in it."—(Memoir of W. E. Aytoun, by Theodore Martin, pp. 35, 58.) To write lays of the Cavaliers, and slashing reviews in *Maga*, and a burlesque such as *Firmilian*, and a good share of Bon Gaultier's ballads, was more nearly and dearly in his way.

son. "Verses! Poetry! Ovid, whom I thought to see the pleader, become Ovid the playmaker! . . . Publius, I will see thee on the funeral pile first." Publius confesses to his exasperated sire that he *has* begun a poem, but not a play. "You have, sir, a poem!" Ovid senior rejoins: "and where is it? That's the law you study. . . . Name me a professed poet, that his poetry did ever afford him so much as a competency." What was Homer himself, as rated by the elder Ovid and his gossips, Luscus, Tusca, Lupus, and the like, but a poor blind rhyming rascal, that lived obscurely up and down in booths and tap-houses, and scarce ever made a good meal even in his sleep, the hungry beggar. Young Ovid implores a truce from these diatribes:

> "Sir, let me crave you will forego these moods:
> I will be anything, or study anything;
> I'll prove the unfashion'd body of the law
> Pure elegance, and make her rugged'st strains
> Run smoothly as Propertius' elegies."

Why, as the old man complains, the young one cannot speak, cannot think, out of poetry; he is bewitched with it. Jonson professes in his Apologetical Dialogue to have brought in Ovid, chid by his angry father for neglecting the study of the law for poetry; and to be warranted by his own words, *Sæpe pater dixit, studium quid inutile tentas?* etc.

Varchi, the historian of Florence, was put to study law at Pisa; but he took to literature immediately upon his father's death. Bernado Segni, who also, wrote *Storie Fiorentine*, was originally a law student at Padua,—the mere mention of which almost suffices to make

"*Enter* PORTIA, *dressed like a doctor of laws,*"

to represent old Bellario and to rout old Shylock. To Padua went Tasso to study that law for which he had so little inclination: he was not out of his teens when he completed *Rinaldo*, in twelve cantos, to the dissatisfaction of his sire, who misliked this flirtation with the Muses when Torquato should be absorbed in matters legal. To Bologna was Petrarch sent to study law, and mighty little to his taste he found it: so finding, no wonder he left it.

Sir Thomas Overbury was entered a Middle Templar, but men have their exits and their entrances. Oliver Cromwell is said to have been entered at Lincoln's Inn, when removed from Cambridge on the death of his father; and a bad use he made of his chambers, by the account of those who disparage him, and whose account of the alleged law proceeding altogether is itself of small account. His son Richard's study of law in the same inn of court was confessedly nominal. Of Selden we read that, by nature unfit or by accident unable to apply himself to the more active business of his profession, he devoted his time to the study of history and antiquities, philology, and moral philosophy.

Antonio de Solis was sent to Salamanca to read law,

but he gave poetry the preference, and turned poet himself.

Gli Vicente, the "Plautus of Portugal," followed the wish of his family in studying law, but soon abandoned it for the stage. Gongora was sent at the age of fifteen to Salamanca, to study the law, which his love of poetry soon impelled him to abandon. La Motte is another example of the law student turning playwright. Corneille himself began to practise at the bar, and little he made of it, as little he took to it. Dancourt threw up legal studies for the stage—for which he wrote six volumes that have had their day. Voltaire was placed with a procureur, but found the legal atmosphere stifling, and ousted himself with all speed. Diderot was similarly placed, but made no advance in law, and read any other books he could lay hold of, and anon shook off office trammels altogether. Tom D'Urfey forswore law for letters. Samuel Foote began studying Coke, but was truant in a trice. Wycherly in a previous generation had played the same trick. Schiller could not endure the thraldom of law studies. Scribe was even counselled by his guardian, the advocate Bonnet, to abandon the bar for the stage. The success of Thomas Morton's first play made him throw up the bar before he was called to it.

Tycho Brahé was intended for the law by his uncle, who sent him to Leipzig with a tutor; but law soon perished out of the way. Clusius, known as "the martyr of botany," repudiated law at Marburg for philosophy elsewhere. Réaumur's private fortune enabled him to renounce the law for science. Cluverius was despatched to Leyden as a law student; but geography and antiquities won him away, and Joseph Scaliger helped on the winning side. The Neapolitan painter, Solimena, was intended for the law. The celebrated French sculptor, Girardon, was placed with a procureur, but all too soon (his friends thought) became disgusted with law, and devoted himself to art. Sir Nicolas Dorigny, the French engraver, was educated as an advocate. Anker Smith exchanged legal pursuits for engraving. So did that knightly Jacobite, Sir Robert Strange,—though in his case a seafaring life intervened.*

John Banks, the dramatist, was a London attorney, who gave up his profession for play-writing. The result had little of the success of Francis Beaumont, Fletcher's associate, who neglected the law, in *his* time, to more purpose. Matthew Henry began to study the law in Gray's Inn, but speedily relinquished it for divinity. Was not St. Chrysostom himself a lapsed barrister ? Huet, Bishop of Avranche, made the same exchange. So did Charles Leslie, renowned in controversial theology. Dr. George Campbell, of the *Philosophy of Rhetoric*, and the *Dissertation on Miracles*, also from lawyer turned divine. Young was

---

* Mr. Pyne, the artist, was articled to a Bristol solicitor. Oehlenschläger relinquished the stage for the law, and law for literature.

nominated by Archbishop Tenison to a law fellowship in All Souls, but poetry and theology made a poetical divine of him, if not quite a divine poet. Massillon is another example of ex-legal churchmanship; to be a notary was his original destination. Lacordaire has been described as going to the bar determined, as a mere boy, to overwhelm courts, judges, juries, and adversaries with his frantic eloquence: he had just begun to succeed when he left the bar and became a priest.

Valesius, or Henry de Valois, one of the last of that race of scholars in France who died out in the seventeenth century, after a continuous succession from the fifteenth, studied jurisprudence at Bourges, and afterwards practised as a lawyer, to please his father; but soon took to literature exclusively.* Ménage began

---

* Murray, as we are told by Pope, and reminded by Mr. Thackeray, might have been an Ovid, but he preferred to be Lord Chief Justice, and to wear ermine instead of bays. Perhaps, suggests the later author of one of his heroes, or that hero for himself, Mr. Warrington—the George of the *Virginians*, not of *Pendennis*—might have risen to a peerage and the woolsack, had he studied very long and assiduously. "He behaved to Themis with a very decent respect and attention; but he loved letters more than law always; and the black letter of Chaucer was infinitely more agreeable to him than the Gothic pages of Hale and Coke."—*The Virginians*, chap. lxiii.

Mr. Prescott, in his critical memoir of Charles Brockden Brown, after observing that he was certainly not the first man of genius who found himself incapable of resigning the romantic world of fiction and the uncontrolled revels of the imagination for the dull and prosaic realities of the law,—adds, that few indeed, like Mansfield, have been able so far to constrain their " young and buoyant imaginations, as to merit the beautiful eulogium of the English poet; while many more,

life by practising as an advocate,—his father being *avocat du roi.*

The younger Bougainville studied in the university of Paris with a view to the bar; but instead of starting as an advocate at the Palais, he startled his friends by enlisting in the Black Musqueteers, and by publishing a treatise on the integral calculus within a fortnight from his turning *militaire.* Justus van Effen, the so-called Addison of Holland, was a lawyer by profession for awhile. Vico had neither health nor inclination to follow up his early success at the bar. Boileau, self-styled "fils, frère, oncle, cousin, beau-frère de greffier," turned truant to the family traditions:

> "J'allai loin du palais errer sur le Parnasse.
> La famille en pâlit, et vit en frémissant
> Dans la poudre du greffe un poète naissant."

Richard West tells Gray how he is being perpetually stirred up to the remembrance of his father being an eminent lawyer—of his uncle too making some figure in Westminster Hall—and that his grandfather's name will get him many friends; but he has lived in the Temple till he is sick of it, and leaves it, no more of a lawyer than when first he went in. Fontenelle was nominally a law student; but the *belles lettres* were

---

comparatively, from the time of Juvenal downwards, fortunately for the world, have been willing to sacrifice the affections plighted to Themis on the altars of the Muse."—Prescott, *Biogr. and Crit. Essays*, 6.

his loves, and the *Corpus Juris* a bore. The Marquis de Pombal studied for the law at Coimbra, but his vivacity, not to say turbulence of character, cut short the connection. Buffon was entered at the Jesuits' College at Dijon as a student of law; but that study went against the grain with him, and his father "wisely suffered him to follow the path he had chosen," and which led to renown. Of Burke's legal studies nothing appears to be known with certainty; the attractions of literature and politics soon withdrew him from a pursuit of the law as a profession. James Harris (*Hermes*) soon abandoned that pursuit for metal more attractive. David Hume tells us that his studious disposition, his sobriety and industry, gave his family a notion that the law was a proper profession for David; but he owns to having found an "insurmountable aversion to everything but the pursuits of philosophy and general learning;" and while the family believed him to be poring over Voet and Vinnius, it was Cicero and Virgil that he was secretly devouring. Lalande complied with his parents' wish to have him adopt the legal profession, with a lucrative appointment in prospect; but the compliance was partial, and the eventual abandonment complete. Valmont de Bomare originally studied for the bar, but his attachment to natural history drew him away from what he never had cared for.

Quinault followed for a time the profession of the

law, but dramatic poetry was too seductive, and he transferred his allegiance with *empressement*. Metastasio is celebrated for the assiduity with which for a whole year he studied under Paglietti, that "mortal enemy to the Muses." Nicholas Freret studied the law, to please his family, but compensated himself by making history and chronology all his real concern. Yriarte was equally complaisant, but with him bibliography at large was the counter-charm. The lapse of Thomas Rymer had the same plea. Dorat was educated for the bar, but had money enough to devote himself to poetry and the drama, and some twenty volumes are his leavings. The German poet Zacharie neglected law at Leipzig for general literature; and for once a father sanctioned the exchange of interests. Thomas Astle, the antiquarian, was seduced from an attorney's office at Yoxall by a taste for studying antiquarianism general and particular. Samuel Lysons was called to the bar, only to be called away from it by archæological attractions. Bound apprentice to a Bristol attorney, Chatterton preferred manipulating old Rowley, and threatened suicide in order to effect his release. Volney's compliance with his father's wish to see him a law student was transient enough. Smeaton for a time attended the courts of law at Westminster Hall, but the bent of his mind was so opposite that his father at length gave way to his wishes, and that native energy found vent in engineering. It was for no idle trade he left his calling;[*] or rather, indeed, his calling was to his new pursuit. Jeremy Bentham's father had formed the most brilliant anticipations of his son's success in the practice of his profession, and seems to have slowly and reluctantly given in to that son's preference for a less lucrative path to reputation; from the poverty of the young man's early life, it should seem as if the elder one acted on the principle of starving him into compliance. Voltaire is the subject of Mr. Carlyle's picture of the second of two sons of Arouet, that steady, practical, and perhaps rather sharp-tempered old gentleman, of official legal habits and position, "Notary of the Châtelet," and something else, who had destined young François for the law profession; which said François accordingly sat "in chambers," as we call it, and even became an advocate, but did not in the least take to

---

[*] "I left no calling for this idle trade,
No duty broke, no father disobey'd."
POPE: *Prologue to the Satires*.

The Sigismund Smith of a popular fiction is typical of idle-trade-turning in ordinary, on the part of ordinary turncoats. That young man is described as reading for the Bar, and for the first part of his sojourn in the Temple working honestly and conscientiously; but finding that his legal studies resulted in nothing but mental perplexity and confusion, he beguiled his leisure by the pursuit of literature, and found literature not only a good deal easier but much more profitable than the study of Coke upon Littleton, or Blackstone's Commentaries; whereupon by degrees he abandoned himself entirely to the composition of such works as are to be seen, garnished with striking illustrations, in the windows of humble newsvendors in the smaller and dingier thoroughfares of every large town.

advocateship,—took to poetry, and other airy dangerous courses, both speculative and practical; causing family rebukes and explosions, which were without effect upon him. "A young fool, bent on sportful pursuits instead of serious; more and more shuddering at Law. To the surprise and indignation of M. Arouet senior—Law, with its wigs and sheepskins, pointing towards high honours and deep fleshpots, had no charms for the young fool; he could not be made to like Law." *

Le Sage dropped the designation of avocat, and the profits, that literature might to him be all in all. Shadwell (MacFlecknoe) was bred to the law, but the drudgery of the office was beyond his patience, and he became—what Dryden has made of him. Piron, of the *Métromanie*, graduated in law, and practised as an advocate at Dijon, but presently forsook his first love,—if love for it he ever had. Melendez Valdes, the Spanish poet, gave up law to become what Quintana

---

* "M. Arouet senior stood strong for Law; but it was becoming daily more impossible. Madrigals, dramas, . . . satirical wit, airy verse, . . . were what this young man went upon." Consigned to the Bastile for a certain rhymed lampoon, François employed his time, not in repentance, or in serious legal studies, but in writing an epic. Two years later, and he was out with a play, *Œdipe*, which had a run; and by that time Law might be considered hopeless, even by M. Arouet the elder.—See Carlyle's *History of Frederick the Great*, ii. 580, seq.

The then almost unequalled "run" of *Œdipe*, whose author was but twenty-two, is referred to in the previous volume as "greatly angering old M. Arouet of the Chamber of Accounts; who thereby found his son as good as cast into the whirlpools, and a solid Law career thenceforth impossible for the young fool."—(I., 500.)

calls him, "the spoilt child of society and the Muses;" but the relinquishment, for a rarity, was only for a time; and Melendez became after all one of the foremost men at the Spanish bar. The success is a rarity, too: failure, signal and ignominious, is apt to be the lot of those who find a spokesman in George Canning the elder, who, in the proem to his *Anti-Lucretius*, expresses a resolve to forsake his unprofitable dalliance with the Muses, and to be devout to Themis alone henceforth:

> " Then welcome Law ! Poor Poesy, farewell !
> Though in thy cave the loves and graces dwell,
> One Chancery cause in solid worth outweighs
> Dryden's strong sense, and Pope's harmonious lays."

The common experience is expressed in Chetwood's affirmation, writing to his friend Malone,* that no law jargon, no collection of statutes, nor all the Pandects in all the world, can avail to extinguish the passion for the Muse when she has taken what he calls legal possession.

An early taste for versification led the bard of *Grongar Hill*, John Dyer, to relinquish his legal studies. Nicholas Rowe was a law student until he became his own master, whom poetry, however, had

---

* Of Malone himself his biographer remarks, that frequent explorations of black-letter law led him onward to the taste for its poetry and dramatic literature. Sir James Prior signalizes him as a striking example of a life devoted to one literary pursuit. "He forsook law, wealth, and probably station, for unprofitable literature."—*Life of Edmund Malone*, p. 322.

meanwhile mastered. Thomas Southern, preferring poetry to law, served the latter with a *nolle prosequi*. Theobald was another recreant of the same complexion: his father was an attorney, and to his father's business he was bred; but young Lewis took to writing *Electra* and some nineteen other plays; and the end of it was that he booked himself a place in the *Dunciad*. Both the George Colmans were brought up to the law, and took a more or less French leave of it, in favour of letters. Quin was intended for the bar, and for some time had chambers in the Temple.

On leaving Westminster school, Cowper was articled to a solicitor, in whose office he giggled and made giggle; he afterwards had chambers in the Middle Temple, and was called to the bar, and there was legal patronage at his kinsfolk's command; but all this availed him nothing in favour of a pursuit he disrelished, while literature had charms and consolations he did well to cultivate. Hayley studied in Trinity Hall, Cambridge, intending to practise at the bar, but the law was not to his taste, and he discarded it accordingly. Pinkerton was articled to a writer to the signet, and spent (or misspent) five years in his office. William Mitford, the historian, "studied law for a time in the Middle Temple, but found the study distasteful."

Sir William Beechey, the accomplished portrait-painter, was originally articled to a conveyancer. Joseph Highmore quitted the law for the same art.

Pestalozzi was transiently, very transiently, a limb of the law. Bouterwek was diverted from it by the charms of sprightlier book-lore. The learned traveller Tweddell is commended for betaking himself to his law-books for a season with as much application as his aversion would allow. Marshal Ney was articled to a notary.

Andrieux, once so highly popular a lecturer in the Collége de France, and still in repute as an indefatigable author of poems, plays, prose tales, essays, and reviews, was brought up in a proctor's office, and destined for the bar; but though industrious at his legal studies, he wrote verses without stint, and eventually devoted himself exclusively to literary pursuits. Jean D'Arcet, in whose arms Montesquieu died, was educated with a view to his father's profession and office, as a magistrate; but his taste for natural science was too strong for him: in vain his father forbade him to indulge this taste, on pain of being disinherited; he could not, would not give up his favourite pursuits, and his father kept his word, and cast Jean out. The celebrated D'Argens was in like manner designed for the law by his father, who was procureur-général to the parliament of Aix; but the lapse in this instance was less fatal to home affections. Audoin, the naturalist, one of the martyrs of science, was at first educated for the law, but soon renounced it for studies zoological and medical. Balzac, the novelist, was placed with a notary in Paris, but almost from the first he took to writing for the journals.* ·Heine took a degree in law at Göttingen, and proposed to establish himself as an advocate at Hamburg, but the design fell to pieces, like his ancestral faith, or rather his faith in the faith of his ancestors. Larra, the popular Spanish author, was thrown upon the world without resources, by a quarrel with his father (never made up) apparently connected with his abandonment of the study of the law. M. Capefigue turned from law to *belles lettres*, early in his prolific course. Ulrici studied law at Halle, to please his father, but at the first opportunity forsook it, to please himself. Of Donizetti we are told that, being destined for the law, it was somewhat late when he began his musical studies.† Frederic Soulié waited as an *avocat* for briefs, with some patience; but literature was his stay, and became his mainstay. The Norwegian linguist and antiquary, Munch, forsook jurisprudence for the more winsome ways of history and philology.

Don Augustin Duran, the distinguished Spanish critic and essayist, gave up practice at the bar for the

---

* Börne forsook medicine for journalism. Hector Berlioz renounced it for music. Similarly, Dr. Arne, educated at Eton, though but an upholsterer's son, and intended for the law, cherished a craze for music, strong enough to prevail at last.

† Adriano Willaert is another instance in musical history of the like "perversion" from jurisprudence to harmony. J. P. Salomon, again, was trained for the law, but his predilection for music won the day. Tartini, too, was educated at Padua for jurisprudence, but, after no slight expenditure of struggle, his love of music was allowed to assert itself, which it did *con brio*.

dear delights of literature. Castilho, the blind poet of Portugal, was put to the law, without ever taking to it. The Hungarian poet, Vörösmarty, was admitted an advocate at Pesth, but literature became ere long his recognized profession. Spain's most popular of recent poets, Zorilla, was sent to study law at Toledo, but for poetry's sake he gave law the go-by. Emile Souvestre got tired of waiting for advocate's work at Rennes.

William Hone was an attorney's clerk before he took to books—to the selling as well as writing them. Ireland, of the Shakspeare Forgeries, had been articled to a conveyancer: the *Vortigern* fiasco involved his leaving his father's house, as well as abandoning his profession. Dr. Richardson, the philologer, was addicted to law before he was won away from it by philology. Granville Sharp is another of the lapsed. Patrick Fraser Tytler felt the sharp edge of the saw that a good author makes a bad lawyer; and when Law, too jealous (as Mr. Burgon phrases it) to brook the presence of a rival, ultimately forsook him, the parting on his side was certainly without a pang. William Jerdan was put to study law at Edinburgh, but the study was a breakdown, and literature soon had him all to herself. Dr. Lardner was originally in a solicitor's office. Mr. W. C. Bryant gave up law for literature. Leigh Hunt was for some time in the office of an attorney, one of his brothers. Washington Irving studied the law, or was by courtesy supposed to do so, in Judge Hoffman's office; but Salmagundi was more to his taste than Coke and Blackstone,* and though admitted to the bar, it was scarcely to practise there. The like history holds good of John Gibson Lockhart and of John Wilson. Mr. Longfellow stopped short at an earlier point in the course. Mr. Charles Dickens started life in an attorney's office. Alexandre Dumas (the elder) was copying clerk to a provincial notary. Mr. P. J. Bailey soon abandoned the bar for poetical aspirations of which the outcome was *Festus*. Mr. Prescott, the historian, was designed for his father's profession, and engaged accordingly in legal studies for a time. Tom Moore was entered at the Middle Temple. Mr. de Quincey had the right of signing himself a Templar, in the letters he wrote for the *London Magazine*. Mr. T. K. Hervey left the office of a special pleader for literature. Sir Charles Lyell practised at the bar in early life. Mr. Disraeli was for a time subject to the drudgery of an attorney's office. Mr. Eliot Warburton ended almost as soon as begun his practice at the bar. Mr. Shirley Brooks "qualified" to practise as a solicitor. Mr. John Oxenford has the same qualification. Though Mr. Edwin Chadwick looked to the bar as his profession, he formed that early connexion

---

* He writes of himself in his twenty-sixth year, "I felt my own deficiency, and despaired of ever succeeding at the bar. I could study anything else rather than law, and had a fatal propensity to belles-lettres," etc.—See his *Life and Letters*, chap. xiv.

with the newspaper press which, says one authority, "has extended the mental range of many a law student," and, he might have added, cut short the law studies of many another. Mr. Layard speedily gave up his once cherished design of studying for the law: literature and art had already obtained too fast a hold of him. Of Sir William Hamilton we read how soon he abandoned the wearisome pacing to and fro of the Parliament House, and with it the best chance of a brief, for those underground recesses in which were then stored the choice treasures of the Advocates' Library. Mr. Carlyle contributed to Professor Veitch's memoir of Sir William a memorial sketch of him as one who was titularly an advocate, but had no practice, nor sought any; who touched the sketcher with "royal respect" for him in that house of his in Howe Street, in a fine silent neighbourhood, with a north light which was economized by having no curtains to the study, and quartos lying about on the window-sill; where he had gathered his modest means thriftily together, and sat down with his mother and cousin and his store of books, frankly renouncing all ambitions except what Mr. Carlyle then recognized to be the highest and one real ambition in this dark ambiguous world.

XIII.

Lapses in Law, and Commercial Failures.

II. COMMERCIAL FAILURES.

A CHAPTER OF INSTANCES.

BETWEEN the Francis Osbaldistone* of fiction, and his namesake the saint, of Assisi, in fact, there are at least two points of personal and domestic affinity; each was a commercial failure, and each on that account was a thorn in the flesh of his irritated, deprecatory, denunciatory sire. Not that Saint Francis declined commerce for the "beggarly

---

* Fiction at large has its Frank Osbaldistones by the score. "Behold me, then," writes the autobiographer of one of Miss Lee's *Canterbury Tales*, "doomed for my offences, whatever these were, to spend the greater part of the day on a high stool, and to go through all the drudgery of the counting-house, busy with invoices," etc. Leonard Fairfield, in the second of the Caxtonian series, has set his heart upon completing his intellectual education, upon developing those powers within him which yearn for an arena of literature, and he revolts from the routine of trade, to which the advances of his uncle, Richard Avenel, constrain him. "But to his credit be it said, that he vigorously resisted this natural disappointment, and by degrees schooled himself to look cheerfully on the path imposed on his duty, and sanctioned by the

trade" of verse-making; but decline it he did, to ensure the payment of the vows he had vowed to Poverty, his bride. Graphic is Sir James Stephen's account of the disgusted disenchantment of the respectable Pietro Bernardone, thriving merchant that he was, whose imagination—for he had one—was occupied in grouping into forms ever new and brilliant, like spangles shaken in a kaleidoscope, the ideas of bales and bills of lading, of sea risks and of supercargoes, combining with those of loans to reckless crusaders and of the supply of hostile camps, to form one gorgeous El Dorado, until intelligence of the loss of his draperies, his pack-horse, and his son, restored him to the waking world and to himself; and until, however gradually, all too surely, the mind of the old man

---

manly sense that was at the core of his character." Lord Lytton believes that this self-conquest proved the boy to have true genius. "The false genius would have written sonnets and despaired." There is Mrs. Gore's Henry Hamlyn, again, in *The Banker's Wife*, whom the "slavery and abject occupations of a banking-house" appal. "With a decided taste for literature, . . . how was he to reconcile the routine of a city life, or the devotion to business which he knew would be exacted by his father?" There is James Walkinshaw in Galt's *Entail*, whose Highland tinge of romantic enthusiasm, and love of adventure, are found incompatible with mercantile success. There is Mr. Trollope's George Bertram, who, invited to elect a vocation, though affirming literature to be the grandest occupation in the world for a man's leisure, owns it to be "a slavish profession,"—but meets his rich trading uncle's sneer, "Grub Street, eh? Yes, I should think so. You never heard of commerce, I suppose?" with the back-handed hit, "Commerce. Yes, I have heard of it. But I doubt whether I have the necessary genius." The old man looking at him as if doubtful whether or no he was being laughed at, George explains, "The necessary kind of

embraced the discovery that, though dwelling on the same planet, he and his son were inhabitants of different worlds.

Boccaccio was apprenticed to a merchant in Paris, and spent six years there, but his dislike to business induced his father* to sanction his withdrawal, in favour of the canon law: the sight of Virgil's tomb near Naples determined Giovanni's literary vocation for life.

Joost von den Vondel, recognized as "the great national poet of Holland" (1587-1679), served in his

---

genius." And at once the elder takes him up: "Very likely not. Your genius is adapted to dispersing, perhaps, rather than collecting." One may call to mind Coleridge's lines,—

> "Old Harpy jeers at castles in the air,
> And thanks his stars whenever Edmund speaks,
> That such a dupe as that is not his heir ;—
> But know, old Harpy, that these fancy freaks,
> Though vain and light as floating gossamer,
> Always amuse, and sometimes mend the heart:
> A young man's idlest hopes are still his pleasures,
> And fetch a higher price in Wisdom's mart
> Than all the unenjoying Miser's treasures."

Fully qualified was S. T. C. to sympathize with his friend Charles Lloyd, who was intended for his father's Birmingham bank, but who definitely pronounced the tedious and unintellectual occupation of adjusting pounds, shillings, and pence, to suit those alone who had never, eagle-like, or Charles Lloyd-like, gazed on the sun, or, in Joseph Cottle's phrase, bathed their temples in the dews of Parnassus.

* As father, a more genial and congenial one than St. Francis of Assisi was blest withal—the sire of the saint being, in Milman's words, "a hard, money-making man," who took his son into his trade, and was "shocked" by his untradesmanlike ways. "To a steady trader like the father it was folly if not madness."—*Lat. Christ.*, iv. 262.

father's shop, a hosier; and seems to have failed to reconcile the demands of trade with the accomplishments of verse, for the hosiery business languished in his hands. Jeremias de Decker, another Dutch bard of renown, some twenty years his junior, seems to have stuck better to commerce, and only to have devoted leisure hours to the muse.

Tailoring was, by paternal decree, and as a matter of inheritance, Molière's lot; and the father took care to put young Poquelin in the shop betimes. But his maternal grandfather sometimes took the lad to the play; and from each successive visit that youngster returned more and more out of conceit with "the shop," less and less indisposed to welcome *la perspective de sa profession*. He avowed his distaste, and, backed by the grandfather who "spoiled" him, talked his sire into letting him go to school, or college as it was called—collegiate schools our high-polite generation is apt to call much humbler institutions—the college of Clermont, under Jesuit directorship. The father consented, according to Voltaire, with the repugnance of a bourgeois who believed his son's fortune ruined if he took to study. Like the vexed senior in Béranger's chanson of *Le Tailleur et la Fée*:

> "Le vieux tailleur s'écrie: 'Eh quoi! ma fille
> Ne m'a donné qu'un faiseur des chansons!
> Mieux jour et nuit vaudrait tenir l'aiguille
> Que, faible écho, mourir en de vains sons.'"

If a boy have a poetic vein, it is to Locke, in his

Tractate of Education, the strangest thing in the world that the father* should desire or suffer it to be cherished or improved: "it is not likely to promote his fortunes, but rather to make him poor and idle." A busy, active man of business, as a modern essayist remarks, likes to see his boy work while he works, and play while he plays, but he cannot bear to see him think, or, as he usually calls it, dream and loiter. Yet meditation, solitude, and reflection are rightly said to be absolutely indispensable, not only to richness and beauty of character, but to energy in all the higher spheres of action. Such a suggestion, however, it were labour lost to din into the ears of "the strong sons of the world," as Mr. Tennyson styles them, in a passage descriptive, and the description is on both sides typical, of

> "One whom the strong sons of the world despise;
> For lucky rhymes to him were scrip and share,
> And mellow metres more than cent for cent;
> Nor could he understand how money breeds,
> Thought it a dead thing; yet himself could make
> The thing that is not as the thing that is."

The prelude to one of the highest strains that Burns ever penned, *The Vision*, represents him musing regretfully on wasted time, spent at best in "stringing blethers up in rhyme, for fools to sing." Irony inspires and inspirits him as he goes on:

---

* There is an exclamation of M. Sainte-Beuve to the purpose: "Oh! combien je comprends que les parents sages d'autrefois ne voulussent pas de littérateurs parmi leurs enfants!" etc.—*Portraits Littéraires*, i., 436.

> "Had I to guid advice but harkit,
> I might, by this, hae led a market,
> Or strutted in a bank, an' clarkit
>   My cash account:
> While here,* half-mad, half-fed, half-sarkit,
>   Is a' th' amount.
>
> I started, mutt'ring, Blockhead! coof!
> And heaved on high my waukit loof,
> To swear by a' yon starry roof,
>   Or some rash aith,·
> That I, henceforth, would be rhyme-proof
> Till my last breath." †

It is of George Darley, whose *Sylvia, or The May Queen*, Miss Mitford hailed as exquisite—" something between the Faithful Shepherdess and the Midsummer Night's Dream "—that the same lady writes to Mr. Harness: "The author is the son of a rich alderman of Dublin, who disinherited him because he would write poetry; and now he supports himself [1836] by writing in the magazines." John Galt turned author in a merchant's counting-house at Greenock. William Jerdan is described as proving "an indifferent clerk" in a West Indian merchant's counting-house. Mr. Bowdich, the learned traveller, was a partner in his father's mercantile house, but ended a prolonged struggle " both with his own inclinations and with want of suc-

---

* That is to say, sitting lonely, at eventide, by the ingle-cheek, in his auld clay biggin.

† Should glossarial aid be acceptable to any too exclusively "plain English" reader, the footnote offers to explain that *clarkit* means wrote; *sarkit*, provided with shirts; *waukit*, thickened; *loof*, palm of the hand.

cess," by betaking himself to Oxford. Millevoye, the French poet, like postoral Gessner before him, hoped to reconcile a taste for books with the sale of them; but one day he was caught, absorbed in reading, by the bibliopole he served, and was thus sternly addressed: "Young man, you're a reader! You'll never be a bookseller;"—and after two years of *cette tentative infructueuse*, Millevoye renounced the trade. Dr. John Pringle exchanged a mercantile for a medical career, learned and beneficent.

Harsh were the means used by Gifford's master, the Ashburton shoemaker, to wean him from his literary tastes; but what could be done with, and what use could be made of, an apprentice who, for want of paper, used to hammer scraps of leather smooth, and work mathematical problems on them (if not indite sonnets) with a blunt awl? Isaac Disraeli, an only child—and a pale, pensive, timid, susceptible, absent one—was intended by his parents to carry on the traditions of their race, and devote himself to money-making; but, as one of his critics has it, "he early showed that he would disappoint the fond hopes entertained of his becoming a millionaire." The crisis arrived, we are told, when Isaac produced a poem: his father was seriously alarmed: decisive measures were taken to eradicate the evil, and prevent future disgrace; the boy was shipped off to Amsterdam; but anon he informed his father that he declined to be a merchant, and had written a long poem against

Commerce, which was the corruption of man. William Taylor of Norwich was happy in a rich father who, anxious as he had been to see the young man succeed him in a large and prosperous business, favoured his withdrawing from it when once satisfied that William "had an imagination too lively, and a taste too decided for literary pursuits," to succeed in trade; a sanction aided by the father's gratification at his son's speedily attained distinction in literature. James Perry, of the now dead-and-gone, once thoroughly alive and kicking *Morning Chronicle*, developed from a Manchester manufacturer's clerk into editorship of that and other journals.

Louvet, disdaining the commerce of his father, as Lamartine phrases it, "sought the level of his mind in literature"—a sufficiently low level, ethically speaking, if not æsthetically too; for the book he wrote was a celebrated "manual of elegant libertinism," drawn from the corrupted society of the period, and characterized as a reversed ideal of a society which laughs at itself, and which admires itself only in its vice. As contrary to Louvet as day to night was Sir Samuel Romilly, in all that goes to form character, circumstances excepted; the circumstance at least of renouncing commerce. The humble situation of a clerk in his godfather Fludyer's counting-house might have led young Romilly, by his own account, to a very brilliant fortune. "My father therefore determined to fit me for that situation,"—but the design came to nought. The father, as a jeweller, was making twenty thousand pounds a year, and Samuel became his book-keeper—an occupation which never pleased its occupant, except that it allowed him time for reading and rhyming; for the youngster wrote eclogues, songs, and satires, made translations of Boileau, and attempted imitations of Spenser. "My father's business became every day more unpleasant to me,"—and an earnestly expressed wish for change of employment was gratified. To distinguish himself in some literary career was the "chimerical hope" which he had long indulged; and he had once even supposed that he might become illustrious as a poet; but this delusion, for as such he recognized it, was not of long duration.

Francis Jeffrey was at one time in a great fright lest he should be made a merchant; and, preparing for the worst, he wrote a sheet of observations "on a mercantile life," not at all favourable to its tendencies in respect of inducing happiness. He would have made a miserable merchant, Lord Cockburn asserts, for he had a horror of risk, and was void of the spirit of adventure, so that one shilling certain had charms for him which twenty shillings doubtful could not impart. The law, and in Edinburgh, was plainly his destiny; and with him there was no lapse in law, however decided might have been a commercial failure.

Humphrey Wanley, the antiquarian, could stick to

no trade, let them put him to what they would. Thomas Birch, the historico-biographer, was designed for the coffee-mill-making business of his Quaker sire; but the design fell through, overruled by his devotion to books. David Hume was sent to a mercantile house in Bristol in 1734; but finding the "drudgery of this employment intolerable," he cried off, and made off for Rheims.

John Gay began the world as apprentice to a London mercer, and trying his 'prentice hand at literature, forswore the shop. It is entered to the credit account of Volkov, the founder of the Russian theatre, (1729-63,) that, distasteful as his counting-house duties were to him, he was sedulous in discharging them. George Stevens, once renowned for his "Lecture on Heads," deserted at an early age the trade to which he was brought up. Lindley Murray was a deserter from his father's counting-house. John Walker, the Dictionary man, was brought up to trade. Humphry Repton, the first (in time) of Landscape Gardeners, was placed in a merchant's counting-house at Norwich, and afterwards set up on his own account, but poetry, music, and drawing were too effectively seductive. Abraham Sharp was apprenticed to a Manchester tradesman, whom he prevailed upon to cancel his indentures, and set him free to pursue science, at his own charges, if not to his own cost. Tiberius Cavallo, who made a name by his treatises on electricity, soon abandoned commerce for natural philosophy. Fahrenheit had to resist a father's exclusive dedication of him to matters mercantile. Arthur Young was apprenticed to a merchant at Lynn, and often did he lament the money thus wasted, and the time: books were all his solace, and for them he had a huge appetite, and not a bad digestion. In vain the father of Thomas Twining, the clerical translator of and dissertator upon Aristotle's Poetics, strove to keep him to his tea-business. Marmontel's father put him to trade at Clermont, but there was authorship bred in the bone of him, and it would out. Edward Moore deserted the draper's shop, to write *The Gamester*, and edit *The World*. Dr. Parr renounced with disgust the apothecary associations to which he was born and bred. F. H. Jacobi—the philosophic opponent of Kant, and Fichte, and Schelling—was brought up for a mercantile business, and for some time managed to reconcile commerce with literature. Tollens, in his day the most popular of Dutch poets, served behind the counter of his father, a thrifty and thriving dealer in colours, who at first was pleased with his son's facility in song-writing, and then alarmed at its possible influence on his trading prospects. Frederic Schlegel was apprenticed to a mercantile house at Leipzig, but his disinclination and incompetency induced his father to remove him to the more congenial atmosphere of Göttingen. Millingen, the archæologist, was clerk in a banking-house in Paris, but the clerkship was noway to his taste, while the study of Pinkerton and Polybius was. Sismondi's father having lost the whole of his disposable capital in the revolutionary troubles of France, the son had to tear himself from an endeared home for a counting-house at Lyons, where, however, the irksomeness of the employment was compensated by the habits of business he learnt, not to omit an achieved mastery of the mysteries of double entry, and of the courses of exchange.

Napoleon's military historiographer, Jomini, was for nearly a decade of years in a merchant's office.* Armand Carrel was a son of a merchant of Rouen, who intended him for trade: struggling "between the wishes of his family, which pointed to a counting-house, and his own consciousness of faculties suited to a different sphere," he became secretary to M. Augustin Thierry—from whom his mother, as M. Nisard tells us, exacted assurances of her son's success in literature, for the "humble life of a man of letters" seemed decidedly detrimental in her eyes.† Paul de Kock spent several years in a banker's counting-house in Paris, where he began to write for the stage. Auber had once a commercial engagement in London. Moscheles was brought up to the business of his father, who was a prosperous merchant at Prague;

---

* Marshal Lannes was brought up as a dyer.

† "Vous croyez donc, Monsieur, que mon fils fait bien, et qu'il aura une carrière?" "Je réponds de lui," answered the historian, "comme de moi-même."—*Notice sur Carrel, par M. Nisard.*

but young Ignatz won over father and all to favour his dedication to harmonics instead.*

Rosellini, the orientalist, was designed for his father's

---

* In the department of the sister art of painting and sculpture, a long list of seceders from trade might be made out. Albert Dürer, for instance, who, to the great chagrin of his father, gave up the goldsmith's business for high art. Backhuysen, who emerged from an Amsterdam counting-house, the windows of which opened out upon the sea, where there were ships to draw, and with office pen and ink young Ludolph drew them to his heart's delight, until heart he had none left for the ledgers and invoices nearer at hand. James Barry went to and fro with his father as a coasting-trader, and extremely repugnant to the sire were the literary and artistic predilections of the son. Franz Kobell spent four years in a merchant's office before his love for the arts was allowed or enabled to prevail. John Varley, very much against his will, was apprenticed to a silversmith; Kaulbach equally resented being bound to a goldsmith; and Le Keux, to a manufacturer of pewter. John Raphael Smith forsook the counter of a linendraper for painting and engraving. William Linton was in vain placed with a Liverpool merchant, in the hope of being cured of his pictorial passion. Frank Stone entered his father's factory, and continued in it some years after he came of age. David Roberts was apprenticed to an Edinburgh house-painter; and Richard Redgrave spent his youth in the counting-house of his father, a manufacturer. Scott typifies this class of transfer in his Dick Tinto, the tailor's son, who not only exhausted all the chalk in making sketches upon the shopboard, but even caricatured several of old Mr. Tinto's best customers, who began loudly to murmur that it was too bad to have their persons deformed by the vestments of the sire, and to be at the same time turned into ridicule by the pencil of the son; which state of feeling and form of expression led to discredit and loss of custom, until the old tailor, yielding to destiny, and to the entreaties of his son, permitted him to attempt his fortune in a line for which he was better qualified.

Hartley Coleridge observes of old Richard Hogarth, whom therefore he dubs "Poor Richard," that he did not live to see his son a great man, or to see his own prophecies about him frustrated; for doubtless he augured ill of a lad that did not take to his Latin, but wasted time and paper in ornamenting his capitals with lines of beauty, and caricaturing his master and schoolfellows.

business, but an early love of antiquities diverted him, in a double sense. Dr. S. G. Morton, the ethnologist, gave up the counting-house for materia medica and zoological researches.

Martin Barry's strong bent for scientific studies was *too* strong for the family scheme of a mercantile career for him. Mr. Leitch Ritchie's first destination was commerce, and both in Glasgow and London he had engagements with trading firms. Bernard Barton was faithful to the bank; but he inherited to the full, and something over, the literary turn of his father, who reconciled himself with difficulty to the manufactory *his* father left him at Carlisle. "I always," said he, "perused a Locke, an Addison, or a Pope, with delight, and ever sat down to my ledger with a sort of disgust." Polevoy, one of the few authors of mark Siberia can call her own, took unkindly enough to the brandy distillery and the earthenware works in which by birth and breeding he was interested. The late Samuel Lucas, son of a wealthy merchant of Bristol, was brought up with a view to business, but declined it in favour of *belles lettres*. Mr. G. H. Lewes, they tell us, was for some time in a mercantile office, before taking to medicine, and then being taken up with literature.—But this chapter of instances must somewhere have an end; and perhaps here or nowhere, now or never, is the word.

XIV.

Merry Masks and Sad Faces.

AMONG the miscellaneous verses of Mr. Thackeray are some nominally due to the author's faithful old gold pen, that had served him three long years, and drawn thousands of funny women and droll men; and this stanza occurs among these chrysostomic confidences:

> "I've help'd him to pen many a line for bread;
> To joke, with sorrow aching in his head;
> And make your laughter when his own heart bled."

So, in one of the Sketches and Letters attributed by him to Mr. Brown, we read of Tightrope, the celebrated literary genius, who sits down to write and laugh—with the children very likely ill at home—with a strong personal desire to write a tragedy or a sermon, with his wife scolding him, his head racking with pain, his mother-in-law making a noise at his ears, and telling him that he is a heartless and abandoned ruffian, his tailor in the passage, vowing that he will not quit that place until his little bill is settled; under which miserable conditions Tightrope writes off a brilliant funny article, that shall set all the town a-giggling. Giggle the town does, to the top of its bent; and it perhaps assumes the jester to be the heartiest laugher of all. But

> "He shows, if he removes the mask,
> A face that's anything but gay."

Mr. Carlyle has a word to say, in passing, on strophes of "the comic laughter-loving sort; yet ever with an unfathomable earnestness, as is fit, lying underneath: for, bethink thee, what is the mirthfullest grinning face of any Grimaldi,[*] but a transitory *mask*, behind which quite otherwise grins—the most indubitable Death's-head." Harlequin without his mask, as the Lecturer on English Humorists reminded his audience, is known to present a very sober countenance, and was himself, the story goes (of Rich), the melancholy patient whom the doctor advised to go and see Harlequin—a man "full of cares and perplexities like the rest of us, whose Self must always be serious to him, under whatever mask, or disguise, or uniform he presents it to the public." Mr. Thomson, the correspondent of Burns, quotes the same story with another stage-hero for it, when he tells the

---

[*] Thomas Moore, in his Diary, makes a note of the odd effect of seeing a comic personage in ill-humour, as he saw Liston, when dressed for the part of Rigdum Fonidos; and as Washington Irving once described his having seen Grimaldi behind the scenes in a furious rage, with the regular grin painted on his cheeks.

Scotch poet how sorry he is for his melancholy, the while his strains are gladdening and inspiriting broad Scotland: "Like the hypochondriac who went to consult a physician upon his case: 'Go,' says the doctor, 'and see the famous Carlini, who keeps all Paris in good humour.' 'Alas, sir,' replied the patient, 'I am that unhappy Carlini.'" Cowper was fresh from writing *John Gilpin* when he assured Mr. Unwin, by letter, that if he trifled, and merely trifled, it was because he was reduced to it by necessity — a melancholy that nothing else so effectually dispersed, engaging him sometimes in the arduous task of being merry by force; and strange as it might seem, he adds, the most ludicrous lines he ever wrote were written in the saddest mood; and but for that saddest mood, perhaps, had never been written at all. Long years later he tells the same correspondent, "Perhaps you remember the Undertaker's dance in the Rehearsal, which they perform in crape hatbands and black cloaks, to the tune of 'Hob or Nob,' one of the sprightliest airs in the world. Such is my fiddling and such is my dancing; but they serve a purpose which at some certain times could not be so effectually promoted by anything else." Seven years later still he writes to Hayley: "*Non sum quod simulo.* I am cheerful upon paper sometimes, when I am absolutely the most dejected of all creatures."

The foremost literary "entertainer" of his day bore witness, on a last page of one of his first books, to the gloomy depression, the bitter reaction of spirits which the "comic writer" knows too well, in all its acute intensity. "Comedy is crying," is the sententious utterance of Triplet's precocious little Lucy, in the original version of *Masks and Faces*, when the lady visitor is in the poor author's den : "Father cried all the time he was writing his one." Triplet turned as red as fire at this, and exclaimed, "Hold your tongue, I was bursting with merriment." So may royalty play the pretender, as where the king of men, in Racine, longs to take off his mask and have a good cry,—

> "Encor si je pouvais, libre dans mon malheur,
> Par des larmes au moins soulager ma douleur !"

Triste destin des rois! Scott's Lewis the Eleventh is all humour and caustic wit with his distinguished guests; but no sooner have they left the room than the light of assumed vivacity fades from the king's eyes, the smile deserts his face, and he exhibits all the fatigue of an accomplished actor who has just finished the exhausting representation of some favourite part, in which, while upon the stage, he has displayed the most buoyant animation. So with the Regent Murray, in another of Sir Walter's best historical tales, whom we see and hear laughing heartily as he says to the privy councillors, "Farewell, my lords, and hold me in remembrance to the Cock of the North,"—and who then turns slowly round to Roland Græme, while the marks of gaiety disappear from his countenance,* as completely as the passing bubbles leave the dark mirror of a still, profound lake into which a traveller has cast a stone: "In the course of a minute his noble features had assumed their natural expression of deep and even melancholy gravity." All the world's a stage, in this respect, and all the men and women merely players,—hypocrites, in the classical sense: from a very French Agamemnon, *anax andrôn*, or an inscrutable Louis Onze, down to a Sophia Western, finding it so difficult to "force the appearance of gaiety into her looks, when her mind dictated nothing but the tenderest sorrow, and when every thought was charged with tormenting ideas;" or a Doctor Firmin, pink of politeness, and *princeps* (*facilè*) of fashionable physicians, who has to wear the inspiriting smile, to breathe the gentle joke; who is suffering real torture while he is smirking in Lady Megrim's face; and who all day, perhaps, sees no one so utterly sick, so sad, so despairing, as himself; or, once again, a Vivian Grey in gay companionship owing to sadness, and to practise in "the sad opportunity of observing that the face of man is scarcely more genuine, and less deceitful, than these masquerade dresses which we now wear." There is a Mask among

---

* As with the chieftain in Mr. Robert Lytton's most elaborate poem:
"All his countenance, now
Unwitnessed, at once fell dejected, and dreary,
As a curtain let fall by a hand that's grown weary,
Into puckers and folds."

Mrs. Browning's poems, and " I have a smiling face, she said, I have a jest for all I meet,"—but it is the Mask does it, and the smile and the jest are only mask-deep.

> "Behind no prison-grate, she said,
> Which slurs the sunshine half a mile,
> Are captives so uncomforted,
> As souls behind a smile.
> God's pity let us pray, she said.
>   *   *   *   *
> But in your bitter world, she said,
> Face-joy's a costly mask to wear,
> And bought with pangs long nourished
> And rounded to despair.
> Grief's earnest makes life's play, she said."

Mr. Lockhart observes of Scott's demeanour in public during the excitement and festivities of the king's visit to Scotland in 1822, that no one could have suspected from it that he was, during those three or four weeks of revel, daily and nightly the watcher of a deathbed, or the consoler of orphans; striving all the while against "true earnest sorrows, rooted miseries, anguish in grain, vexations ripe and blown." Nor did his son-in-law remember ever to have seen him in such a state of dejection as when attending at Lord Kinedder's funeral; yet was that one of the noisiest days of the royal festival, and Scott had to plunge into some scene of gaiety the moment after he returned; and his exclamation as he and Lockhart halted in Castle Street,[*] where Crabbe's mild placid

---

[*] So with Harley L'Estrange in the novel, whom, as he dismounted at his father's door, you would hardly have supposed to be the same

face appeared at his window, was,—"Now for what our old friend there puts down as the crowning curse of his poor player in the Borough—

> 'To hide in rant the heartache of the night.'"

Two of the liveliest characters in *Lucile* are heavy-laden by their author with

> "A sadness which each found no word to explain.
> Whatever it was, the world noticed not it
> In the light-hearted beauty, the light-hearted wit.
> Still, as once with the actors in Greece, 'tis the case,
> Each must speak to the crowd with a mask on his face."

La Confession du Comte Grifolin takes this form, in the penwork of Rivarol:

> "C'est trop cacher mes traits sous un masque trompeur;
> Le rire est sur ma bouche et la mort dans mon cœur."

None too rare in the letters of Leigh Hunt are such passages as that in which he owns his state of health to be so bad (in 1832), that he does not tell his nearest connections how much he suffers from it: "and often while I am entertaining others in company, such a flow of melancholy thoughts comes over me, that their laughter if they knew it would be changed to tears." Add an execution in the house for forty shillings, and great family sufferings apart from considerations of fortune, to make the gruesome gruel

---

whimsical, fantastic, though deep and subtle humorist he had just before, in company, been showing himself—for his expressive face was now unutterably serious; but the moment he entered the house, his face was again radiant and gladsome—brightening the whole room like sunshine.

thick and slab, as well as bitter as gall. Mr. Trollope somewhere speaks of wit as the outward mental casing of the man, which has no more to do with the inner mind of thoughts and feelings than have the rich brocaded garments of the priest at the altar with the asceticism of the anchorite below them, whose skin is tormented with sackcloth, and whose body is half flayed with rods. He says of the mental efforts which men make, that those which they show forth daily to the world are often the opposites of the inner workings of the spirit. There is many a man, Lord Lytton has said, whom we call friend, and whose face seems familiar to us as our own; yet, could we but take a glimpse of him when we leave his presence, and he sinks back into his chair alone, we should sigh to see how often the smile on the frankest lip is but the bravery of the drill, only worn when on parade.

> "Amidst the throng in merry masquerade,
> Lurk there no hearts that throb with secret pain?"

The query is Byron's, and he knew but one answer to it. Elsewhere he sings of the sigh suppressed, corroding in the cavern of the heart, making the countenance a mask of rest, and turning human nature to an art. Finding him invariably lively when they were together, Moore often rallied him on the gloomy tone of his poetry, as assumed; but his constant answer was, and Moore avowedly soon ceased to doubt of its truth, that, although thus merry and full of laughter with congenial spirits, he was, at heart, one of the most melancholy wretches in existence. Byron on one occasion complacently quotes the testimony of his wife, after a particularly brilliant evening in society,—"At heart you are the most melancholy of mankind; and often when apparently gayest." Elsewhere he cites approvingly the remark of Grimm, that Raynard and most other comic poets were *gens bilieux et mélancoliques.*

XV.

Pangs in Print.

OFTEN did Mr. Thackeray, in laughing at the early sorrows of the heart, assure his readers that an unhappy love which finds a vehicle in prose or rhyme is a very bearable malady. There are exceptions to this rule,[*] though as a competent objector to it allows, why persons who have felt very deeply should give utterance to their sorrow is often difficult to say; "but real emotion is something unmistakeable, and we can tell its presence in an instant." The exceptions as usual go to confirm the rule. *Curæ leves loquuntur, ingentes stupent:* light griefs find utterance, the great ones are speechless. Dryden, following Chaucer, tells us that

> "Light sufferings give us leisure to complain;
> We groan, but cannot speak, in greater pain."

And in one of his dedications he refers to Ovid, going

---

[*] Expression of feeling is different with different minds, as Mr. Longfellow says; it is not always simple, for instance; some minds when excited, naturally speak in figures and similitudes, but do not on that account feel less deeply.

to his banishment, and writing from shipboard to his
friends, who were to excuse the faults of his poetry
by his misfortunes, since good verses never flow but
from a serene and composed spirit. The Cornélie of
Corneille exclaims, and in her (and his) grand way,

> " N'attendez point de moi de regrets, ni de larmes ;
> Un grand coeur à ses maux applique d'autres charmes.
> Les faibles déplaisirs s'amusent à parler,
> Et quiconque se plaint cherche à se consoler."

Misery observes no oratory, says an old writer.
Whenever the hero of tragedy is able to express his
pain in antitheses and ingenious allusions, we may,
with Schlegel, safely reserve our pity ; this sort of
conventional dignity being, as it were, a coat of mail
which prevents the pain from reaching the inmost
heart. Not that the German critic fails to recognize
the "miracle effected by poetry," which has its indescribable sighs, its immediate accents of the deepest
agony, in which there still runs a something melodious : it is only a certain full-dressed and formal
beauty which he rejects as incompatible with the
greatest truth of emotional expression. Metaphysical
Dr. Thomas Brown designates metaphor as the figure
of passion, and simile the figure of calm description ;
on which showing, in the drama, as the most faithful
poetic representation of passion, the simile should
be of rare occurrence, and never but in situations
in which the speaker may be considered as partaking
almost the tranquillity of the poet himself. Dr. Brown

cites as an instance of error in this respect the scene in *Cato*, where Portius, at the very moment in which Lucia, his beloved, has just bid him farewell for ever, and when he is struggling to detain her, traces all the resemblances of his passion to the flame of a fading lamp,—making us feel immediately, that a lover who could so fully develop a comparison, and a comparison, too, derived from an object the least likely to occur to him at such a moment, could not be suffering any very great agony of heart.* Gresset was right to disclaim, in his neatest and most serious versification, the purpose of setting his sorrow to the music of verse; being sad in earnest, how could he in sad earnest versify his greif?

> "Pour moi, de ma douleur profonde
> Trop pénétré pour la chanter," etc.

In Milton's *Lycidas*, as Warton admits, there is perhaps more poetry than sorrow. Johnson refuses to regard it as the effusion of real passion; for passion runs not after remote allusions, and neither plucks berries from the myrtle and ivy, nor calls upon Arethuse and Mincius, nor talks of rough satyrs and fauns with cloven heel. "Where there is leisure for fiction there is little grief." South in one of his

---

* With regard to metaphor, on the other hand, "if we attend to what occurs in real life, we shall find that metaphor, far from being unnatural, is almost a necessary part of the language of emotion, and that it is then that the language of prose makes its nearest approach to the language of poetry."—*Phenomena of Simple Suggestion*.

discourses approves the known saying, that ordinary slight griefs complain, but great sorrows strike the heart with an astonished silence. "Thorns make a crackling blaze, and are quickly gone; but great wood lies a long time, and consumes with a silent fire. A still grief is a devouring grief, such a one as preys upon the vitals, sinks into the bones, and dries up the marrow." That wound is of all others the most deadly, that causes the heart to bleed inwardly. Says Elwina, in the tragedy of *Percy*,

> "The sorrow's weak that wastes itself in words:
> Mine is substantial anguish—deep, not loud."

There are a good many symbols, even, that are more expressive than words; in illustration of which Dr. Oliver Holmes refers to a young wife he knew, who, having to part with her husband for a time, did not write a mournful poem; indeed, she was a silent person, and perhaps hardly said a word about it; but she quietly turned of a deep orange colour with jaundice. A great many people in this world, he adds, have but one form of rhetoric for their profoundest experiences,—namely, to waste away and die. To apply another passage: When a man can versify, his paroxysm of feeling is passing. When he can rhyme, his anguish has slackened its hold.. Don Quixote bids Sancho sleep, while himself gives vent to his sorrow in a little madrigal of his own composing: "Methinks," quoth Sancho, "that a man cannot be suffering much when he can turn his breath to verse-making." It had often been observed, before Gibbon repeated the observation, that the highest agitation of the mind is such as no language can describe, since language can only paint ideas, and not that "sentimental, silent, almost stupid," excess of rage or grief which the soul feels with such energy, that it is not master of itself enough to have any distinct perceptions: such passion baffles all description; but when this storm subsides, passion is as fertile in ideas, as it was at first barren. It is a significant entry in Mackenzie's record of the super-sentimental experiences of his Man of Feeling in general, and of one of them in particular, that "In a day or two he [Harley] was so much master of himself as to be able to rhyme upon the subject. The following pastoral," etc., etc. Independently of the mediocrity of many of the poetical effusions interspersed throughout Mrs. Radcliffe's novels, they often assume what Professor Moir calls a ludicrous air, from their contrast with the circumstances which occasion them: under all situations of anxiety and distress, paper, pencils, and poetical enthusiasm are never wanting to her heroines; indeed it is observable that the poetical sensibilities of these much-tried ladies generally become more lively after any domestic calamity, such as the death of a parent; much as Beau Clincher's exuberance of spirits was "accounted for by the fact that he was in mourning for his father." The late Professor Blunt was thinking of *Lycidas* when

he said that in the paroxysms of grief no man thinks of writing verses of any kind; the rhymes of a ballad-monger would then be as much out of place as the strains of a Theocritus: we exclaim, as King David does, "My son! my son!" When the paroxysm is past, every man will write such verses (if he write them at all) as the ordinary turn of his mind dictates; men act and speak under suffering agreeably to the manner in which they act and speak in general.*
"Ma douleur serait bien médiocre, si je pouvais vous la dépeindre," writes Madame de Sévigné to her daughter; "aussi je ne l'entreprendrai pas aussi." But the *bien médiocre* is, for art purposes, for rhymes and elegy-factors, for sonneteers and madrigal-makers, the very golden mean. When the *douleur* has reached that stage, it becomes the property of the artist in verse, and he can then describe and depict and *dépeindre* with effusion, counting the feet of his verses correctly the while, and polishing them off as he goes along.

---

* "Milton lamented his friend in the language of romance: who would on that account deny that the poet's sorrow was unfeigned?" (See J. J. Blunt's review of *Todd's Milton*.)

Take again the suggested case of Marmontel—(and between Marmontel and Milton pretty nearly the whole and sole resemblance consists, as with Fluellen's famous analogy of Macedon and Monmouth, in the initial capital M.): Marmontel was, by habit, a reader and writer of plays; and therefore, when he loses his favourite child, and witnesses the affliction of his wife, he betakes himself to composing, (so he tells us,) as an analogous subject, the opera of Penelope. This was very French; but his distress was undoubtedly sincere, subdued enough however in good time to be put into recitative and arie.—*Quarterly Review*, xxxvi., 47.

Walter Savage Landor reasons out the philosophy of the question in one of his fragmentary relics of song :

> "So then, I feel not deeply ! if I did,
> I should have seized the pen and pierced therewith
> The passive world !
>   And thus thou reasonest ?
> Well hast thou known the lover's, not so well
> The poet's heart ; while that heart bleeds, the hand
> Presses it close. Grief must run on and pass
> Into near Memory's more quiet shade
> Before it can compose itself in song.
> He who is agonized and turns to show
> His agony to those who sit around,
> Seizes the pen in vain : thought, fancy, power,
> Rush back into his bosom ; all the strength
> Of genius cannot draw them into light
> From under mastering Grief ; but Memory,
> The Muse's mother, nurses, rears them up,
> Informs, and keeps them with her all her days."

When Corinne's grief was at its height, in vain she sought for words, or else she wrote unmeaning ones, that dismayed her on perusal, as would the ravings of delirium. Hers were now but long unvaried wailings ; her expressions are characterized by her author as "too impetuous, too unveiled," as those of misery, not of talent. To write well, observes Madame de Staël, we ought to feel truly, but not (as Corinne did) heart-breakingly. "The best of melancholy poetry is that inspired by a kind of rapture, which still tells of mental strength and enjoyment." Real grief she declares to be a foe to intellectual fertility ; it produces a gloomy agitation, that incessantly returns to the same point, like the knight who, pursued by an evil genius, sought a thousand roads for escape, yet always found himself at the spot from which he started. What mourner, exclaims Addison,

> "ever felt poetic fires?
> Slow comes the verse that real woe inspires:
> Grief unaffected suits but ill with art,
> Or flowing numbers with a bleeding heart."

In his annotations on Ovid he taxes that poet with thinking he never can draw tears enough from his reader, as though we could be at the same time delighted with the poet's talent and concerned for the person who gives it pathetic expression: *lamentationes debent esse breves et concisæ.* The bard of *In Memoriam* tells us,

> "I sometimes hold it half a sin
> To put in words the grief I feel;
> For words, like Nature, half reveal
> And half conceal the soul within.
>
> But, for the unquiet heart and brain,
> A use in measured language lies;
> The sad mechanic exercise,
> Like dull narcotics, numbing pain."

Rasselas uttered his woe-worn musings with a plaintive voice, but with a look that indicated something of complacence in his own perspicuity, and that he received some solace of the miseries of life, from consciousness of the delicacy with which he felt, and the eloquence with which he bewailed them. "Qu'on ne s'y trompe pas," says Sainte-Beuve; "les douleurs célébrées avec harmonie sont déjà des blessures à peu près cicatrisées, et la part de l'art s'étend bien avant jusque dans les plus réelles effusions d'un coeur qui chante." The artist, like other men, as Mr. Dallas argues, must get his experience of life through suffering, and sometimes he suffers much and long; but the power of expressing himself in art implies, if not perfect relief, a certain recovery *—implies that he has so far got the better of his trouble as to be curious about it, and able to dandle it. Those who cherish the luxury of woe, he goes on to say, of course will not admit this: it is a pleasure to them to think that they are utterly miserable; the idea of solace is distasteful to them; and when, to convict them of their error, they are asked, " Why, then, are ye so tuneful?" the question seems as heartless as that of the rustic in the fable, who said to the roasting shell-fish, " Oh, ye Cockles! near to death, wherefore do ye sing?" Notwithstanding such self-deception, then, the fact remains, as enounced by Euripides, that "if the poet is to give pleasure, he must compose in pleasure." Mr. Chambers remarks of some of the pathetic songs of Burns to Clarinda, that although they could not have been written without an earnest, however transient, feeling on the part of the author, it would be a great mistake to accept them as a literal expression of pas-

---

* Your Breughel, as Mr. Carlyle has it, paints his sea-storm, not while the ship is labouring and cracking, but after he has got on shore, and is safe under cover.

sion : * "We ought to make a considerable allowance for the extent to which the poet's mind is actuated by mere considerations of art and the desire of effect." † Byron duly journalizes his conviction, that to write so as to bring home to the heart, the heart must have been tried,—but, perhaps, ceased to be so. While you are under the influence of passions, you only feel, but cannot describe them,—any more than when in action, you could turn round and tell the story to your next neighbour. "When all is over,—all, all, and irrevocable,—trust to memory; she is then too faithful." Of Byron's own celebrated *Fare thee well*, many affirmed at the time that it was a mere showy effusion of sentiment, as difficult for real feeling to have produced as it was easy for fancy and art. To this opinion his biographer owns himself to have been inclined, so "suspicious" appeared to him the sentiment that could, at such a moment, indulge in such verses. But Moore changed his mind when he came to examine the memoranda, in which Byron described, "in a manner whose sincerity there was no doubting,

---

* " Et que sont les paroles," cries Balzac's Valentin, weeping over his Pauline : " Plus tard j'essayerai de te dire mon amour, en ce moment je ne puis que le sentir."—*La Peau de Chagrin*. The sentiment is pretty nearly at one with Rogers's couplet—altered and adapted for the nonce :

"But not till Time has smoothed the ruffled breast,
Are those impassioned hopes and fears express'd."

† "The *Ae Fond Kiss* appears in a different light. The tragic tale seems there concentrated in a wild gush of eloquence direct from the poet's heart."—Chambers' *Life and Works of Burns*, vol. iii., p. 209.

the swell of tender recollections under the influence of which, as he sat one night musing in his study, these stanzas were produced,"—the tears, as he said, and as the aspect of the MS. implied, falling fast over the paper as he wrote them. Some years later we find him writing to Mr. Murray, "As for poesy, mine is the *dream* of the sleeping passions; when they are awake, I cannot speak their language, only in their somnambulism, and just now they are not dormant." Wisely and well Mr. Lewes says of the composition of *Werther*, that the true philosophy of art would, *à priori*, lead us to the conviction that, although Goethe cleared his "bosom of the perilous stuff" by moulding this perilous stuff into a work of art, he must have essentially outlived the storm before he painted it,—conquered his passion, and subdued the rebellious thoughts, before he could make them plastic to his purpose.* The poet cannot see to write when his eyes are full of tears; cannot sing when his breast is swollen with sighs, and sobs choke utterance. "He must rise superior to his grief before he can sublimate his grief in song. The artist is a master, not a slave; he wields his passion, he is not hurried along by it; he possesses, and is not possessed." Ably developed to the same effect is the doctrine that Art enshrines

---

* And this *à priori* deduction is verified by the rigour of dates, which forces Goethe's biographer to the conviction that *Werther*, although taken from the poet's experience, was not written while that experience was being lived.—*Life and Works of Goethe*, i. 210.

the great sadness of the world, but is itself not sad: the storm of passion weeps itself away, and the heavy clouds roll off in quiet masses, to make room for the sun, which, shining through, touches them to beauty with its rays. While pain is in its newness, it is pain, and nothing else; it is not Art, but Feeling.* To soothe the spirit though the heart be shaken, is the emollient privilege of song, writes Mr. Quillinan:

> "Not with the griefs that all to pain belong
> The mourner sits beneath the cypress tree
> Whereon the melancholy lyre is hung
> That turns to sighs the breeze's minstrelsy:
> When tears to music flow, their fall is anguish-free."

---

* In fine, "Goethe could not write *Werther* before he had outlived Wertherism."

XVI.

Ready Writers.

PLUTARCH, ever fond of parallels, and so of contrasts, puts in contrast the poetry of Antimachus[*] and the portraits of Dionysius—alike in traces of effort, and redolent of the lamp—with the paintings of Nicomachus[†] and the verses of Homer, alike struck off with readiness and ease. Cicero compliments his brother, Quintus Tullius, on having despatched four tragedies in sixteen days. Horace refers to, not in the way of compliment, a certain Cassius, whose custom it was to compose four hundred verses every day. If this was the Cassius of Parma who is said to have been burned with his books, one can easily understand how easily he came by his funeral pile. The poem composed by Statius the younger, in honour of the marriage of Aruntius Stella, was professedly completed in two days, though containing two hundred and seventy-seven hexameters,—and Martial is sup-

---

[*] Who laboured at epics in the days of Socrates.
[†] Who, says Pliny, painted with a swift as well as masterly hand.

posed to have glanced at this epithalamium in an epigram on verse-making convivial and compulsory. Varus, another name of some note (but that not much) in the decline of Latin poetry, signalized himself by writing two hundred lines every day. The facility with which Galen wrote is proved by the great extent and diversified range of his *opera necnon opuscula omnia*.

Cicero may or may not have been ironical in "complimenting" his brother on his speed in composition. Any compliment addressed to him upon his own, he would have had the right to take seriously. During his retirement as a bereaved father, he wrote more books than M. Villemain finds it easy to follow in imagination: "On a peine à concevoir combien d'ouvrages il écrivit pendant ce long deuil." Without speaking of the Tusculan disputations and the treatise on Laws, which are still extant, in however mutilated a form, he finished within the same year his *Hortensius*, so dear to St. Augustin, his *Academics*, in four books, and a funeral eulogium on Porcia, Cato's sister. Reflecting on this *prodigieuse facilité*, always combined with the most severe perfection, the French critic just named can find in all literature nothing more astounding than the genius of Marcus Tullius Cicero.

Would Tully have complimented his brother, had the rate of his dramatic productions been that of Lope de Vega or of Hardy? Hardy bargained with the French comedians of his day—and he was nearly as much the creature of a day as they were—to keep them supplied with as many new plays as ever they could wish for; and that he kept his word may be inferred from a complacent boast in the preface to his fifth volume, that he had written more than six hundred dramas. Jodelle, again, who was frequently charged by Henry II. to provide the French court with dramatic *divertissements*, is known to have devoted no more than ten forenoons to any one of his tragedies, while his comedy of *Eugène* was finished in four sittings. As for Lope de Vega, well may Mr. Ticknor treat his characteristic facility as akin to improvisation. He is said to have dictated verse more rapidly than an amanuensis could take it down, and to have written out in two days a play which a copyist could scarcely manage to transcribe within the same time. The Homeric epithet of *inarithmeticable* is perhaps the fittest descriptive of his sum total.

Dryden's rival, "fat hulking Shadwell," dashed off his comedies as fast as he could write. In one year, 1678, Dryden himself published six complete plays, with what Johnson terms a celerity of performance which, though all Langbaine's charges of plagiarism should be allowed, shows such facility of composition, such readiness of language, and such copiousness of sentiment, as since the name of Lope de Vega perhaps no other author had ever possessed. On the other hand, Dryden avowedly spent a fortnight in composing and correcting the Ode on St. Cecilia's

Day. But what is this, Johnson exclaims, to the patience and diligence of Boileau, whose *Equivoque*, a poem of only three hundred and forty-six lines, took from his life eleven months to write it, and three years to revise it? Boileau, however, could openly compliment, and perhaps inwardly envied, the rapidity with which Molière composed:

> "Rare et sublime esprit, dont la fertile veine
> Ignore en écrivant le travail et la peine."

Rousseau was free to own, in regard of his four letters to M. de Malesherbes (in 1762), which he dashed off *sans brouillon, rapidement, à trait de plume,* and without so much as reading them over before committing them to the press, that they were probably the only thing he wrote with ease his whole life long. Jean Jacques, with all his morbid excess of vanity, seems to have been not vain enough—perhaps for once he was too proud—to emulate Voltaire's boast of doing a tragedy at the rate of more than an act a day. There is a dash at least of the pride that apes humility in Byron's avowal to Moore, ("what I would not say to everybody,") that he wrote *The Bride of Abydos* in four days, and *The Corsair* in ten. He professes to take this to be a most humiliating confession, as proving his own want of judgment in publishing, and the public's in reading, things which "cannot have stamina for permanent attention."* The German

---

* The four days of the *Bride* refer, it seems, to the first sketch only. But the *Corsair* was, from beginning to end, by Moore's

novelist Hoffmann's works were written with what by Mr. Carlyle is called "incredible speed"; and many are the marks they bear of haste; indeed it is seldom that any piece is perfected, or its "brilliant and often genuine elements blended in harmonious union." The same critic comments on the high proficiency of Scott in what he terms the "extempore style" of writing,— Sir Walter's rapidity being extreme, and "the matter produced excellent, considering." Mr. Carlyle hails it as a valuable faculty, this of ready writing, and even affirms that for Scott's purpose it was clearly the only good mode; for by much labour he could not have added one guinea to his copyright, nor could the reader on the sofa have lain a whit more at ease. "It was in all ways necessary that these works should be produced rapidly; and, round or not, be thrown off like Giotto's O." But, on the other hand, the critic would not be himself if he failed, at the same time, strenuously to urge that, in the way of writing, no great thing was ever or will ever be done with ease, but with difficulty. He bids ready writers with any faculty in them lay this to heart: it is not with ease

---

testimony, struck off at a heat. Nearly two hundred lines a day were the average in this instance—a rate of production that, his biographer says, would be altogether incredible, if we had not Byron's own, *plus* John Murray's, word for it. "Such an achievement,—taking into account the surpassing beauty of the work,—is perhaps wholly without a parallel in the history of genius." Moore takes it to show that "*écrire par passion*," as Rousseau expresses it, may be a shorter road to perfection than any that Art has ever struck out.

that any man shall do his best, in any shape. "Virgil and Tacitus, were they ready writers? The whole Prophecies of Isaiah are not equal in extent to this cobweb of a review article." Shakspeare, it is admitted, may be supposed to have written with rapidity, but not till he had thought with intensity. And herein, we are assured, truly lies the secret of the matter: such swiftness of mere writing, after due energy of preparation, is doubtless the right method. "The hot furnace having long worked and simmered, let the pure gold flow out at one gush. It was Shakspeare's plan: no easy writer he, or he had never been a Shakspeare." Milton, again, the same authority sharply distinguishes in the same way from the mob of gentlemen who write with ease; nór did he attain Shakspeare's faculty of ever writing fast *after* long preparation, but struggled while he wrote. Did Dante write easily,—he that saw himself "growing lean" over his Divine Comedy? Did Petrarch? Goethe tells us he "had nothing sent him in his sleep;" and Schiller, as an unfortunate and unhealthy man, "*könnte nie fertig werden*," never could get done.* But

---

* "Cease, therefore, O ready writer, to brag openly of thy rapidity and facility; to thee (if thou be in the manufacturing line) it is a benefit, an increase of wages; but to me it is sheer loss, worsening of my pennyworth: why wilt thou brag of it to me? Write easily, by steam if thou canst contrive it, and canst sell it; but hide it like virtue!" And then Mr. Carlyle quotes Sheridan's *mot* about easy writing being sometimes ineffably hard reading; and adds, that it is always sure to be rather useless reading, which indeed (to a creature of few years and much work) he reckons to be the hardest of all.

to recur to Scott. His rapidity Mr. Carlyle takes to be a proof and consequence of the solid health of the man, bodily and spiritual; a proof of his soundness of nervous system, his practicality of mind, and of his having the knack of his trade. In the most flattering view, rapidity is thus accepted as betokening health of mind; but much also, perhaps most of all, will depend on health of body. William Cobbett is cited, one of the healthiest of men, as a greater improviser than even Walter Scott. Pierre Bayle is cited, as the writer of enormous folios, "one sees not on what motive-principle; he flowed on for ever, a mighty tide of ditch-water; and even died flowing, with the pen in his hand." But to Mr. Carlyle's thinking, the most unaccountable ready-writer of all, probably, is the common editor of a daily newspaper. Mr. Thackeray, however, awards the palm to the fashionable authoress. The thousands of pages that Lady Flummery has covered with ink he declares to be past belief. The readiest of ready pens has she: her Pegasus gallops over hotpressed satin so as to distance all gentlemen riders:* like Camilla, it scours the plain—of Bath, and never seems punished or fatigued; only it runs so fast that it leaves all sense behind it. Contrast

---

* "You must have remarked, madam, in respect of this literary fecundity, that your amiable sex possesses vastly greater capabilities than ours, and that while a man is painfully labouring over a letter of two sides, a lady will produce a dozen pages, crossed, dashed, and so beautifully neat and close, as to be wellnigh invisible."—*Character Sketches.*

Miss Mitford's "It is a tremendous undertaking!" on actually beginning a novel; "for I write with extreme slowness, labour, and difficulty; and, whatever you [Haydon] may think, there is a great difference of facility in different minds. I am the slowest writer, I suppose, in England, and touch and retouch perpetually." Many years later we find her telling another correspondent, "For my own part, I am convinced that without pains there will be no really good writing. I find the most successful writers the most careful." And she asserts herself still so difficult to satisfy, that she has written a long preface (of some forty pages) to her collected dramatic works three times over, many parts far more than three times; and can foresee that there will still be much to do when the proofs go through her hands. To Mr. J. S. Mill, as editor of a quarterly review, M. de Tocqueville, as a contributor, writes: "You must think me very slow. You would forgive me if you knew how hard it is for me to satisfy myself, and how impossible for me to finish things incompletely." He has always thought, he says, that the public has the right to require authors to strain their powers to their utmost, and he endeavours to act up to this duty.

Plutarch cites the case of Agatharcus the painter bragging of the celerity and ease with which he despatched his pieces, to whom Zeuxis replied, "If I boast, it shall be of the slowness with which I finish mine."* It is quite possible to overdo this. Samuel Rogers is known as one of the authors who have taken too much pains with their writings: the *Pleasures of Memory* employed him seven years, *Columbus* fourteen, *Human Life* six, *Italy* fourteen; and even after the publication of these poems he did not cease to correct them. In these days of hasty composition, it has been said, one cannot but respect so much patience and so much concentrated labour, and well-known maxims would lead one to anticipate that very great excellence would be the result. A sage authority believes these maxims to be, in most cases, erroneous, and that such extremely slow production is very rarely favourable to the production of works of genius. "Writers forget what they mean to say. Who can answer for the exact shade of thought which he intended to express nine years ago?" A student of the most celebrated poems of Mr. Rogers discovers many expressions out of which a patient elaboration has extracted the whole meaning, and many paragraphs of which the first flow has been destroyed by interpolated thoughts and gradually modified ideas. Bembo, perhaps the most distinguished of the Ciceronians of the *renaissance*, is said to have had in use forty portfolios, into each of which passed

---

* "For ease and speed in the execution seldom give a work any lasting importance, or exquisite beauty; while, on the other hand, the time which is expended in labour, is recovered and repaid in the duration of the product."—Plutarch, *Life of Pericles*.

in succession every page he wrote, that it might be subjected step by step to all the corrections (call them stripes,—forty, *not* save one) of his exacting taste. Malherbe was another Rogers in fastidious slowness. He would spoil half a quire of paper in composing and decomposing and recomposing a stanza. It is reckoned that, during the twenty-five most prolific years of his life, he composed no more than, on the average, thirty-three verses per annum. Of Balzac* (the seventeenth century one, not the nineteenth,) it has been said that he took as much pains to pen a paragraph as the ancient sculptors did to make a god. Some of the *Maximes* of La Rochefoucauld were amended more than thirty times, before he could compass the precision of express he deemed indispensable. As Mr. Carlyle is free to allow, in his *Life of Schiller*, there is a purism in taste, a rigid fantastical demand of perfection, a horror at approaching the limits of vulgarity, which obstructs the frank impulse of the faculties, and, if excessive, would altogether deaden them. But the opposite excess he contends to be much more frequent, and, for high endowments, infinitely more pernicious. " That too much care does

---

* Malherbe and Balzac are credited with having founded in French literature the polished style, "dans l'enfantement duquel on arrive de la pensée à l'expression, lentement par degrés à force de *tâtonnements* et de *ratures*."—Sainte-Beuve, *Portraits de Femmes*, p. 20. Balzac once told the Chevalier de Méré that he could not satisfy himself with the diction of a certain little note he had to write to a provincial mayor, until he had spent four mornings over it.

hurt in any of our tasks is a doctrine so flattering to indolence, that we ought to receive it with extreme caution." Of all our authors he takes Gray to be perhaps the only one that from fastidiousness of taste has written less than he should have done; while there are thousands that have erred the other way.

Sir Joshua Reynolds made the just observation, that, although men of ordinary talents may be highly satisfied with their productions, men of true genius never are. Cowper quotes the remark applaudingly in one of his letters; and to Cowper himself the remark has been particularly applied, for he took infinite pains with his verses, and was seldom satisfied with them in the end. The practical value of all this toil and care is well said by Mr. Robert Bell to be exhibited instructively in the result; his labour obliterated all traces of labour; shaping his thoughts, after repeated experiments, into just and natural forms, he made them come out with an appearance of the most unpremeditated ease. The little poem, of three stanzas only, *On a Goldfinch*, he kept under the revising process for several months, and polishing it, he tells us, as a lapidary "rubs away the roughness of a stone." "I never suffer a line to pass," he says on another occasion, "till I have made it as good as I can." But he set too just a value upon time to emulate the finical scrupulosity attributed to Waller, who, says Fenton, spent the greater part of a summer in correcting a poem of ten lines—which precious decade was inscribed in her Grace of York's copy of Tasso. Southey, midway in *Madoc*, declared himself convinced that the best way of writing* is to write rapidly, and correct at leisure: "*Madoc* would be a better poem if written in six months, than if six years were devoted to it." Of *Thalaba* he writes, when finished, and half ready for the press: "I am polishing and polishing, and hewing it to pieces with surgeon severity. Yesterday I drew the pen across 600 lines." 1200 lines in a week were the quickest run (in sailors' phrase) that he ever made, he tells Mr. Landor; adding, "But this is nothing to what you have accomplished," in *Count Julian;* "and your manner involves so much thought (excess of meaning being its fault), that the same number of lines must cost thrice as much expense of passion and of the reasoning faculty to you than [? as] they would to me." It is observable how strenuous Southey was in disclaiming, after a certain period of life, the facility and speed of composition imputed to him. To one of his publishers he writes in 1835: "It is long since I have been a rapid writer: the care with which I write, and the pains which I take in collecting materials and making myself fully acquainted with the subject before me, render it impossible that I should be so." And two years later he assures his excellent friend old Mr. Bedford,

---

* Voltaire says in his commentaries on Corneille, that an author may write with the rapidity of genius, but should correct with scrupulous deliberation.

"As for eagerness of composition, my dear Grosvenor, whatever ardour of that kind I once possessed has long since been expended. For many years whatever I have written has been composed slowly and deliberately." The *Colloquies* were for long years in hand, and he even asserted of perhaps every paper he wrote for the *Quarterly Review* after the first six or eight numbers, that it cost him thrice the time in composing that it would have cost any one else, to say nothing of the time employed in reading for the specific subject. Dr. Johnson was for advising every young man beginning to compose, to do it as fast as he can, to get a habit of having his mind to start promptly; so much more difficult is it to improve in speed than in accuracy. Dr. Watson's avowed preference for accuracy, lest one should get bad habits of composing in a slovenly manner, only moved Johnson to a "Why, sir, you are confounding *doing* inaccurately with the *necessity* of doing inaccurately. A man knows when his composition is inaccurate, and when he thinks fit he'll correct it. But if a man is accustomed to compose slowly, and with difficulty, upon all occasions, there is danger that he may not compose at all, as we do not like to do that which is not done easily; and, at any rate, more time is consumed in a small matter than ought to be." Dr. Watson thought to pose Johnson by the stubborn fact that Blair took a week to compose a sermon. "Then, sir," rejoined the English doctor, "that is for want of the habit of composing quickly, which I am insisting one should acquire." Dr. Blair's credit being creditably dear to Dr. Watson, the latter explained that the reverend Hugh was not composing all the week, but only such hours as he found himself disposed for composition. "Nay, sir," was Johnson's reply, "unless you tell me the time he took, you tell me nothing. If I say I took a week to walk a mile, and have had the gout five days, and been ill otherwise another day, I have taken but one day." And he went on to say, he, the author of the *Rambler*, the poet, pamphleteer, dictionary doctor, and what not, that he had himself composed about forty sermons: that he had begun a sermon after dinner, and sent it off by post that night. He wrote forty-eight of the printed octavo pages of his *Life of Savage* at a sitting; but then he sat up all night. Six sheets in a day had he written of translation from the French. Boswell's interpolated remark, in the capacity of a good listener, that we all must have observed how one man dresses himself slowly and another fast, met with his great friend's approving assent. "Yes, sir; it is wonderful how much time some people will consume in dressing; taking up a thing and looking at it, and laying it down, and taking it up again. Every one should get the habit of doing it quickly. I would say to a young divine, ' Here is your text; let us see how soon you can make a sermon.' Then I'd say, ' Let me see how much better you can make it.' Thus I should see both his powers and his judgment." Voltaire bragged to Bernis of having composed his tragedy of *Cassandre* (previously entitled *Olympie*) in six days, and calling it *L'Œuvre de six jours* accordingly; whereupon Bernis counselled him to bestow another six days' labour on improving, correcting, and revising the style and details of his piece. Be it admitted, however, with the leading French critic of the age of Scribe, Balzac, and Georges Sand, that, all due limitations presupposed, " la fertilité," including *la facilité*, " est une des plus grandes marques de l'esprit." It is of the first of the names just now cited that Sainte-Beuve has said, that to be writing plays was, with M. Scribe, in his earlier years, a trade as well as a talent, but that, in later years, to judge by the rapidly increasing number of them and their sustained success, to go on writing plays had become his pleasure and hobby,—nay, a necessity to him, and a part of his nature.

Like Southey, that very different man and writer, Sydney Smith, when he had any subject in hand, was indefatigable in reading, searching, inquiring, seeking every source of information, and—perhaps in this respect, *un*like Southey—discussing it with any man of sense or cultivation who crossed his path (for here the opportunities as well as the disposition of the canonical diner-out and clerical man of the world were in salient contrast with those of the recluse of Greta Hall). But having once mastered it, as Lady

Holland tells us, Sydney Smith would sit down and commit his ideas to paper with the same rapidity* that they flowed out in his conversation,—no hesitating, no erasures, no stopping to consider and round his periods, no writing for effect, but a pouring out of the fulness of his mind and feelings, for he was heart and soul in whatever he undertook. He mused well before he took pen in hand; but while he was musing, the fire burned, and anon he spake with his pen, *currente calamo;* and as he penned, the fire, as it were, ran along the paper.

Faria, the Portuguese author, whose ardour in literature hastened his end, wrote daily, by his own account, twelve sheets, and plumed himself on such facility in rhetorical turns and flourishes, that in a single day he could compose a hundred different addresses of congratulation and condolence. Fénelon composed *Télémaque* in three months, and there were not ten erasures in the original MS. The like facility is ascribed to Gibbon, after his first volume; and Isaac Disraeli couples with him the author of the *Wealth of Nations*, copiously dictating in fluent ease as he paced the room. Charles Dibdin's facility of composition is celebrated in the production of nine hundred

---

* "His power of abstraction was so great that he would begin to compose, with as much rapidity and ease as another man would write a letter, those essays which are before the world, . . . and this in the midst of all the conversation and interruptions of a family party, with talking or music going on."—*Memoir of the Rev. Sydney Smith*, i. 115.

songs. What has been called the finest of Oriental romances, Beckford's *Vathek*, was professedly composed (in French too) at a single sitting,—the writer being then in his twentieth year, before completing which he published *Vathek*, and was famous. How Diderot wrote long works within the week, sometimes within almost the four-and-twenty hours, surprising proofs are on record,—only to provoke a caustic critic to the remark that internal evidence makes such feats quite credible, most of Diderot's works bearing the clearest traces of extemporaneousness; *stans pede in uno*. The German sentimentalist La Fontaine[*] wrote with such velocity (he did, as Mr. Carlyle words it, some hundred and fifty weeping volumes in his time) that he was obliged to hold in, and "write only two days in the week." The same critic makes merry, in his sombre way, over that prince of all playwrights, Kotzebue, who "could manufacture plays with a speed and facility surpassing even Edinburgh novels"—for his muse is said, like other doves, to have hatched twins in the month. M. de Rémusat wrote his two plays on the Crusaders and on St. Domingo insurrection, ten acts, in twelve days; that is, as admiring reviewers compute it, an act a day, and after each drama a day to read it over: "on ne saurait entrer d'un

---

[*] Of his more celebrated French namesake M. Sainte-Beuve observes that he prepared himself "par une longue et laborieuse éducation, à cette facilité merveilleuse qu'il garda jusqu'aux derniers jours de sa vieillesse."—*Portraits Littéraires*, i. 491.

pied plus léger dans la rapidité romantique." Both plays were lions for the season in the salons of high-bred Paris: dead lions now, this many a day. Rapidity, "as of pulsing auroras, as of dancing lightnings," is made a special characteristic of John Sterling, by his guide, philosopher, and friendly biographer, who admires his incredible facility of labour, and of putting his thoughts on paper "with a swift felicity, ingenuity, brilliancy, and general excellence, of which, under such conditions of swiftness, I have never seen a parallel. Essentially an *improviser* genius; as his father too was," the slashing Captain of the *Times*. Charles Brockden Brown's facility is called by Mr. Prescott "unpardonable precipitancy"—three of his romances (and he wrote *Wieland, Arthur Mervyn*, and *Edgar Huntly;* not that these were the three,) being thrown off in the course of one year—written with the printer's devil literally at his elbow; one being begun before another was completed, and all of them before a regular, well-digested plan was devised for their execution. A judicious critic of our own day complains of almost all our novel-writers as writing too fast,— some indeed making a boast of never recopying a line, and of wasting but a small amount of time on corrections of the most elementary kind; these it is who talk of sending off to the printer the first draft, just as they have scrawled it down,[*] without recasting or

---

[*] There are good names on record by way of justificatory precedent in this respect. Sydney Smith, we know, hardly ever altered or cor-

reconsideration, as they would talk of anything else they held praiseworthy, not seeing that they are pronouncing their own condemnation when they betray their carelessness. "This easy writing is terribly hard reading, and does no one any credit—neither the writer who puts it forth without a blush, nor the public which accepts it without complaint." If it were not for a faithful few who do really take pains, and make of their work a labour of love, the critic here quoted would despair of our present race of novelists, considering the system on which they work to be so essentially untrue to art that no real good does or can result from it.

---

rected what he had written; indeed he is said to have been so impatient of this, as hardly to bear the trouble of even looking over what he had penned. Frequently he would throw the manuscript down on the table as soon as written, and say, "There, it is done; now, Kate, do look it over, and put dots to the i's, and strokes to the t's"—and then would sally forth to his morning's walk. But it was something that he did, even by proxy, care for these complementary attentions to his "copy." To many, his inferiors, foul copy is fair.

XVII.

Labor Limae.

THERE is no love lost, it would seem, between those who in composition always keep the file going, and the bolder, hastier, more dashing spirits who write off at a heat, and despise correction or revision, and hate the fastidious, finical ways of the file altogether. The high-flyers whose motto or maxim is, *Stet:* "what I have written, I have written," have no patience with the indefatigable emendators who never can let well alone. And those to whom the *labor limæ* is by instinct and by habit a labour of love, regard the impetuous scamperers who claim to be above such labour, as themselves almost below contempt.

Perhaps the elect representatives of Italian literature in its most elegant moods and tenses, are *facilè principes* in their manipulation of the file. Petrarch's lyrical pieces, which, as a foreign critic says, like miniatures, from their minuteness, demand the highest finish of detail, were by him corrected with an all but "inconceivable" expenditure of pains; some of them appearing, from the memo-

randa which he has left, to have been submitted to
the file for weeks, nay months, before he dismissed
them. "His fine ear disposed him to refuse all
but the most harmonious combinations of sound."
Prescott notes it as a curious fact, that notwithstanding the apparent facility and graces of Berni's
style, it was wrought with infinite care: some of his
verses were corrected from twenty to thirty times;
and many of his countrymen found out their mistake
in imitating it, when they mistook its familiarity of
manner for facility of execution. It has been told of
Bembo's scrupulous care to give his compositions the
utmost finish, that he kept forty portfolios, into which
every sheet entered successively, and was only taken
out to undergo his corrections, before it entered into
what Mr. Hallam expressively calls the next limbo of
this purgatory.

Dionysius of Halicarnassus, speaking of the exquisite finish given by Plato and Isocrates to their style,
compares their works rather to pieces of fine chasing
or sculpture than of writing; and a modern critic
takes the minuter workmanship of chasing, the sort of
gem-engraving which this seems to imply, to be aptly
descriptive of the elaborate compositions of Isocrates,
who was said to have employed more years in writing
the panegyric on the Persian War alone, than
Alexander took to conquer all Asia. Nor was this
excessive labour deemed incompatible with the
highest excellence in oratory, at least with the cul-

tivation of all its graces. As for Plato, whom no one can charge with littleness, with miniature beauties, with sacrificing force and dignity to polish, and of whose diction it was indeed said, that the Father of the gods, had he spoken in Greek, would have used no other language but Plato's—*his* language, though compared by Cicero to the inspirations of poetry, and by Quinctilian to those of the Delphic oracle, was by no means, as an Edinburgh Reviewer reminds us, poured forth with the readiness which the admirers of modern fluency term Nature, and in which they think a true genius for eloquence consists, although it is only a habit acquired by a mechanical process. So far from pouring out his mighty flood like our modern *improvisatori*, he continued to his eightieth year correcting and new-moulding the language of his Dialogues; and after his death there was found a note-book, in which he had written the opening words of his *Republic* several times over, in different arrangements. Lord Brougham argues from the redundant repetitions in the fourth Philippic of Demosthenes, the pains which that great orator had bestowed upon the composition of each part, and the value which he set upon the result; the choice and the disposition of the words, even in passages apparently of inferior importance, having been demonstrably a work of mature deliberation, and of some difficulty. Nor are critics ever tired of referring to Virgil dictating a number of verses in the morning, spending the day in revising, correcting, and reducing them, and comparing himself, if we may take the word of Aulus Gellius for it, to a she-bear licking her misshapen offspring into shape.

> "Some curious painter, taught by art to dare,
> (For they with poets in that title share)
> When he would undertake a glorious frame
> Of lasting worth, and fadeless as his fame,
> Long he contrives, and weighs the bold design,
> Long holds his doubting hand ere he begin,
> And justly, then, proportions every stroke and line,
>   And oft he brings it to review,
> And oft he dares deface, and dashes oft anew."

So writes John Oldham, in honour of his contemporary Ben Jonson, defending him from critics who "called that slowness which was care and industry," and expressing a hearty wish to share his shame, if diligence be deemed a fault, and if to be faultless must deserve their blame. With rigour Ben arraigned each guilty line, nor spared one faulty phrase because 'twas *his*. Students of the literature of those days have adverted with amazement to the pains and polishing bestowed by Fairfax on his version of Tasso, his first stanza in particular, after it had been printed, being emended again and again. The Cambridge MS. of Milton's *Lycidas* has numerous passages that had been erased and re-written—sometimes re-written twice; rarely are there many consecutive lines, Professor Masson says, without some verbal alteration; and invariably the alteration is for the better. In the interval between writing it and the publication of the printed text, Milton had evidently, his biographer concludes, hovered over the "rathe primrose" passage with fastidious fondness, touching every colour and fitting every word till he brought it to its present perfection of beauty. Etienne Pasquier finds honourable mention for not having committed his writings to the press until after five-and-twenty years of sedulous digestion. He polished and ré-polished them *à longues pauses,* "mille et mille fois passant et repassant l'œil sur eux," his namesake Nicolas tells us, "en se hâtant lentement." *Festinans lentè.* Malherbe is proverbial for his taking a year to write a strophe. Voiture used to rally Vaugelas on the time and trouble he took over a very small matter; saying that he would never make an end of it; that while he was polishing one part, the French language was undergoing change enough to necessitate his re-writing the whole of the rest—like Martial's barber, who took such a time over a beard, that before he had come to an end with it, a new beard was in palpable progress.

> "Entrapelus tonsor dum circuit ora Luperci,
> Expungitque genas, altera barba subit."

So, while Vaugelas loiters, *altera lingua subit.* The Abbé d'Olivet says of Patru, that "le soin excessif qu'il apportoit à la correction de ses ouvrages, lui donnoit le temps de vieillir sur une période." Pascal spending twenty days in perfecting a single letter (to a Provincial); La Rochefoucauld spending fifteen years *à enfanter un petit volume* of 200 pages; La

Bruyère passing his whole life long in preparing his *Caractères* (and only claiming them as his after Theophrastus), and approving himself an author that posterity must respect even to his colons and commas, as well as for the exquisite choice of his words and the admirable turn of his phrases; these are stock quotations for all time.

Shaftesbury declares the *limæ labor* to be the great grievance of his countrymen. "An English author would be all genius." Already in those days there were representatives of Churchill, to whom blotting out and correcting were so hateful that he told his publisher it was like cutting away one's flesh. He had no notion, he, of what Young calls

> "filing off the mortal part
> Of glowing thought with Attic art."

He would have gone along with Cobbett in his counsel, self-applied at least, "Never think of what you write; let it go; no patching."* Niebuhr's rule is a sort of parallel passage: "Try never to strike out any part of what you have once written down. Punish yourself by allowing once or twice something to pass, though you see you might give it better." Jean Paul Richter, a riotous innovator in style, yet recalls with a sigh of

---

* But then Cobbett adds, and the addition (sometimes ignored by those who quote him) is material: "As your pen moves, bear constantly in mind that it is making strokes which are to remain for ever." Cobbett's own writings are cited by Archdeacon Hare as a proof of the excellence of his rule: what they may want in elegance, they more than make up for in strength.

regret the "once upon a time" in Germany when a Lessing, a Winckelmann, filed their periods like Plato or Cicero, and Klopstock and Schiller their verses like Virgil or Horace; when, as Tacitus, "we thought more of disleafing than of covering with leaves—a disleafing which, as in the vine, ripens and incites the grapes." Correction, he complains, had come to seem as costly to his contemporaries of the craft, "as if, like Count Alfieri, we had them to make on printing-paper, at the charges of our printer and purse. The public book-market is to be our bleach-green; and the public, instead of us, is to correct; and then, in the second edition, we can pare off somewhat, and clap on somewhat." That some authors cannot correct, Bayle holds for certain: they compose with wisdom, but exhaust all their force, he says: when they come to review their works, they fly with but one wing; the first fire does not return. To More, the Platonist, correction was a much greater labour than composition. It is curious to contrast the case of a Scaliger (Julius) writing with such accuracy that his MSS. and the printed copy corresponded page for page, and line for line; and of a Tasso, whose MSS., still preserved, are illegible from the vast number of their corrections.* Professedly concerning himself with

---

* See the chapter on Literary Composition, in the *Curiosities of Literature.* Mr. Disraeli gives a facsimile of one page of Pope's Homer, to show how continual were his corrections and critical erasures. He refers, too, on the same topic, to Madame Dacier perpetually retouching

neither orthography nor punctuation, Montaigne says, "Whoever shall know how lazy I am, and how indulgent to my own humour, will easily believe that I had rather write as many more essays, than be bound to revise these over again for so childish a correction." "I add, but I correct not," is elsewhere his explicit declaration. A superstitious regard to the correction of his sheets is mentioned by Johnson as one of the peculiarities of Richard Savage, and a paradoxical one enough it may seem in him. He often altered, revised, recurred to his first reading or punctuation, and again adopted the alteration; he was dubious and irresolute without end, his biographer tells us, as on a question of the last importance, and after all was seldom satisfied: the intrusion or omission of a comma was sufficient to discompose him, and he would lament an error of a single letter as a heavy calamity. In one of his letters relating to the printing of some verses, he remarks, that he had, with regard to the correction of proofs, "a spell upon him;" and indeed the anxiety with which he dwelt upon the minutest and most trifling niceties deserved no other name, in Johnson's robust reckoning, than that of fascination.

---

her version—some parts of which were translated in six or seven manners, not without the frequent note in the margin, "I have not done it yet." Isocrates too is mentioned, spending ten years on one of his works; and Virgil, pronouncing his Æneid imperfect after eleven years' labour; and Dion Cassius spending twelve on his history; and Diodorus Siculus thirty on his. Thirty were spent by Vaugelas on his Quintus Curtius, though of his six or seven versions, the first was, by competent critics, thought to be the best.

Pope is characterized by the same biographer of the poets, as one of those few whose labour is their pleasure: he never passed a fault unamended by indifference, nor quitted it by despair. "It was as pleasant to me to correct as to write," says Pope himself, in the Preface to his Works. Swift frequently revised the first impression of his works; and the numerous interlineations and erasures which his editors record, bear witness to his desire to amend his composition to the utmost of his power. Far from speedy was Goldsmith in his verse-making, whatever he might be and do in prose, for pot-boiling or other purposes. His *Deserted Village*, as may be seen in Mr. Forster's Life of him, was paused over, altered, polished, and refined. Bishop Percy is cited as noting the delightful facility with which Goldsmith's prose flowed forth unblotted with erasures, as a contrast to the labour and pains of his verse interlined with countless alterations. Ten lines (from the fifth to the fifteenth) of the poem above-named occupied him an entire forenoon, and after reading them to a friend who called in upon him, "Come," he added, "let me tell you this is no bad morning's work." That "come," had all the cheery meaning, accent, and *abandon* of the French *allons donc*.

Cowper assures Unwin that to touch, and retouch, is, though some writers boast of negligence, and others would be ashamed to show their foul copies, the secret of almost all good writing, especially in verse. "I am never weary of it myself, and if you would take as much pains as I do, you would have no need to ask for my corrections." With all that indifference to fame for which he sincerely asked credit, Cowper confessedly took the utmost pains to deserve it. Considering the taste of his day to be refined and delicate to excess, and feeling certain that to disgust this delicacy of taste by a slovenly inattention to it, would be to forfeit at once all hopes of being useful, he gives this as the reason, in another letter to Mr. Unwin, why, although he has written more verse within one year (1781) than perhaps any man in England, he has finished and polished, and touched and retouched with the utmost care.

Johnson attributes this peculiarity to Gray as a writer, that he did not write his pieces first rudely, and then correct them, but laboured every line as it arose in the train of composition. The converse, this, of Southey's precept and example; for we find him assuring Scott, while on the look-out for the publication of *Marmion*, that "no man of real genius was ever yet a puritanical stickler for correctness," and that "the best artists, both in poetry and painting, have produced the most. Give me more Lays, and correct them at leisure for after editions—not laboriously, but when the amendment comes naturally and unsought for." It never does to sit down doggedly to correct, he adds; and that might be Gray's opinion too. At any rate Gray is known to have found the *limæ labor* irksome and unsatisfactory,—witness the many unfinished pieces he left behind him, such as the *Agrippina*, the *Ode to Vicissitude*, the fragment on *Education and Government*, etc. Being once asked why he had never finished the last-named piece, he replied, Because he could not; and then explained that, having been used to write chiefly lyric poetry, short enough to allow of polish with care in every part, he could now scarcely write in any other manner; the labour of similar polish in a long poem would hardly be tolerable. Mr. Mathias got a similar answer when he asked Gray why he had written so little poetry: "Because of the great exertion it cost him in the labour of composition." He belonged to the Fresnoy school of finishers,—or, as young ladies might term it, finishing-school; that Fresnoy to whose poem on the art of painting Pope's couplet refers :

> " How finished with illustrious toil appears
> This small, well-polished gem, the work of years ! "

Twenty years, namely ; not a year less.

Although Hume is represented as having written with such ease that he hardly ever corrected, it is shown by Lord Brougham to have been exactly the reverse ; the manuscript of his History bearing marks*

---

* John Foster writes to a friend in reference to the MS. of his essays: "I wish, for the proof that I have been *sometime* laborious, that you could see this manuscript." Later, again, he urges the incompetency of a reader to do justice to the labours of an author, unless himself one ; and affirms the very many times that he has spent a whole day in

of composition anxiously laboured, words being written and scored out, and even several times changed, until he could find the expression to his mind. The MS. of his Dialogues is written in the same manner, and even his letters show the like tokens of care and reconsideration.

Gerard Hamilton, whose conversation was so easy and agreeable, was in composition laboriously affected; "a literary fop of the most determined cast," Sir James Prior calls him; for a stop omitted, a sentence not fully turned, or a word that upon reflection could be amended, was quite enough to warrant the recall of a note to a familiar acquaintance. So with his speeches in the House, which he not only got by heart[*] but rehearsed in private; one of these three hours long, is known to have been inflicted on a friend three several times. Burke polished his *Reflections on the French Revolution* with extraordinary care, more than a dozen revises being thrown off and destroyed, by

---

adjusting two or three sentences amidst a perplexity about niceties which would be far too impalpable to be even comprehended, if one were to state them, by the greatest number of readers. "Neither is the reader aware how often, after this has been done, the sentences or paragraphs so adjusted were, after several hours' deliberation the next day, all blotted out. The labour of months lies in this discarded state in the manuscripts," etc.—(To the Rev. Joseph Hughes, April, 1805.)

[*] Sheridan, in like manner, always prepared his speeches; the highly-wrought passages in the Begum speech were written beforehand and committed to memory. Great practice, strong passion, and a fervid imagination may, observes Mr. G. P. Marsh, confer the gift of unstudied eloquence, but the orations which after-ages read with applause are almost never the result of unpremeditated effort.

Dodsley's account, before the writer could please himself. And yet, after all this, we have Francis, the presumed original of Junius, once for all wishing Burke would let him teach him how to write English. "Why will you not allow yourself to be persuaded that polish is material to preservation?" Accustomed to dictate letters with apparently careless facility, Burke is described as, on the contrary, fastidious with whatever he wrote for the press. "Great pains and frequent and careful revisions were expended . . . blots and erasures were so numerous as to render his manuscripts frequently difficult to decipher." Of Canning, his biographer tells us, that with a broad sense of great faculties in others, he was himself fastidious to excess about the slightest turns of expression. He would correct his speeches, and amend their verbal graces, till he nearly polished out the original spirit. His alterations were often so minute and extensive, that the printers are said to have found it easier to recompose the matter afresh in type than to correct it. The late Bishop Lonsdale, whom the Lichfield diocese found in no merely conventional sense a father in God, was forced, latterly, by pressure of diocesan business, to give up, as a rule, writing new sermons, and to be content with altering his old ones; and his son-in-law and biographer deems it hard to understand how he managed to see his way, always without hesitation, through such a labyrinth of corrections as some of them exhibit. He was never satisfied with anything he wrote so long as he could see how it might be done better; and he used, Mr. Denison tells us, "to alter his sermons in pencil in the vestry, and even in the pulpit, before he began preaching." Dr. Burney used to press the services of his daughters in elaborating his History of Music, employing them in copying and recopying his "painful" manuscripts, "tracing over and over again the same page when his nicety of judgment suggested fresh alterations." Jacob Bryant, who figures prominently in the Diary pages of Dr. Burney's daughter, is therein commemorated for a similar scrupulousness of polish; his avowal being that he copied everything over, himself, and that three transcribings were the fewest he could ever make do; but, generally, nothing went from him to the press under seven.

Jeffrey refers to Sheridan's way of dallying fondly with the ideas of which he was most proud, and employing himself so very patiently in polishing the diamonds which had been brought to light by the richness of his native vein,—quite a different kind of work from that of a drudge, who can do nothing extempore; for instances of this elaboration are common in writers the farthest removed from all suspicion of slowness or penury of invention. Ariosto, the most original and prolific of the continental poets, is said to have written the first stanza of his *Orlando* ten or twelve times over; just as the same daring and ready hands which "covered the Roman frescoes with their swift and unchangeable creations, have left innumerable traces of the minutest labour and most fastidious corrections, in the finishing of other works, over which, in a different mood, it was their pleasure, or their fancy, to linger."* Ben Jonson's Gallus thus characterizes Virgil, taking his cue from Horace :—

> " And yet so chaste and tender is his ear,
> In suffering any syllable to pass,
> That he thinks may become the honour'd name
> Of issue to his so examined self,
> That all the lasting fruits of his full merit,
> In his own poems, he doth still distaste ;
> As if his mind's piece, which he strove to paint,
> Could not with fleshly pencils have her right."

Buffon caused his *Époques de la Nature*, which he published in 1778, in his seventy-first year, and which is accounted the most perfect of his works, to be recopied no fewer (we are assured) than eighteen times.

Nothing, it has been said, can be more instructive than the manner in which M. Victor Cousin† confronts Rousseau's manuscripts with his printed works, showing, as he does, from corrections and erasures, by what

---

* The Earl of Dudley, in his letters to the Bishop of Llandaff, says of the MS. of Ariosto, preserved at Ferrara, that the inspection of it will greatly confirm the opinion of those who think that consummate excellence, united to the *appearance* of ease, is almost always the result of great labour. "The corrections are innumerable. In several passages where, as they now stand, the words and thoughts seem to flow along with the most graceful facility, and the rhyme to côme unsought for, have been (sic) altered over and over, till scarce a line of the first draught has been allowed to remain."

† In his *Fragments et Souvenirs* (1858).

successive steps Jean Jacques brought his style to perfection.* Thomson evidently considered the choice of language a matter of paramount importance, and to this object, says a biographer, he almost exclusively devoted the remarkable labours of revision he bestowed upon *The Seasons*. Endless were the changes he made in that poem from first to last—retrenchments, expansions, additions, verbal alterations, and transpositions.

> "But how severely with themselves proceed
> The men who write such verse as we can read!
> Their own strict judges, not a word they spare,
> That wants or force, or light, or weight, or care,"

says Pope,† in imitation of Horace (*At qui legitimum*

---

* Leon Curmer, the French publisher, used to tell an amusing story of Balzac, who had promised with enthusiasm to contribute to his projected periodical, *Les Français peints par eux-mêmes*, but grew cold, and kept so, after once the hot fit of delight in the novel speculation had passed away. Curmer could get nothing from him. At last, on the eve of publication, the printer's messenger was sent to Balzac's lodgings, with strict injunctions not to come back empty-handed. The envoy returned with three or four slips of paper, on which a few lines had been hastily scribbled. Curmer, however, knew his man. The manuscript was speedily in type, and a proof was despatched to the author. Balzac returned it, double its former size, with erasures, corrections, and additions crossing each other between the lines in inextricable confusion. Eight times was the process repeated, and at last the memorable "monograph" entitled *Nos Épiciers* was the result. "The corrections of that proof," Curmer used to say, "cost me one thousand francs; but I sold twenty thousand copies of the first number."

† Contrast with Pope's dictum the free-and-easy faith and practice of Chapelle :

> "Tout bon habitant du Marais
> Fait des vers qui ne coûtent guère,
> Moi c'est ainsi que je les fais,

cupiet fecisse poema, etc.) The manuscripts of La Fontaine the fabulist are rife with erasures and alterations; the same pieces are copied and recopied over and over again, and often with happy corrections. " You will think there is no end to my villanous emendations," is the opening sentence of one of Byron's letters from abroad to Lord Holland, full of revisions and retouchings. And of one favourite passage in the *Bride of Abydos* we are told by Moore that it was sent in successive scraps to the printer, correction following correction, and thought re-enforced by thought. Numerous examples are given of "that retouching process by which some of his most exquisite effects were obtained," and, notwithstanding his eagerness and facility, of his "anxious care in correcting." Waller's couplet is of standard application, though the application may be made ambiguous:

> " Poets lose half the praise they should have got,
> Could it be known what they discreetly blot."

Rogers himself informed the clerical reporter of his

> Et, si je voulois les mieux faire,
> Je les ferois bien plus mauvais."

Charles Nodier, in some stanzas *qu' à deux ou trois mots près aurait pu signer La Fontaine*, in Sainte-Beuve's judgment, thus "endorses" the sentiment of Chapelle, and follows in his wake :—

> " C'est ainsi que parlait Chapelle,
> Et moi je pense comme lui.
> Le vers qui vient sans qu'on l'appelle,
> Voilà le vers qu'on se rappelle.
> Rimer autrement, c'est ennui."

table-talk that he was for nine years engaged on the *Pleasures of Memory*, nearly as many on *Human Life*, and for sixteen on *Italy*. Hazlitt guessed as much from what he called the "finical finish" of the lines, which he was convinced were produced with labour and toil, (Sydney Smith's accouchement *mot* is hardly too good to be true of them,) and afterwards polished with painful industry. Rogers would have been proud to adopt the avowal of Henri Beyle (De Stendhal), that often and often he spent a quarter of an hour in reflecting whether to place an adjective before its substantive or after. Robert Hall, on the other hand, lamented as a serious defect his fastidious habit of recasting whole sentences and pages; improving, rejecting the improvement, and repenting the rejection. The resultant air of stiffness and formality in his writings was vexatious to him. Isaac Taylor remarks on the simple Hymns of his sister Jane, in his interesting memoir of that devout and honourable woman, that if one might judge by the aspect of the manuscript copy—its intricate interlineations and multiplied revisions, it would seem that many of them cost the author more labour than any other of her writings. A Quarterly Reviewer, who disavows the belief that compact perspicuity can ever be sustained without much care and reflection, contends, nevertheless, that different writers conduct the mechanism of composition in different fashions, and that the negative evidence of an unblotted page is worth next to nothing.* Citing the instances of "the two most graceful prose writers, on a large scale," of the last generation, he refers to their MSS. as showing few erasures. But the one, he remarks, had so extraordinary a memory that he could finish a chapter during a ride, and then set it down so as hardly to need revision;—the other not only kept commonplace books in which every thought that occurred to him as likely to be useful afterwards, was entered and indexed, but wrote out every separate paragraph on a scrap, and worked it up in pencil before he trusted his pen with a syllable of what we can now compare with the print. "If the pencilled fragments had been preserved, then we should have had a curious study," such as in the autograph of Ariosto, which marks what the reviewer styles the unrelenting sacrifice of a thousand lofty and figurative expressions, in exchange for a chaste simplicity, to the imitation of which Galileo ascribed his own success in making science attractive. It is for a Jean Paul to say that the file shapes, but begets no beauties; that not merely the poet, but his poem, is born, not made. Lamartine affirmed those to be the greatest minds of all which commit almost nothing to writing, being (like Virieu, of whom he was speaking

---

* How as to the positive evidence of a blotted page? Courtois essays to prove the mediocrity of Robespierre's talent by the numerous corrections, the multiplied erasures, with which he "surcharged" his MSS. This proof seems to M. Daunou a little strange; *he*, on the other hand, should have thought that Robespierre overlooked at least half the passages he ought to have run his pen through.

at the time) never satisfied with their works, and preferring to keep them ever in a state of conception within their breasts, rather than produce anything imperfect, and profane their ideal by giving it a form. Lamartine himself wrote enough to disprove his claim to rank with these highest spirits of all. Chateaubriand, when anxious to do his best, was extremely systematic in revising his compositions on relays of prepared paper, sized and sorted with methodical precision; a detailed report of the process being given by his secretary, the Comte de Marcellus, in the preface to his memoir. Béranger prided himself on the manifold correction, up to absolute correctness, of his phrases, and the *grande exactitude* of his rhymes. He watched with extreme vigilance the aspect of those who listened to a reading of his yet unpublished *chansons*,—took jealous note of their slightest gesture, their faintest utterance, "afin de reconnaître les passages qui exigeaient changement, correction ou rature entière." Paul Louis Courier was scrupulously painstaking in all he wrote, private letters included, lest anything should proceed from his pen which savoured of negligence and incorrectness. *Ecrivain chatié et minutieux*, M. St.-Marc Girardin calls him. However apparently negligent some of Henri Beyle's pages may be, they were none the less wrought out with prolonged toil—all his books, says M. Prosper Mérimée, having been several times copied and recopied before he sent them to press. Alfred de Vigny, as M. Gustave Planche has assured us, very seldom yielded himself to the first *élan* of his thought, but was distrustful of the caprice of his inspirations. When once he had set to work upon what he thought was good metal, that would bear good workmanship, and therefore deserved it, he would not put the metal aside until he had chased his meaning upon it to the top of his bent, to the limit of his power. 'It was not enough for him to give, as a clever lapidary might, a luminous transparency to the gem he had cut ; he was for pushing farther his travail and triumph. He would enrich the jewel with figures instinct with movement and life, interlacing their arms, animating their gestures, and emulating the precision and *finesse* of Florentine art.

XVIII.

Book-built Castles in the Air.

DR. REID, in his chapter on Simple Apprehension in general, finds occasion to enforce the truth, or truism, for it is what "everybody knows," that it is one thing to conceive, another thing to bring forth into effect; one thing to project, another to execute: a man may think for a long time what he is to do, and after all do nothing. "Conceiving, as well as projecting or resolving, are what the schoolmen call 'immanent' acts of the mind, which produce nothing beyond themselves." Wordsworth has exemplified in his own instance, while a definitely great poem was being indefinitely planned by him, the vast aspirations and "no effects" of the merely projecting mind; telling us, in his autobiographical *Prelude* how he indulged high hopes to endue with outward life the "airy phantasies" that had for years been floating loose in his imagination; and how the hopes were discouraged,—welcome light dawning from the east, only to disappear and mock him with a sky that ripened not into a steady morning :—

> "If my mind,
> Remembering the bold promise of the past,
> Would gladly grapple with some noble theme,
> Vain is her wish; where'er she turns she finds
> Impediments from day to day renewed."

Whatever the structure of his book-building fancy, it came to nought in those days,—was a mere cloud-compact formation, a poet's castle in the air:

> "the unsubstantial structure melts
> Before the very sun that brightens it,
> Mist into air dissolving."

Thus his days were passed in contradiction, with no skill to part vague longing, "haply bred by want of power," from paramount impulse not to be withstood; or again to distinguish a timorous capacity from prudence, and infinite delay from circumspection. And so it went on, until in the bitterness of his spirit he counted it

> "Far better never to have heard the name
> Of zeal and just ambition, than to live
> Baffled and plagued by a mind that every hour
> Turn'd recreant to her task; took heart again,
> Then felt immediately some hollow thought
> Hang like an interdict upon her hopes."

This was his lot; for either still he found some imperfection in the chosen theme, or so much wanting in himself of absolute accomplishment, that he recoiled and drooped, and sought repose in listlessness from vain perplexity, unprofitably travelling toward the grave.

As Molière's Dorine reminds Damis,

> "On n'exécute pas tout ce qui se propose ;
> Et le chemin est long du projet à la chose."

Leigh Hunt tells us of his father, that he was always scheming, never performing; always looking forward to some romantic plan which was sure to succeed, and never put in practice. "My poor father! . . . I believe he wrote more titles of non-existing books than Rabelais." Coleridge is a signal example of the potential mood of projectors. His scheming faculty was prodigious. Like his air castle-building prototype in the *Castle of Indolence*,

> "Oft as he traversèd the cerulean field,
> And marked the clouds that drove before the wind,
> Ten thousand glorious systems would he build,
> Ten thousand great ideas filled his mind;
> But with the clouds they fled, and left no trace behind."

Mr. Peacock seems to have been girding at S. T. C. under the mask of Mr. Flosky, in *Nightmare Abbey*, who dilates on the distinction of fancy and imagination as one of the most abstruse and important points of metaphysics, and adds, "I have written seven hundred pages of promise to elucidate it, which promise I shall keep as faithfully as the bank will its promise to pay." As with the perennial promiser in a French satire—

> "Il promet l'Énéide, où régnent tant d'appas;
> Il promet, il promet : que ne promet-il pas?"

In 1826 we find Coleridge, from his correspondence with Lamb, seriously meditating a poetical pantomime. The posthumous collection of his letters shows him to have been projecting numerous and diversified plans for relieving himself in money matters—one being a scheme of systematic contributions to *Blackwood*, the first of which duly appeared in the October number of 1821, and was to have been followed offhand by a sketch of the history and philosophy of superstition, with other attractive disquisitions, but No. 2 never came to the birth. Familiar to every student of his writings are such passages as this, in a marginal note to Southey's Life of Wesley, in the chapter devoted to the Moravians: "These bewilderments of the first Moravians suggested to me, which I still hope to execute, an essay on the nature and importance of Taste (φιλοκαλία) in religion.—S. T. C." In his prospectus of *The Friend* he makes special reference to his having, at different periods of his life, not only planned, but collected the materials for, many works on various and important subjects; so many, indeed, that the number of his unrealized schemes and the mass of his miscellaneous fragments had often furnished his friends with a subject of raillery, and sometimes of regret and reproof. Sainte-Beuve remarks of a certain French notable, whose powers notably surpassed his performance, "On voit dans son exemple de riches facultés qui se perdent, et des talents distingués qui s'altèrent et s'abîment faute d'emploi; on est involontairement attristé." The alias of the heading of Sainte-Beuve's critical causerie is, *Un Paresseux*. And when Coleridge set himself to account for, or explain away, as best he might, his own failures to carry out his large and varied schemes.

he said that, waiving the mention of all private and accidental hindrances, he was inclined to believe that his want of perseverance had been produced in the main by an over-activity of thought, "modified by a constitutional indolence," which made it more pleasant to him to continue acquiring, than to reduce what he had acquired to a regular form. Southey writes to him from Bristol in 1802, "As to your Essays, etc., etc., you spawn plans like a herring; I only wish as many of the seed were to vivify in proportion." A year later we have a memorable letter from Coleridge to Southey, which contains the magnificent plan of a work almost too vast to have been conceived by any other person—so at least the proposed *Bibliotheca Britannica*[*] is spoken of by Mr. Cuthbert Southey, who introduces the letter with a sighful "Alas! that the plans of such a mind should have been but splendid dreams." Southey, in his reply, assures his friend that his plan is too good, too gigantic, and quite beyond *his*, Robert the Rhymer's, powers. "If

---

[*] By design a History of British Literature, bibliographical, biographical, and critical—six or eight of the earlier volumes to consist entirely of separate treatises, each giving a critical biblio-biographical history of some one subject. S. T. C. was to get up Welsh and Erse for the occasion, and to be off by the autumn to Biscay, to "throw light on the Basque." Then for an exhaustive review of our poets and prose writers; then a history of metaphysics, theology, medicine, alchemy, common law, canon law, and Roman law, from Alfred to Henry VII.; in other words, a history of the dark ages in Great Britain. Then the later metaphysics and ethics, the philosophy of theology, the arts and sciences,—and where an end?

you had my tolerable state of health, and that love of steady and productive employment which is now grown into a necessary habit with me, if you were to execute and would execute it, it would be, beyond all doubt, the most valuable work of any age or any country; but I cannot fill up such an outline. No man can better feel where he fails than I do; and to rely upon you for whole quartos! Dear Coleridge, the smile that comes with that thought is a very melancholy one; and if Edith saw me now, she would think my eyes were weak again, when, in truth, the humour that covers them springs from another cause." Ben Jonson's Madrigal might sit or stand for S. T. C. so far as this characteristic of effect defective goes:

> "*Mad.*—I have almost done. I want but e'en to finish.
> *Fit.*—That's the ill-luck of all his works still.
> *Pen.*—What?
> *Fit.*—To begin many works, but finish none."

Good Joseph Cottle's Reminiscences teem with records of "Mr. C.'s" fertility in scheming books, and failure to produce them. "His mind was in a singular degree distinguished for the habit of projecting." New projects and plans, the worthy publisher testifies, at this period of their Bristol alliance, followed each other in rapid succession, and while the vividness of the impression lasted, the very completion could scarcely have afforded the projector more satisfaction than did the vague design. "To project, with him, was commonly sufficient. The execution, of so much consequence in the estimation of others, with him was a secondary point." He once read to Mr. Cottle, from his pocket-book, a list of eighteen different works which he had resolved to write, and several of them in quarto, not one of which he ever brought into being. Each of these works he could have talked, for he often poured forth as much as half an octavo volume in a single evening, and that in language sufficiently pure and connected to be at once available as printer's copy. One of his letters from Stowey, in 1796, expatiates on a projected epic. "I should not think of devoting less than twenty years to an epic poem. Ten years to collect my materials and warm my mind with universal science ;"—for he would not only be a tolerable mathematician, but would thoroughly understand mechanics, hydrostatics, optics, astronomy, botany, metallurgy, fossilism, chemistry, geology, anatomy, medicine ; then the mind of man ; then the minds of men, in all Travels, Voyages, and Histories. So would he spend ten years; the next five in the composition of the poem, and the last five in the correction of it. As S. T. C. never wearies of scheming, so neither does Joseph Cottle of deploring that one whose views were "so enlarged as those of Mr. Coleridge, and his conceptions so Miltonic," should have been satisfied with scheming; and that he did not, "like his great prototype, concentrate all his energies, so as to produce some one august poetical work, which should become the glory of his country." Such incidental notes as the following are of perpetual recurrence, at suggestive intervals of time, in Mr. Cottle's pages: "Mr. C. told me that he intended to translate the whole of Lessing. I smiled. Mr. C. understood the symbol, and smiled in return." *Risum teneat quis?* Sir Humphry Davy is quoted a page or two later, to tell how Coleridge "talked of beginning three works.... What talent does he not waste in forming visions, sublime, but unconnected with the real world!" Subsequently, and during the initial stage of the opium dynasty, Mr. Cottle finds him "full of future activity, projecting new works, and particularly a new Review, of which he himself was to be the editor." Seven or eight years afterwards, we have Mr. C. the projector writing to Mr. C. the publisher about his scheme of "a series of Odes on the different sentences of the Lord's Prayer," and especially his desire to finish his "greater work on 'Christianity, considered in Philosophy, and as the only Philosophy.'" All the materials he has, in no small part, reduced to form, and written, he says, "but, oh me! what can I do, when I am so poor," etc., and then comes the familiar request for a loan. Southey mentions that Coleridge counted on defraying his Pantisocratic emigration expenses by the sale of (the italics are Southey's) "his *projected work*, 'Specimens of Modern Latin Poems,' for which he had printed proposals, and obtained a respectable list of Cambridge subscribers." In one of his letters from Germany to Mr. Wedgewood, Coleridge says he has made "very large collections for a 'Life of Lessing,'" and that he has bought thirty pounds' worth of books, chiefly metaphysics, "with a view to the one work to which I hope to dedicate, in silence, the prime of my life." And again next year: "I am now working at my 'Introduction to the Life of Lessing,' which I trust will be in the press before Christmas." Later again: "I mentioned to you at Upcott a kind of comedy that I had committed to writing in part. This is in the wind." Too true a phrase, that last one. To another of the Wedgewood family, some two years afterwards, he sends word that in a few weeks he goes to press with a volume on the prose writings of Bishop Hall, Milton, and Jeremy Taylor; and that he intends to immediately follow it up with an essay on the writings of Dr. Johnson and Gibbon, in which two volumes he flatters himself he shall present a fair history of English Prose. "If my life and health remain, and I do but write half as much, and as regularly, as I have done during the last six weeks, this will be finished by January next; and I shall then put together my memorandum-book on the subject of Poetry." In the same letter he adverts to his having, since his twentieth year, meditated an heroic poem on the Siege of Jerusalem by Titus. "This is the pride and the stronghold of my hope, but I never think of it except in my best moods. The work to which I dedicate the ensuing years of my life, is one which highly pleased Leslie, in prospective, and my paper will not let me prattle to you about it," and, he might have added, my infirmity of will forbids Leslie or any one else being ever pleased with it, except in prospective. Amid other projected miscellanies to which he put his name, *nominis umbram*, may be noticed a book on Morals, in answer to William Godwin ; a translation of Wieland's *Oberon ;* a set of lectures on Female Education ; a treatise on the Corn Laws ; a History of German belles lettres ; a disquisition on the Progressiveness of all Nature ; another, on the Principles of Population ; the completion of *Christabel ;* a poem on the Nativity, of three hundred lines, and a ballad of some three hundred and forty; a treatise on the culture of German Boors ; an essay on writing in Newspapers, etc., etc. Well might Charles Lamb in that inimitable letter of his to Manning, in China, give this imaginary, yet none too imaginative, notice of Coleridge, by hypothesis prospectively deceased : "Poor Col,—but two days before he died, he wrote to a bookseller proposing an epic poem on the 'Wanderings of Cain,' in twenty-four books. It is said he has left behind him more than forty thousand treatises in criticism, metaphysics, and divinity, but few of them in a state of completion." Nor was Mr. de Quincey, so like Coleridge in some subjective aspects of character, as well as in certain objective experiences in life, unlike him in respect of an addiction to magnificent scheming, and there an end. The English

Opium-eater has told us, in his *Confessions*, how he had devoted the labour of his whole life, had dedicated his intellect, blossoms and fruits, to the slow and elaborate toil of constructing one single work, to which he had "presumed to give the title of an unfinished work of Spinoza's,—viz., *De Emendatione Humani Intellectûs*." His powers paralysed by opium-eating, this enterprise was now, as he describes it, locked up as by frost, like any Spanish bridge or aqueduct begun upon too great a scale for the resources of the architect; and instead of surviving him, as a monument of wishes at least, and aspirations, and long labours, dedicated to the exaltation of human nature in that way in which God had best fitted him to promote so great an object, it was likely to stand a memorial to his children of hopes defeated, of baffled efforts, of materials uselessly accumulated, of foundations laid that were never to support a superstructure, of the grief and the ruin of the architect. Well, the baffled projector then tried a change of plan, and took to political economy; Mr. Ricardo's book rousing him to an almost ecstasy of emulation; in which mood he devised and drew up his "Prolegomena to all Future Systems of Political Economy." This exertion, however, was but a momentary flash; as the sequel showed. The *Confessions* duly tell how arrangements were made at a provincial press, about eighteen miles distant from the Grasmere recluse, for printing this work of his, an additional compositor being retained for some days, and the work being twice even advertized, so that its (prospective) author felt himself to be, in a manner, pledged to the fulfilment of his intention. But he had a preface to write, and a dedication, which he wished to make impressive, to Mr. Ricardo; and all this he found himself quite unable to accomplish. So the arrangements were countermanded, the compositor dismissed, and the "Prolegomena" rested peacefully by the side of its elder and more dignified brother. The books that Mr. de Quincey, first and last, tantalized his admirers by projecting, in divers and diverse lines of authorship—now a gerat history, now an exhaustive philosophy of the mind, now an elaborate fiction,—were many enough to indicate his nearness of kin to Coleridge and Herder, both of whom he has somewhere termed "men of infinite title-pages;" indeed, he used to mention his hearing Coleridge own that his title-pages alone (titles, that is, of works meditated but unexecuted) would fill a large volume; and of Herder he takes it to be clear that, if his power had been commensurate with his will, all other authors must have been put down, and that many generations would have been unable to read to the end of his works.

Good cause had the Cardinal of Ferrari, in the case of Benvenuto Cellini, to warn the royal patron of that versatile genius,* that "men of genius who have noble

---

* Nor was his Eminence the only unfriendly friend at court of Cellini. "How is it possible," urged a whole chorus of other voices, on another occasion, "that your sacred Majesty can employ Benvenuto to make

and sublime ideas in their own art, are very ready to engage in grand enterprizes, without duly considering when they can bring them to a conclusion." Still, the names and instances yet to be cited are often distinguishable enough in degree, if not in kind, from the Coleridge and De Quincey type.

Dryden projected an epic poem on the exploits of King Arthur; and had he been enabled to accomplish such a work, it would have been undoubtedly, affirms Scott, a glorious monument of English genius, as well as record of native heroism. But *res angusta domi*, and conspiring causes, made glorious John abandon the scheme, and it was reserved for a later laureate, whose star had not even risen when Sir Walter's set.

Among the papers of Sir William Jones found after his death, one contained a list of what a biographer calls his "Oriental literary projects," and very ample these were. The ancient geography of India, a botanical description of Indian plants, a grammar of Sanscrit, a dictionary of the same (to be compiled from thirty-two original vocabularies, etc.), a treatise on the ancient music of the Indians, another on the Indian art of medicine, a dissertation on the Philosophy of the ancient Indians, a translation of the

---

you twelve statues of silver, when he has not yet finished one? If you engage him in so great an undertaking, you must resolve to give up the other plans which you are so much bent upon, because a hundred men of first-rate talents would be unable to finish all the great works which this one enterprising genius has taken in hand."—*Life of Benvenuto Cellini*, l. iii., ch. v., vii.

Véda, another of the Puránas, the History of India, the History of Arabia, the History of Persia, a Dictionary of pure Persian, a History of the Tartar nations, translations of Hariri, Nizami, and Confucius, —*cætera desunt*, but these too have to be entered as *desiderata*. Be it clearly recognized, however, that Sir William was no mere schemer, but a very hard worker indeed.

Dr. Johnson refers to Mallet as having never written a single line of his projected life of Marlborough: he groped for materials, and thought of it, till he had exhausted his mind. "Thus it sometimes happens that men entangle themselves in their own schemes." Johnson himself could scheme on a large scale, with nothing to come of it. He once conceived the design of writing the Life of Oliver Cromwell,—interested in tracing his extraordinary rise to the supreme power, from so obscure a beginning. Another project of Johnson's was a work to show how small a quantity of "real fiction" there is in the world; and that the same images, with very little variation, have served all the authors who have ever written. Goldsmith was a sanguine projector, and an eager undertaker of literary engagements he was only too ready to break, —to break his word of promise to the hope, at least, if not to the ear. The most congenial and indulgent of his biographers admits that he certainly gave reason for distrust among the booksellers, by the "heedlessness with which he conducted his literary undertakings. Those unfinished, but paid for, would be suspended, to make way for some job that was to provide for present necessities." It was towards the very last that he proposed *A Survey of Experimental Philosophy*, in two volumes, to be published by subscription; but the plan of subscriptions came to nothing, and the projected *Survey* was never executed. The head, as Washington Irving says, might yet devise, but the heart was failing poor Oliver; his talent at hoping, which gave him buoyancy to carry out his enterprizes, was almost at an end.

Dr. Warton excused himself from contributing to his sometime pupil, Bishop Burgess's, *Conspectus*, by the plea, that in all intervals of leisure he never lost sight, for a moment, of what he calls "my own great work, the *History of Grecian Poetry*." The signal failure to fulfil this scheme moved Dr. Harford to emit the trite reflection, how humiliating to human pride it is to compare the projects of superior minds with their actual achievements. A clever essayist on Chameleons pictures to the life that too versatile being, in his human development, taking up a history of civilization in a dozen volumes, or some equally impressive work: the size of the scheme, the writer's gigantic design and colossal fulfilment, the glimpse which it gives of the long vista of time and the great procession of the ages, stir his imagination to boiling point. We see him crowding his table with heavy tomes, atlases, charters, and nondescript aids and appliances, that are to go to the making of the brief chronicle of humanity, the annals of mankind sublimated. " The world of the chameleon's friends is on the tiptoe of expectation. Good wishes fall thick around the undertaking ; encouragement flows' in on every side ; no stimulus is wanting." But lo ! as we gaze and wonder and clap our hands, the scene has already changed ; the historic muse is suddenly deposed, and her very image, like that of the fallen Sejanus, is dragged as with a hook through the mire of a new contumely. The schemer has changed his mind and his subject ; turns now, say, to politics ; and the politician, once upon the stage, magically expels the historian and the philosopher with a fork, and has *his* scheme, piping hot, and bigger than ever, only resembling the others in the common and inevitable destiny of coming to nought.

Dr. Channing used to avow a hope of being spared to execute a work of some extent, for which he had made preparation ; but time flies away—is his complaint—"and nothing is done but the accumulation of more materials, and my plan continues to grow, while the space for accomplishing it is contracted." But he sees this to be the history of a thousand students,—especially of his profession ; and he can also see how certainly it is well for the world that so many schemes of authorship prove abortive.

That brilliant man of society, and vivacious wit, Rivarol, with his considerable acquirements, and with his great mastery over the French language, gave signal promise of becoming something more; and the fragments which he has left are cited to show that, as a critic or historian, he might have been one of the chief ornaments of French literature. But his inveterate idleness prevented him from doing more than write the preface and conceive the plan of a new and elaborate dictionary of the French language, and his biographers have simply to tell the tale of years that passed away without his producing anything more important than a few essays and fragments, even after he had, not for the first time, avowed his entire devotedness to literary pursuits. For what scores and centuries of authors of every complexion might stand good, *mutatis mutandis*, what Swift, far advanced in life and broken in health, says of himself in one of his letters to Pope: "Yet, what is singular, I never am without some great work in view, enough to take up forty years of the most vigorous, healthy man: although I am convinced that I shall never be able to finish three Treatises that have lain by me several years, and want nothing but correction." *Haud intellecta, senectus* creeps apace, stealthily, on men like Patrick Fraser Tytler, leaving their meditated *magnum opus* a bodiless idea. "I have promised," writes that far from idle historian, in 1830, to his wife, "to write a popular history of the Reformation of Religion, which will extend to at least four volumes." Fifteen years later he was married again, but the big history remained a big scheme. Referring to it at this later date, Mr. Burgon of Oriel says that " He had been for years meditating, as he more than once told me, a great work which, if he had been spared to execute it, would have been a truly valuable contribution to letters ; I mean, a History of the Reformation." But even the execution of his original intention to bring down his History of Scotland to the Union of the Kingdoms, had to be relinquished. In Mr. Tytler's case, however, failing health and premature decay must be duly taken into the account ; and these were with him discernible enough to mark him off by an almost hard and fast line from the mere dreamy, dozing, dilettante do-nothings, whose vocation is air-castle building, whether of cards or of books. No affinity had he with the Canon in *Consuelo*, who, a wit, a fluent speaker, and an elegant writer, had long promised, and would probably continue to promise all his life, to write a book on the laws, privileges, and immunities of his order. Surrounded, as Georges Sand depicts him, by dusty quartos which he had never opened, this most promising of canons had not as yet produced his own, and it was obvious never would do so. Two secretaries he employed, but their employment was unconnected with their office ; they talked a great deal about this famous book, and expected it very much, of course. Indeed, this non-existent book had procured for its author a reputation for learning, perseverance, and eloquence, of which he was in no haste to produce proofs ; not, we are given to understand, that he was by any means incapable of justifying the good opinion of his brethren, but merely because life was short, meals were long, the toilet indispensable, and the *far niente* delicious. Besides all this, the canon loved horticulture and doated on music. With so much to do, how could he have found leisure to write a book? And then again, as Madame Dudevant shrewdly says, it is so pleasant for a man to talk of a book that he has not written, and so disagreeable, on the other hand, to speak of one that he has. He tells Consuelo how overborne and overdone he is by his vocation and avocations, how hampered by engagements of all kinds, how "enslaved," above above all, " by an enormous, a frightful task, which I have imposed upon myself. I am writing a book on which I have been at work for thirty years, and which another would not have completed in sixty—a book which requires incredible study, midnight watchings, indomitable patience, and profound reflection. I think it is a book that will make some noise in the world." But is it nearly finished ? asks Consuelo. "Why, not exactly," replies the canon, who desires to conceal from himself the fact that he has not yet made a beginning of it.

Nathaniel Hawthorne somewhere dreams of a splendid library, the volumes of which are inestimable, because they consist not of actual performances, but of the works which the authors only planned, without ever finding the happy season to achieve them.* The shelves are crowded; for every author is assumed by the dreamer to have shaped out in his thoughts more and far better works than those which have actually proceeded from his pen.

At the picnic beside the Roaring Brook, Mr. Churchill, in *Kavanagh*, makes known to the company his long-cherished purpose of writing a poem called "The Song of the Saw-mill," and enlarges on the beautiful associations of flood and forest connected with the theme. He delights himself and his audience with the fine fancies he means to weave into his poem. He is Professor Longfellow's type of one forced to teach grammar who would fain have written poems; from day to day, and from year to year, the trivial things of life have postponed the great designs which he feels capable of accomplishing, but never has the resolute courage to begin. Thus he dallies with his thoughts and with all things, wasting his strength on trifles, like the lazy sea, that plays with the pebbles on the beach. For a while the project of a new magazine of mark and likelihood absorbs him; but the project is dropped, and Mr. Churchill being thereby deprived of his one hundred and fifty thousand readers, lays aside the few notes he has made for his papers on the Obscure Martyrs, and turns

---

* Eg., the untold tales of Chaucer's Canterbury Pilgrims, the unwritten cantos of the *Faerie Queene*, the conclusion of Coleridge's *Christabel*, etc.

his thoughts again to his previous design of a great Romance. But time speeds on, and chapters upon chapters later we find him employing his leisure hours in anything and everything save in writing his Romance. A great deal of time he daily consumes in reading the newspapers, because it is necessary, he says, to keep up with the age; and a great deal more in writing a Lyceum lecture, on what Lady Macbeth might have been, had her energies been properly directed. He has also made some little progress in a poetical arithmetic, but relinquishes it because the school committee think it not practical enough; and still the vision of the great Romance moves before his mind, august and glorious, a beautiful mirage of the desert. When Kavanagh revisits him, at the close of the story, he finds him precisely where he left him; not advanced one step; the same dreams, the same longings, the same aspirations, the same indecision; a thousand things planned, and none completed. While he muses, the fire burns in other brains; other hands write the books he dreams about.*

---

* "And your Romance,—have you been more successful with that? I hope it is finished, or nearly so?" "Not yet begun," said Mr. Churchill. "The plan and characters still remain vague and indefinite in my mind. I have not even found a name for it."—*Kavanagh*, chap. xxx.

XIX.

A Run upon a Book.

A THOUGHTFUL writer owns to having never thought very highly of the special gift which appears to belong to particular writers of obtaining for their works what the French call a "mad success." He reckons the books which are read in every family and sold on every bookstall, which furnish platform speakers with half their arguments and all their illustrations, and which convert the fortunate author or authoress into the lion of the season, to have very seldom much substance; or, if they have, it is not to their substance, he contends, but to their popular defects that the rage for them is owing. The reason of this he takes to be, that the region of the mind to which such books address themselves is that which lies uppermost, and which has least permanence about it. In such cases, thousands of amiable and communicative people are ready to say, "my own sentiments, better expressed;" and as they like to get an excuse for talking about their sentiments, they find one in praising the books and the authors by whose means their wish has been humoured. Now it is not, we are reminded, by standing on the same level with the rest of mankind, and repeating their transient commonplaces in a piquant style, that lasting reputations are won, or works of permanent importance completed. "An author who looks beyond money and popularity must be, to some extent, in advance of his neighbours." Then again a real work of art is not to be understood at a moment's notice; it will grow upon the world, and educate the minds of the public at large to appreciate its beauty, and will thus have a "sounder and more lasting popularity a few years after its production than it had at first." Our present concern, however, is not with the justification of any special craze for any particular book, but with examples of the craze itself, as manifested at sundry times and divers manners, in the history of literature at large.

There is, for example, Madame de la Fayette's *Princesse de Clèves*, which, from the day of its appearance (in 1678) was the topic of all talk and all letter-writing in lettered France,* and out of it. Bussy and Madame de Sévigné wrote about it; everywhere people were on the *qui vive* as to the authoress. Fontenelle read the romance four times while yet the

---

* From 1649 to 1654, all France, from one end to the other, from highest court circles to the lowest of the *bourgeoisie* with any culture or care for reading at all, was in a craze about the *Grand Cyrus* of Mdlle. de Scudéry. Each one of the ten big volumes, in the order of its appearance, was, to borrow Victor Cousin's diction, not merely read, but snatched at, hurried away with, devoured.

gloss of novelty was upon it. Boursault drew matter for a tragedy from it. Valincourt indited a whole volume of criticisms upon it, which was attributed to Père Bonhours himself; and a certain Abbé de Chames replied by another little tome, or tomelet, that was ascribed to Barbier d'Aucourt, a renowned critic of those days, who habitually took up the cudgels against the *spirituel jésuite* aforesaid. Some dozen years earlier the *Maximes* of M. de La Rochefoucauld caught readers "comme un rhume." A previous century had hailed in Marot's *Psaumes et cantiques*, or holy song-book for harpsichord or voice, what Disraeli the elder calls a "gay novelty," and no book, says the historian of literary curiosities, was ever more eagerly received by all classes. In the fervour of that day, Clement Marot's Psalms sold faster than the printers could take them off their presses. The sacred poems of Du Bartas, a captain in the service of the young king of Navarre, were also welcomed *avec transport*.

The *Amadis*, as a Spanish scholar says of it, touched the right spring in the Castilian bosom, so that its popularity was great and immediate—edition succeeding edition, to the admiration of all admirers. Of the *De Imitatione Christi* there are said to be thirty translations in Italian, and no fewer than sixty in French,—a proof, as De Quincey accepts it, of the prodigious adaptation of the book to the religious heart of the fifteenth century; for, excepting the Bible, and excepting that alone, in Protestant lands, "no book known to man has had the same distinction. It is the most marvellous bibliographical fact on record." The sixty are not editions, observe, but separate versions. As to mere editions, not counting the early MSS. for half a century before printing was introduced, those in Latin amount to two thousand, and those in French to one thousand.* The public "flung itself" (is Michelet's phrase) on the *Adagia* of Erasmus,—the shop in the Rue St. Jacques where it was on sale, being never empty of buyers, and edition following edition, each bulkier than the one before. No *chef-d'œuvre*, the French historian asserts, was ever the object of so much enthusiasm as this book of proverbs.

There was a constant struggle in the chief towns of Germany, during Luther's early campaigns, for the slightest of his pamphlets or *opuscula*. The sheet, yet wet, was brought from the press under some one's cloak, and passed from shop to shop. Even during the sitting of the Diet of Worms, and before the departure of the emperor, Luther's works were in brisk supply as well as demand in the public streets, and the sheets were snatched from the press to appease the greed of hungry readers. Latter-day critics find it

---

* To Mr. de Quincey it is very clear that this astonishing popularity, so entirely unparalleled in literature, could not have existed except in Roman Catholic times, nor subsequently have lingered in any Protestant land. It was, he maintains, the denial of Scripture fountains to thirsty lands which made this slender rill of Scripture truth so passionately welcome.

difficult to account for the immense success of *Ye Schyppe of Fooles*—the great work of Sebastian Brant (*Narrenschiff*)—at the time of its publication. That was in 1497, at Basil, and the first edition, though on account of its woodcuts it could not have been a very cheap book, was sold off at once. " Edition after edition followed, and translations were published in Latin, in Low German, in Dutch, in French, and English. Sermons were preached on the *Narrenschiff*: Trithemius calls it *divina satira;* Locher compares Brant with Dante ; Hutten calls him the new law giver of German poetry." Some historians ascribe its success to the woodcuts, which are allowed to be certainly very clever, and may be Brant's very own ; yet even a Turner, it is remarked, has failed to render mediocre poetry popular by his illustrations, and there is nothing to show that the caricatures of Brant were preferred to his satires. But then we have to remember the time in which he wrote. What, asks a critic who recognizes the utter unlikelihood of Brant's poem achieving a success in our day, what had the poor people of Germany to read toward the end of the fifteenth century ? " Printing had been invented, and books were published and sold with great rapidity. People were not only fond, but proud, of reading books. Reading was fashionable, and the first fool who enters Brant's ship is the man who buys books." Now the books then offered for sale were not very exhilarating ; and there was room, and to spare, in the reading world, for such a work as the *Ship of Fools*. It is known as the first printed book that treated of contemporary events and living persons, instead of old German battles and French knights; and "people are always fond of reading the history of their own times;" and this was just such a satire as ordinary people would read with zest. So the ship had a prosperous voyage, with flying colours.

The Earl of Surrey's works—for their audacity in venturing to reprint which, in 1714, the booksellers apologized—went through four editions in two months, and through seven more within the thirty years after their appearance in 1557, besides appearing in garlands, broadsheets, and miscellanies. Copies were multiplied in manuscript as well. The *Arcadia* of Sir Philip Sidney was universally read and eulogized at the time of its publication, and is held to have given perhaps a greater impulse to the national taste for the romantic style of fiction than any single work before or after it. The bachelor Sampson Carrasco bears record of the run upon the *Adventures of Don Quixote*, that a copy of it was to be found in every nobleman's antechamber, and in the hands of every page off duty; that if one lay it down, another took it up; one asked for it, another snatched it; it was in the thoughts of the upper ten thousand, and in the mouths of the million. For Le Sage's Asmodean romance the rage was extreme; people could not wait for the printer's sheets to be bound, and court *seigneurs* disputed possession of a last copy at the point of the sword.*

Forty-seven editions in rapid succession testified to the prodigious success of the *Eikon Basiliké* at home, while numerous translations carried the echo throughout Europe. Such an extent of distribution in an age of readers so limited, as well as the duration of the interest connected with a question so personal, is regarded by De Quincey as the strongest testimony extant of the awe pursuing so bold an act as the judicial execution of a king.

The partisans of Racine are eager to proclaim the fact that his *Andromaque* made a sensation nearly as great as that of the *Cid*. The *Folle querelle* of Subligny affords piquant proof of this popularity; Racine's play being the subject of every conversation in the family into which he transports us; they all dispute over it; servants as well as masters are full of it, and can speak or think of nothing else. Cook,

---

* "Messieurs, I have but a single copy left," the bookseller assured his two rival customers. "Then it's mine," cried one. "No, mine!" exclaimed the other, "for I asked for it first." "Perhaps you did, but then I was inside the shop when you were only just at the door." "I have got hold of the copy, and won't part with it except in pieces." "Messieurs," interposed the bookseller, "I can never allow a book like that to be torn to pieces." "Well, the *Diable boiteux* is worth a sword thrust or two; so come on, and let us fight for it." "Agreed; and he that gets the worst of it shall be too far gone to read the *Diable boiteux*, and the other may then carry it off whole." So off they went to have out their fight on the Quai de la Tournelle. The only ascertained result of the combat was, that it sealed the success of the book, and put more editions in request.

coachman, lackey, stable boy, all must have their say on the subject; and the contagion bids fair (or foul) to extend to the cat and dog of the house.

La Bruyère's *Caractères*, not expected to sell at all, sold well enough offhand to secure a handsome marriage portion for the publisher's daughter. The popularity of Montesquieu's *Lettres Persanes*, published in 1721, was so great, that, according to the author, booksellers used to go about the streets, catching every one by the sleeve, and begging, "Pr'ythee, write me some Persian Letters."

In a letter to Mann in 1744, Horace Walpole says: "We are now mad about tar-water, on the publication of a book that I will send to you, written by Dr. Berkeley, Bishop of Cloyne. The book contains every subject from tar-water to the Trinity; however, all the women read and understand it no more than they would if it were intelligible. A man came into an apothecary's shop the other day: 'Do you sell tar-water?' 'Tar-water!' replied the apothecary, 'why I sell nothing else.'" In a subsequent epistle the writer recurs to "Dr. Berkeley's mad book on tar-water, which has made everybody as mad as himself."

Bernardin de St. Pierre's books had *un succès d'enthousiasme*. And the Abbé Barthélemy, with his polished, elegant, chilly young Greek (Anacharsis), had *un succès à la Bernardin de Saint-Pierre*. Prodigious, too, in its way, and in its day, was the success of *Les*

Liaisons dangereuses of La Clos, above all in the salons, where its appearance was a literary event.

> "That was a hit!
> The world is murmuring like a hive of bees;
> He is its theme—to-morrow it may change."

M. Demogeot says of the *Encyclopédie* that the eighteenth century recognized itself in that picture. It was a work impatiently looked out for, and welcomed with transport. Composed of twenty-two volumes in folio, four thousand two hundred and fifty copies were published, and not one remained on hand at the booksellers'. The last copies were eagerly caught up at the price of eighteen hundred livres, and a second edition was at once talked of. As Rousseau's Dijon Discourse made what Grimm calls "a kind of revolution in Paris," so the circulation of his later writings was "unprecedented," and when his *Nouvelle Héloïse* appeared, the booksellers were speedily sold out; the book was lent to read at the charge of twelve sous per volume, and only one hour allowed for the perusal. In the case of Swift's *Gulliver*, the price of the first edition was raised before the second could be printed, so urgent was the demand.

When Necker, in 1781, published his celebrated *Compte Rendu*, or Report on the Finances of France, the eagerness to obtain it was, in Mr. Buckle's words, "beyond all bounds;" six thousand copies were sold the first day; and the demand still increasing, two presses were kept constantly at work in order to satisfy the public curiosity.*

Writing of the reception of his brother's *Reflections on the Revolution in France*, Richard Burke tells Shackleton, "Seven thousand copies have been sold in six days, and to all appearance as many more will be soon demanded." Within the first year, Sir James Prior tells us, nineteen thousand copies were sold in England, and about thirteen thousand in France; the whole number of English copies disposed of within a few years being estimated at more than thirty thousand—and this at a time when the demand for books of any kind was a mere fraction of what it has since become. "Some experienced booksellers have said that the sale was greater than that of any preceding book whatever of the same price." Lord Lytton, in one of his stories, pictures a knot of politicians in eager conversation respecting a new book which had been published a day or two before, but which had already seized the public attention with that strong grasp which constitutes always an era in an author's life, sometimes an epoch in a nation's literature. "We need scarcely say that a book which makes this sort of sensation must hit some popular feeling of the hour, supply some popular want. Ninety-nine times out of

---

* Necker's daughter, Madame de Staël, says that eighty thousand copies were sold. Grimm describes the sensation produced as *sans exemple*. And Ségur speaks of the work as being in every abbé's pocket, and on every lady's table.

a hundred, therefore, its character is political." No work, says Mr. Robert Bell, was probably ever read with greater avidity than Dryden's *Absalom and Achitophel*. It passed through five editions in a year. "The effect it produced was unprecedented," though it failed of its immediate object, which was to prejudice the public mind against Shaftesbury, then awaiting in the Tower the presentation of the bill of indictment against him. It was thought "unprecedented" in 1711, that four large editions of Swift's *Conduct of the Allies* were exhausted in a week. It is boasted, writes Johnson, that between November and January, eleven thousand volumes were sold; a great number at that time, when we were not yet a nation of readers. The vast success of Gay's *Beggar's Opera* is noted in the notes to the *Dunciad* as unprecedented and almost incredible —the favourite songs being transcribed on ladies' fans and on dwelling-house screens. Of Sacheverell's celebrated sermon in 1709, forty thousand copies were sold in a few days.

Galiani's *Dialogues sur le Commerce des blés* had a most brilliant success, in 1770. The ladies of Paris raved about the pet production of their pet abbé, and fancied they understood it, *elles en raffolaient, elles croyaient comprendre;* they were all deep in the shallows of political economy, while the fit lasted and the fire held out. Gessner's Idyls, translated by Huber, obtained a prodigious success in France: the journals, books of beauties or elegant extracts, the keepsakes and almanacs of the muses, were deluged with translations and imitations in verse, of the version in prose. Sainte-Beuve remarks that Gessner, the bookselling-printer (*libraire-imprimeur*) of Zurich, became one of the idols of sentimental youth, just as that other printer, Richardson, was, for his *Clarissa*. Gibbon professes to be at a loss, in his Memoirs, how to describe the success of his History, without betraying the vanity of the historian: the first impression was exhausted in a few days; and a second and third edition was scarcely equal to the demand; the book was on every table, and almost on every toilette. The fame of that redoubtable horseman, *John Gilpin*, has been described as spreading over the kingdom, like a fire when it seizes on a prairie: the ballad was speedily minted into lines and phrases that passed current like ancient proverbs. It was reprinted again and again in a variety of forms, Cowper's biographers tell us; it became an indispensable feature in playbills on benefit nights at all the London and provincial theatres,[*] and prints representing John Gilpin flying past the Bell at Edmonton were sold by thousands. When Cowper brought out the *Task*, he suggested to his publisher that the circulation of that lengthy poem might be helped on by printing the now famous bal-

---

[*] The rage for it dated, in fact, from the recital of it by Henderson the actor,—the effect on his audience (in Freemasons' Hall) being described as perfectly electrical. Mrs. Siddons is said to have "lifted up her unequalled dramatic hands, and clapped as heartily as she herself used to be applauded in the same manner."—*Southey's Life of Cowper*.

lad at the end of the volume; but Johnson objected that this would only be to reprint a piece that was already hackneyed in every magazine, and in every shop, and at the corner of every street.

The fact that Hayley's *Triumphs of Temper* was for some years the reigning fashion in England, and passed, in an incredibly short space of time, through a great number of editions, is taken by Mr. Robert Bell to afford humiliating evidence of the public taste in the latter part of the eighteenth century.*

Baron Trenck received a very large sum for the Memoirs he published after the death of Frederick the Great; and his book was translated into almost all European languages. Mrs. Piozzi is thus made, by Peter Pindar, to snap at Boswell for his asking who praised *her* reminiscences of their great common friend:

> "Thousands, you blockhead!—no one now can doubt it,
> For not a soul in London is without it.
> The folks were ready Cadell to devour,
> Who sold the first edition in an hour."

St. Pierre's *Paul et Virginie*, though at first snubbed

---

* That a work "so jéjûne in design and so poor in execution" did not, however, escape sarcasm even in the zenith of its reputation, Sheridan's couplet remains to show:

> "Miss keeps her temper five long cantos through—
> Egad, 'tis more than half your readers do."

Of which, again, Byron's is a literal enough imitation:

> "Triumphant first, see *Temper's Triumphs* shine!
> At least I'm sure they triumphed over mine."

and scouted in high society, anon became all the rage,
edition following edition, and imitation imitation—
fifty within a single year. Translations of Schiller's
Robbers soon appeared in almost all the languages of
Europe; while in Germany the enthusiasm it excited
was extreme. Mr. Carlyle speaks of the young author
as bursting upon the world like a meteor: surprise,
for a time, suspended the power of cool and rational
criticism; and in the ferment produced by the universal discussion of this single topic, the poet was
magnified beyond his natural dimensions, great as
they were. The *Promessi Sposi* of Manzoni sold to
the extent of six hundred copies within the first fortnight (figures that signify a good deal), and at once
became the rage; all Milan was in a fever of purchase
and perusal.

The *Astronomical Discourses* of Dr. Chalmers ran
to nine editions within a year; and, according to Dr.
Hanna, never previously, nor ever since, has any
volume of sermons met with such immediate and
general acceptance. The *Tales of My Landlord* had
a month's start in the date of publication, and even
with such a competitor it ran an almost equal race.
Not a few curious observers are said to have been
struck with the novel competition, and watched with
lively interest the almost neck to neck course, for a
whole year, of Scotland's great preacher and her great
novelist.

Lacordaire said of the *Essai sur l'Indifférence* of his

master, Lamennais,—so sudden and so deep was the impression produced by it,—that in a single day he rose like a new Bossuet above the horizon. The *mot* may recall Byron's epigrammatic memorandum, on the sudden success of *Childe Harold:* " I awoke one morning and found myself famous." The first edition of that poem was disposed of instantly, and Byron became the theme of every tongue, and from morning (*that* morning) till night " the most flattering testimonies of his success crowded his table," with which movement the pressure on his publisher duly kept pace. Scott's poetical reputation was already sensibly declining; but Lockhart records how well he remembers, being in 1812 a young student at Oxford, how the booksellers' shops there were beleaguered for the earliest copies of *Rokeby*, and how he that had been so fortunate as to secure one was followed to his rooms by a tribe of friends, all as eager to hear it read as ever horse-jockeys were to see the conclusion of a match at Newmarket; and indeed it comes out that not a few of those enthusiastic gownsmen had bets depending on the issue of the struggle, which they considered the elder favourite as making, to keep his own ground against the fiery rivalry of *Childe Harold*.

The late Mr. Senior, in his article on Mrs. Stowe in the *Edinburgh Review*, pronounced the sale of *Uncle Tom's Cabin* to have been the most marvellous literary phenomenon the world had witnessed. By the end of November 1852, 150,000 copies had been sold in

America; and in September of that year, the London publishers furnished to one house 10,000 copies a day for about four weeks, and had to employ a thousand persons in preparing copies for the general demand. Without attempting to follow it beyond 1852, he speaks of more than a million of copies having then been sold in England; "probably ten times as many as have been sold of any other work, except the Bible and Prayer Book." In France, one publisher alone sent out five editions in different forms; and before the end of 1852 it had been translated into Italian, Spanish, Swedish, Danish, Dutch, Flemish, German, Polish, and Magyar. Dutch translations there were two, and German twelve. Dramatized in twenty forms, it was acted in every capital in Europe, and in the Free States of America.—And no doubt Messrs. Longman could a tale unfold of the wondrous demand first and last for Lord Macaulay's History, including odd statistics of its "unauthorized" sale in "the States" and elsewhere. And so could the house of Strahan, of the run upon the laureate's last, and penultimate, and antepenultimate volumes of verse; not to go on speculating on what Mr. Murray could tell us of the rush for Mr. Darwin's newest deliverance, or Messrs. Blackwood of the applications for early copies of George Eliot's return to provincial life and story,—as, indeed, are not these things, and the like of these, to be inferred from the pithy announcements which from time to time head Mr.

Mudie's advertisements, to wit, One Thousand Copies of this particular new book, before it is in the binder's hands, and Two Thousand Copies of that, long before the compositor has neared the end of the last chapter?

XX.

Enthralling Books.

SYDNEY SMITH pronounces the main question as to a novel to be—did it amuse? were you surprised at dinner coming so soon? did you mistake eleven for ten, and twelve for eleven? were you too late to dress? and did you sit up beyond the usual hour? In some families, remarks a more recent reviewer, where over-excitement of the youthful mind is carefully avoided, it is the custom to read aloud one chapter of a tale every successive evening. Of course he has his example at hand of a book in the case of which no one would go to bed with a painful feeling of indignation at the story being interrupted,—just as Sydney Smith had his instance to show of a novel which answered the test extremely well—producing unpunctuality, making the reader too late for dinner, and the rest. On the other hand, to finish a book at a sitting is not always a compliment pure and simple to its powers of entertainment : for there is justly said to be many a high-wrought story through which the reader, as it were, gallops breathlessly to the end : we do not lay it down, because, if we once laid it down, we should not take it up again; we hurry on to the catastrophe, but we neither dwell on particular portions while reading, nor do we look back to it again when once finished. This sort of qualification made, it is, of course, the crowning triumph of a book, novel or whatever else, to possess the reader as with

<blockquote>" a presence that is *not to be put by* "</blockquote>

till the last page is come, too soon; and the degree of the book's success may be said to depend, generally speaking, on the nearness with which it approximates to this ultimatum. We shall offer a miscellany of instances both of the positive and the comparative degree.

There is Dean Swift, for example, taking up a volume of Congreve's plays, that his man Patrick had got for his own reading; looking into it, and in his own words, " in a mere loitering read in it till twelve, like an owl and a fool: if ever I do so again: never saw the like." These broken sentences are in the Journal to Stella. Later on we read in the same: "I borrowed one or two idle books of *Contes des Fées*, and have been reading them these two days, although I have much business upon my hands." The Dean himself is complimented by Lord Bathurst with the assurance that whenever any of Dr. Swift's tracts fell in his way, my lord was never easy till he got to the end of them. Such compliments, sometimes quite sincere, are common enough in universal literature. Horace Walpole's are often couched in this strain, as where he begins a letter to Pinkerton, who had sent him his *Letters on Literature,* fresh from the press: "Since I received your book, sir, I scarce ceased from reading till I had finished it." So Mr. Bancroft writes to Washington Irving on receiving from that author the life of his great (Christian) namesake: "Your volume, of which I gained a copy last night, ... shortened my sleep at both ends." And again, four years after, on receiving a later instalment of the work, writes the same to the same, "I did not go to bed till I had finished all the last half of the volume." If the book was shorter, the compliment was more complete, in the instance of Leigh Hunt's assurance to Mr. Frederick Locker: "You may judge how pleased, as well as surprised, I was with your fresh and gallant manner, when I tell you I read the book through before I went to bed."—Smollett declared Lady Mary Wortley's letters to be so bewitchingly entertaining, that he defied the most phlegmatic man on earth to read one without going through with them. Judge of Mrs. Piozzi's transport when she heard of the King having sent for her Anecdotes of Dr. Johnson at ten o'clock at night, and sitting up all night reading it. And what greater compliment could well be paid to the interest of Rousseau's *Emile,* than the fact that so punctiliously methodical a Professor as Immanuel Kant was for two or three days kept from his diurnal promenade—always taken at precisely the same hour —by reading that didactic fiction?

Nor would Washington Irving have haggled for a more flattering tribute to his History of New York (Knickerbocker's) than was paid it by Coleridge in taking it up before his companion, C. R. Leslie, went to bed, and making all but, if not quite, an end of it before the artist got up again. The eccentric Harms, who, it seems, was afterwards opposed to Schleiermacher on many points, records in his autobiography how he walked home one Saturday afternoon with the Discourses of that philosophic divine (and, some think, divine philosopher) under his arm; how he began to read, and declined to be disturbed by visitors, and read far into the night, and finished the book. "After that I slept for a few hours. On Sunday morning I began again from the beginning, read again the whole forenoon, and recommenced after dinner; and then came a sensation in my head as if two screws had been clapped upon my temples." Evidently, and in more senses than one, Schleiermacher was too much for him. So, in one way at least, was Goethe's Young Werther for Zimmermann, who describes himself as having lost not one minute in devouring *Werthers Leiden*, but as being so wrought upon and agitated by the first volume, that he had no choice but to let a fortnight elapse before he was calmed down enough to read the second—the reading of which, when it did come off, was, like that of the first, *l'affaire d'un instant*. Similarly, Hartley Coleridge tells us that if ever he was deeply interested in the course of a story, the interest was so violent as to be painful; he feared—he shrank from the conclusion, or else he forestalled it. But Hartley explicitly avows that he never felt in history or fiction that sort of curiosity which will not suffer you to lay a book down; and that he never exactly devoured a novel.

Mechitar, the reviewer of Armenian literature, was noted in early life for never parting with any book that came into his hands until he had read it through. Pellisson, in one single night, read the Memoirs of Queen Marguerite of Navarre twice through. Addison records his first getting a copy of Budgell's translation of Theophrastus, which he could not lay by till perused to the very last page. Lord Chancellor Thurlow, being detained by a thunderstorm at a country inn, and asking the hostess whether she had any books in the house, is said to have tossed aside the Bible she brought him, and to have sworn at Horsley's Sermons, —which last, however, to cure idleness by short distraction, his lordship began to read, and was so enthralled by the unknown divine that he read on, long after the rain was over, and carried it with him to the carriage steps—whence he threw the book back to the hostess, wishing he might be—something unpleasant —if he didn't make that fellow a bishop; and he was as good as his word. Not a little the Lord Chancellor pleased Boswell by telling him he "could not help" reading through his Hebridean Journal. "I surely have the art of writing agreeably," is Boswell's comment on the occasion.

Fanny Burney owns herself to have felt the very "highest delight" she was capable of feeling, on being told that Burke doted on *Evelina;* that he began it one morning at seven o'clock, and could not leave it a moment, but sat up all night reading it. Months afterwards, when some one, in Fanny's presence, asserted that Gibbon had read the whole five volumes in a day, "'Tis impossible," cried Mr. Burke; "it cost me three days; and you know I never parted with it from the time I first opened it." In high glee, too, she records in her Diary the fact of Sir Joshua Reynolds beginning her *Evelina* one day when he was too much engaged to go on with it; but, "so much caught" was he, that he could think of nothing else, and was quite absent all the day, not knowing a word that was said to him; and, when he took it up again, found himself so much interested in it, that he sat up all night to finish it. Well known is the story of Sir Joshua meeting in Devonshire with Johnson's Life of Savage, before he knew anything of the author, and beginning to read it while he was standing with his arm leaning against a chimneypiece: how the book seized his attention so strongly, that, not being able to lay it down till he had finished it, he found his arm completely benumbed when he tried to alter his position. Johnson had gone as far as he could to write the book at a sitting; forty-eight of the printed octavo pages he had written without a break—sitting up all night to do so. Many a reader has got through Beckford's *Vathek* at a sitting, but very few authors indeed could or would emulate Beckford's feat of writing it at one. True the sitting was a long one, for it lasted three days and two nights, and it cost him a severe illness—which, some will think, and perhaps he thought, served him right.—Johnson himself professes to have read through Fielding's *Amelia* without stopping. Burton's *Anatomy of Melancholy*, he said, was the only book that ever took him out of bed two hours sooner than he wished to rise. Boswell describes the Doctor's eager appropriation, at a dinner-party too, of Charles Sheridan's book on the then recent Revolution in Sweden—seeming to read it ravenously, as if he devoured it; keeping it wrapt up in the table-cloth in his lap during the time of dinner, " from an avidity to have one entertainment in readiness when he should have finished another "—resembling indeed, if Mr. Boswell may be allowed so coarse a simile, a dog who holds a bone in his paws in reserve, while he eats something else which has been thrown to him. Charles Sheridan at any rate would have been gratified at the sight, whatever Mr. Dilly and his guests may have been. Captain Carleton's Memoirs is another book that enthralled Johnson's attention. Lord Eliot sent him a copy, as containing the best account on record of the Earl of Peterborough; and the Doctor told Sir Joshua Reynolds that he was going to bed when it came, but became so interested in it that he sat up till he had read it through.

Hazlitt has an essay on time-pieces and repeating watches, to the latter of which he declares himself to be no friend—remarking that the only pleasant association he has with them is the account given by Rousseau of some French lady, who sat up reading the *New Heloïse* when it first came out, and ordering her maid to sound the repeater, found it was too late to go to bed, and so continued reading on till morning. Yet how different, he adds, is the interest excited by this story from the account elsewhere given by Jean Jacques of his sitting up with his father reading romances, when a boy, till the two were startled by the swallows twittering in their nests at daybreak, and the father cried out, half angry and ashamed—*Allons, mon enfant, je suis plus enfant que toi!* With what characteristic zest Hazlitt describes in another essay his own rapt perusal of the *Nouvelle Heloïse*, on his birthday too, and at the inn at Llangollen—and in sitting up half the night to read *Paul and Virginia*, which he picked up at an inn at Bridgwater, after being drenched in the rain all day Equally vivid are Sir Walter Scott's local as well as personal recollections of his first acquaintance with Percy's Reliques—but the story has already been told on a previous page, how he sat in the garden, and devoured Percy under a big plane tree, and ignored dinner-time, though his was the hearty boy appetite of thirteen, and had to be sought for with anxiety, and was found still absorbed in the Reliques. Of Spenser he says that he could, at the same age, have read him on for ever. (So could Southey, to whom Landor confesses on that subject, "But me he mostly sent to sleep.") The number of those whom Scott by his own writings has kept from sleep, would probably equal that of which any other writer can boast. John Murray asked Lord Holland his opinion of the Tales of My Landlord, just out; and was answered, "Opinion! We did not one of us go to bed last night—nothing slept but my gout." Goethe's daughter-in-law told Scott's son-in-law, that when her father got hold of one of the Waverley Novels, there was no speaking to him till he had finished the third volume: he was worse than any girl at a boarding-school with her first romance.

In Moore's Diary may be read frequent entries of complacent authorship, making mention of Lady Glengall sitting up till seven in the morning to finish his *Life of Byron*; and of Lady Lansdowne telling him she was too late to receive her guests, thanks to his absorbing *Epicurean*; and of Lady Lyndhurst saying to him across the table, at a dinner-party, "A friend of mine nearly broke his neck over your book yesterday"—the explanation being that this friend was anxious to finish the *Epicurean*, and was reading it in his curricle, when the horses all but ran away with him.

Lady Mary Wortley Montagu, at all times a lover of reading, describes in a letter from Venice, the eagerness with which she opened a box of books from England, and how she, "falling upon Fielding's works, was fool enough to sit up all night reading." Four years later we find her captivated by "the Parish Girl, which interested me enough not to be able to quit it till it was read over." Here is another example: "Candles came, and, my eyes grown weary, I took up the next book, merely because I supposed from the title it could not engage me long : it was Pompey the Little, which has really diverted me more than any of the others, and it was impossible to go to bed till it was finished." In her ready and frequent sacrifices of sleep to such occupation, Lady Mary was almost the equal of Marguerite, Queen of Navarre, who, whenever she got hold of a book she cared for,—and that was often enough,—having made a beginning, could have no rest till she had come to the end, however long the book might be; frequently neglecting both food and sleep in favour of this absorbing interest: "et bien souvent en perdoit le manger et le dormir." Renowned in story, and even in history, are the *grandes dames* in Paris, and the provinces,—duchesses and marchionesses,—who received at evening a copy of the *New Heloïse*, and were surprised by daybreak dawning on them as they sat in their slippers by the fireside, devouring the eloquent protestations of Julie and Saint-Preux.

When Rousseau himself read aloud his Confessions, at the Marquis of Pezai's, the *lecture* lasted seventeen hours, interrupted only by two very curt repasts— *deux repas forts courts*—without the voice of the reader, or the eyes or ears of the assembly, betraying one symptom of fatigue. The story related with much complacency by Jean Jacques of Madame de Talmont reading his Julie, is perhaps but another and more authentic version of a similar one already mentioned. This lady received a copy on the day she was going to a ball at the Opera: after supper, she dressed, and, waiting for the time for starting, took up this new romance. At midnight she ordered her horses to be put to the carriage, and went on reading. A servant brought word the carriage was ready, but got no reply. After a while came others of her household to tell her it was two o'clock. There was no hurry, she answered; and went on reading. The minutes fleeted by, her watch stopped, and she rang to ask the time; —it was four in the morning. That being the case, it was too late to go to the ball, she said; let her horses go back to the stable. She undressed, and passed the rest of the night in reading on and on. Rousseau was eager to make the acquaintance of a *grande dame*, a princess even, who had been so enthralled by a work of his. What would he not have given to have seen her under the spell, when, to apply a stanza of Wordsworth,

"Never did pulse so quickly throb,

> And never heart so loudly panted;
> She look'd, and could not choose but look
> Like some one reading in a book—
> A book that is enchanted."

Rare indeed is the chance of such a book as Mercator's *Logarithmotechnia* finding such a reader as Dr. Wallis, who writes of it, on its first appearance, to Lord Brounker, "I could not quit it till I had completed its perusal."

General Mitchell, the author of the Life of Wallenstein, recalls, in his reminiscences of Peninsular service from 1810 to 1812, his being one of a party who passed a stormy night, while encamped on the heights above Siñacora, in reading the *Lady of the Lake*, then only just published. As a special favour it had been lent to them for that night only; and though their cloaks were scarcely effectual in keeping their one candle from being blown out, they did not break up until every word of the book, notes and all, had been conscientiously and greedily read. Professor Wilson records his reading Galt's *Entail* through, from beginning to end, in one day, the day it was published. Sir William Hamilton is said to have got hold of Carlyle's *French Revolution* about three in the afternoon, and not to have been able to lay it aside till four in the morning—thirteen hours at a stretch. When Macaulay was once told by the author of *Vanity Fair* that he had never read *Clarissa*,—"Not read 'Clarissa'!" he cried out. "If you have once thoroughly entered on 'Clarissa,' and are infected by it, you can't leave it." And he referred to an experience of his in India, when passing one hot season at the hills, where were the governor-general, and chief secretary, and the commander-in-chief, and their wives. He had *Clarissa* with him; and, as soon as they began to read, the whole station, he said, was in a passion of excitement. "The governor's wife seized the book, and the secretary waited for it, and the chief-justice could not read it for tears." Mr. Thackeray does not appear to have caught the infection. But he does record one instance of his being enthralled by a book he could not put by. "How well I remember the delight and wonder with which I read 'Jane Eyre' —sent to me by an author whose name and sex were then alike unknown to me; the strange fascinations of the book; and how with my own work pressing upon me, I could not, having taken the volumes up, lay them down until they were read through!" And we know that when the manuscript of *Jane Eyre* was taken home by one of the publishers' "readers,"—he, a clear-headed Scotchman, not given to enthusiasm, became so absorbed in it as to sit up half the night to finish it: a fact which, taking this reader's temperament into account, went far to decide Messrs. Smith and Elder to accept the work at once.—The last book read before his death by that accomplished and refined critic the late W. C. Roscoe, was the *Idylls of the King*—and it was on a hot day in June, when he could not even move his head without pain, that he read it eagerly through, as he lay on a sofa beside which his biographer, that was to be, sat at work. Too ill to speak much, he yet devoured the book at a single meal.

Fiction has its pertinent examples to illustrate what we have been exemplifying from real life.

When Mr. Croftangry, the literary aspirant, in one of Scott's prefatory chapters, leaves his work to be "glanced over" by his legal acquaintance Mr. Fairscribe, he does so with a sort of persuasion that if once the phlegmatic lawyer began his lucubrations, he would not be able to rise from them till he had finished the perusal, nor to endure an interval betwixt his reading the last page, and requesting an interview with the author. When the interview does come off, the old lawyer adverts to the acquaintance he has just been making with Schiller's plays,—a copy of which he had found in his daughter Kate's workbasket. "I sat down, and, like an old fool, began to read; but there, I grant, you have the better of Schiller, Mr. Croftangry." "I should be glad, my dear sir," exclaims the latter, "that you really think I have approached that admirable author: even your friendly partiality ought not to talk of my having excelled him." "But I do say you have excelled him, Mr. Croftangry, in a most material particular. For surely a book of amusement should be something that one can take up and lay down at pleasure; and I can say, justly, I was never at the least loss to put aside these sheets of yours when business came in the way. But, faith, this Schiller, sir, does not let you off so easily. I forgot one appointment on particular business, and I wilfully broke through another, that I might stay at home and finish his confounded book."—One of the most sensible of Miss Austen's heroes is fain to own that he could not lay down again the *Mysteries of Udolpho* when he had once begun it: "I remember finishing it in two days, my hair standing on end the whole time." This he mentions in connection with his assertion that the person, of either sex, who has no pleasure in a good novel, must be intolerably stupid. Uncle Adam, in Miss Ferrier's *Inheritance*, is presented to us as one of those "excellent but mistaken" people, in whose mind novels and mental imbecility are inseparably united: novel writers he has always conceived to be born idiots, and novel readers something still lower in the scale of intellect. This is the old man who comes across the first volume of *Guy Mannering*, and with the deepest sense of humiliation is irresistibly carried along by the force of the story. Heywood, the priest, in *Aspen Court*, is found intently reading, while out walking, by Carlyon, who wonders where such engrossing books are to be met with nowadays. "No, the art has gone out," says the clergyman, and shows him Rabelais. "Rabelais. Ah, I understand you overlooking the milestones," is

Carlyon's reply.—And once more; in Mr. Charles Reade's first matter-of-fact romance, we have Fry, the gaoler, so absorbed in *Uncle Tom's Cabin* as to be for the first time in his life behind time; while Hawes, the governor of the gaol, appropriates the volume in order to see what could be the story which had prevailed so far over the stern realities of system as to derange that piece of clockwork called Fry. And Hawes too becomes absorbed, and devours the story till his candles burn down in their sockets, and send him to bed four hours beyond his time.

XXI.

Unread and Unreadable.

HOW many there are, exclaims Dr. Thomas Brown, in his *Philosophy of the Human Mind*, who willingly join in expressing veneration for works which they would think it a heavy burthen to read from beginning to end! And indeed he regards this circumstance, when the fame of an author has been well established, as rather adding to his reputation than lessening it; because the languor of a work cannot be felt by those who never take the trouble of perusing it, and its imperfections are not criticized, as they otherwise would be, because they must be remarked before they can be pointed out; while the more striking beauties, which have become traditionary in quotation, are continually presented to the mind. The Edinburgh Professor recognizes, accordingly, a muchness of truth in the principle, whatever injustice there may be in the application, of Voltaire's sarcasm on Dante, that "his reputation will now continually be growing greater and greater, because there is now nobody who reads him."

When George Warrington speaks to the Baroness Bernstein of his grandfather loving Shakspeare so much, that Madame Esmond had not a word to say against her father's favourite author,—" I remember," the old lady assents. " He could say whole pages by heart ; though, for my part, I like Mr. Congreve a great deal better.* And then, there was that dreadful, dreary Milton, whom he and Mr. Addison pretended to admire!" cries the aged Beatrix, tapping her fan. Herr Professor Teufelsdröckh, explaining the notable phenomenon of some notable personage being worshipped because he *is* worshipped,—one idolater, sheep-like, running after him, because many have already run,—adds shrewdly this note of interrogation : " Nay, on what other principle but this hast thou, O reader (if thou be not one of a thousand) read, for example, thy Homer, and found some real joy therein?" †   " But what will you say," writes my

---

* Nina Gordon, of the Dismal Swamp story, frankly owns to Edward Clayton, "Well, I don't like Shakspeare. There! I'm coming out flat with it. In the first place, I don't understand half he says ; and then they talk about his being so natural. I'm sure I never heard people talk as he makes them," etc. Clayton admires the young lady's sincerity in uttering her thought." " I have often heard ladies profess an admiration for Shakspeare that I knew couldn't be real. I knew that they had neither the experience of life, nor the insight into human nature, really to appreciate what is in him ; and that their liking for him was all a worked-up affair, because they felt it would be very shocking not to like him."—*Dred*, chap. xx.

† Of Mr. Carlyle himself, the author of *Recreations of a Country Parson* has the grace, or want of it, to freely confess that he cannot for the life of him see anything to admire in the writings of that man of genius

Lord Chesterfield, "when I tell you truly, that I cannot possibly read our countryman Milton through? ... Keep this secret for me: for, if it should be known, I should be abused by every tasteless pedant, and every solid divine, in Europe." It is not every expositor of Plato that is ready to affirm with Mr. Lewes that Plato is, with regard to matter, a somewhat tedious, as well as a very difficult writer: "this is the reason of his being so little read: for we must not be deceived by the many editions." Often mentioned and often quoted at second-hand, he is rarely read, except by professed scholars and critics. "Men of culture usually attack a dialogue or two out of curiosity. Their curiosity seldom inspirits them to further progress." Chaucer again: in what terms some speak of him! exclaims Thomas Moore, "while I confess I find him unreadable."* And it comforted this confessor to find Lord Lansdowne glad to hear him say so, as he had always in silence felt the same. As for the tragedies of Voltaire, even † M. de

---

"I tried to read *Sartor Resartus*, and could not do it. . . . I confess, further, that I would rather read Mr. Helps than Milton. . . . I value the *Autocrat of the Breakfast-table* more highly than all the writings of Shelley put together."—*Leisure Hours in Town*, chap. v.

* Isaac Barrow is another of the British Classics for whom Moore owns to a pronounced distaste. "Mr. Fox always spoke of Barrow with enthusiasm, and upon the strength of this opinion I bought his sermons, but found him insufferably dry; at least as far as I read, which was not very far."—Moore's *Diary*, April 3, 1819.

† *Even*, referring to nationality, not to the individual man. It is a distinguished Frenchman who pronounces the tragedies of the cleverest

Tocqueville could not read them: he told Mr. Senior so, who further asked him, "Can you read the

of Frenchmen simply unreadable. Now it is a Scotchman, and no less a man than Dr. Adam Smith, who declares one at least of Voltaire's tragedies, the *Mahomet*, to be the summit of dramatic genius. No wonder then if the great political economist avowedly "did not admire Shakspeare," preferring the precise and monotonous rhythm of the French tragedy to the sublimities of the divine Williams.

Professor Anthon is satisfied that Horace would not have admired Shakspeare; that he would have considered Addison and Pope as much finer writers, and would have included Falstaff, Autolycus, Sir Toby Belch, and all the clowns and boasters of the Stratford genius, in the same censure which he bestows on the *Plautinos soles*, and the *Mimes* of Luberius. According to Malone, our second King George, as indiscriminate in his disrelish for poets and poetry as for painters and painting, uttered once the querulous query, "Who is this Pope, that I hear so much about? I cannot discover what is his merit... I hear a great deal, too, of Shakspeare; but I cannot read him, he is such a *bombast* fellow." This Pope protested in his day, and that was King George's day, against the jealous extravagances of Shakspeare-worship:

"On Avon's bank, where flowers eternal blow,
If I but ask, if any weed can grow,....
How will our fathers rise up in a rage,
And swear, all shame is lost in George's age!"

Hume is known to have had not the least relish for Shakspeare, nor any sense of his transcendent merit. His criticism on him in the history is said to have been originally much more severe and tasteless than now appears,—it having been much qualified and softened by Lord Kames, who, says Boswell, "feared the historian would have been disgraced by confessing total insensibility to what the English nation has so long and so justly admired." A piquant paragraph in Swift's Narrative of the Frenzy of John Dennis relates how the said Dennis being in company with Lintot the bookseller, and Shakspeare being mentioned as of a contrary opinion to Mr. Dennis, the latter "swore the said Shakspeare was a rascal, with other defamatory expressions, which gave Mr. Lintot a very ill opinion of the said Shakspeare." Ill opinions of him, equally well grounded and rational, have been rife in the bookselling and bookbuying world, first and last. Artemus Ward has a characteristic chapter

Henriade!" "No, nor can anybody else," was the reply. C. R. Leslie mentions Mr. Rose observing at

on Wax Figures *versus* Shakspeare, in which, on the nothing like leather principle, that racy showman maintains that "wax figgers is more elevatin than awl the plays ever wroten. Take Shakespeer for instunse. Peple think heze grate things, but I kontend heze quite the reverse to the kontrary." So the sententious Wizard of another dead-and-gone humorist argues, "Shakspeare's all very well in his way,—but he couldn't do the doll-trick. What's Macbeth to the pancake done in the hat, or the money in the sugar-basin? Answer me that, now,—what's Macbeth to them?" He pauses for a reply, and having got the sort of one he wanted, this authority proceeds: "But Shakspeare's going down, sir; he's not the card he used to be; the people begin to cut him, and he'll be at the bottom of the middle pack before long." It is curious to mark the diversity of characters as well as classes that incline thus to disparage and depreciate Shakspeare. Now we have a Byron sneering at "one Shakspeare" and "his plays so doating,

"Which many people pass for wits by quoting;"

and again, in another canto, himself quoting and at the same time taking an unkindly cut at him; at any rate, at all and sundry his worshippers:

"'To be, or not to be; that is the question,'
Says Shakspeare, who just now is much in fashion."

Now we have a renowned New England preacher, Dr. Hopkins, speaking of himself as finding no attraction in either Milton or Shakspeare. Now we have a great Polish scholar, Sniadecki, well up in English, avowing his distaste for Shakspeare, "much of whose writings" he declares to be "at present unintelligible even to educated Englishmen." Now it is a Talfourd—but, to be sure, in early youth, and as such typical, or representative—owning himself (in retrospective review) incapable of appreciating the deep humanities of Shakspeare, and resting and expatiating by preference in the brocaded grandeurs of Dryden, Rowe, and Addison; much as, yet ever with a difference, George the Third owned to a very lukewarm interest in Shakspeare, while O'Keeffe he applauded to the echo. Most of his countrymen, it has been plausibly alleged, read our "great national poet" after the same fashion that Sancho Panza saw Dulcinea, by *hearsay:* they hear some of his dramas at the theatre, and get a relish for them when spiced and sauced with

Abbotsford that he had never known anybody who had read Voltaire's *Henriade* through. Scott replied "I have read it, *and live;* but, indeed, in my youth I read everything."

Mrs. Browning confesses humbly before gods and men that she, reviewer of the Book of the Poets,

---

the high-seasoning of stage effect, scenery, machinery, decorations, and declamations; while in point of fact not a few playgoers, it is believed, would admit with Farmer George their preference of the farce-writer of to-day to the Shakspeare of all time, had they His Majesty's candour as well as his coarse taste. The Slickville clockmaker, turned attaché at the Court of St. James's, is supremely sarcastic on the fact that "in the high life I've been movin' in lately, we must swear by Shakspeare whether we have a taste for plays or not,—swaller it in a lump, like a bolus, obscene parts and all, or we have no soul." Samuel Rogers is well known to have had little real admiration for the greatest of poets, and we hear of his frequently reading aloud from Ben Jonson's *Discoveries*, "I remember the players have often mentioned it as an honour to Shakspeare, that in his writings, whatsoever he penned, he never blotted out a line. My answer hath been, 'Would he had blotted out a thousand!'" Mr. Hayward speaks of the strong emphasis always laid by Rogers on the concluding sentence, and of his one morning challenging the company to produce a passage from Shakspeare which would not have been improved by blotting; how, after picking many beautiful specimens to pieces, he was with difficulty silenced by the one beginning, "How sweet the moonlight sleeps upon this bank." Perhaps he thought of his own bank, and was mollified accordingly. Byron should have said to Rogers what he said to Moore, "Well, after all, Tom, don't you think Shakspeare was something of a humbug?" The Viscount in *Martin Chuzzlewit* brands him as "an infernal humbug" outright. Byron, by the way, is the original of the speaker in Mr. Disraeli's *Venetia*, to whose thinking Shakspeare was but an inspired adapter for the theatres, which were then not as good as barns; a mere botcher-up of old plays, who probably never wrote a single whole play himself, whose "popularity is of modern date, and may not last." Cadurcis is impatient of the indiscriminate admiration for all that bears his name, and at seeing a regular Shakspearian fall into ecstasies with what this detractor calls trash worthy of a niche in the *Dunciad.*

never did and never could read to the end of Akenside's *Pleasures of the Imagination*, albeit she had read Plato: "some pleasures, say the moralists, are more trying than pains." The works of Hume, Gibbon, Robertson, Beattie, Soame Jenyns, and generally all those volumes which "no gentleman's library should be without," are crowded by Elia into the same category with books which are no books, *biblia a-biblia*, such as Court Calendars, Directories, Pocket-books, Draught-boards (bound and lettered on the back), Scientific Treatises, Almanacs, and Statutes at Large. Else Elia asserts his entire ability to read anything which he calls a book : he has no repugnances : Shaftesbury is not too genteel for him nor Jonathan Wild too low. With the above exceptions—adding such others, however, as the Histories of Flavius Josephus, and Paley's Moral Philosophy, "I can read almost anything," is Lamb's complacent assertion ; and in making it he blesses his stars for a taste so catholic, so unexcluding. Mr. Carlyle breathes a sigh over those unfortunate persons who have sat, for long months and years, obstinately incurring the danger of locked-jaw, or suspension at least of all the thinking faculties, in stubborn perusal of Whitlocke, Heylin, Prynne, Burton, Lilburn, Laud, and the like,—"all flat, boundless, dead and dismal as an Irish bog." Compared with the labour of reading through Dr. Nares' three quarto volumes on Burleigh and his Times, Macaulay declared all other labour—the labour of thieves on the treadmill, of children in factories, of negroes in sugar plantations —to be an agreeable recreation. And he went on to cite the story of the criminal in Italy who being suffered to make his choice between Guicciardini and the galleys, chose the history; but the war of Pisa was so much too much for him that he changed his mind, and went to the oar. Guicciardini, though certainly not the most amusing of writers, Macaulay pronounced to be a Herodotus or a Froissart, when compared with Dr. Nares, whose volumes he alleged to exceed all other human compositions, not merely in bulk, but in specific gravity also; and who, on every subject discussed by him, produced three times as many pages as another man, while one of his pages "is as tedious as another man's three." Pointing to three large volumes of *Voyages to the South Sea*, which were just (1784) come out, "Who," demanded Dr. Johnson, "will read them through? A man had better work his way before the mast than read them through; they will be eaten by rats and mice before they are read through." Goldsmith rules that all odes upon winter, or any other season, all epodes and monodies whatsoever, shall be deemed too polite, classical, obscure, and refined to be read, and entirely above human comprehension. And elsewhere he pictures the surroundings of a philosophical beau, whose library is preserved with the most religious neatness, and is a repository of scarce books, which bear a high price, because too dull or useless to become common by the ordinary methods of publication. Such have not even the melancholy merit claimed for another class of the Unread, by Pope in his Imitations of Donne:

> "These are good works, 'tis true, we all allow,
> But oh! these works are not in fashion now:
> Like rich old wardrobes, things extremely rare,
> Extremely fine, but what no man will wear."

The official books that deck or depress green-cloth tables are, *par excellence*, and even *ex officio*, unreadable literature. Such as the row that stood on the table of a Record Office of Mr. Trollope's painting, placed lengthways on their edges; the Post Office Directory, the Court Circular, a Directory to the Inns of Court, a dusty volume of Acts of Parliament which had reference to Chancery accounts; "and there were some others; but there was no book there in which any Christian man or woman could take delight, either for amusement or for recreation." When Mr. Jobling, waiting at the lawyer's office, asks the clerk if he can "give a fellow anything to read in the meantime," Smallweed suggests the Law List. But Mr. Jobling declares, with much earnestness, that he "can't stand it." Scott's Nigel would fain borrow some sort of book, to pass away the night withal, in his Alsatian lodgings; but there is nothing available in the Trapbois household save the Whetstone of Witte, being the second part of Arithmetic, by Robert Record, with the Cossike Practice and Rule of Equation; which promising volume Nigel declines to borrow. Yet there are modern sensation novels, sensational of malice prepense, of which criticism is fain to assert that it would be better for the reader (suppose one shut up by the rain in a small inn in Westmoreland), and less wearisome too, if he threw them into the fire, and passed the time on his hands in refreshing his memory of the multiplication table, or in studying last year's almanac.

Individual avowals of inability to read through any particular book of note, or to read at all certain classes of books of no note, have their interest, according to the noteworthiness of the recorder. Leigh Hunt, although a not easily daunted reader, avowed that he never read an entire play of either Ford or Massinger, so repelled he felt by the conventionalism of their style, and their unnatural plots and characters. M. de Sacy avows of the *Leben Jesu* of Strauss, that, despite the sensation it had made, he could not (unless in a derogatory sense) ever make an end of it. "Moi je déclare avec franchise qu'il m'a été impossible d'en supporter la lecture jusqu'au bout." Mr. Caldwell Roscoe believed himself to be speaking for a large constituency when he asserted of *King Arthur* that no poet could have written it, and no reader gifted with the humblest susceptibility to imaginative impressions be deceived by it: he, the nominal "reader" may be puzzled to explain why it is not poetry, but his native instincts infallibly prove that negative, on this critic's showing: "he may not be able to say why it is unreadable, but he will not read it." Had the author of it some actual personage in his mind's eye when, in one of his later books, he laughed at "Professor Long's great work upon limpets, two vols. post octavo," an uncut copy of which in a public library moves philosopher Waife to the reflection that if limpets were but able to read printed characters in the English tongue, this work would have more interest for them than the ablest investigations upon the political and social history of man : " But the human species is not testaceous ; and what the history of man might be to a limpet, the history of limpets is to a man"? Let but those volumes reach the shelves of the library uncut, and uncut, it is assumed, they will remain to the crack of doom. The late Rev. John Eagles testified to having seen in the window of the largest bookseller in a large city the following temptations for any aspirants to knowledge : " Hurd's Horace, 4 vols. ; Harwood's Classics, 2 vols. ; Shenstone's Poems, 2 vols. These books will be given away to any one who will undertake to read them." Godwin's *St. Leon*, and two others, on the same terms, and "eight vols. of Spectator" followed—terms, ditto. Captain Cuttle may be remembered as making it a point of duty to read none but very large books on a Sunday, because this had a more staid appearance; and as having therefore bargained, years ago, for a prodigious volume at a bookstall, five lines of which tome confounded him at any time,—insomuch that he had not yet ascertained of what subject it treated. Equally well, perhaps, with Barry Cornwall,

> "We might spare the too deep dissertations
> Which nobody reads,
> The Essays (on something or nothing)
> Which nobody needs."

Noticeable among the entries on Charlotte Bronte's list of *Legenda*, is the counsel (and confession annexed), "For history, read Hume, Rollin, and the Universal History, if you *can:* I never did." Burns, on the other hand, got up his ancient history from still drier sources; for no book, Dr. Currie tells us, was so voluminous as to slacken his industry, or so antiquated as to damp his researches. Sir Samuel Romilly relates how his excellent and learned friend George Wilson once prevailed on Lord Ellenborough to endeavour to read Adam Smith on the *Wealth of Nations;* and how this went no farther than an endeavour; for, after sundry unavailing efforts, not less strenuous and conscientious than bootless, Lord Ellenborough returned the book, with a declaration that he found it impossible to read it. Of an earlier fiction by the since popular author of *A Daughter of Heth,* a Saturday Reviewer affirmed, that in comparison with it any sort of literature, a Blue-book bursting with statistics, or say the Scotch Registrar's monthly Reports, or a book of sermons by an Evan-

gelical Irish Episcopalian pastor, would be light
reading; there would at least be something for the
mind to lay hold of in either of these,—the calculating
faculties would be stimulated by the Blue-book, and
if the sermons did nothing else they might at least
arouse a sense of wonder; but over the pages of the
novel in question you had no relief, and the mind,
instead of being stimulated or aroused, became flaccid
and sodden. In the same style of banter is treated
such an utterly different style of book as Mr. Finlason's
Dissertation on the History of Hereditary Dignities—a
book which one erudite reviewer professes to have
made several attempts in perfect good faith to read,
but human nature being frail, he had fairly broken
down as often as he made the attempt. He specifies
the possibility of a law book pure and simple being
very dull, which yet may by an effort be read through
on occasion, not only by a lawyer, but by a layman
of fairly robust digestion; and that an historical
narrative may be very dull, and yet that a sense of
duty may carry a man through it, the whole craft
of reviewers is cited to show. "Nay, it is rumoured
that men have read Diodorus Siculus from beginning
to end and still abide, alive and well. But Mr.
Finlason is beyond us." Another recognized order
of the unreadable is that deprecated by Macaulay in
his depreciating query, What man of taste and feeling can endure *rifacimenti*, harmonies, abridgments,
expurgated editions? Who, he asked, ever cut open

Mrs. Siddons's Milton? Who ever got through ten pages of Mr. Gilpin's translation of John Bunyan's Pilgrim into modern English? Of Sidney's *Arcadia* Professor Masson says that it would be mere pretence to allege that it could be read through now by any one not absolutely Sidney-smitten in his tastes, or that, compared with the books which we do read through, it is not intolerably languid. Lecturing upon Boyle's *Parthenissa* at Edinburgh's Philosophical Institution, and quoting the initial sentence, the same professor frankly confessed, "You must not suppose that I have gone many pages into the Romance beyond this introductory sentence;" and anon referring to Hannibal, Masinissa, Mithridates, Spartacus, and other old-world worthies who are brought into the story, the lecturer adds, " How they came into the story, or what the story is, I cannot tell you ; nor will any mortal know, any more than I do, between this and doomsday." Grant the *Arcadia* perfect after its sort ; grant the *Parthenissa* faultless of its kind ; the faultlessness would but suggest what Boileau says about *ne trouvant en Chapelain*

"Autre défaut sinon qu'on ne le saurait lire."

Much in the same way does Macaulay charge upon Spenser's *Faerie Queene*, as pervading the whole of it, "one unpardonable fault, the fault of tediousness." We become sick, he protests, of cardinal virtues and deadly sins, and long for the society of plain men and women. Of the persons who read the first canto, not one in ten, by his reckoning, ever reaches the end of the first book, and not one in a hundred perseveres to the end of the poem. "Very few and very weary are those who are in at the death of the Blatant Beast." And the uncongenial critic doubts whether, if the last six books (said to have been destroyed in Ireland) had been preserved, any heart less stout than that of a commentator would have held out to the end. Maybe he would have deemed not inapplicable the spirit of Churchill's reference to a quite distinct type of literature—

> " Though solid reasoning arms each sterling line,
> Though Truth declares aloud, 'This work is mine,'
> Vice, while from page to page dull morals creep,
> Throws by the book, and Virtue falls asleep."

Klopstock, the so-called German Milton,[*] Cole-

---

[*] Page after page, almost sheet after sheet, even in the reduced type of foot-notes, might be taken up by enumerating, out of a very grand total indeed, cognate examples of this trick of phrase, used so vaguely, cheaply, and unscrupulously. Schiller has been called the Æschylus of Germany, with what a judicious critic styles that blind designation which, seeing two points of resemblance (both being dramatists, and the most admired of their time), instantly concludes the resemblance of the whole. (In his exhaustive, aphoristic, and rhetorical modes of writing he is rather, it is suggested, to be compared to Euripides, of the two.) Anna Byns, famous in Flemish literature, was called by her co-religionists the Sappho of Brabant, inappropriately enough, observes a reviewer of M. Delepierre's book, for her poems, though energetic in style, pure in language, and harmonious in versification, were entirely of a religious cast. Sulpicius Severus received the title of the Christian Sallust, and he might with equal justice, submits a recent critic, have claimed that of the Christian Tacitus. Ferreira is the Portuguese Horace Charles I. used to call William Dobson the English Tintoret. Hyacinthe Rigaud, despite his lack of simplicity and purity of style, as well as difference in

ridge's very German Milton, has at least this one point of resemblance to the English one, that the

mode of colouring and management of chiaroscuro, is "the French Vandyck." Dobson, aforesaid, is known and cited, *pace* King Charles, as "the English Vandyck." Galanino, of the Carracci school, is sometimes called the Italian Vandyck. Greuze is, forsooth, the French Hogarth. Cuyp is more allowably the Dutch Claude. Inigo Jones is the English Palladio. Walpole designates George Jamesone as the Vandyck of Scotland. Zurbaran is the Spanish Caravaggio; and good critics have said that he has equal nature and power, with less vulgarity than his original. Admirers have hailed in Thomas Worlidge the English Rembrandt. Martos has been called the Russian Canova, and Quaglio the German Canaletto, and Pierre Puget the Michel Angelo of France, and William Pitts the English Cellini, and Pierre Patèl the French Claude, and Nasmyth the English Hobbima, and David Allan the Scottish Hogarth.

Moschensch is spoken of as the German Quevedo. It must have been a satirist that called D'Urfé the French Sir Philip Sydney. Wergerland was claimed to be the Byron of Norway; Dr. Latham calls him rather her (Ebenezer) Elliot-Ossian. Klementyna Hoffmanowa is sometimes called the Polish Miss Edgeworth. Thomasina Buntsen is accepted as the Danish Miss Austen. Holberg is hailed as the Danish Butler. Krilof is the Russian La Fontaine. Gil Vicente in the Plautus of Portugal. Lord Lytton calls Montaigne the Horace of Essayists, not only because of the subjective and personal expression of his genius, but for his genial amenity, and combination of sportiveness and earnestness. Torrentius (Van der Beken) was styled by his contemporaries the Christian Horace. Gogol is the recognized Homer of Russian life. Warton calls Thomas Tusser the British Varro. Pushkin is the Russian Byron, as Mickiewicz is the Polish. Zagoskin they dub the Russian Walter Scott. As John Home was once, or was to be, the Shakspeare of Scotland, so was Dr. William Wilkie her Homer ("save us and pless us!") Justus van Effen is the Addison of Holland. Vida was styled the Christian Virgil. Meli is the modern Theocritus. Petöfi is the Burns of Hungary, and Mena the Spanish Ennius, and Parny the French Tibullus, and Morales the Leland of Spain, and Shakhovsky the Russian Kotzebue, and Sze-Ma-Tséen the Chinese Herodotus, and Stagnelius the Swedish Shelley, and Mrs. Sigourney the American Hemans. Edward I. is "the English Justinian." Admirers of Deak have hailed in him the Hungarian Pym.

many find him unreadable; while it may safely be alleged that *all* English readers leave him unread. It has been said, indeed, of Milton, that the way to answer all objections to him is to take down the book and read him; and the saying is quoted with apparent acceptance by an eminent reviewer who yet affirms of Gibbon that the way to reverence *him* is not to read him at all, but look at him, from outside, in the bookcase, and think how much there is within; what a course of events, what a muster-roll of names, what a steady solemn sound. "You will not like to take the book down, but you will think how much you could be delighted if you would." Lessing's epigram may be designedly as well as in effect double-edged :

> "Klopstock is great, sublime, the German Milton :
> All praise the bard ; but will they read him ?—No.
> Us common men who walk without a stilt on,
> If you will read, we'll let your praises go."

Judge Haliburton's Attaché complains that "we must go into fits if Milton is spoke of, though we can't read it if we was to die for it, or we have no tastes." And in a later work the same author maintains that few people read *Paradise Lost* for any other reason than that they feel ashamed to confess their ignorance, and want of appreciation of the poem. Men do not like to be considered heretics, he remarks, and are therefore compelled to conform to the received opinion, instead of confessing the difficulties they have in wading through the beauties of Milton. "If they dared to do so, they would say they infinitely preferred *Hudibras;* but, alas! they have not courage to speak the truth." Dr. Johnson told Beattie* that he never read Milton through till he was obliged to do it, in order to gather words for his Dictionary.

* Who himself observes, in a letter to Sir William Forbes, that very small indeed is the number of those who have any sense of the beauties of Milton; yet everybody admired Milton, because it was the fashion.

Southey's fast friend (in the fine old, not the slangy modern sense of fast) Mr. Grosvenor Bedford, in excusing himself from undertaking a review of Milton to which Gifford was urging him, freely confessed he did not understand him sufficiently to be "in the same raptures, which our countrymen, in general, think it a national duty to feel." It is easier to dictate such a complet as this of Boileau's than to fulfil it in spirit and to the letter,—

"Aimez donc ses écrits, mais d'un amour sincère;
C'est avoir profité que de savoir s'y plaire."

XXII.

Booking a Place for all Time.

BYRON in one of his wilder sallies pauses to muse on the probable doom of his verse; whether the fame of it is destined to cease

> "While the right hand which wrote it still is able,
> Or of some centuries to take a lease."

It was partly, if not mainly, because Scott felt the prudence of giving way, as a poet, before Byron's confessedly more forcible genius, that he gave up poetry,—himself cheerfully and manfully avowing, (it would not have been himself else,) that he had had his day with the public, and that, being "no great believer in poetical immortality," he was very well pleased to rise a winner, without continuing the game until possibly beggared of any credit he had acquired. Now most authors, as Mr. Carlyle has said, speak of their "fame" as if it were a quite priceless matter; the grand ultimatum, and heavenly Constantine's banner they had to follow, and conquer under. But this is how any such author is apostrophized by that plain-spoken philosopher: "Thy 'fame'! Unhappy mortal, where will it and thou both be in some fifty years? Shakspeare* himself has lasted but two hundred; Homer (partly by accident) three thousand: and does not already an eternity encircle every Me and every Thee?" Johnson's carelessness as to fame Mr. Carlyle accounts a most striking fact in his history; token of sound heart and understanding head. Johnson himself has said in one of his *Rambler* essays, that few indeed are the kinds of composition from which an author, however learned or ingenious, can hope a long continuance of fame; adding, that he who has carefully studied human nature, and can well describe it, may with most reason flatter his ambition. Bacon, for instance, among all his pretensions to the regard of posterity, seems to have pleased himself chiefly with his Essays, which "come home to men's business and bosoms," and of which, therefore, he declares his expectation

---

* When the Shepherd in the *Noctes* puts the question to North, will their great countryman Scott live as long as Shakspeare?—why should he not? is Christopher's answer; why, *he*, Wilson, and his compotator Hogg, "will live as long as Shakspeare," he flatters himself and his friend; but it is not mere length of life, he goes on to say, but intensity and universality of life, that constitutes true immortality. "Gude—gude," the Ettrick Shepherd is prompt to assent; "In ae sense, a' that's prented may live for ever; in anither sense, amaist a' that's prented dies. Common owthors leeve but in their byucks—and every time ye shut his byuck, it may be said that ye put a common owthor to death, or imprison him in a cell. He is in oblivion. But once in ages an ages an owthor is born—Homer, Shakspeare, Scott—wha leeve na in their byucks alone, though edition after edition keeps perpetually pourin' out o' the press—but omnipresent in the regions o' Thocht and Feelin' as sunshine fills the day."—*Noctes Ambrosianæ*, vol. iii. p. 90.

that they "will live as long as books last." We
authors, Chateaubriand says for Self and Company,
put forth our pretensions to hold converse with future
generations by our thoughts; but "we are ignorant,
as I believe, of the dwelling-place of posterity, and
we make an error in the address. When we are laid
in the silent tomb, death will freeze our words so
keenly with his icy breath, that they will not melt,
like the frozen words mentioned by Rabelais." But
how continually do the words predecease (as they say
in Scotland) the author of them! Mr. Yellowplush
hit hard the contemporary dramatist who consoled
himself with the assurance of finding as many friends
in the next age as he had found (critical) enemies in
this: "You hope to find frends for your dramatic wux
in the nex age? Poo, I tell you that the nex age will
be wiser and better than this; and do you think that
it will imply itself a reading of your trajadies? . . .
You ot to have a better apinian of human natur."*
And the Editor of the Yellowplush Papers, in his own
more correct English, admonishes "a man who aspires
to immortality," that Horace clipped and squared his
blocks more carefully before he laid the monument
which *imber edax*, or *Aquila impotens*, or *fuga temporum*,

---

* Charles James recurs to the sore point: "And, then, for the nex
age. Respected sir, this is another diddlusion, a grose misteak on your
part. . . . These plays immortial? . . . Do you know the natur of
bear? Six weeks is not past, and here your last casque is sour—the
public won't even now drink it."—*Epistles to the Literati.*

might assail in vain; and that even Ovid, when he raised his stately, shining heathen temple, had placed some columns in it, and hewn out a statue or two which deserved the immortality that he prophesied, "somewhat arrogantly," for himself. But let not all be looking forward to a future, and fancying that *incerti spatium dum finiat ævi,* our books are to be immortal. "If all the immortalities were really to have their wish, what a work would our descendants have to study them all." It was on observing some names of little note recorded in the *Biographia Britannica* that Cowper wrote the lines,

> "Oh, fond attempt to give a deathless lot
> To names ignoble born to be forgot!
> In vain, recorded in historic page,
> They court the notice of a future age:
> These twinkling tiny lustres of the land
> Drop one by one from Fame's neglecting hand;
> Lethean gulfs receive them as they fall,
> And dark oblivion soon absorbs them all.
>
> So when a child, as playful children use,
> Has burnt to tinder a stale last year's news,
> The flame extinct, he views the roving fire—
> There goes my lady, and there goes the squire,
> There goes the parson, O illustrious spark!
> And there, scarce less illustrious, goes the clerk!"

Horace Walpole assures a distant correspondent, in 1748, that the pains that people, who have a mind to be named, are forced to take to be very particular, would convince him* how difficult it is to make a

---

* "As famous as you think your Mr. Mill, I can find nobody here who ever heard his name," etc. (Walpole to Mann, Jan. 26, 1748.)

lasting impression on such a town as London; and a quarter of a century later we find the Complete Letter-writer acknowledging Lady Ossory's complimentary verses about his "immortal fame," with the remark that his immortal fame may walk perhaps to the publication of the next monthly magazine: "In serious earnest, I do think it is such an impertinence in every little scribbler in a parish to accept new year's gifts of immortal fame from their friends, that, at the risk of ingratitude, I must protest against the practice."* In advanced age he writes to Mr. Pinkerton, on the subject of a collected edition of his, Walpole's, works, that he is content to swim for a moment on the passing current, aware how soon it will hurry him into the ocean where all things are forgotten. Printing, that secures existence (in libraries) to indifferent authors of any bulk, he compares to those cases of Egyptian mummies which in catacombs preserve bodies of one knows not whom, and which are scribbled over with characters that nobody attempts to read, till nobody understands the language in which they were written. He claims to know throughly well how trifling his own writings are, and how far below the standard that constitutes excellence: "as for the

---

* "He can nevertheless promise immortality to his correspondent Mason, whom he congratulates (June 26, 1778) on the prospect of becoming famous across the Atlantic—of knowing, indeed, that he will become a classic in a free and rising empire; that his lines will be repeated on the banks of the Oroonoko, and that Ossian's "Dirges" will not.

shades that distinguish the degrees of mediocrity, they are not worth discrimination; and he must be very modest, or very easily satisfied, who can be content to glimmer for an instant a little more than his brethren glowworms." Shiploads of fashionable novels, we are reminded, of sentimental rhymes, tragedies, farces, diaries of travel, tales by flood and field, are swallowed monthly into the bottomless pool; and every month increases the number, as it were by arithmetical progression, almost menacing to become geometrical. Why do none of them last longer than "snow-flake on the river," or, as Carlyle puts it, "the foam of penny-beer"? His answer is, Because they *are* foam.

> "The list grows long of live and dead pretenders
> To that which none will gain."

The placarded dead-walls of Paris, during the fever and fury of the first Revolution, set the most graphic historian of it a-moralizing on the aspect of an everyday, ever-fresh Periodical Literature: to-day swallowing yesterday, and then being in its turn swallowed of to-morrow, "even as Speech ever is. Nay what, O thou immortal Man of Letters, is Writing itself but Speech conserved for a time? The Placard Journal conserved it for one day; some Books conserve it for the matter of ten years—nay, some for three thousand; but what then? Why, *then*, the years being all run, it also dies, and the world is rid of it." Man's literary "immortality indeed, and whether it shall last half a lifetime or a lifetime and half, is not that a very considerable thing? Immortality, immortality:— there were certain runaways whom Fritz the Great bullied back into the battle with a *R——, wollt ihr ewig leben,* Unprintable Offscouring of Scoundrels, would ye live for ever?" So again in the closing chapter of *Past and Present* the author has his fling at "Fame" as being, for fools and unreflective persons, very noisy, and talking of her "immortals," and so forth. "Her 'immortals'! Scarcely two hundred years back can Fame recollect articulately at all; and there she but maunders and mumbles. She manages to recollect a Shakspeare or so; and prates, considerably like a goose, about him; and in the rear of that, ... it was all blank." Goose-like possibly would those be called who even to Shakspeare himself should apply, in a hope full of immortality, and with a terminal note of admiration rather than interrogation, his own lines—

> "How many ages hence
> Shall this our lofty scene be acted over,
> In states unborn, and accents yet unknown?"

The very existence of the works of William Dunbar has been hailed as a signal proof of "the immortality of real merit;" for we know not at what precise time he was born, nor when he died, and his very name is not, with one solitary exception, to be met with in the whole compass of our Literature for two hundred years; nor was it till after the lapse of three centuries that his poems were collected and published—to secure him the reputation, among his own countrymen, of being one of the greatest of Scotland's poets. Rehabilitations with this result, or anything like this, are rare. The common lot is suggestive rather of the French critic's reflection: "Qu'est-ce de prétendre tirer de l'oubli? Nous ressemblons tous à une suite de naufragés qui essaient de se sauver les uns les autres, pour périr eux-mêmes l'instant après." And then how uncertain, after all, as a historian of Athens exclaims, is the great tribunal of posterity,—often as little to be relied upon as the caprice of the passing day! For an example he cites our possession of "the worthless Electra of Euripides," while all is lost, save the titles and a few sententious fragments, of thirty-five comedies of that Epicharmus,[*] who, by all accounts, must have been a man of extraordinary genius, and of very thoughtful and accomplished mind.

"That suit in Chancery, which some persons plead
In an appeal to the unborn, whom they,

---

[*] Wordsworth says or sings of Time, who spares pyramid pointing to the stars, that he yet

"Hath preyed with ruthless appetite
On all that marked the primal flight
Of the poetic ecstasy
Into the land of mystery.
No tongue is able to rehearse
One measure, Orpheus! of thy verse;
Musæus, stationed with his lyre
Supreme among the Elysian quire,
Is, for the dwellers upon earth,
Mute as a lark ere morning's birth."

> In the faith of their procreative creed,
> Baptize Posterity, or future clay,"

to Byron seemed but a dubious kind of reed to lean on for support in any way:

> " Since odds are that Posterity will know
> No more of them, than they of her, I trow."

One is grimly mindful of Byron's musing when there meet the eye or occur to the memory such words as Dryden lavishes in the *Threnodia Augustalis*, where he craves acceptance of " our pious praise, 'tis all the subsidy the present age can raise,

> " The rest is charged on late posterity ;
> Posterity is charged the more,
> Because the large abounding store
> To them, and to their heirs, is still entailed by thee."

Necker had two courses, or plans, *projets*, to offer for the salvation of France, in 1802, either of which the First Consul was free to choose. But what if the First Consul elected to choose neither? In that case the shelved statesman had but to appeal to posterity; and he did so. "Il en appelle à l'avenir et au bon sens qui, tôt ou tard, selon lui, est le maître de la vie humaine." Sainte-Beuve has a remark on its being curious to see how generations to come are commonly endowed presumptively with the good sense we, of the present, are supposed to be without. It is the fashion, observes an English essayist, to speak of posterity as if it were a court of ultimate appeal which is sure, sooner or later, to correct the unjust sentence of contemporary generations. "Misunderstood genius on all occasions invokes it loudly. Literary authors expect that after their death they will be read more fairly." Posterity, however, in the wide sense of the term, is not a tribunal that is in the habit of redressing injustice, or dealing very flatteringly with the memories of people who have failed to please their own generation; and it is only too demonstrable that the majority of sensitive creatures who are so anxious for the approbation or admiration of after-ages, never succeed in being remembered, still less in being praised. "Posterity is not malignant, it is true. But then, on the other hand, it is terribly candid. The sensitive persons who are so averse to critics, and who pant for what they call kindly criticism—that is to say, to be allowed, like the Abyssinian peasants, to go about with perpetual pats of butter on their heads—will not get butter in the quantities they would like from posterity." If posterity notices them at all, the grim surmise or shrewd suspicion is that it will be in the sort of way in which a surgeon delivering a clinical lecture notices his subject. Given a belief in purgatory, what more substantial form of purgatory, we are asked, could be invented for great men than to have to sit still inside their tombs and listen to the dissecting criticisms passed on their memories by the world?

Gibbon, towards the close of his autobiography, indulges the fond desire, the pleasing hope, that one day his mind will be familiar to the grandchildren of those who are yet unborn. In what he expressly styles "the first of ancient or modern romances," Fielding's masterpiece, "this proud sentiment," he says, "this feast of fancy, is enjoyed by the genius of Fielding," who invokes the bright love of fame to fill his ravished fancy with the hope of charming ages yet to come; and to teach him not only to foresee but to enjoy, nay even to feed on future praise. "Comfort me by the solemn assurance that when the little parlour in which I sit at this moment shall be reduced to a worse-furnished box, I shall be read with honour by those who never knew nor saw me, and whom I shall neither know nor see." Earlier in his memoirs Gibbon bestowed a passing mention on his ancestor John, who "expected immortal fame" from a small volume of heraldry of his compiling. *Ventura fatebitur ætas*, John Gibbon took for granted, what a capital genealogist he was. His more illustrious descendant expressed a like hope in his own instance, as well in familiar letters as in formal composition for the press. "I sometimes reflect with pleasure that my writings will survive me," he tells Lord Sheffield in 1789. We are all fond of fame, he muses, in his Essay on the Study of Literature, but each man differs from the rest in his mode of attachment to it; one author prefers the praise of his contemporaries, death puts a termination to his hopes and fears, the tomb that encloses his body may, for what he cares, bury his name; another leaves his name as a legacy to the most remote posterity, and is pleased to think, as Edward Gibbon was, that a thousand years after his death, the Indian on the banks of the Ganges, or the Laplander in the midst of the ice-field, will read his works, and envy the age and country that witnessed his existence. No one, however, could be better qualified or disposed than Gibbon to relish every such satirical sally as Boileau's,—

> " Vous vous flattez, peut-être, in votre vanité,
> D'aller comme un Horace à l'immortalité.
> Et déja vous croyez dans vos rimes obscures
> Aux Saumaises futurs préparer des tortures.
> Mais combien d'écrivains, d'abord si bien reçus,
> Sont de ce fol espoir honteusement déçus ! "

The poetaster snubbed by Despréaux being presumably of the calibre of that Lord Thurlow who seemed to fear that our language might break down under him, or not last long enough to convey the burden of his song to distant ages, when he thus began certain verses addressed to Lord Holland:

> " I think, my Lord, to build a verse,
> Which, if our language hold,
> Shall through the sides of darkness pierce,
> And to all time unfold," etc.

Hardly is the keenest of satirists exempt from the yearning, or superior to the fallacies of hope. Churchill's aspiration was:

> " Let one poor sprig of bay around my head
> Bloom whilst I live, and point me out when dead ;
> Let it (may Heaven, indulgent, grant that prayer !)
> Be planted on my grave, nor wither there ;

> And when, on travel bound, some rhyming guest
> Roams through the churchyard, whilst his dinner's dress'd,
> Let it hold up this comment to his eyes—
> 'Life to the last enjoy'd, here Churchill lies ;'
> Whilst (oh, what joy that pleasing flattery gives !)
> Reading my works, he cries—' Here Churchill lives.'"

Enough of Satire, are the words next ensuing ; and Charles Churchill would have wished that *Jam satis* to be understood as preceding the aspiration just cited, in which he was as serious as so frivolous a person, not to write it parson, could be.

Little Pedlington has its Immortals ; and Jubb is of them. Shall not the house he dwelt in become a shrine for the pilgrims of posterity ?

> " A something inward tells him that his name
> May shine conspicuous in the rolls of Fame ;
> The traveller here his pensive brow may rub,
> And softly sigh, ' Here dwelt the tuneful Jubb.'"

But authors who obtain immortality are not always first-rate, Ernest Maltravers somewhere observes. He is answered that they are first-rate in their way, even if that way be false or trivial ; they must form a link in the great chain of a nation's authors, which may be afterwards forgotten by the superficial, but without which the chain would be incomplete. And thus, if not first-rate for all time, they have been first-rate in their own day, and in their own way. De Montaigne and Maltravers discuss the subject on another occasion; and the latter moralizes on the tendency of the desire of distinction to grow upon us, till excitement becomes disease. Scarcely, as he puts it, do we win the applause of a moment, ere we summon the past and conjecture the future: our contemporaries no longer suffice for competitors, or our own age for the Court to pronounce on our claims: we call up the dead as our only true rivals, and appeal to posterity as our sole just tribunal. Writing to Swift and Pope as poets, Bolingbroke says, "You teach our self-love to anticipate the applause which we suppose will be paid by posterity to our names; and with idle notions of immortality you turn other heads besides your own." Swift replies, that the desire of enjoying fame in after-times is owing to the spirit and folly of youth: "but with age we learn to know that the house is full, that there is no room for above one or two at most in an age, through the whole world." Few, however, as are the names that may outlive the life that now is theirs, the thoughts of every man who writes, as a modern writer consoles himself with thinking, are made undying: others appropriate, advance, exalt them; and millions of minds, unknown, undreamt of, are required to produce the immortality of one. The million, meanwhile, go every man to his own place. Lord Macaulay found signal amusement in turning over recent volumes of periodical works to see how many immortal productions had, within a few months, been gathered to the poems of Blackmore and the novels of Mrs. Behn; how many "profound views of human nature," and "exquisite delineations of fashionable manners," and "high imaginings," the world had already contrived to forget; the names of the books and of the writers being even then buried in as deep an oblivion as the name of the builder of Stonehenge,—though he had indeed reared a lasting pile,* and they had not. Even for recognized merit of no mean order, the doom of oblivion is irreversible; as with those who, in Victor Cousin's words, "brillent un moment dans leur siècle sans arriver jusqu'à la posterité." Chateaubriand once asked M. de Marçellus if he knew why antiquity has left us in literature nothing but masterpieces, or at least very remarkable productions ; nor paused for a reply, but went on to give as the reason, that Time, the best of critics, has dealt out justice to mediocrities, by putting them out of sight, out of mind.

De Quincey somewhere ridicules 'the regret of Mathias that Dr. Parr did not write the history of his times, to be like that of Tacitus, "an everlasting memorial to posterity," by observing that posterity is very difficult to get at ; that whatever other good qualities posterity may have, accessibility is not one of them ; that a man may write eight octavos, specially

---

* Prior speaks of those who, trying to catch the shade of immortality, wishing on earth to linger, and to save part of its prey from the devouring grave, are fain

"A fancied kind of being to retrieve,
And in a book, or from a building, live.
False hope ! vain labour ! let some ages fly,
The dome shall moulder, and the volume die."

But how many volumes, of how many generations, has Stonehenge outlived, and will.

addressed to posterity, and get no more hearing from "the wretches" who compose it, than had he been a stock and they been stones. It takes a judicious Hooker to write a book of which a Pope of Rome shall say, in admiration of the *Ecclesiastical Polity*, " His books will get reverence by age, for there are in them such seeds of eternity, that if the rest be like this, they shall last till the last fire shall consume all learning." Our King James I. emulated the style of His Holiness, by saying, with all the authority of the royal divine he claimed to be, " Though many others write well, yet in the next age they will be forgotten; but doubtless there is in every page of Mr. Hooker's book the picture of a divine soul, such pictures of truth and reason, and drawn in so sacred colours, that they shall never fade, but give an immortal memory to the author." That author himself was not the man to reckon on literary immortality, or in any sense to adopt the style of the philosopher of *Alma*,—

> " For, standing every critic's rage,
> I safely will to future age
> My system, as a gift, bequeath,
> Victorious over spite and death."

À très-peu dans chaque époque est-il donné de survivre. Ovid's boast is echoed by many a poetaster, " exegi monumentum ære perennius,"—but the echo dies a very natural death, only not still-born. The vaunt of Ennius is capped by many a puny braggart, where he desires none to lament him dead, because he is and shall be a living presence among men, and ever on their lips : *volito vivu' per ora virum;* but the brag finds no verification in the next age, or even in the next year. It has been said that the parable of the wheat and the tares is as applicable in literature as in theology : Let both grow together till the harvest ; for the sieve of Time is just to every book, and to each page of every book ; the chaff will surely be blown away in good time, and the wheat gathered in for the use of future generations. An essayist on the vanity and glory of literature encounters the objection that if, in so vast a majority of cases, the hope of immortality is a dream, it does not much matter how men write—success, though ephemeral, being the great point. Though immortality, he answers, be out of the question, a gentle decay and serene old age have always been thought a desirable thing, rather than a sudden and violent dissolution. "Immortality is not to be thought of; but *euthanasia* is not to be despised." Not of this mind was Percival Stockdale : *euthanasia* he accounted a thing not to be thought of, for such writings as his; and anything short of absolute immortality, a thing to be despised. "Before I die, I think my literary fame may be fixed on an adamantine foundation," wrote the venerable man, ("vivacious spectre," Isaac Disraeli calls him,) whose name now is provocative only of the languid query, Who *was* Percival Stockdale? Young poets are haply more excusable than such a very old one, in cherishing very exaggerated opinions of the powers of verse to confer immortality. William Roscoe, in his early poem of *Mount Pleasant*, aspired to immortalize Liverpool with and by himself.

> "The shades of Grongar bloom secure of fame;
> Edgehill to Jago owes its lasting name.
> When Windsor forest's loveliest scenes decay,
> Still shall they live in Pope's unrivall'd lay.
> Led on by hope, an equal theme I choose,
> O might the subject find an equal Muse!
> Then shall her name the force of Time defy,
> When sunk in ruin, Liverpool shall die."

Does Edgehill to Mr. Jago owe its lasting fame? If Mr. Jago's *quantum* of immortality was for Mr. Roscoe a *quantum suff.*, there is no more to say, but happy man be his dole.

Jeremy Bentham in his old age uttered a wish that each of the years yet remaining to him could have been shifted severally to the end of each of the ages which should follow his decease; that so he might be witness of the influence exercised on successive generations by his works. But, formally at least, this aspiration was modest enough; results being its object, and not the direct vitality of his penwork *per se*. The aspiration, such as it was, however, set a French critic upon moralizing on the vanity of human wishes. *Hélas! vivront-ils si longtemps, ces ouvrages de Jérémie?* The same critic it is who in another of his books, and they are to be counted by the dozen,

constructs in fancy a pyramid much bigger than that of Cheops, of the books that nobody reads, and of which scarcely a round hundred of bibliomaniacs know even the bare names. "Croyez donc à l'immortalité des œuvres imprimées!—Que votre vanité, vos griefs, vos passions essaient de vaincre à coups de plume le temps, qui s'avance et qui reduit en poussière tous les souvenirs humains!" The beautiful Isabella Andreini, one of Mr. Adolphus Trollope's decade of typical Italian women, sought to "avoid death," and thought to do so, too, by some hundred and fifty little treatises on such topics as friendship, love, and war, jealousy, constancy, and marriage,—toiling on in the long night hours, in pursuit of immortal fame.*
Henri Beyle could laugh away at Diderot promising immortality to M. Falconnet, sculptor; yet was it this Henri Beyle who said, "Perhaps I shall be famous in 1960;" and even congenial critics of his own clime and time have taken note of his veritable thirst for renown, and have asserted the utter unlikelihood of his being known a hundred years after his death by any book he ever wrote,† or by anything else, if

---

* "A given number of hours on the treadmill would probably be deemed by most extant men far more endurable than a similar number spent in reading the pages thus industriously put together. Nevertheless, if these sentences can help her on for a year or two more in her fight against oblivion, she is heartily welcome to the lift."—*A Decade of Italian Women*, ii. 216.

† As for his *romans*, M. Cuvillier-Fleury says, "Je n'en souhaiterais la lecture qu' à mes ennemis, si j'en avais."—*Dernières Etudes historiques et littéraires*, ii. 304.

anything at all, than some few of the hasty billets that dropped from his pen. The mere fact of every successive age leaving something durable behind it, obviously renders the attainment of a literary immortality a task of increasing difficulty. "Time must at length have his hands filled," as a Quarterly Reviewer says; in other words, it is impossible that the public mind can hold in view an unlimited number of writings, the permanence of which depends upon their being very generally read.

Almost pathetic is the indomitable confidence of Southey's appeals to posterity to do him justice, whether as poet or historian. The editor of the *Review* which occupied the best part of his time, and was the main source of his income, none too kindly girded at him, after he was gone, for his eternally proclaiming the conviction that whatever he wrote was destined to be classed by posterity with the very highest creations of genius and skill. Certainly his published letters afford material for the charge. Let us glance at a few out of many. To Mr. May he writes in 1803: "I have a full and well-founded faith in the hope you express, that my reputation will indeed stand high hereafter. Already I have enough, but it will be better *discriminated* hereafter. . . . . I already receive the reward of my own applause, and shall receive the highest rewards as the feelings and truths which I shall enforce produce their effect age after age, so long as our language and our literature endure." Concerning *Thalaba*, he writes to Miss Barker in 1805, "Die when I may, my monument is made. Senhora, that I shall one day have a monument in St. Paul's is more certain than I should choose to say to everybody; but it was a strange feeling which I had when I was last in St. Paul's, and thought so. How think you I shall look in marble?" In 1811 he writes to his uncle Hill: "With regard to *Kehama*, I was perfectly aware that I was planting acorns while my contemporaries* were setting Turkish beans." "As I feel no want of any profit from those works, which are for futurity, I am completely indifferent concerning their immediate success." To Mr. Grosvenor Bedford, in 1814: "I have long been convinced that I am one of those poets who must die before it is the fashion to buy their works." To his brother, Captain Thomas Southey, he has this to say of *Roderick*, in 1815: "The poem is of far too high a character to become popular, till time has made it so. It is like an acorn upon Latrigg now. The thistles and the fern will shoot up faster, and put it out of sight for a season, but the oak will strike root and grow." To Mr. Moxon, the publisher, in 1833: "My day and popularity will come when I shall have said good night to the world." Most of these references are to his poems; but equally confident was he of becoming with posterity a really standard historian.

---

* Referring to Scott in particular,—25,000 copies of whose *Lady of the Lake* had been printed, Southey mentions, against 500 of *Kehama*.

He versifies this conviction in one of the stanzas of a proem dedicated to the Princess Charlotte, ushering in *The Lay of the Laureate*:

> "Sometimes I soar where Fancy guides the rein,
> Beyond this visible diurnal sphere;
> But most with long and self-approving pain,
> Patient pursue the historian's task severe;
> Thus in the ages which are past I live,
> And those which are to come my sure reward will give."

Time is in no hurry, thus far, to verify the good man's forecast. The future he counted upon is still a paulo-post future, or even less definitely proximate than paulo-post implies. But after all, in an age like ours, when complaints are rife, and reasonable, of the tendency to write exclusively for circulating libraries, anxiety to conciliate posterity is hailed by the judicious as a possible corrective, so far as it goes, which may not be very far. Satirical dissertators on the delusions or illusions of those who are "waiting for the verdict" of posterity, are yet found to admit that everybody desirous of seeing literature flourish is interested in promoting among literary men and women the delightful and innocuous thought, that there is, for all and each of them, a posterity which will be really pleased to read and study what they have composed.

XXIII.

Traces and Tokens of True Fame.

"THAT is true fame," said Coleridge, when he found a little worn-out copy of *The Seasons* lying on a window-seat in the Linton inn, where he and Hazlitt, on their jaunt from Nether-Stowey down the Bristol Channel, "put up" at midnight, and next morning "breakfasted luxuriously" in an old-fashioned parlour, on tea, and toast, eggs, and honey, (we seem to overhear William Hazlitt's smack of the lips at each item in the carte,) within sight of the hive whence the honey had been taken, and a garden full of thyme and wild flowers that had produced it. A sort of parallel passage occurs in quite another set of reminiscences on Hazlitt's part,—the discourses by Dr. Chalmers on Modern Astronomy being this time the book truly famous. He says these sermons ran like wildfire through the country, were the darlings of watering-places, were laid in the windows of inns, and were to be met with in all places of public resort; and he calls to remembrance his finding the volume in the orchard of the inn at Burford Bridge, near Boxhill, and passing a whole and very delightful morning in reading it, without quitting the shade of an apple-tree.

That was true fame, the poet himself was fain to believe, when Ariosto, being once stopped among the Apennines by a band of robbers, was protected by his name and reputation; for the outlaws, on learning who was their captive, honoured him with demonstrative respect, and offered to escort him whithersoever he would.

To find his *Cid* translated not only into Italian, and German, and Flemish, but into the language of Spain —from which he had borrowed the piece—was a vast satisfaction to Corneille; and a still better token of true fame, in his own land, was the fact that it became proverbial to say, in several provinces of France, "That's as fine as the *Cid*." The fame at once secured by Butler's *Hudibras* is proved by its being minted into proverbs and bonmots: no book, says Mr. Robert Bell, was so much read, no book so much cited. Archbishop Trench considers that we have a fair measure of an author's true popularity—that is, of the real and lasting hold which he has taken on his nation's heart—in the extent to which his writings have supplied the nation with "household words." Father Prout says of Horace, that if to be quoted and requoted, until every superficial inch of his toga has become (from quotation) threadbare, constitutes perpetuity of poetical existence, according to the theory of Ennius (*volito vivu' per ora virum*), such life has been pre-eminently vouchsafed to the songster of Tivoli. But there are poets and poets; Horace scarcely comes within the canon enounced by Hood's street Sir Oracle, that

> "when a piece of poetry has stood its public trials,
> If pop'lar, it gets printed off at once in Seven Dials,
> And then about all sorts of streets, by every little monkey
> It's chanted like the 'Dog's-meat man,' or 'If I had a donkey,'"

Mr. Catnach's canon is scarcely of canonical authority, as *Quod semper, quod ubique, quod ab omnibus.* But his flimsy broadsheets are in some cases second only to your printed pocket-handkerchiefs, as seals and tokens of true fame. We have seen on a previous page how Bernard Barton wrote to Crabbe, in 1845, that many years ago he had indited some long-since forgotten verses for a Child's Annual, to accompany a print of little boy Doddridge learning Bible history. His own words are: "Some one has sent me a child's penny cotton handkerchief, on which I find a transcript of that identical print, and four of my stanzas printed under it. This handkerchief celebrity tickles me somewhat. Talk of fame! is not this a fame which comes home, not only to 'men's business and bosoms,' but to children's noses into the bargain!" What, though one Tom Churchyard called this an indignity, an insult, and, in Suffolk phrase, looked "scorny" at it, —protesting that he would cuff any urchin whom he caught making a "wipe" of one of his sketches. Our *gentil Bernard* is not so nice. "I write verses to be read," is his avowal: "it is a matter of comparative indifference to me whether I am read from a fine-bound book, on a drawing-room table, or spelt over from a penny rag of a kerchief by the child of a peasant or a weaver. So, honour to the cotton printer, say I, whoever he be; that bit of rag is my patent as a household poet." The late Mr. Albert Smith made a foot-note of the gratification he felt at seeing a pocket-handkerchief exposed for sale at one of the stalls surrounding Milan cathedral, imprinted with the principal characters from his first story.*

Chateaubriand dilates on the expressive tokens of the popularity of his *Atala*—such as his finding even in the little wayside inns coloured engravings of the principal characters, who were also to be seen exhibited in wax, in little wooden boxes, on the quays, just as at fairs they exhibit images of the Virgin and the saints. He saw his female savage, with a head-dress of cock's feathers, at a theatre of the Boulevards. Parodies, burlesques, caricatures, assailed him, to his infinite glorification, on every side. Further on in the *Mémoires d'outre-tombe* we come across such passages as this: "I arrived at Avignon on the eve of the Festival of All Saints. A child offered me some books which he was hawking about for sale—I bought at

---

* Two years later he was again interested in seeing that an Italian translator had placarded the name of the poor parish orphan in that story against the walls of the Ducal Palace of Venice.

once three counterfeit editions of a little romance named *Atala!*" The next refers to his Genius of Christianity: "The most vivid pleasure that I have ever experienced has been that of finding myself honoured with marks of serious interest both in France and in foreign lands. It has sometimes happened to me, while reposing myself in a village inn, to see a father and mother enter with their son; they brought me their child, they said, in order that he might thank me." It was not vanity, protests one of the vainest of authors, which caused him the gratification he felt on such an occasion as this. What did it avail to his vanity, he asks, that some worthy but obscure rustics should come to tell him of their gratitude in such a place, where no one could hear them? But he took care they should be heard, as far and wide as popular *feuilleton* and sensational memoirs could ensure the hearing.

When Don Quixote speculated on the possible need of a commentary to make the first part of his Adventures intelligible, "Not at all," answered the bachelor, Sampson, "for it is so plain, so easy to be understood, that children thumb it, boys read it," etc.; "in short, it is so tossed about, so conned, and so thoroughly known by all sorts of people, that no sooner is a lean horse seen than they cry, 'Yonder goes Rosenante.'" That was true fame. *Le Diable Boiteux* of Le Sage had what the French call a mad success; the story is stale, even in these pages, of the crossing of swords in a bookseller's shop for the last copy of the second edition; and of Boileau threatening to dismiss his *petit laquais* for yielding to the fascination of a private copy. Of *Werther*, Mr. Lewes says that perhaps there never was a fiction which so startled and enraptured the world; as in Germany it became a people's book, hawked about the streets, printed on miserable paper, like an ancient ballad; so in the Chinese empire, Charlotte and Werther were modelled in porcelain. The flimsy paper and coarse type are veritable tokens of fame; just as, in Elia's judgment, (who maintains that Thomson's *Seasons* looks best a little torn and dog's-eared,) the sullied leaves and worn-out appearance, nay, the very odour (beyond Russia), if we could not forget kind feelings in fastidiousness, of an old circulating library *Amelia* or *Vicar of Wakefield*, are beautiful to a genuine lover of reading. For they speak of the thousand thumbs that have turned over their pages with delight,—of the lone sempstress whom they may have cheered after her long day's needle-toil, running far into midnight, when she has snatched an hour, ill spared from sleep, to steep her cares, as in some Lethean cup, in spelling out their enchanting contents. Who would have them a whit less soiled? he asks: what better condition could we desire to see them in? Their raggedness is true fame.

When Sir Walter Scott was at Sheffield, together with his travelling companion and namesake, young Gala, in 1815, he sallied out early in the morning to provide himself with a planter's knife of the "most complex contrivance and finished workmanship," as Mr. Lockhart describes the desideratum. Having secured one to his mind, and which for many years after was his constant pocket-companion, he wrote his name on a card, "Walter Scott, Abbotsford," and directed it to be engraved on the handle. At breakfast he mentioned this purchase, and young Gala was at once desirous to secure a similar tool, and made his way to the shop accordingly. Having bought a knife to his mind, and in turn written his name for the engraver, the master cutler eyed the signature for a moment, and exclaimed —"John Scott of Gala! Well, I hope your card may serve me in as good stead as another Mr. Scott's has just done. Upon my word, one of my best men, an honest fellow from the North, went out of his senses when he saw it: he offered me a week's work if I would let him keep it himself; and I took Saunders at his word." Sir Walter used to talk of this as one of the most gratifying compliments he ever received in his literary capacity; and these were many. Mr. Lockhart refers elsewhere to the "very particular satisfaction" he showed at seeing a mason reading to his comrades, as they sat at their dinner, by a new house on Leith Walk, the reprint of his "Visionary" (political essays), in 1820. No less grateful to him than the testimony of the Sheffield cutler's dear acquisition of his signature on a visiting card, was the mark of homage to his genius paid in London some years later, by a sergeant of dragoons, also his compatriot. On the night after the coronation of George the Fourth, Sir Walter had to return home on foot from the banquet at Westminster, between two and three in the morning (he had missed his carriage), and he found himself, together with a young friend, locked in the crowd near Whitehall, amid such tumult and pressure as alarmed the latter on account of Scott's lame limb. A space for the dignitaries and bigwigs was kept clear at that point by the Scots Greys; and Sir Walter appealed to a sergeant of the force to be allowed to pass by him into the open ground in the middle of the street. The man answered curtly that his orders were strict—that the thing was impossible. While he was endeavouring to persuade the sergeant to relent, some new wave of turbulence approached from behind, and his companion called out in a loud voice, "Take care, Sir Walter Scott, take care!" The stalwart dragoon, on hearing the name, exclaimed, "What! Sir Walter Scott? He shall get through anyhow!" He then addressed the soldiers near him, "Make room, men, for Sir Walter Scott, our illustrious countryman!" The men responded, "Sir Walter Scott!—God bless him!" He was in a moment within the guarded line of safety. That was true fame, again, which Allan Cunningham records, when Scott was in London during his last illness, in 1832: walking home late one night, "honest Allan" found several working men standing together at the corner of Jermyn Street, and one of them asked him—as if there was but one death-bed in London—" Do you know, sir, if this is the street where he is lying?"

An American traveller bringing news to Byron, in 1813, that his rhymes were very popular in the United States, an entry in the poet's diary gives special welcome to the announcement: " These are the first tidings that have ever sounded like *fame* to my ears—to be redde on the banks of the Ohio!" He declares the greatest pleasure he had ever derived, of this kind, to have been from an extract from Cooke the actor's journal, stating that in the reading-room at Albany, near Washington, he perused *English Bards and Scotch Reviewers*. " To be popular in a rising and far country has a kind of *posthumous* feel, very different from the *éclat* and fête-ing, buzzing and party-ing compliments of the well-dressed multitude." A year later he exulted in a *Java Gazette*, in whose columns there was a controversy respecting the comparative merits of himself and Moore,—to whom he writes on the subject : " Only think of our . . . setting paper warriors in array in the Indian seas. Does not this sound like fame—something almost like *posterity ?* It is something to have scribblers squabbling about us 5000 miles off, while we are agreeing so well at home." * Moore, again, in one of his letters from

---

* Some six or seven years afterwards we find Byron recurring with obvious complacency to this evidence of true fame. For in his thirty-second year he expatiates in his diary on the pleasant memory of that

America, exultingly tells his mother how even a poor watchmaker at Niagara, who did a very difficult job for him, insisted that the little bard should not think of paying him, but accept it as the only mark of respect he could pay to one he had heard so much of, but never expected to meet with. "This is the very nectar of life, and I hope, I *trust*, it is not vanity to which the cordial owes all its sweetness." And in after-years were not his lays' sung, or said to be sung, by moonlight, in the Persian tongue, along the streets of Ispahan? Even more delighted, apparently, was Moore, now verging on his grand climacteric, at an incident after the Literary Fund dinner in 1842, when a pelting shower overtook him and Washington Irving just as they got out together in the street, and cabs were being caught up in all directions. "Our plight was becoming serious, when a common cad ran up to me, and said, 'Shall I get you a cab, Mr. Moore? Sure ain't *I* the man that patronizes your melodies?'" Fetch a cab he did, and after closing the door, he whispered confidentially in the poet's ear, "Now mind, whenivir you want a cab, Misthur Moore, just 'call for Tim Flaherty, and I'm your man." Misthur Moore hereanent exclaims: "Now, this I call *fame*, and of somewhat a more agreeable

---

Java Gazette: "There is *fame* for you at six-and-twenty! Alexander had conquered India at the same age; but I doubt if he was disputed about, or his conquests compared with those of Indian Bacchus, at Java."
—*Byron's Diary*, Jan. 15, 1821.

kind than that of Dante, when the women in the street found him out by the marks of hell-fire on his beard. (See Ginguené.)" Is not some such story told of John Wilkes, in the days of Wilkes and Liberty? The days, namely, when "Wilkes and Liberty" was on every wall; sometimes on every door, and on every coach (to enable it to get along); as a genial gossip records, it stamped the pats of butter, the biscuits, the handkerchiefs; in short, had so identified one word with the other, that a wit, writing to somebody, begun his letter with, "Sir, I take the Wilkes and Liberty to assure you." Grammarians might take this for a pleasant illustration of hendiadys.

Lady Anne Barnard exulted in what she styled "the noble exhibition of the 'Ballad of Auld Robin Gray's Courtship,' as performed by dancing dogs under my window,"—the authorship of the ballad being as yet a vexed or an open question; for the canine histrionics "proved its popularity from the highest to the lowest, and gave me pleasure while I hugged myself in my obscurity."

La gloire is a very French word, and thing; and Balzac loved to expatiate on his experience of it. He would tell, for instance, how when once travelling in Russia with some friends, night overtook him, and hospitality was asked and granted at a château, where the châtelaine and the ladies her guests were eager in welcome; one of the latter, however, hurried away at the moment of the travellers' entrance, to speed the preparation of refreshments, and as she reentered the room, holding in her hand the dish of cakes she was to offer to the new-comers, the first words she heard were, "Eh bien, Monsieur de Balzac, vous pensez donc. . . ." Whereupon, straightway, in joyous surprise, she made a sudden movement, let the dish drop from her hands, and all was smash and ruins at her feet. *N'est-ce-pas là la gloire?* is Balzac's complacent demand. Was not *that* true fame?

Dr. Channing's lectures on Self-culture and on the Elevation of the Labouring Classes brought him a letter of thanks from a Mechanics' Institute in England, where they were reprinted,—on receiving which he said, with glowing countenance and beaming eyes, "This is honour, this is honour." On his table was then lying, his biographer tells us, a letter written by command of "the monarch of one of the mightiest nations of Europe," to thank him for a copy of his writings; but the humbler recognition, in the handwriting of a rough miner, moved him more deeply than the courteous praises of the great, the admiration of scholars, or even the warm appreciation of friends. Towards the close of his life we find him saying, "It is when a nurseryman forgets his plants and customers to express his interest in my views, and a retired Quaker family is moved by my presence, that I become conscious that I have found my way to the hearts of my fellow-creatures. This is better than fame, a thousand times."* He rated it as Tintoretto would have rated the sobs of the old man whom William Collins observed at Venice, absorbed in gazing on the great colourist's "Crucifixion." For some time our English painter, himself struck speechless as he looked at it by sunset, had supposed himself alone in the room; but the half-suppressed sobs, audible from the lower and darker end of that room, betrayed the meek presence of an old man, dressed in the worn rusty cossack of the lower order of Italian country curate, who was standing there with his wan hands clasped upon his breast, the tears rolling down his cheeks, and his eyes fixed immovably on the majestic composition before him. And there he stood still, in seeming unconsciousness of aught without, when the room was left to him alone.

In the glee of her heart Miss Mitford plies her old friend Sir William Elford with proofs of the popularity of *Our Village*, in 1825. Columbines and children have been named after Mayflower, it seems; stage coachmen and postboys point out the localities; schoolboys deny the possibility of any woman having written the cricket-match without schoolboy help, and such men as Lord Stowell send to her for a key.

The popularity of the late Mr. Apperley, "Nimrod," as a writer on sporting topics was unique in its day.

---

* To Miss Martineau he writes, in 1842: "Have I told you what pleasure I have felt from the expressions of gratitude which I have received from mechanics in your country, for my efforts to elevate the labouring classes? I find my books circulate among them freely, and awaken some enthusiasm. To *me* this is *fame*."

When a ship once arrived at Calcutta from England, Colonel Nesbitt, who then hunted the Calcutta hounds, hurried down to the beach, and asked, "What news?" "There are new ministers in," was the reply. "Hang the new ministers," cried the Colonel; "Is Nimrod's Yorkshire Tour arrived?" A man, says Nimrod, relating the anecdote himself, "must be dead to fame to be insensible to such a compliment as this."

Not the less a signal because an indirect token of renown is such a one as that noticed by Professor Masson, in his lectures at the Philosophical Institution at Edinburgh, with regard to the fact of Mr. Dickens being so eminently in request for phrases, fancies, and general illustrations, among the very writers who are or were, more or less, for writing him down. Take, said the Professor, any periodical in which there is a severe criticism of Mr. Dickens's latest publication; and, ten to one, in the same periodical, and perhaps by the same hand, there will be a leading article setting out with a quotation from him that flashes on the mind of the reader the thought which the whole article is meant to convey, or containing some allusion to one of his characters which "enriches the text in the middle, and floods it an inch round with colour and humour."*

---

* The present writer once amused himself by collecting, before ever he came across the above remark, a profuse variety of such illustrations from Mr. Dickens, as used in the pages of probably the very ablest and perhaps the most severe of current Reviews ; and the profusion be

The author of *Recreations of a Country Parson* has described in detail his sensations on coming across a copy of *Fraser* well thumbed at the pages which contained an article of his. "With much satisfaction I perceived that the pages which bore that article were remarkably dirty. Indeed, I do not think I ever saw dirtier pages, and by a subtle process of ratiocination I arrived at the conviction that those dirty pages must have been pressed by many hands, while the lines they bore were read by many eyes. My first emotion was one of exultation. I am a popular author! thought I to myself. And . . . the extreme novelty of the reflection produced a pardonable elation." Other thoughts of a modifying, qualifying, and disquieting sort followed; but with these we are not here concerned, although, like nearly all from the same pen, they expressly claim to be of a "concerning" kind.

came piquant in its very excess; the instances so grew and multiplied, the "allusions" became so numerically redundant, that after filling a few sample pages with them in close foot-note type, it was expedient to give up, but with the case proved over and over again. One of the best-abused of authors was, in the same journal, out and out *the* best-quoted one, and in that capacity was for ever turning up.

XXIV.

Transparent Authorship; or, The Man betokened by the Book.

WASHINGTON IRVING begins his Life of Goldsmith with the remark that there are few writers who have so eminently possessed the gift of identifying themselves with their writings: we read his character in every page, and grow into familiar intimacy with him as we read. His pages are indeed shown to be little more than transcripts of his own heart, and picturings of his fortunes: many of his most ludicrous scenes and incidents having been drawn from his own blunders and mischances; while he seems to have been buffeted into almost every maxim imparted by him for the instruction of his reader. Now Goldsmith is one of the instances specially cited by Lord Lytton to exemplify his thesis, that the man who writes a book is immeasurably above the book. What, he asks, does Garrick's sneer prove; that Goldsmith wrote like an angel, and talked like poor Poll? It only proved that the player could not follow the poet. "A man who writes like an angel cannot always talk like poor Poll." That Goldsmith, in his peach-coloured coat, awed by a Johnson, bullied by a Boswell, talked very foolishly, our Caxtonian philosopher can very well understand; but let any gentle reader, he suggests, of human brains and human heart have got Goldsmith all to himself over a bottle of madeira, in Goldsmith's own lodgings— talked to Goldsmith lovingly and reverentially about *The Traveller* and *The Vicar of Wakefield;* and confidently the assertion is made that he would have gone away with the conviction in poor Oliver immeasurably greater than those faint and fragmentary expressions of the man which yet survive in the exquisite poem and the " incomparable " novel.* A very popular writer and brilliant converser once observed to the one just quoted, that the poet Campbell reminded him of Goldsmith—so inferior was his conversation to his fame. " I could not deny it, for I had often met Campbell in general society, and his talk had disappointed me. Three days afterwards, Campbell asked me to come and sup with him *tête-à-tête.* I did so. I went at ten o'clock. I stayed till dawn; and all my recollections of the most sparkling talk I have ever heard in drawing-rooms, afford nothing to equal the riotous affluence of wit, of humour, of fancy, of genius, that the great lyrist poured forth in

---

* " Take a great book, and its great author; how immeasurably above his book is the author, if you can coax him to confide his mind to you, and let himself out!"—*Caxtoniana,* part vi.

his wondrous monologue." Monologue is the word advisedly used; for he had it all to himself. Moral, or deduction: If the whole be greater than a part, a whole man must be greater than that part of him which is found in a book.

The cases where artists do not resemble their works are with reason alleged to be numerous enough to prevent the admission of a rule asserting the contrary; of which view Perugino, Rubens, Vandyke, Tintoretto, Salvator Rosa, and others are cited as apposite examples. So with poetry. What in Milton's nature, it is asked, corresponded to the terrible and sensual phases of his poetry? What likeness is there between the guzzling, flirting Klopstock, and the pious penman of the *Messiah?* And so with the musician. "Where is the analogy between the heavy, gluttonous Handel and the inspired strains which came from his pen —between the trivial and farcical Mozart, and the sublime heights of the Jupiter Symphony and *Don Giovanni?*" On the other hand, how few instances there are, after all, as computed in *The Student*, of even a seeming discrepancy between an author's conduct and his books; and we are referred to the life of Schiller, to see how completely his works assimilate with his restless, questioning, and daring genius,—the animation of Fiesco, the solemnity of Wallenstein, being alike emblematic of his character: "his sentiments are the echo to his life." Then again Walter Scott and Cobbett in contrast: could Cobbett's life have been that of Scott, or Scott's character that of Cobbett? May you not read the character of the authors in their respective works, as if the works were meant to be autobiographies? Lord Lytton points to Warburton as a signal illustration of the "proud and bitter bishop" in his proud and bitter books; to Sir Philip Sidney as the *Arcadia* put into action (Campbell's phrase); to the wise and benevolent Fénélon, the sententious and fiery Corneille, the dreaming and scarcely intelligible Shelley; and ask of these, are not their works mirrors of their own natures? To the same critical eye, Johnson, with his pompous vigour, his prejudice and his sense, his jealousies and his charity, his habitual magniloquence in nothings, and his gloomy independence of mind, yet plebeian veneration for rank, is no less visible in the *Rambler*, in *Rasselas*, in *Taxation no Tyranny*, and in the *Lives of the Poets*, than in his large chair at Mrs. Thrale's, his lonely room in the dark court out of Fleet Street, or his "leonine unbendings with the canicular soul of Boswell." Dante, Petrarch, Voltaire, are among the other names cited—to name whom is enough, it is assumed, to remind the reader that if he would learn their characters, he has only to read their works. The life of Paul Louis Courier is suggested, again, as singularly in keeping with the character of his writings. Talking at Paris with some of his friends, the author of the Caxton essays excited their astonishment at his accurate notions of the brilliant pamphleteer's character: "You must have known him," they said. "No; but I know his works." So far, in this critic's judgment, from there being truth in the vulgar notion that the character of authors is belied in their works, their works are, to a diligent inquirer, their clearest and fullest illustration—an appendix to their biography far more valuable and explanatory than the text itself. Authors, in fact, by his contention, are the only men we ever do really know,—the rest of mankind die with only the surface of their character understood.

The foremost in fame of modern French critics remarks of the Abbé Prévost, that in his writings may be found the most complete and authentic idea of his mind and disposition. Prévost has himself said, with an acknowledged *mélange* of complacency and humility which is not without a grace of its own, "On se peint, dit-on, dans ses écrits; cette réflexion serait peut-être trop flatteuse pour moi." He is right, says Sainte-Beuve, who holds, notwithstanding, that this rule of judging of an author by his books is no unjust one, especially with regard to Prévost and to those who, like him, join a tender soul and lively imagination to a weak character; for if our life often makes only too evident what we have become, our writings show us at least as we would be.

No author of the second class, in M. Nisard's judgment, exemplifies so distinctly as Vauvenargues the truth of the maxim that "le cachet d'un ouvrage lui vient moins de l'esprit que du caractère d'un écrivain." La Rochefoucauld, his ancestor direct, was another example of the truth. If La Rochefoucauld was so excellent in speculation, and so equivocal in action, it was, M. Nisard says, because he put more of his mind (*esprit*) in what he did, and more of his character in what he wrote. A man's books may not always speak the truth, but, as Mr. Thackeray asserts, they speak his mind and character in spite of himself. Goethe has told us, emphatically, that all his works are but fragments of the grand confession of his life. Whence the application to him of what Horace* says of Lucilius, that he trusted his secrets to books as to faithful friends.

Sir Egerton Brydges says he never took up a book which he could read without wishing to know the character and history of the author—his feelings, temper, disposition, modes of thinking, habits, etc. The author of *The Doctor* quotes Sir Egerton's wish, and

---

*   " Ille velut fidis arcana sodalibus olim
            Credebat libris ; . . . quo fit, ut omnia
            Votiva pateat veluti descripta tabellâ
            Vita senis."

The Horace of Ben Jonson thus Englishes his own words, in free colloquy with Trebatius :

" He, as his trusty friends, his books did trust
   With all his secrets ; . . . .
   So that the old man's life, described, was seen
   As in a votive tablet in his lines ;
   And to his steps my genius inclines."

meets it, under his professional mask, with a "methinks my feelings, my disposition, and my modes of thinking are indicated here as far as a book can indicate them." Sir Egerton had said that if it could be proved that what one writes is no index to what one thinks and feels, then it would be of little value and no interest; expressing his confidence, however, that such delusive writers always betray themselves: sincerity has always a breath and spirit of its own. And Southey adds that if his book have not that breath of life, it must be still-born.

Of Plutarch it has been said, that the character of the man is as familiar to us from his writings as if we possessed the most elaborate biography of him. Applicable to him is what Sainte-Beuve says of a distinguished Frenchman of the last century: "Il est un de ceux qui, de profil ou de face, se sont le plus volontiers dépeints et réfléchis eux-mêmes dans leurs écrits." Unconscious self-revelation is noted as remarkably full and explicit in De Foe, because, not penetrating into the interior of other men, he was thrown very much on the resources within himself: all his characters are woven out of the same thread, and however differing in many ways, are, in certain characteristics, and those the most deep-seated, like one another, and like the author. "It is the innermost part of his nature which a man can least shake off in his writings."

M. Cuvillier-Fleury prefaces his reviewal of M.

Edmond About by an account of his making the acquaintance of that *spirituel* author in vacation time, and *tête-à-tête*. Not that he had ever seen him, or exchanged a single word with him; but M. About's works spoke for him; and the reader-critic professes to have knowledge of no author whose portrait it is easier to draw after having become acquainted with his books.

Despite the real likeness between the book and the man, as a rule, the vulgar will not fail to be disappointed, as the *New Phædo* essayist remarks, because they look to externals; and the man composed the book not with his face, dress, or manners, but with his mind. Others, however, than the mere and sheer vulgar may be excused if they take a sort of amused interest, now and then, in the superficial discrepancies observable between certain authors, as men, and the impression formed of them, as men, by readers intent on descrying their manner of manhood in their books. Of Henry Hallam a writer of distinction observed, at the time of his death, that the reader of his weighty (not heavy) works, impressed with the judicial character of the style both of thought and expression, imagined him a solemn, pale student, and might almost expect to see him in a judge's wig; whereas the stranger would find him the most rapid talker in company, quick in his movements, genial in his feelings, earnest in narrative, rather full of dissent from what everybody said, innocently surprised when he found himself agreeing with anybody, and pretty sure to blurt out something awkward before the day was done—but never giving offence, because his talk was always the fresh growth of the topic, besides that his manners were those of a thoroughbred gentleman.* Rückert's portrait is accounted out of keeping with the ideal formed of him by most of his readers; for the poetical optimist, the tender and cheerful singer of love's spring, was, we learn (from Dr. Beyer), a man of lofty stature and athletic frame, with a commanding presence and an eagle eye; a man who, though most amiable in his domestic circle, loved seclusion, was uncompromising in his antipathies, and only to be approached with considerable precaution. John Martin Miller, the German novelist, whose *Siegwart* and other stories were so amazingly popular in his own country towards the close of the eighteenth century, disappointed, on personal acquaintance, many who expected to find in him an impassioned enthusiast—so different was the chilly manner and reserved tone of the man, from the excessive sensibility and fervour of the writer. Zhukovsky, the Russian poet, was notably as gay and sprightly in society as in his writings he was disposed to be mild and meditative.

---

* "In a capital sketch of a dinner-party to which Sydney Smith went late, Hallam was one of the figures: 'And there was Hallam, with his mouth full of cabbage and contradiction;' a sentence in which we see at once the rapid speech and action, and the constitutional habit of mind."—*Biographical Sketches*, by Harriet Martineau, p. 393.

Colonel Hamley tells us of his introduction to Professor Aytoun, that from the tone of his critical and political papers, at once gay and bold, and the chivalrous cast of his poetry, the notion of the professor conceived by the colonel was that of a man alert, self-confident, and self-asserting, with a jovial, resolute bearing, whereas the real professor, "sober in gait, slow and gentle of voice, and with a student-like stoop in his shoulders, advanced as shyly as a young girl," and received the other's "attempted compliments" with a reserve that might have implied they were displeasing, but which "was in truth only a thin crust over a very genial, affectionate nature." The Hungarian poet Kisfaludy was always of a cheery, joyous disposition, though his poems are characterized by a pervading tone of pensive melancholy.* We are assured in the case of Miss Landon (L. E. L.) that the romantic melancholy of her poems was entirely imaginative: in private life she was full of mirth, and her talk all vivacity and brisk enjoyment.

But why with swelling instances swell the chapter of instances yet more? To proclaim yourself disappointed with an author of note, it has been said, is usually to condemn your own accuracy of judgment, and your own secret craving after pantomimic effect. To those "extreme sceptics" who doubt whether it is

---

* He describes this himself as a national Hungarian characteristic : "It may be said the Hungarian even dances in tears."

possible to deduce anything as to an author's character from his books, Mr. Walter Bagehot addresses the reminder, that surely people do not keep a tame steam-engine to write their books; and if those books were really written by a man, he must have been a man who could write them,—must have had the thoughts which they express, have acquired the knowledge they contain, have possessed the style which gives them expression. "The difficulty is a defect of the critics. A person who knows nothing of an author he has read, will not know much of an author whom he has seen." Of Shakspeare this critic was writing when he penned these words, and of Shakspeare it is that Canon Kingsley says, in reference to the lack of a biographer, and indeed of materials for a biography, in his case, that it is questionable whether a biography, as such things go, would be of any use whatever to the world ; since the man who cannot, by studying Shakspeare's dramas and sonnets, attain to some clear notion of what sort of life he must have led, would not see him much the clearer for many folios of anecdoté. For after all, we are put in mind, the best biography of every sincere man is sure to be his own works: here he has set down, "transferred as in a figure," all that has happened to him, inward or outward, or rather all which has formed him, produced a permanent effect upon his mind and heart. "Of the honest man this holds true always; and almost always of the dishonest man, the man of cant, affectation, hypocrisy; for even if he pretend in his novel or his poem to be what he is not, he still shows you thereby what he thinks he ought to have been, or at least what he thinks that the world thinks he ought to have been, and confesses to you, in the most naïve and confidential way, like one who walks in his sleep, what learning he has or has not had; what society he has or has not seen; and that in the very act of trying to prove the contrary." On this account, it is urged, the smaller the man, or woman, and the less worth deciphering his biography, the more surely will he show you his essential as well as accidental self; and whether his books treat of love or political economy, theology or geology, it is there, the history of the man legibly printed, for those who care to read it.

XXV.

The Style bespeaks the Man.

AS the style is, argues a clever dissertator upon it, so, more or less, is the man. If his information be shallow, and his general habit of mind flippant, shallowness and flippancy will, it is asserted, mark what he writes. "His power of expression will, in a great measure, coincide with his powers of reasoning, imagination, and intellect. If he writes obscurely, it is mainly because he thinks obscurely, the picture he draws for the reader being simply reflected from the image within. What pleases and satisfies himself, must, he thinks, be equally satisfactory to others." Style is therefore held to be to a great extent an index of the value of what a man has to say. Exceptions* are of course freely recognized : an ignorant, shallow man, may possibly so far master the difficulties of composition, as to attain some facility of expression, and avoid many gross errors ; just as, in the same way, a man brimful of information may

---

* Apply, for example, what Hazlitt says of Fawcett the actor : "His style was laboured and artificial to a fault, while his character was frank and ingenuous in the extreme."—*Essay on Criticism*.

possibly be unable to clothe his ideas in any suitable dress. But the exceptions are as usual taken to prove the rule; and the rule is, that as the style is, so is the man.

Qualis homo talis oratio, was one of the sayings of Erasmus. "A man's style," says a more modern writer, "is the most complete expression of his entire moral nature." *Stylus virum arguit.*

Buffon is often quoted as having said, "Le style c'est l'homme," the style *is* the man. Mr. Lewes so quoted him in the original edition of his *Biographical History of Philosophy;* and in a later one he left the passage as it stood, for the sake of correcting the all but universal error. He had in the meantime detected it to be an error by the simple process of reading Buffon's actual words, which some French writer, he suggests, having misquoted from memory, thousands have repeated without misgiving, "although the phrase is an absurdity." He refers us, accordingly, to Buffon's Discours de Réception à l'Académie; where, speaking of style as that alone capable of conferring immortality on works, because the matter was prepared by preceding ages, and must soon become common property, whereas style remains a part of the man himself, the illustrious Academician adds, "Ces choses sont hors de l'homme ; le style est de l'homme même." There is, observes Mr. Lewes, an immense difference between saying *le style c'est l'homme*, and *le style est de l'homme.*

Marivaux said that style has a sex, and that women may be recognized as such by a phrase.

Lecturing to ladies on English composition, Canon Kingsley referred to a warning Professor Maurice had given him, when he undertook the lectureship—that the lecturer's object in teaching them about "styles" should be that they might have no style at all. The ladies are exhorted, however, not to be afraid of letting the peculiarities of their different characters show themselves in their styles; their prose may be the rougher for it, but it will be at least honest, "and all mannerism is dishonesty, an attempt to gain beauty at the expense of truthful expression which invariably defeats its own ends, and produces an unpleasant effect, so necessarily one are truth and beauty." But mannerism, they are instructed, can be only avoided by the most thorough practice and knowledge; half-educated writers are always mannerists; while, as the ancient canon says, "the perfection of art is to conceal art"—to depart from uncultivated and therefore defective nature; to rise again through art to a more organized and therefore more simple naturalness. Elsewhere he says that style, as the expression of thought, will depend entirely on what there is within to be expressed, on the character of the writer's mind and heart—which is implicitly allowed by us in the epithets we apply to different styles; as where we talk of a vigorous, a soft, a frigid, an obscure style; not meaning that the words and sentences in themselves are vigorous, soft, weak, or even obscure (for the words and their arrangement may be simple enough all the while), but intimating the quality of the thoughts conveyed in the words—that a style is powerful, because the writer is thinking and feeling strongly and clearly ; weak or frigid, because his feelings on the subject have been weak or cold ; obscure to you, because his thoughts have been obscure to himself. " Expression is literally the pressing out into palpable form that which is already within us." The habitual mode of utterance must, as Mr. Herbert Spencer puts it, depend upon the habitual balance of the nature. Let the powers of speech be fully developed, however; let the ability of the intellect to utter the emotions be complete ; and fixity of style will disappear. " The perfect writer will express himself as Junius, when in the Junius frame of mind ; when he feels as Lamb felt, will use a like familiar speech ; and will fall into the ruggedness of Carlyle, when in a Carlylean mood." Now he will be rhythmical, and now irregular; here his language will be plain, and there ornate ; sometimes his sentences will be balanced, and at other times unsymmetrical ; for a while there will be considerable sameness, and then again great variety. His mode of expression naturally responding to his state of feeling, there will flow from his pen a composition changing to the same degree that the aspects of his subject change.*

---

* " As now, in a fine nature, the play of the features, the tone of the voice and its cadences, vary in harmony with every thought uttered ;

Admitting to the full the excellence of Southey's style within his own range of subjects, De Quincey, himself a consummate master of style, used to maintain that Southey's defects in this particular power were as striking as his characteristic graces. Let a subject arise in which a higher tone is required, of splendid declamation, or of impassioned fervour, and Southey's style would, his critic affirmed, immediately betray its want of the loftier qualities as flagrantly as it asserted its power in the unpretending form best suited to his level character of writing, and his humbler choice of themes. For instance, were a magnificent dedication required, moving with a stately and measured solemnity, and putting forward some majestic pretensions, arising out of a long and laborious life; were a pleading required against some capital abuse of the earth—war, slavery, oppression in its thousand forms; were a *Defensio pro Populo Anglicano* required; Southey's was not, by De Quincey's contention, the mind, and, by a necessary consequence, Southey's was not the style, for carrying such purposes into full and memorable effect. His style was *therefore* good, because it was suited to his themes. He wrote plain, manly, unaffected English; what he thought, what he felt, what he was.

John Ward, the reverend Stratford-upon-Avon

so, in one possessed of a fully developed power of speech, the mould in which each combination of words is cast will similarly vary with, and be appropriate to, the sentiment."—*The Philosophy of Style*, by Herbert Spencer.

diarist, journalizes this apophthegm: that "a man is not better known by his face than by his writing, if he draws his discourse out of his own braine, and is not a book botcher." Among the *Pensées*, again, of M. Joubert, we come upon this one: "Il y a une sorte de netteté et de franchise de style qui tient à l'humeur et au tempérament, comme la franchise au caractère." M. Gustave de Beaumont cites the "hundred-times-repeated mot that the style is the man," only to offer the demur, that this is hardly true of the style of a book in which the author observes himself, and exerts all his skill to exhibit himself as he wishes to appear; but it is nearer the truth, he remarks, with respect to letters, which are written as one speaks, and because one cannot speak. "They sometimes show the intellect of the writer; they always reveal his heart and disposition." Professor Marsh speaks of "the aphorism popularly, but perhaps erroneously, ascribed to Buffon, 'The style is the man,'" as a limited application of the general theory, that there is such a relation between the mind of man and the speech he uses, that a perfect knowledge of either would enable an acute psychological philologist to deduce and construct the other from it. But Southey, in *The Doctor*, affirms that he must be a desperate mannerist who can be detected by his style, and a poor proficient in his art if he cannot at any time so vary it as to put the critic upon a false scent. Indeed he takes every day's experience to show that they who assume credit to themselves, and demand it from others for their discrimination in such things, are continually and ridiculously mistaken. Miss Mitford declared, half a century ago, that in point of style, all men now write pretty much alike,—the good days being quite bygone when the very arrangement of the words showed, as in Walton, in Addison, and in Johnson, almost as much as the thoughts they embodied, of the writer's disposition.* The late Alexander Smith was emphatic to the same effect. He complained in particular of our current periodical literature as commonplace, just as a man's countenance is commonplace which has no marked and prominent feature, no individuality of expression, no difference in any material degree from the countenances of his fellows. Indeed he goes so far as to make the deliberate assertion that all the defects of our present literature may be summed up in a word—want of style. It is by their styles, he urges, that writers are recognized, just as it is by their gait, their bearing, their tones of voice, and their numberless individual peculiarities that you recognize men in the street or in the house. Every sentence of the great writer, he contends, is like an autograph : there is no chance of

* To Sir William Elford she writes in 1814: "The diffusion of education, and partly, perhaps, the general habit of education, has done this with your sex ; but style, I think, though not bearing the impress of the individual in men, is still as much the criterion of mind and temper in women, as when 'the 'Spectators' reflected, as in a mirror, the blameless purity of Addison, and the 'Ramblers' showed, as in a majestic cast, the strength and sublimity of Dr. Johnson."—*Life and Letters of Mary Russell Mitford,* i. 293.

mistaking Milton's large utterance, or Jeremy Taylor's images, or Sir Thomas Browne's quaintness, or Charles Lamb's cunning turns of sentence; these are as distinct and individual as the features of their face or their signatures. "If Milton had endorsed a bill with half a dozen blank-verse lines, it would be as good as his name, and would be accepted as good evidence in court. If Lamb had never gathered up his essays into those charming volumes, he could be tracked easily by the critical eye through all the magazines of his time." The identity of these men, it is insisted,* can never be mistaken; every printed page of theirs is like a coat of arms, every trivial note on ordinary business like the impression of a signet ring.

Gibbon commences his autobiography with the promise, "The style shall be simple and familiar; but style is the image of character, and the habits of correct writing may produce, without labour or design, the appearance of art and study." And in describing how he set about composing the first volume of his history, he tells us in another place, "The style of an author should be the image of his mind, but the choice and command of language is the fruit of exercise." Many were the experiments he owns to have made before he could hit the middle tone, as he reckons it,

---

* Try, suggests Dr. John Drown, to put Horace, or Tacitus, Milton, Addison, or Goldsmith, Charles Lamb, or Thackeray, into other words, and you mar, if not kill the thought—they cease to be themselves.— *Horæ Subsecivæ*, 214.

between a dull chronicle and a rhetorical declamation. Small risk ran he of consignment to Ben Jonson's category of "*Jejuna, macilenta, strigosa.—Ossea et nervosa.* Some men, to avoid redundancy, run into that; and while they strive to have no ill blood or juice, they lose their good. There be some styles, again, that have not less blood, but less flesh and corpulence. These are bony and sinewy; *Ossa habent, et nervos.*" That language most shows a man, is another of Jonson's "Discoveries"—*speak, that I may see thee.* It springs out of the most retired and inmost parts of us, he says, and is the image of the parent of it, the mind. "No glass renders a man's form or likeness so true as his speech. Nay, it is likened to a man; and as we consider feature and composition in a man, so words in language; in the greatness, aptness, sound, structure, and harmony of it." Elia characterized his own essays as villanously pranked in an affected array of antique modes and phrases. They had not been *his*, if they had been other than such; and better it is, Lamb maintains, that a writer should be natural in a self-pleasing quaintness, than to affect a naturalness (so called) that should be strange to him.

One of the biographers of Agrippa d'Aubigné, having finished his portraiture of the man of action, and in action, proceeds to discuss him as thinker and writer; and thus he prefaces this section of his work: "Si le style, comme l'a dit Buffon, est l'homme même, on ne saurait attendre d'un tel personnage qu'un style

d'un accent prononcé et d'une originalité saisissante."
Nor is such expectation belied. M. Léon Feugère
descries in the style of D'Aubigné the imperfections
and especially the *intempérance* so markworthy in the
man; hence his redundancies, trivialities, brusqueries,
and *rudesses*. Often and often the grim captain treats
grammar as he treated his foes, writing just as he
acted, with headlong ardour, and hurling forth his
phrases in a sort of reckless improvisation. He who
thinks decidedly, it has been said, will write clearly,
if not forcibly; he who has made up his mind what
he is going to say, can say it; and thus an Edinburgh
Reviewer defines the difference between Lord Eldon's
and Lord Collingwood's mode of writing to be neither
more nor less than that which existed to the last
between the energetic Seaman and the hesitating
Judge. The incomparable simplicity of style of
Herodotus—his spontaneous and natural mode of
telling a story—the naturalness of manner which
makes his narrative so clear and transparent, and
rarely allows the shadow of a doubt to rest upon his
meaning; in all this is traced the counterpart of his
"clear, candid spirit,"—his style being, as one of his
critics observes, as far removed from the rather osten-
tatious display of Xenophon as from the studied and
sombre reticence of Thucydides.

Sydney Smith has been named as sometimes forming a striking exception to " Buffon's famous dogma,
Le style, c'est l'homme;" for in his case the man was

always natural, simple, and essentially English, whereas the style was often forced, factitious, composite, and (to borrow his own word) cosmopolite. Buffon's famous dogma is of stereotyped service on both sides the Channel, and as often as not it is cited by way of exception; as where Heinrich Heine maliciously remarks,—" Buffon said, *Le style, c'est l'homme.* M. Villemain is the living refutation of this maxim. His style is elegant and pure." Churchill derides altogether the claim of critical insight and discernment of personal identity, derived from style alone; secure from vulgar eyes, the nameless author passes in disguise;

> "But veteran critics are not so deceived,
> If veteran critics are to be believed.
> Once seen, they know an author evermore,
> Nay, swear to hands they never saw before.
> . . . .
> How doth it make judicious readers smile
> When authors are detected by their style;
> Though every one who knows this author, knows
> He shifts his style much oftener than his clothes!"

XXVI.

Personality in Fiction.

A VERY puzzle it seems to many in our day how ever the voluminous platitudes of Mademoiselle de Scudéry's romances could obtain vogue, and be actually and greedily in demand, once, and only once upon a time. One plausible reason assigned is the fact, that all the personages who figured in these *romans* were her flesh and blood contemporaries; all were drawn in detail from real life; their names were known to all, their portraits and characters were recognized, from the great Cyrus himself, in whom men descried the great Condé, to Doralise, who was Mdlle. Robineau. "Tous ces personnages, même les plus secondaires," says M. Sainte-Beuve, "étaient connus dans la société ; on se passait la clef, on se nommait les masques." Masquerade work of this kind was a piquant attraction. There was a peculiar zest in seeing the world one lived in painted as it was, in seeing the people one daily met and observed and had to do with introduced all alive into a work of fiction, and there made to talk with *esprit* and *finesse*. So it was with D'Urfé, and almost every other *romancier* of the time; they all put their acquaintance into their books, as well as put themselves, and perhaps the adventures of their youth; though in D'Urfé's case, at least, all this was so combined, disguised, and, in Patru's phrase, *romanced*, that only the author himself could supply the clue to the labyrinth.

Personality in fiction is old as the old comedy of Athens at least, when "such was the licence of the muse," as Goldsmith words it, that, far from lashing vice in general characters, she boldly exhibited the exact portrait of every notorious man of the day—omitting no circumstance of his external appearance,—his very air, attire, manner, and even his name. Varying in degree, this personality licence has never lost its hold on writer or reader. Demand begets supply, and supply again begets demand. Ever and anon a Fielding (not that Fieldings are many) has to put forth a deprecatory protest, as in the Preface to *Joseph Andrews*, that the author has no intention to vilify or asperse any one; and that albeit scarcely a character is introduced which is not taken from personal observation, yet has the utmost care been used to obscure the persons by such different circumstances, degrees, and colours, that it would be impossible to guess at them with any approach to certainty. In the body of that same book he questions not but some of his readers will

know the lawyer in the stage coach, the moment they
hear his voice, and that the wit, the prude, and indeed
all the rest of the characters, will be severally identified offhand. To prevent, therefore, any such malicious applications, he makes a point of then and
there declaring, once for all, that he describes not
men, but manners; not an individual, but a species.
If asked, Are not the characters then taken from life?
he answers Yes, and that he has written little more
than he has seen. The lawyer he affirms to be not
only alive, but to have been so these four thousand
years, and, if God will and the world last, likely to
live as many more. Indeed he is confined to no one
religion, profession, or country.* Whether Pope's
Atticus be, or be not, a true portrait of Addison, is
now, says one of Pope's critics, of as little consequence as whether Justice Shallow be a correct resemblance of Sir Thomas Lucy; the character is true—its
prototype is to be found in every generation; happy
will it be when the picture has no living original.

Walking one day in company with Rousseau, Bernardin de St. Pierre asked Jean-Jacques whether he
did not mean Saint-Preux for his very self. "No,"

---

* "It is therefore doing him little honour to imagine he endeavours
to mimic some little obscure fellow, because he happens to resemble
him in one particular feature, or perhaps in his profession. . . .
This places the boundary between, and distinguishes the satirist from
the libeller: the former privately corrects the fault for the benefit of the
person, like a parent; the latter publicly exposes the person himself, as
an example to others, like an executioner."—*Joseph Andrews*, book iii.,
chap. i.

was the reply; "Saint-Preux is not exactly what I have been, but what I have wished to be." Almost all poetizing romancers may say the same. Corinne, says M. Sainte-Beuve, is, for Madame de Staël, what she fain would be, and what, after all,—difference in the grouping of art allowed for—she actually was. The character of Pechorin, the misanthropic militaire, disgusted with life, in the Russian novelist Lermontov's best-known work, is said to have been intended by the author for himself; and this was faintly denied in much the same manner, suggests one critic, that Byron at times denied his own identity with Childe Harold. Plenty of people are or have been preposterously positive that Vivian Grey is Mr. Disraeli; and Pelham, Lord Lytton; that, in fact the authors would be disappointed to find there could be any question as to the personal identity. That Madame de Staël was willing to be thought her own heroine, is credible enough. Madame Necker de Saussure tells us that "Corinne est l'idéal de Madame de Staël; Delphine en est la réalité durant sa jeunesse." Delphine became for her a touching personification of her years of pure sentiment and tenderness at the moment of her leaving them behind—what Sainte-Beuve calls a last and heartrending farewell (*un dernier et déchirant adieu*), on the threshold of her new career, "au début du regne public, à l'entrée du rôle européen et de la gloire." All the characters in *Delphine* were, at the time, presumed to be copies from life. M. de Lebensei, that Protestant gentleman with English manners, and intellectually remarkable in so exceptional a degree, was Benjamin Constant. Madame de Vernon was made out to be a portrait, *en femme*, of the most celebrated French politician of the day. Madame de Cerlèbe, devoted to domestic life, to the gentle uniformity of household duties, and taking infinite pleasure in the work of educating her children, was Madame Necker de Saussure. And so on. Miss Brontë was charged, by no unfriendly critic, with being scarcely herself aware how faithfully she drew from the life; her close adherence to the matter of her own limited experience being shown by the fact that her pictures were recognized as portraits. Hence were traced not only defects in her workmanship, but a "gross infraction of social rights," to the wrongfulness of which she seemed to be "singularly blind." True, her portraits were not exact, but this, it is contended, only did the greater mischief: they were sufficient to identify those who were unfortunate enough to have become the subjects of her keen examination, and the variation did only the further injustice of conveying a false impression of them. In one of her letters she does indeed assure a lady friend, "You are not to suppose any of the characters in *Shirley* intended as literal portraits. It would not suit the rules of art, nor of my own feelings, to write in that style. We only suffer reality to *suggest*, never to dictate. The heroines are abstractions, and the heroes also." But this very letter is cited by Mr. Roscoe as containing a proof, notwithstanding her express disclaimer of literal portrait-painting, that she did copy pretty closely external indications of character, as well as of her alleged failure to seize the inner spirit. The Autocrat of the Breakfast-table is free to own his fears that were he ever to write the story he wants to write, the amount of personality in his fiction would be fatal to the peace of his friends, and so to his own. He is "terribly afraid" he should show up all his friends ; for is not that what all story-tellers do? And he is afraid all his friends would not very well bear showing up, since they have an average share of the common weaknesses of humanity, which he is pretty certain would come out. For, of all that have told stories among his people, he can hardly recall one who has not drawn too faithfully some living portrait that might better have been spared.

A Saturday Reviewer claims to see in *Vivian Grey* and its kindred romances all the prognostics of their writer's destiny : there stand in ineffaceable characters his moral code, his political creed, and the ideal policy of the future statesman. True, human nature is at best a puzzle, and man's inner self changes with circumstances, and the juvenile indiscretions of a novelist should not be taken as too full an exposition of the method and belief of the matured man. But there are books, it is contended, which are a complete index to the mind that created them. "It is because we know the author that we know that the work is indubitably his. It is for the very reason that Mr. Disraeli reminds us so forcibly of his novels that we accept them as a fair commentary on his career." Indeed, another critic asserts, with perfect confidence of the truth of his statement, although it is confessedly impossible to produce direct evidence of that truth,— because it would involve personality to attempt to do so,—that in a large proportion of novels written in the present day, the characters are only the author set in different lights, and the novel itself virtually a literary adaptation of the ingenious device formerly exhibited at the Polytechnic, where a sort of arbour, made of mirrors, was so arranged, that when any one entered he saw his own face in twenty different attitudes, and from as many points of view: one showed the back of his head and the cut of his shoulders, another his profile, a third his hair, a fourth his ear, cheek, and the back view of his whiskers, a fifth the lower surfaces of the chin, upper lip, nostrils, and eyelid. Just in the same manner the characters in a novel are shown to be the author as he felt when in high spirits, the author in a sceptical state of mind, the author when he determined to devote himself to common-sense and practical life, the author in love, the author when he had lost his illusions, and every now and then the author on his death-bed. There is, however, nothing which novelists deprecate so eagerly as the imputation that their heroes are meant for themselves.*

Just as Tieck has essayed to discern the actual man Shakspeare in some subordinate characters of his plays,—in Horatio, for instance, and Antonio, and other persons of worth, if not of much weight in the piece,—so have contemporary critics affected to trace the benevolent traits of Sir Walter Scott in Mordaunt Morton and similar rather colourless personages. M. Sainte-Beuve writes: "S'il s'est peint dans quelque personnage de ses romans, ç'a été dans des charactères comme celui de Morton des *Puritains* ["Old Mortality"], c'est-à-dire dans un type pâle, indécis, honnête et bon." The same critic denies that any such conjecture will hold good in the case of Molière. He snubs without hesitation the attempts to prove Alceste to be a portrait of M. de Montausier, the *bourgeois gentilhomme* to be Rehault, Harpagon to be the Président de Bercy. He has no patience with the ingenious blunderers who *will* find the Comte de Grammont in one comedy, and the Duc de La Feuillade in another. He pooh-poohs peremp-

---

* "Every one who has the common instincts of manliness and propriety must feel that for any man to sit down deliberately to draw his own portrait, and to make public his own recollections—recollections probably to which he justly attaches an all but sacred value—to make capital out of his affections, and to communicate confidentially to the world thoughts which he would never have the impudence to communicate to an individual—is an action which can only be described as grossly indecent, and unworthy of any man who values independence and self-respect."—*Saturday Review*, vii. 12.

torily the amateurs of anecdotage, the Dangeau tribe, the Tallemants and Guy Patins, who identify the faces behind the stage masks. Alceste, *le misanthrope*, he contends, is no more M. de Montausier than he is Molière, or than he is Boileau, whom he equally resembles in some feature or another. Trissotin is the Abbé Cotin only for a moment. The characters of Molière, in short, are not copies, but creations. Mr. Thackeray, in his Book of Snobs, amusingly repudiated the charge of personal portraiture. "No, we are not personal in these candid remarks. As Phidias took the pick of a score of beauties before he completed a Venus, so have we to examine, perhaps, a thousand Snobs, before one is expressed upon paper." Dryden sought, in his prologue to the *Man of Mode*, to exonerate Etherege from aiming at any particular coxcomb in his famous portrait of Sir Fopling Flutter:

"Yet none Sir Fopling *him* or *him* can call:
He's knight o' the shire, and represents ye all;"—

but it was sufficiently notorious at the time that Beau Hewitt was the original.

It was generally believed that Smollett painted some of his own early adventures under the veil of fiction; but the public, says the best of his biographers, and one who outdid him in his own art, carried the spirit of applying the characters of a work of fiction to living personages much farther perhaps than the author intended. "Gawkey, Crabbe, and Potion were assigned to individuals in the west of Scotland; Mrs. Smollett was supposed to be Narcissa; the author himself represented Roderick Random (of which there can be little doubt); a bookbinder and barber, the early acquaintances of Smollett, contended for the character of the attached, amiable, simple-hearted Strap; and the two naval officers under whom Smollett had served, were stigmatized under the names of Oakum and Whiffle." All the more keenly the public appears to have relished the book for the zest of its presumed personalities. To Mr. Disraeli an unfriendly reviewer assigns the invention of the contrivance of "libellous descriptions of political or religious opponents," and on him is fixed the responsibility of placing it in the hands of others stupider but more malignant than himself. "The sketches of living men inserted in *Coningsby* and other novels of the same set were scarcely redeemed from vulgarity by their wit;" and they were, the reviewer maintains, necessarily unjust—the method pursued by their author being to delineate the side of an adverse politician's character which is open to the world's gaze, and then to fill up that part concealed from it by strokes in harmony with the portion seen. The result is described as generally a picture of perfect baseness, which was inevitably untrue, inasmuch as the conclusion suggested by the largest experience is that the traits of a man's nature which a political enemy does not see are exactly those which redeem it, and do in fact commend it to his friends. Georges Sand's *Elle et Lui*, and Paul de Musset's *Lui et Elle*, have been signalized as illustrating all too completely the horrible injustice of the system of attacking private character in novels.* The discredit which attaches to each of these books and authors is traceable to the portraits which they have drawn of the persons whom they respectively wished to exhibit to the world at large in infamous colours. Now it is boldly alleged to be in fact hardly possible to imagine a state of things in which it can be otherwise than a crime to make a personal enemy into the hero of a novel—it not being in human nature to withstand the temptation to injustice which such a proceeding affords, while the injustice is aggravated by every circumstance which gives excellence to the novel; for effectiveness, and not accuracy of statement, is the object at which novelists invariably and necessarily aim.

When the *Dowager* of Mrs. Gore appeared, reviewers said how easy it would be to assign to the *dramatis personæ* prototypes in the world of fashion; indeed it was scarcely possible to avoid them; but then it was only in so far as regards the particular trait, not as respects the entire personage. In the same character might be found peculiarities derived

---

* The representative of Mme. Sand, for instance, in *Lui et Elle*, "is guilty of a string of atrocities perhaps even more disgraceful than those which Mr. Disraeli attributed in *Coningsby* to Mr. Croker."—*Saturday Review*, viii. 133; cf. xlii. 417.

from distinct originals, and combined with much that was of general, not individual, application. Mrs. Gore delivers herself of this candid avowal in the preface to one of her revised and reprinted fictions: "Experience has convinced me that the strictures of my friends Lord and Lady Holland were just; and that nothing can be more objectionable than the introduction of real characters into a work of fiction—confusing the mind of the young or careless reader, and creating a semi-vitality, half flesh, half marble, like that of the Prince in the Arabian Tale." Referring, in his admirable memoir of his aunt, Miss Austen, to the surmises of some readers that she took her characters from individuals with whom she had been acquainted,* the Rev. J. E. Austen-Leigh treats such a supposition as surely betraying an ignorance of the high prerogative of genius, to create out of its own resources imaginary characters who shall be true to nature and consistent in themselves. The creator of Mr. Woodhouse and Mrs. Elton, of Mr. Collins and Miss Bates, of Mrs. Jennings and John Thorpe, "did not copy individuals, but she invested her own creations with individuality of character." Her own relations, we are assured, never recognized any individual in her characters; though her nephew can call to mind several of her acquaintance whose peculiarities

---

* "They were so lifelike that it was assumed that they must once have lived, and have been transferred bodily, as it were, into her pages."
—*Memoir of Jane Austen*, p. 200.

were very tempting and easy to be caricatured, but of whom there are no traces in her pages. And it is on record that she herself, when questioned on the subject by a friend, expressed a dread of what she called such an "invasion of social proprieties."*

In his kindly, genial way, shrewd withal, and twinkling with fun, Sir Walter Scott confessedly drew profiles, if not whole faces, and sometimes full-length figures from real life. He avows in his autobiography, for instance, that in his father's old friend, George Constable, he had observed many of those peculiarities of temper which long afterwards he tried to develop in the character of Jonathan Oldbuck.† Mr. Lockhart ends his notices of the residence at Sandy Knowe with observing, that in Sir Walter's account of the friendly clergyman who so often sat at his grandfather's fireside there, we cannot fail to trace many features of the secluded divine, Cargill, in *St. Ronan's Well.*

---

* She said that she thought it quite fair to note peculiarities and weaknesses, but that it was her desire to create, not to reproduce. "Besides," she added, "I am too proud of my gentlemen to admit that they were only Mr. A. or Colonel B." Not, however, that Jane Austen supposed her imaginary characters to be of a higher order than exist in nature; for she said, when speaking of two of her great favourites, Edmund Bertram and Mr. Knightly: "They are very far from being what I know English gentlemen often are."—*Ibid.*, p. 203.

† "It is very odd, that though I am unconscious of anything in which I strictly espied the *manners* of my old friend, the resemblance was nevertheless detected by George Chambers, Esq., solicitor, London, an old friend both of my father and Mr. Constable, and who affirmed to my late friend, Lord Kinedder, that I must needs be the author of The Antiquary, since he recognized the portrait of George Constable."
—*Autobiography of Sir Walter Scott*, chap. i.

The style of life and manners in the household of Joshua Geddes of Mount Sharon, and his amiable sister, in some of what are aptly called the sweetest chapters of *Redgauntlet*, is a slightly decorated edition, it appears, of what Scott witnessed under the hospitable roof of Mrs. Waldie of Henderside,—whose many kind attentions to him are said to have left strong traces on every page of his works in which he has occasion to introduce the Society of Friends. Mr. Lockhart has no sort of doubt that William Clerk was, in the main, Darsie Latimer, while Scott himself unquestionably sat for his own portrait in Alan Fairford. According to Mr. Shortreed, Willie Elliot of Millburnholm was the great original of Dandie Dinmont. David Ritchie was the acknowledged prototype of the Black Dwarf. George Thomson, or *Dominie Thamson*, appears to have been no way inclined to quarrel with the universal conviction of his having sat for Dominie Sampson,—or at any rate "furnished many features for the inimitable personage whose designation so nearly resembled his own." Of Matilda, in *Rokeby*, we find Sir Walter writing to Miss Baillie that she was attempted for an actual person, then deceased ; and that he felt particularly flattered with his gifted correspondent's distinguishing that character from the others, which are in general mere shadows.*

---

* His biographer and son-in-law has no sort of doubt that the lady in question was the object of Sir Walter's own unfortunate first love ; and as little, that in the romantic generosity, both of the youthful poet

In his Introduction to Chronicles of the Canongate, he takes occasion to state generally, but explicitly, that although he deemed historical personages free subjects of delineation, he had never in any instance violated in his fictions the respect due to private life. It was indeed impossible, he allowed, that traits proper to persons, both living and dead, with whom he had intercourse in society should not have risen to his pen; but he had always, he protests, made it his study to generalize the portraits, so that they should still seem, on the whole, the productions of fancy, though possessing some resemblance to real individuals. Confessedly, his attempts had not in this last particular been uniformly successful; there being men whose characters are so peculiarly marked, that the delineation of some leading and principal feature, inevitably places the whole person before you in his individuality.

From various indications, the attentive reader of *Henry Masterton*, its author surmised, would doubtless discover that the character of Frank, the hero's elder brother, was not drawn from imagination, even were no such admission made on the part of the portrait-painter. Individual traits of character are the property of every person who observes and attempts to portray human nature; but the writer in question

---

who fails to win her higher favour, and of his chivalrous competitor, we have before us something more than "a mere shadow."—*Lockhart's Life of Scott*, chap. xxv.

claimed credit, "from his own peculiar views of what is right in society," for refraining from painting what may be called full-length pictures of anybody he had actually known, except in two or three instances, in all of which, as in the case of Frank Masterton, the original had long been dead before the pen which essayed to depict him had begun its task.

Hartley Coleridge has somewhere said that the question should be, not, Is the picture taken from individual life? but, Does its effect require that the individual likeness be recognized? This he proposes as the test that distinguishes legitimate satire from lampooning, a Hogarth from a caricaturist, a Fielding from a fashionable novelist. Fielding's name he mentions rather than Scott's, because in Sir Walter's works there is no character that could possibly be meant for any living individual, which the original might not be proud to acknowledge. Almost the concluding lines of Crabbe's *Borough* are these:

> "Nor be it ever of my portraits told—
> 'Here the strong lines of malice we behold.'
>   *   *   *   *
> This let me hope, that when in public view
> I bring my pictures, men may feel them true;
> 'This is a likeness,' may they all declare,
> 'And I have seen him, but I know not where;'
> For I should mourn the mischief I had done,
> If as the likeness all would fix on one."

XXVII.

Fiction appealing to Facts.

IT has been said that perhaps an author is never wise to claim credit for veracity in his fictions: accidentally, a story may be as veracious as possible, but it is certainly unwise to insist on its being believed; for while a story, regarded only as a fiction, commonly meets with gentle treatment at the hands of its reader, directly its veracity is insisted on it is regarded from another point of view. It is pronounced a mistake to suppose that the interest is heightened by our belief in the real existence of the persons introduced : interest is heightened or depressed according to the author's skill in surrounding his personages with the atmosphere of real life, but in no other way. Of one of our most popular lady novelists it has been said that her aim is to make her reader think each character a portrait, and each event real : she particularizes the height of her hero, as if she were on oath, as "five feet ten, or ten and a half;" and as she thus proceeds she frequently pauses to assure us that she is speaking literal truth, not borrowing from imagination. An at least equally popular writer of the rougher sex, has been taxed or twitted with indulging in a like plea, by way of defence for what is strongly sensational in his stories: he "assures us that all his personages and all their misdeeds are strictly historical." Marvellous as his incidents may be, he asseverates again and again that they rest on facts which have happened within his own knowledge. "Bah! I tell you I have known these people," is the summary reply with which he dismisses an imaginary objector—and he has objectors other than imaginary—to the probability of his story. But the impulse to justify one's figment improbabilities by an appeal to facts seems irresistible, even to masters and mistresses of fiction. Dante exclaims midway in the twenty-fifth canto of *L'Inferno*—

> "If, O reader I now
> Thou be not apt to credit what I tell,
> No marvel; for myself do scarce allow
> The witness of mine eyes."

Lord Lytton prefaces his grim story of *Lucretia* with an explicit affirmation that, incredible as it might seem, the crimes therein recorded had taken place within the seventeen years immediately preceding. There had been, he protested, no exaggeration as to their extent, no great departure from their details: "the means employed, even that which seems most far-fetched (the instrument of the poisoned ring), have their foundation in literal facts. . . . In those most salient essentials which will most, perhaps, provoke the reader's incredulous wonder, I narrate a history, not write a fiction." Balzac deals in a different spirit with the anticipated charge against his *Père Goriot*, that the author is extravagant in his inventions: "Eh-bien, sachez-le ! ce drame n'est ni une fiction ni un roman : *All is true*, il est si véritable, que chacun peut en reconnaître les éléments chez-soi." R. H. Dana prefaces his *Buccaneer* poem with this among other paragraphs : " I will not say of my first tale, as Miss Edgeworth sometimes does of her improbabilities, 'This is a fact ;' but thus much I may say : there are few facts so well vouched for, and few truths so fully believed in, as the account upon which I have grounded my story." Dr. O. Wendell Holmes announced in the preface to his *Elsie Venner*, that while the story was in progress he received the most startling confirmation of the possibility of the existence of a character like that which he had here drawn as a purely imaginary conception. Milverton, of *Friends in Council*, iterates, with at least as much emphasis as discretion, his design of writing a true story, "at least one which I know has happened in the world's history." Ellesmere derides his announcement, and is satirical on his choice, in the case of *Realmah*, of an opportunity for inventing things that cannot be contradicted ; while another, and still more, far more matter-of-fact critic, pleads for the story not to be pitched in impossible latitudes and longitudes, for to the plain, practical pleader, that a story should have some semblance of reality is a great comfort. " Mine is all real," answers Milverton, "and must have happened :

in fact, I know it did happen." Farther on, when Ellesmere takes exception to the Realmah style of thinking and talking, its author replies: "I can only tell you what I know to have occurred. I may use modern terms . . .; but what I know is, that I shall give a most true account of the thoughts and doings of the great Realmah." Ebenezer Elliott is eager to assure his readers that there is not in his poetry one good idea that had not been suggested by some real occurrence, or by some object actually before his eyes, or by some remembered object or incident, etc. Byron's mocking laugh is heard through the stanzas beginning:

> "There's only one slight difference between
> Me and my epic brethren gone before,
> And here the advantage is my own, I ween, . . .
> They so embellish, that 'tis quite a bore
> Their labyrinths of fables to read through,
> Whereas this story's actually true.
>
> If any person doubt it, I appeal
> To history, tradition, and to facts,
> To newspapers, whose truth all know and feel," etc.

And here he is again, much later in his narrative, but unaltered in tone, tune, and metre:

> "Besides, my Muse by no means deals in fiction :
> She gathers a repertory of facts,
> Of course with some reserve and slight restriction,
> But mostly sings of human things and acts—
> And that's the cause she meets with contradiction ;
> For too much truth, at first sight, ne'er attracts."

Mr. Dickens gives prominence, in his chapter on Nurse's Stories, to a certain "female bard," as he designates her, who made a standing pretence which greatly assisted in forcing him, the coy listener, back to a number of hideous places he would by all means have avoided. This pretence was, that all her ghost stories had occurred to her own relations. Politeness towards a meritorious family, as he puts it, therefore prohibited his doubting them, and they acquired an air of authentication that impaired his digestive powers for life.* One is apt to feel something of the same recalcitrant politeness in regard to the novelists who assert the absolute *vero* of their *ben trovato*. Constantly in contemporary fiction are we meeting with such preliminary precautions and interpolated assurances as the following, in one of the most popular of current stories: "My story is a true one,—not only true in a general sense, but strictly true as to the leading facts which I am about to relate,—and I could point out, in a certain county, . . . the very house in which the events I shall here describe took place." Judicious critics ever and anon refer with a sense of weary deprecation to the "strange but very common delusion" that it is a great advantage to a writer of fiction to be able to assure his readers that the facts he narrates have actually occurred in real life—that

---

* Feebly endeavouring to explain away one apparition, "on Mercy's retorting with wounded dignity that the parlour-maid was her own sister-in-law, I perceived there was no hope." So with another rationalizing essay or explanatory hypothesis: "But my remorseless nurse cut the ground from under my feet, by informing me that She was the other young woman," etc.—*The Uncommercial Traveller*, xv.

the village apothecary is still alive who supplied the pretty bigamist with poison, or that a nightcap may be seen in Madame Tussaud's Exhibition with the hero's own blood, warranted, upon it. This theory is presumed to have reached perhaps the climax of its absurdity when, a few years since, a well-known authoress half-apologized for the harassing and repulsive character of the facts she described, but justified herself on the ground that they were strictly true. This, it is agreed, would have been an admirable excuse if the lady had been giving evidence in a witness-box, or had been exposing the horrors of vivisection in the hope that public opinion would enforce their abolition. But it is "obviously no sort of excuse for a novelist, unless indeed he can plead, like the Ancient Mariner, that he is under some mysterious and irrepressible impulse to tell his tale of woe. As an artist working in the regions of imagination, he has it in his power to select or invent whatever facts best suit his purpose, provided they be in due conformity to the laws of nature and the principles of his art." He is in no way concerned, let him take the critic's word for it, with the question whether or not they have taken place in real life; and the singular fashion of insisting upon their actual occurrence is surmised to be due to a modern rage for wild and grotesque stories in which sensation is purchased at the cost of all ordinary notions of probability,—a writer feeling the necessity of somehow convincing his readers that his story is not the tissue of unnatural absurdities that it looks; "just as a bad sign-painter is obliged to print, in staring capitals, the name of his picture, in order that you may not mistake a horse for an ass." A reviewer of a book of this class prognosticated that if the mania for sensation should last, it might become the fashion for a certain order of novelists to appear, with a long array of witnesses, before a magistrate, and solemnly prove the truth of all the statements which they advance. If troublesome in one way, this system would save a world of trouble in another. "A novelist who could place on his title-page a magisterial certificate testifying that all he had written was strictly in accordance with fact, would not of course be expected to maintain that general semblance of conformity to the laws of nature which we now expect in a genuine work of art." Mr. Adolphus Trollope's *Gemma* was stamped as a spoilt story, by his adoption of the principle that it is a merit in a novelist to adhere closely to fact ; he not only giving us carefully to understand that the chief events recorded in it had really occurred, and that at the time of publication there were people still alive who well remembered them, but on one occasion even accounting, not to say apologizing, for the unheroic conduct of his hero by reminding us that he was "telling the tale as it was told to him," and that he could not alter facts. In an evil hour, he was told, it seemed to have occurred to him that he had better adhere closely to the original story, in order that he might enjoy the barren triumph of assuring his readers that it was strictly true.

"'Tis true, 'tis pity, pity 'tis 'tis true,"

in that sense, and to that extent. Sometimes in the æsthetics of art, even as in the paradoxes of jurisprudence, the greater the truth the greater the libel. As a thing may in common parlance be too good to be true, so in art it may be too true to be good.

XXVIII.

Author's Den.

IT was a strange apartment, we are told, of Teufelsdröckh's den,—full of books and tattered papers, and miscellaneous shreds of all conceivable substances, "united in a common element of dust." Books lay on tables, and below tables; here fluttered a sheet of manuscript, there a torn handkerchief, or nightcap hastily thrown aside; ink-bottles alternated with breadcrusts, coffee-pots, tobacco-boxes, periodical literature, and blucher boots. Only some once in the month, old Lieschen, the Herr Professor's bed-maker and stove-lighter, half-forcibly made her way into the den, with broom and duster, and (Teufelsdröckh hurriedly saving his manuscripts) effected a partial clearance, a jail-delivery of such lumber as was not literary. "These were her *Erdbeben* (earthquakes), which Teufelsdröckh dreaded worse than the pestilence; nevertheless, to such length he had been forced to comply." *

---

* In the flush of young authorship, Basil, in Mr. Wilkie Collins' story of that name, thus airs his plans, and prospects, and *de jure* peculiarities, and testifies to his sister's sympathy with them all: " I

Lord Cockburn relates of the venerable Adam Ferguson, Edinburgh's historian of Rome, and predecessor

am engaged in writing a historical romance. Clara has read the first half-dozen finished chapters, and augurs wonderful success for my fiction when it is published. She is determined to arrange my study with her own hands; to dust my books and sort my papers herself. She knows that I am already as perfect and precise about my literary goods and chattels, as indignant at any interference of housemaids and dusters with my library treasures, as if I were a veteran author of twenty years' standing; and she is resolved to spare me every apprehension on this score, by taking all the arrangements of my study upon herself, and keeping the key of the door when I am not in need of it." (Chap vi.)

Mr. Thackeray has a fellow-feeling for the sorrows of Fitzroy, in one of his minor tales. "No sooner was he gone . . . than the women pounced upon his little study, and began to put it in order. Some of his papers they pushed up over the bookcase, some they put behind the Encyclopædia, some they crammed into the drawers,' etc.; and a few chapters later we read of the mother-in-law, how "in Fitz's own apartments she revelled with peculiar pleasure. It has been described how she had sacked his study, and pushed away his papers, some of which, including three cigars, and the commencement of an article for the *Law Magazine*, 'Lives of the Sheriffs' Officers,' he has never been able to find to this day."

When Porpora, in *Consuelo*, one day sees his papers, usually scattered upon the harpsichord in indescribable disorder, ranged (by Consuelo's care) in symmetrical piles, he assumes his valet to be the author of this exasperating intervention, and invokes confusion upon him, for his love of order, accordingly. These valets are all alike, he exclaims; and this one has had the impertinence to touch the master's manuscript. "Forgive him, master," Consuelo pleads; "your music was in perfect chaos." "I know my way in that chaos!" is the reply: "I could get up at night and find any passage of my opera by feeling in the dark: now I know nothing about it; I am lost; it will cost me a month's hard work to put it to rights again." Consuelo then owns herself the culprit, and asks him if her painstaking arrangement and protection of the loose sheets, may not save them from summary destruction by a stroke of the duster, or a sweep of the broom. "But what need was there to sweep and dust my chamber?" the irate old composer demands; he had lived in it hitherto

to Dugald Stewart in her chair of moral philosophy, that he invariably locked the door of his study when he left it, and took the key in his pocket; and no housemaid got in till the accumulation of dust and rubbish made it impossible to put the evil day off any longer; and then woe on the family. If Dr. Thomas Brown, the successor of Dugald Stewart, was aware of Adam Ferguson's jealous resentment of intermeddling hands, in the cause of order, possibly the old professor was in the mind's eye of the young one, when the latter philosophized on the fact of one's feeling more indignant at petty injuries than at great ones. The very magnitude of an evil, he argues, lessens the vividness of the mere feeling of resentment by dividing, as it were, its interest with other intermingled feelings. Thus, an injury which deprives us of half our estate, presents to us many objects of thought, as well as the mere image of the injurer; but when a servant, "in his excessive love of order, has laid out of our way a volume which we expected to find on our table," the evil is not sufficiently great to occupy or distract us; and we see, therefore, the "whole un-

---

to his own satisfaction, without ever letting any one enter it. Unhealthy, say you, to sleep in a room which is not aired and cleaned every day? Bah!

Dinah Morris, dusting in Adam Bede's room, hesitates as she nears the papers on the table, though pained to see so much dust upon them. "Seth, is your brother wrathful when his papers are stirred?" "Yes, very, when they are not put back in the right places," said a strong deep voice, not Seth's.

pardonable atrocity," of that over-diligence which is so teasing in its results. The mild Scotch doctor's style would befit John Dennis in his Frenzy,—that John Dennis whom Swift has cruelly pictured in his den—the whole floor covered with manuscripts as thick as a pastrycook's shop on a Christmas Eve—while on the table were some ends of verse and of candles, a gallipot of ink with a yellow pen in it, and a pot of half-dead ale covered with a Longinus. When Mr. Oldbuck of Monkbarns has led his new friend and visitor to the top of the winding staircase which leads to his own room, his first exclamation, on opening the door, is, "What are you about here, you sluts?" Whereupon a dirty barefooted chambermaid throws down her duster, detected in the heinous fact of arranging the *sanctum sanctorum*, and flees out from the face of her incensed master; while the young lady who has been superintending the hazardous operation, timidly stands her ground, and offers the plea, "Indeed, uncle, your room was not fit to be seen, and I just came to see that Jenny laid everything down where she took it up." " And how dare you, or Jenny either, presume to meddle with my private matters ?" is Mr. Oldbuck's retort ; for he is as professed a good hater of *putting to rights* as Dr. Orkborne, or any other self-willed and self-sufficing student. One paragraph in Benjamin Franklin's serio-comic Account of the Custom of Whitewashing, as inexorably enforced and indomitably practised by Yankee housewives, good women and true, recognizes an alleviation of the husband's distress, in the fact of his generally having the privilege of a small room or closet for his books and papers, the key of which he is allowed to keep, and which is considered a privileged place, standing like the land of Goshen amid the plagues of Egypt. But then, he must, says Franklin, be extremely cautious, and ever on his guard; "for should he inadvertently go abroad and leave the key in his door, the house-maid, who is always on the watch for such an opportunity, immediately enters in triumph with buckets, brooms, and brushes; takes possession of the premises, and forthwith puts all his books and papers *to rights* —to his utter confusion and sometimes serious detriment." The Launcelot Langstaff, Esq., of *Salmagundi*, is described as holding in more utter abhorrence than any living creature what is usually termed a notable housewife: sooner would he see one of the weird sisters flourish through the keyhole on a broomstick, than one of the servant-maids enter the door with a besom. In one of his whim-wham essays he says things the reverse of complimentary of "an ugly old woman who last spring was employed by Mrs. Cockloft to whitewash my room and put things in order; a phrase which, if rightly understood, means little else than huddling everything into holes and corners, so that if I want to find any particular article, it is like 'looking for a needle in a haystack.' Not recognizing my visitor, I demanded by what authority she wished me a 'happy new year'? Her claim was one of the weakest she could have urged, for I have an innate and mortal antipathy to the custom of putting things to rights." So had Dr. Priestley; and not without cause to show for it. While occupied in his first and most important investigation on the nature of the air, and anxiously watching the results of a particular experiment, to be reported at the annual meeting of the Royal Society, he was inopportunely called away from home, and unavoidably detained for several days. He had left his gases, contained in inverted glasses, immersed in water, Mrs. Priestley being strictly charged that no one should touch them; and knowing what foes good housemaids are to philosophers, he had rung the bell, and himself specially enjoined the housemaid to disturb nothing in his study. *She* seems to have construed the injunction against disturbance into a precept that all should be put in order; so, to work she went, with a will; zeal without knowledge impelled her; and when Mrs. Priestley returned from a walk, profound was her dismay at finding all the gas glasses removed, carefully wiped, and put by on the shelf, the water thrown away, and the gas of course escaped.—"This is very wrong," exclaims Maynard, the recluse student, in Jerrold's drama of *The Housekeeper*, when he finds Felicia in his study, arranging his books and papers: "I told you never to enter my study." "I was only putting the things to rights," is her apology. And he bids her receive this as a solemn charge: "Never attempt to put anything to rights in this room—I prefer confusion." Then she urges a "But, sir, only look at the cobwebs and spiders!"— only to meet with the snubbing rejoinder that he is partial to cobwebs, and encourages spiders. Mr. Charles Reade begins a chapter of his admirable *Cloister and Hearth* with this discriminating notice of the hero's good housewifely mother: "A Catherine is not an unmixed good in a strange house.... She has scarce crossed the threshold ere the utensils seem to brighten; the hearth to sweep itself; the windows to let in more light; and the soul of an enormous cricket to animate the dwelling-place." But this cricket, he goes on to say, is a Busy-body; and *that* is a tremendous character: it has no discrimination; it sets everything to rights, and everybody. Now many things, Mr. Reade admits, are the better for being set to rights, but everything is not: everything is the one thing that won't stand being set to rights; except in that calm and cool retreat, the grave.

XXIX.

Book-shelves of all Dimensions.

ONE is interested in reading of the large or small libraries of eminent men, be their eminence what it may, whether in degree or in kind. Richard de Bury, Durham's great bishop of the fourteenth century, who kept in his palace an establishment of bookbinders, stationers, and illuminators, and who borrowed every book he could not buy, and caused it to be copied with all care, is said to have finally become possessed of more volumes than all the other bishops of England put together. In Colbert's library, a most extensive and valuable one, the manuscripts alone amounted to 14,300 volumes (which his grandson afterwards sold to the King). Not the least readable passages in Pepys' Diary are those which detail his gradual accumulation of additions to his bookshelves; as where he records a visit to St. Paul's Churchyard, to his bookseller's, where he called for twenty books, to be the product of "about 40s. or £3," which he had gained that day in the office by his stationer's bill to the King, and how he found himself at a great loss where to choose, "and do see how my nature would gladly return to the laying out of money in this trade. Could not tell whether to lay out my money for books of pleasure, as plays, which my nature was most earnest in, but at last, after seeing Chaucer, Dugdale's History of Paul's, Stow's London, Gesner, History of Trent, besides Shakspeare, Jonson, and Beaumont's plays, I at last chose Dr. Fuller's Worthys, the Cabbala, or Collections of Letters of State, and a little book, 'Delices de Hollande,' with another little book or two, all of good use or serious pleasure;* and Hudibras, both parts, the book now in greatest fashion for drollery, though I cannot, I confess, see enough where the wit lies," any more than our candid Samuel could see the merit of Shakspeare at his best, compared with certain then popular playwrights at their worst. A year later we read: "To my bookseller's, and there did give thorough direction for the binding of a great many of my old books, to make my whole study of the same binding, within very few." Hearty would be the zest with which he would display this decorative unity to his friends, though not in the spirit of La Bruyère's †

---

* Pepys's harmonized version of grave and gay is noticeable. He has just before described his nature as "most earnest" in love of plays; and here again we have "serious pleasure." He would fain be no trifler in his pursuit of the pleasurable.

† "Il me reçoit dans une maison où, dès l'escalier, je tombe en faiblesse d'une odeur de maroquin noir dont ses livres sont tous cou-

tasteless collector. Next day but one, here he is again: "To my bookseller's, and there took home Hook's book of Microscopy, a most excellent piece, and of which I am very proud." By-the-bye, he also took home a hare with him that day, purchased on his homeward route, and was cured of the colic by carrying about a jointed foot thereof. Next month again : " To Paul's Churchyard, there to see the last of my books bound ; among others, my ' Court of King James,' and 'The Rise and Fall of the Family of the Stewarts ;' and much pleased I am now with my study ; it being, methinks, a beautiful sight." By the end of July, 1666, it comes to this, that he has to call in "Simpson, the Joyner ; and he and I with great pains, contriving presses to put my books up in: they now growing numerous, and lying upon one another on my chairs, I lose the use to avoid the trouble of removing them, when I would open a book." Midway in September there are mishaps and misgivings. "Mightily troubled, even in my sleep, by missing four or five of my biggest books, Speed's Chronicle and Maps, and the two parts of Waggoner (? Wagenaer, *Speculum Nauticum*), and a book of cards. . . . My

---

verts. Il a beau me crier aux oreilles, pour me raninuer, qu'ils sont dorés sur tranche, ornés de filets d'or, et de la bonne édition, me nommer les meilleurs l'un après l'autre, dire que sa galerie est remplie, etc., . . . ajouter qu'il ne lit jamais, qu'il ne met pas le pied dans cette galerie," etc. La Bruyère retires with the resolve, "et ne veux, non plus que lui, visiter sa tannière, qu'il appelle bibliothèque."— *Caractères*, chap. xxiii.

books do heartily trouble me." Midway in December his record is : " Spent the evening in fitting my books, to have the number set upon each, in order to my having an alphabet of my whole, which will be of great ease to me." In the following April he is " away to the Temple, to my new bookseller's, and there I did agree for Rycaut's late History of the Turkish Policy, which cost me 55*s.*; whereas it was sold plain before the late fire for 8*s.*, and bound and coloured as this is, for 20*s.*; for I have bought it finely bound and truly coloured, all the figures, of which there was but six books done so, whereof the King and Duke of York, and Duke of Monmouth, and Lord Arlington, had four. The fifth was sold, and I have bought the sixth." *Io anche!* Again (April 15, 1667) : "I to my new bookseller's, and there bought ' Hooker's Polity,' the new edition [containing eight books instead of five, *plus* the Life by Izaak Walton], and Dugdale's ' History of the Inns of Court,' of which there was but a few saved out of the fire, and Playford's new Catch-book, that hath a great many new fooleries in it." The Ecclesiastical Polity and the new Catch-book in the same parcel : Mr. Pepys' taste is catholic. January 10th, 1667-68, brings him "to my new bookseller's, Martin's ; and here did meet with Fournier, the Frenchman, that hath wrote of the Sea Navigation, and I could not but buy him, and also bespoke an excellent book, which I met with there, of China. The truth is, I have bought a great many books lately to a great value; but I think to buy no more till Christmas next, and those that I have will so fill my two presses, that I must be forced to give away some, or make room for them, it being my design to have no more at any time for my proper library than to fill them." But, alas for a confirmed book-buyer's resolve to buy no more this side Christmas. Mr. Pepys does buy, and his purchase is hardly to his credit, but then happily he don't mean to keep it: (Feb. 8) "To the Strand, to my bookseller's, and there bought an idle, rogueish French book, which I have bought in plain binding, avoiding the buying of it better bound, because I resolve, as soon as I have read it, to burn it, that it may not stand in the list of books, nor among them, to disgrace them if it should be found." After which entry the Pepysian purchases of books, pretty well cease to find mention in the Diary.

We have seen *ce cher Samuel* in a bookseller's shop, embarrassed as to what choice to make, twenty volumes being the limit. To have lowered the limit, reducing it to its lowest terms, might or might not have increased his perplexity of choice. Many are the speculations extant in print, as well as continually recurrent in daily life, as to what books one would choose if restricted to some two or three. Let us glance at some of these. The Book of books is not to be lightly touched in this chance medley; let it be assumed that every believer in it would and must fix on that first, and apart from all others. "I have but one book," said poor Collins, in his crazy days, " but that is the best."

Speaker Onslow, in a note to Burnet's *History of his own Times*, says of Archbishop Sharp (of York) : " He was a great reader of Shakspeare. . . . He used to recommend to young divines the reading of the Scriptures and Shakspeare." Indeed he said that the Bible and Shakspeare made him Archbishop of York. Miss Mitford would rather give up all the other books that ever were written, retaining Shakspeare's alone, than sacrifice his and retain all the works of all other authors. But next to him she owned herself babyish enough to like the *Arabian Nights*. A distinguished French authoress said, that were she condemned to select three volumes for her whole library, the three would be, Bacon's Essays, the Bible, and Shakspeare.

The case has often been playfully imagined, observed Mr. de Quincey, that a man were restricted to one book ; and, supposing all books so solemn as those of a religious interest to be laid aside, many are the answers which have been pronounced, according to the difference of men's minds. Rousseau, on such an assumption, made his election for Plutarch.[*] Theodore Gaza, again, of note in the revival of letters,

---

[*] It was not altogether his taste, argues De Quincey, or his judicious choice, which decided Jean Jacques, but his limited reading,—influenced, too, by his thoroughly French education, though himself not French ; and he had the "usual puerile French craze about Roman virtue, and republican simplicity, and 'all that.' So that *his* decision goes for little."—De Quincey, *Philosophy of Herodotus* (1842).

being asked, in case of a general destruction of books, what author he would wish to save from the cataclysm, answered, Plutarch. It was her copy of Plutarch that Charlotte Corday reserved out of all her books, when starting from Caen on her mission of doom.

Schleiermacher said that were he called upon to save three works of antiquity only, not including the Bible, they should be no other than Homer, Herodotus, and Plato. Some people call Schleiermacher himself the German Plato. It was not the English Schleiermacher, nor an English one, though of the same "cloth," that owning once to an effusive little soul feminine and clerical-hero-worshipper his habit of carrying a book, a particular book, in his pocket, for reading in leisure hours, was greeted by his eager listener with an "Ah, yes," not without a hush of real awe in her voice,—" the Bible, of course!" Unluckily, it was the *Physiologie du Goût*. Clerics as well as laymen are not too sure to elect the book of books from all other books at all times. Miles Standish is typical in this respect, at a certain contingency of choice:

"Fixed to the opposite wall was a shelf of books, and among them
Prominent three, distinguished alike for bulk and for binding;
Bariffe's Artillery Guide, and the Commentaries of Cæsar, . . .,
And, as if guarded by these, between them was standing the Bible.
Musing a moment before them, Miles Standish paused, as if doubtful
Which of the three he should choose for his consolation and comfort,
Whether the wars of the Hebrews, the famous campaigns of the
    Romans,
Or the Artillery practice, designed for belligerent Christians.
Finally down from its shelf he dragged the ponderous Roman."

An eccentric Englishman whom Mr. Mereweather met in Java, and asked if he did not find it dull staying so long in a tiger-trap, with a rifle, sitting there as a bait, waiting for the beast, said, No, he took a book to beguile the time; and being asked what branch of literature, now, he selected for this critical position, gave as his favourite work, the *Sorrows* (or Sufferings, *Leiden*, it ought to be translated) *of Werther*. Home critics credit this gentleman with being also a student of another famous German hero—Baron Munchausen.

A philosophic writer, supposing the case of a man in Alexander Selkirk's position, empowered to import one book, and no more, into his insular hermitage, maintains the necessary exclusion of the most powerful of human books, for the following reason,—that in the direct ratio of its profundity will be the unity of any fictitious interest; a *Paradise Lost*, or a *King Lear*, could not agitate or possess the mind as they do, if they were at leisure to "amuse" us. So far from relying on its unity, the work which should aim at the *maximum* of amusement, ought, he argues, to rely on the *maximum* of variety. In that view it is that De Quincey urges the paramount pretensions of Herodotus; since not only are his topics separately of primary interest, each for itself, but they are collectively the most varied in the quality of that interest, and they are touched with the most flying and least lingering pen,—Herodotus being, of all writers, the most cautious not to trespass on his reader's patience.

After the Bible, Luther knew of no better books than the Fables of Æsop, and the writings of Cato. The favourite books of Charles the Fifth were an Italian translation of Thucydides, and the Memoirs of Philippe de Comines. Bishop Sanderson's pet triad consisted of Aristotle's Rhetoric, the *Secunda Secundæ* of Thomas Aquinas, and the *De Officiis* of Cicero, which last, as we learn from Izaak Walton, the fine old prelate had read over not less than twenty times, and could, when past seventy, repeat without book. It was with the Odes of Horace in his hand that Richard Hooker was found tending sheep by his old pupils, Edwin Sandys and George Cranmer; that was the good man's *vade mecum*. And one is always interested to know what book any good or any great man has been apt to advance to that degree of intimate companionship.

Alexander the Great called the Iliad a portable treasure of military knowledge; and the copy corrected by Aristotle, kept by day in a rich casket found among the spoils of Darius, (hence called in Plutarch* the "casket" copy,) he used to lay by night under his pillow with his sword. Plato was so fond of the mimes of Sophron that he had a copy of them under his pillow when he died. The only books that Dion

---

* "A casket being one day brought him, which appeared one of the most curious and valuable things among the treasures and the whole equipage of Darius, he asked his friends what they thought most worthy to be put in it? Different things were proposed; but he said, 'The Iliad most deserved such a case.'"—Plutarch, *Life of Alexander*.

Chrysostomus took with him into exile in what is now Moldavia, were the *Phædon* of Plato, and Demosthenes περὶ Παραπρεσβείας. The great Chrysostom is said by Aldus Manutius to have slept with the comedies of Aristophanes under his pillow.

Boniface made the treatise of Ambrose on the advantages of death his constant companion. Starting on a mission to Friesland, not for the first time, we read of him girding round him his black Benedictine habit, and depositing his Ambrose *De Bono Mortis* in the folds of it. This mission led to his martyrdom; and hagiology has its record of his copy of the *De Bono Mortis*, covered with blood, which was exhibited at Fulda, as a relic, during many succeeding centuries.

The *Gemma Ecclesiastica* of Giraldus Cambrensis was the book which the great Pope Innocent prized above all books. Next to his Bible and his Aristotle, like the student of Oxenford in the *Canterbury Tales*, as Mr. Brewer tells us, he kept the precious deposit at his bed's head,—deaf to entreaties for a loan of it,* on the part of cardinals and bishops. John II. of Castile used to have Mena's poems lying on his table, as regularly as his prayer-book.

---

* But a shrewd critic surmises that Pope Innocent may have kept the book to himself for fear of exposing the nakedness of the land,—unwilling that the world at large should know any part of the Church Universal to be in the state in which Giraldus seems to have found the Archdeaconry of St. David's.

A manuscript of the *Divine Comedy* was the constant companion of Michael Angelo, who was the first illustrator of Dante: it lay on his easel by day, and was thrust under his bolster by night. The treatise of Grotius *De Jure Belli et Pacis* was a favourite book of Gustavus Adolphus, who always carried it with him. Charles II. carried *Hudibras* about in his pocket.* Madame de Maintenon writes to Mdlle. de Lenclos, in 1666, to bid her present her compliments to M. de La Rochefoucauld, and tell him that the book of Job, and the book of *Maximes*, were her elect, her select, her sole reading. Of that little book of *Maximes*, Chesterfield tells his son that he would have him keep it as a *vade mecum*, and look into it, for some moments at least, every day of his life. On another occasion the noble lord advises Philip to let Madame de Sévigné's letters be one in his itinerant library. In *Waverley*, Sir Walter Scott makes capital—that is to say, gets interest out of— the story of an unfortunate Jacobite, who, escaping from gaol, was retaken as he hovered round the place, in the forlorn hope of recovering his favourite Titus Livius. Allan Ramsay exhorted the tenantry of Scotland, farmers of the dales, and storemasters

---

* "Butler," says Dennis, "was starved at the same time the King had the book in his pocket."
"Was not his book," says Colley Cibber, "always in the pocket of his prince?"

of the hills, to make a daily companion of his collection of proverbs, hoard of the wise sayings of their forefathers, to let them have a place on every bookshelf, "and may never a window-sole through the country be without them." That was the book he would choose for himself, and for them.

Robespierre used to carry Gessner in his pocket, when wandering under the trees of Meudon; a choice which induces some reflections by Lamartine on this strange contrast between the sentimentalism of the book and the cold obduracy of the peripatetic reader, who had thus the reveries and contemplations of a languid dreamer, amid scenes of unrelenting proscription and wholesale death.

André Chenier made the *Analecta* of Brunck, which appeared in 1776, his *livre de chevet et son bréviaire*.* Toussaint l'Ouverture made the works of his fellow-slave, Epictetus, his favourite manual.

In the library which Napoleon carried with him, there was a perpetual presence of Ossian, Werther, the New Heloïse, and the Old Testament; which Chateaubriand regards as indicative of the chaos in the Emperor's brain, where matter-of-fact ideas mingled

---

* He would expatiate upon it almost with the fervour of the elder Mr. Shandy on the subject of Slawkenbergius. "At matin, noon, and vespers, was Hafen Slawkenbergius his recreation and delight; 'twas for ever in his hands; you would have sworn, sir, it had been a canon's prayer-book, so worn, so glazed, so contrited and attrited was it with fingers and with thumbs, in all its parts, from one end even unto the other."—*Tristram Shandy*, vol. iii., ch. xlii.

with romantic sentiments, serious studies with the caprices of fancy. The book reserved by Chateaubriand himself, when he was forced to sell his country house and library, was a little Homer in Greek. A bigger Homer in Pope's English was the pet companion of our historian of Port Royal, in early life: "This book was never out of my pocket, except when in my hand,"—and the keen pleasure derived from it is asserted to have absorbed all others.

Frederick William IV., while Crown Prince of Prussia, sent word to Moore that he always slept with a copy of *Lalla Rookh* under his pillow. So at least the poet records in simplest good faith, and not at all in the fibbing style of malicious Peter Pindar, when that irrepressible assailant of Farmer George asserted that

"My verse so much His Majesty bewitches,
That out he pulls my honoured odes,
And reads them on the turnpike roads—
Now under trees and hedges—now in ditches,"

that is to say, when thrown out, "which often is the case," in hunting. Edward Irving used to refer in mid-life to "the venerable companion of my early days—Richard Hooker," with a copy of whose *Ecclesiastical Polity* he made delighted acquaintance in a farm-house near Annan. The late Dr. James Hamilton, writing from Broadstairs in 1849, professes to have continually in his pocket on starting for a seaside ramble a volume of his "unwearying companion," Spenser's *Faerie Queene.*

Coleridge declared that the book most frequently in his hands of any in his ragged book-regiment, was Southey's *Life of Wesley;* and to Southey he bequeathed his copy of it, on account of its marginal annotations. One of these contains the grateful apostrophe: "O dear and honoured Southey! this is the favourite of my library among many favourites, this the book which I can read for the twentieth time with delight, when I can read nothing else at all." A copy of the Iliad (which had belonged to the Abbé Barthelemy) was avowedly Paul Louis Courier's society, his sole companion, in the bivouac and the watch. J. M. W. Turner's travelling library consisted of Young's *Night Thoughts*, Izaak Walton, and some inferior translation of Horace.

But to return to the starting-point of the bookshelves of various note-worthies,—a starting-point abused from its proper meaning into the improper one of starting aside.

The musical Padre Martini had in his library some 17,000 volumes, of which 300 were MSS. of great rarity. Farinelli has the credit of having enabled him to purchase such a collection. Zaluski is by repute the largest private collector on record—more than a quarter of a million of volumes. Cavendish, the natural philosopher, fixed his "immense" library at a distance from his house, that he might not be disturbed by those who came to consult it. John Meerman, the Dutch historian, collected a library that was sold by auction for 131,000 florins.

Large as his own library was, Southey has his expression of interest in and liking for a small collection, when the collector is a simple lover if not a hard student of books; a Daniel Dove, for instance, whose "books were few in number, but were all weighty either in matter or in size;" consisting as they did of the Morte d'Arthur in the fine black-letter edition of Copeland; Plutarch's Morals, and Pliny's Natural History, "two goodly folios, full as an egg of meat;" the whole works of Joshua Sylvester (a name accented on the antepenultimate); Jean Petit's History of the Netherlands, Sir Kenelm Digby's Discourses, Stowe's Edward III., the Pilgrim's Progress, two volumes of Ozell's translation of Rabelais, Latimer's Sermons, and the last volume of Fox's Martyrs. When Montaigne, in the *Imaginary Conversations*, takes Joseph Scaliger into his library, the latter assumes it to be the antechamber to his library: "Here are your everyday books." "Faith! I have no other," is Montaigne's reply: "These are plenty, methinks; is not that your opinion?" "You have great resources within yourself," Scaliger answers, "and therefore can do with fewer."

"*Montaigne.*—Why, how many now do you think here may be?
Scaliger.—I did not believe at first that there could be above four-score.
Montaigne.—Well! are fourscore few? Are we talking of peas and beans?
Scaliger.—I and my father (put together) have written well-nigh as many."

But Julius Cæsar and Joseph are in no sense first cousins of Michael of the Mount.

Sainte-Beuve tells us of Soumet, *le beau* * *Soumet*, that he had, in all, only some seven or eight books in his library: Homer, the Æneid, Dante, Camoëns, Tasso, Milton, and *La Divine Épopée*, which, according to him, was a sufficing substitute for all previous *épopées*, and dispensed with all need of any future ones. "En fait de poëme épique, il n'y avait plus qu'à tirer l'échelle après lui." M. Soumet's epic has long since met the fate of epics a thousand and one.

When the great Dr. Radcliffe was asked by his Oxford visitor, Dr. Bathurst, the president of Trinity College, where was his library, he is said to have pointed to a few vials, a skeleton, and a herbal in one corner of his room, exclaiming with emphasis, "There, sir, is Radcliffe's library." Yet this was the man who left forty thousand pounds for the building of a library at Oxford, which he endowed with an annual stipend, of £150 for the librarian, £100 per annum for repairs, and the same sum for the purchase of books and manuscripts relating to the "science of physic"— under which term are comprehended anatomy, botany, surgery, and natural philosophy. The *mot*, "There, sir, is Radcliffe's library," reads like a varia-

---

* Not in the sense of Adam Smith's use of the term, when, to a friend who expressed surprise at the elegant binding of his books—the selection and decoration of which was his main amusement—the Doctor said, "You must have remarked that I am a beau in nothing but my books."

tion suggested by what Bonaventure said by way of answer to Thomas Aquinas, when the Angelical Doctor asked the great Franciscan to show him the library from which he had derived his remarkable stores of knowledge: Bonaventura pointed to the Crucifix, and said he had learnt all that he knew there. Then again there is the story of Descartes. Asked, while pursuing his anatomical studies, where was his library, the philosopher deemed it enough to show the querist a calf under dissection. Mackintosh, indeed, expressly classes Descartes under the "unreading" philosophers, who avoided books, lest they might stand between them and nature. Leibnitz was another, professedly, of these independent, self-relying spirits. An Italian admirer spent three weeks with him at Hanover, and was thus addressed by him at parting: "Sir, you have often been so good as to intimate that you regard me as a man of some knowledge. I will now show you the sources whence I drew it all." And taking his guest by the hand, he led him into his study, and showed him all the books he had. They were Plato, Aristotle, Plutarch, Sextus Empiricus, Euclid, Archimedes, Pliny, Seneca, and Cicero. If his library was small, Leibnitz seems, however, to have made good use of the few authors he consulted; and is known to have spent the best part of his nights as well as days in reading,—passing months together in his study, with injunctions against being interrupted.

Cowper bids Hayley, in 1792, bring with him any

books he thinks may be useful for the elder poet in his present labours; and adds: "And in truth, if you think that you shall want them, you must bring books for your own use also, for they are an article with which I am *heinously unprovided;* being much in the condition of the man whose library Pope describes as

> 'No mighty store!
> His own works neatly bound, and little more.'"

Patrick Henry's library is said by his biographer to have consisted at his death of only a few odd volumes. Kant had no more than some 450 volumes, the greater part of which consisted of presents: his access, officially, to the royal library of Königsberg made him practically indifferent to private stores; moreover, Hartknoch, his publisher, indulged him with the first sight of every new book that appeared. Perhaps 300 volumes are the number that De Quincey descried in a recess in Wordsworth's little parlour, at his first visit to the cottage afterwards his own. These occupied a little homely painted bookcase, fixed into a shallow recess on the side of the fireplace; ill bound they were, or not bound at all—in boards, sometimes in tatters; many of them imperfect as to the number of volumes,* as well as mutilated as to the number

---

* Like Mr. Benjamin's, in *Tom Jones.* "A book!" cries Benjamin, "what book will you have? Latin or English? I have some curious books in both languages; such as *Erasmi Colloquia,* Ovid *de Tristibus, Gradus ad Parnassum;* and in English I have several of the best books, though some of them are a little torn: but I have a great part of Stowe's *Chronicle;* the sixth volume of Pope's *Homer;* the third

of pages. Charles Lamb's library was eagerly inspected in 1824 by H. C. Robinson, who says of it in his Diary : " He has the finest collection of shabby books I ever saw ; such a number of first-rate works in very bad condition is, I think, nowhere to be found." Lord Cockburn tells us of Jeffrey's "library," that for a lover of books, and for one who had picked up a few, his collection was most wretched ; and so ill-cared-for that the want even of volumes never disturbed him.* He might almost, on this showing, have been represented by Pordage, in Oldham's imitation of Juvenal's third satire,—

"A box without a lid served to contain
Few authors, which made up his Vatican."

The English Opium-eater pictures himself, or at least bids the reader of his Confessions picture him, in a room seventeen feet by twelve, and not more than seven and a half feet high, in the Grasmere cottage that had been Wordsworth's before. It is ambitiously perhaps, but not unjustly, termed "the library," in his family talk ; for it happens, says he, " that books are the only article of property in which I am richer than

---

volume of the *Spectator;* the second volume of Echard's *Roman History ;* the *Craftsman ;* *Robinson Crusoe ;* Thomas à Kempis ; and two volumes of Tom Brown's works." (Chap. lxxxiv.)

* The science of binding he knew nothing about, and therefore despised, and most of his books were unbound. " These slatternly habits all arose from his believing that books were only meant to be read ; and that, therefore, so as their words were visible, nothing else was required."—*Life of Lord Jeffrey,* i., 368.

my neighbours. Of these I have about five thousand, collected gradually since my eighteenth year." Six thousand was the number of volumes, *très-variés*, which composed the *bibliothèque* of Voltaire. It afterwards became the property of Catherine the Great. Mrs. Chapone exclaimed, on hearing of Dr. Burney's difficulties about residence in Chelsea, and his fears of a removal, on account of his twenty thousand volumes, —" Twenty thousand volumes! bless me! why, how can he so encumber himself? Why does he not burn half? for how much must be to spare that never can be worth his looking at, from such a store! And can he want to keep them all? I should not have suspected Dr. Burney, of all men, of being such a Dr. Orkborne!" Perhaps Dr. Burney once thought as Mrs. Chapone did; but the lust of accumulating is imperious with gratification. Love for one's library is apt to grow with the growth of that library, however overgrown, or indeed the more because so overgrown. And even to a comparatively lukewarm collector of books, mere length of life ensures, year by year continually, a steady increment of volumes that surprises* in the long run, if it does

---

* One of John Foster's letters, on the eve of a removal, is concerned with, and expresses his concern at, the transit from Dourton towards Bristol of "a great number of packages of books. . . They have constituted one entire waggon load, and a material portion of two others. I was myself hardly aware of the quantity which had been brought by degrees into this dark den, till they were thus summoned all out from their obscure lodgments in chests, corners, and dust ; whence they have come

not bewilder, or even depress by its own weight, the senescent possessor. Nay, though he begin to collect on a rather large scale late in life, the aggregate soon waxes bulky beyond belief. Sydney Smith is an instance of the late-in-life book-buyer, who, having once made a substantial beginning that way, goes on that way rejoicing. His daughter testifies that one of the earliest uses he made of his increase of wealth when preferred to Combe Florey, was to enlarge his library; and that his books, which at Foston for many years had humbly occupied only the end of his little dining-room, now boldly spread themselves over three sides of a pretty odd room, dignified by the name of library. He used to say, "No furniture so charming as books, even if you never open them, or read a single word."

---

forth, reproaching me with an expense carried, for a succession of years, beyond all conscionable bounds." In other letters, however, he is at pains to justify himself as to his expenditure on even the most expensive of books.

To his aged mother he wrote, in the year of her death, a particular description of the "dark den" aforesaid. It was in a long garret, which in all its length was crowded and loaded with papers and books, intermingled with dust that was never swept away; and along the middle space of the floor he walked backwards and forwards for several hours daily,—to the systematic neglect of outdoor exercise.

XXX.

Good-bye to One's Books.

BOSWELL sentimentalizing rather lackadaisically on the strange unwillingness man feels to part with life, independent of serious fears as to futurity, and citing the instance of a reverend friend who felt a special uneasiness at the thought of leaving his study and his books, was answered by Johnson, "That is foolish in him. A man need not be uneasy on these grounds; for, as he will retain his consciousness, he may say with the philosopher, *Omnia mea mecum porto.*" True, replied Boswell, we may carry our books in our heads; but still there is something painful in the thought of leaving for ever what has given us pleasure. And he recalled his being years ago in melancholy mood, nay "distressed," at the thought of going into a state of being in which Shakspeare's poetry did not exist; and how an admired lady humoured his fancy, and actually relieved him by saying, "The first thing you will meet in the other world will be an elegant copy of Shakspeare's works presented to you." And Dr. Johnson is said to have smiled benignantly at this, and to have appeared not to disapprove of the notion.

In the Diary of John Evelyn we read how, on his visit to a synagogue of the Jews at Amsterdam, he looked through a narrow crevice of one of the sepulchres in the burying-ground, and "perceived divers books lye about a corpse, for it seems when any learned Rabbi dies, they bury some of his books with him." Even so would many a Christian bibliophile be buried; or rather, perhaps, instead of some, he would take all his books with him, if he could. To Henry Crabb Robinson, a guest at Keswick in 1816, Southey said, with great feeling, as he showed him his books, that he sometimes regarded them with pain, thinking what might hereafter become of them. Mr. Herman Merivale owns to the sense of a solemn and rather oppressive feeling, which attends an exposure of books for sale by auction, where the death is recent, and where the owner and collector was a man of this world, taking an interest in the everyday literature which occupies most of us more or less. There, for example, is the dead man's last unbound number of the *Quarterly*, where at such a page the paper-cutter rested from its work, the marginal notes ended, the influx of knowledge stopped, the chain of thought was snapped, the mental perceptions darkened. Can it be, the moralizing speculatist muses, that the active mind of our fellow-worker ceased then and there from that continuous exertion of so many years, and became that we wot not of—a living Intelligence, still of ourselves it may be, but removed into another sphere, with which its habitual region of labour—the cycle in which it moved and had its being—had no connection whatever? Must it be, as Charles Lamb so quaintly expresses it, that "knowledge now comes to him, if it come at all, by some awkward experiment of intuition, and no longer by this familiar process of reading?" It was to Baxter himself, in his *Dying Thoughts*, a grievous thought, that, in dying, he must depart, not only from sensual delights, but from the more manly pleasures of his studies, and from all the delights of reading; that he must leave his library, and turn over those pleasant books no more. Not he the man to be insensible, even at the last, to the yearning wistfulness of Elia's lament: "And you, my midnight darlings, my Folios! must I part with the intense delight of having you (huge armfuls) in my embraces?" Wistful as the piteous outcry of moribund Mazarin in his library,—*Il faut quitter tout cela!* "Que j'ai eu de peine à acquérir ces choses! puis-je les abandonner sans regret?... *Je ne les verrai plus ou je vais.*" It is only the spirit of Sir Thomas More, raised by Southey, that holds out the hope of what Macaulay calls a Paradise Press, in which all the best English works are reprinted as regularly as in Philadelphia,—*Thalaba* and *Kehama* presumably among the number. Southey himself must often have felt what Wordsworth feelingly describes:

> "Tremblings of the heart
> It gives, to think that our immortal being
> No more shall need such garments; and yet man,
> As long as he shall be the child of earth,
> Might almost 'weep to have' what he may lose,
> Nor be himself extinguish'd, but survive,
> Abject, depress'd, forlorn, disconsolate."

Samuel Rogers had next to no sympathy with any such vagaries of wistful forecast. Displaying his literary treasures once to H. Crabb Robinson, the latter asked him, in his frank way, "What is to become of them?" "The auctioneer," said Rogers, "will find out the fittest possessor hereafter. He who gives money for things, values them." H. C. R.'s feelings, Dr. Sadler tells us, were exactly the reverse. He had the greatest anxiety that nothing which had belonged to him should be sold.* A Commonplace

---

* In this respect resembling, although in the salient points of character utterly without resemblance to, the languid, self-occupied Mr. Ochterlony, in *Madonna Mary*, who says of his cherished possessions, when aware that a warrant of death is out for speedy execution against him,—says it, gasping for breath, as he eyes them regretfully, and appeals to his heir: "One can't take them with one, and you will not care for them much, Hugh; . . . but I'd rather you did not sell them, if you could make up your mind to the sacrifice." (Chap. xxx.)

In *Romola*, again, Tito has to employ all his most plausible sophistry to try to reconcile his wife to the dispersion by sale of her father's endeared library. "If I believed it could now pain your father to see his library preserved and used in a rather different way from what he had set his mind on, I should share the strictness of your views." But a little philosophy, he submits, should teach us to rid ourselves of those air-woven fetters that mortals hang round themselves, spending their lives in misery under the mere imagination of weight. Is not the very dispersion of valuable books, Tito would ask his Romola, "in hands that know how to value them, one means of extending their usefulness?" Was not the loss of Constantinople the gain of the whole civilized world?—See *Romola*, ii. 132.

Philosopher's advice is, Enjoy your parcel of new books when it comes; cut the leaves peacefully, and welcome in each volume a new companion; but do not worry yourself by the reflection that when you die, the little library you collected may perhaps be scattered; and the old friendly-looking volumes fall into no one knows whose hands; perhaps be set forth on outdoor bookstalls, or be exhibited on the "top of a wall, with a sack put over them when it begins to rain, as in a place which I have seen."

During the four years' struggle which ended in his bankruptcy, William Roscoe, as the kindly biographer of Northern Worthies phrases it, "alienated those treasures of art and learning which it had been the pride and pleasure of his life to gather together." Books and pictures all went, rather to testify his honour, than to satisfy creditors. And nothing, it has been said, can better show the composure or the vigour of his mind, under these trials, than the admired sonnet with which he took leave of his library:—

> "As one who, destined from his friends to part,
> Regrets their loss, yet hopes again erewhile
> To share their converse and enjoy their smile,
> And tempers, as he may, affliction's dart—
> Thus, loved associates! chiefs of elder art!
> Teachers of wisdom, who could once beguile
> My tedious hours, and brighten every toil,
> I now resign you, nor with fainting heart: *

---

* Late in his last illness, John Foster's son exulted in the thought of being soon in a world where knowledge will beam into the soul without

For, pass a few short years, or days, or hours,
And happier seasons may their dawn unfold,
And all your sacred fellowships restore ;
When, freed from earth, unlimited its powers,
Mind shall with mind direct communion hold,*
And kindred spirits meet, to part no more."

the slow labour of difficult acquisition. This seems to have comforted his father under sad reflections on the now sensibly lessened interest he felt in his own accumulation of valuable books. "He needs now no such means of knowledge. And how many things by this time he knows which no books can tell ! "

* A clerical northern worthy, farther north, begins a thoughtful discourse on the words of apocalyptic vision, "And I saw no temple therein," with the confession that this sentence falls somewhat blankly on the ear, and is somewhat of a disappointment. For he finds a first feeling of sadness in the assurance, as he bethinks him that the most pleasing feature in the most pleasant summer landscape, is the spire of the country church rising above green trees into the blue sky—a little sanctuary amid its quiet expanse of green graves ; and that the noblest edifices in the world are, as they ought to be, the temples dedicated to divine worship,—cathedrals, "unutterably solemn and majestic." His first feeling is of strangeness, in the intimation that the place where in this world, as worshippers, we have known most of the peace of heaven, should not be there. But soon he recognizes the reason, and is reconciled by the reasonableness of it : no temple in heaven, because all heaven is hallowed into a most true temple by the all-pervading presence of our God and Redeemer.

Acton Bell's tenant of Wildfell Hall owns to an inability to contemplate with delight the prospect of losing familiar endearments in a sea of glory ; but can see and say, notwithstanding, that as we grow up, children and childish that we are, our minds will become so enlarged and elevated that we shall come to regard as trifling the objects we now so fondly cherish. In his *Hall of Fantasy*, Nathaniel Hawthorne is eloquent with regrets at the destiny of this "poor old Earth" herself—at the doom of that very earthliness, which no other sphere or state of existence can renew or compensate -the innumerable enjoyable things of earth, which must perish with her. He fears, in his quaintly meditative way, of melancholy nearly all compact, that no other world can show us anything just like this. As for purely moral enjoyments, the good will find them in every state of being ; but where the material and the moral exist together, what is to happen then? Might it not be lawful to regret one's books, for instance, even in the groves of Paradise? If it be objected that in all this he speaks like the very spirit of earth, imbued with a scent of freshly-turned soil, he only cares to answer, that it is not that he so much objects to giving up these enjoyments on his own account, but he hates to think that they will have been eternally annihilated from the list of joys. Another muser bids him doubt not that man's disembodied spirit may recreate Time and the World for itself, with all their peculiar enjoyments, should there still be human yearnings amid the eternal and infinite—while owning himself dubious whether we shall then be inclined to play such a poor scene over again.

INDEX.

A.

Abelard, 20
About, Edm., 412
Addison, 3, 56, 85, 109, 202, 246, 251, 351
Akenside, 356
Alfieri, 11
Ampère, 79
Andreini, Isab., 386
Andrieux, 216
Antoninus, Marcus, 63
Apperley, C. J., 402
Arblay, Mdme. d', 82, 339
Ariosto, 268, 289, 293, 391
Arne, Dr., 217
Arouet, 211, 213
Aubigné, Agr. d', 425
Aubrey, 1
Audoin, 216
Austen, Jane, 348, 439
Author's Den, 452 sq.
Authorship in the Act, 1 sq.
Authorship, Transparent, 405 sq.
Autobiography, Unconscious, 415
Aytoun, W. E., 48, 203, 414

B.

Bacon, Lord, 369
Bagehot, W., 66, 185, 190, 415
Bailey, P. J., 219
Baillie, Joanna, 74, 188
Balzac, H. de, 216, 253, 290, 400, 446

Barnard, Lady A., 400
Barrow, Isaac, 352
Barton, B., 28, 197, 234, 392
Bayle, 77, 145, 262, 280
Beaumont, F., 207 ; G. de, 422
Beckford, W., 272, 340
Beethoven, 118
Behn, Afra, 24
Bembo, 264, 276
Bentham, Jer., 212, 185
Béranger, 11, 170, 224, 294
Berni, 276
Beyle, H., 292, 294, 386
Black, W., 361
Blair, Dr. H., 268
Blake, Wm., 112, 187
Blunt, Prof. J. J., 249
Boccaccio, 223
Boileau, 29, 156, 209, 259, 379
Bolingbroke, 81, 86, 381
Bonald, De, 181
Bonaly, 123
Boniface, 468
Book-built Castles in the Air, 269 sq.
Booking a Place for all Time, 368 sq.
Bookish, 51 sq. ; in Talk, 79 sq.
Book Marks : Local and Incidental, 115 sq. Marginal and Miscellaneous, 99 sq.
Books, Enthralling, 334 sq.
Books, Good-bye to One's, 480 sq.
Book-shelves of all Dimensions, 459 sq.

INDEX

Bookworm, Trail of the, 84 sq.
Boswell, James, 31, 81, 369, 480
Bougainville, 209
Boyd, A. K. H., 351, 404, 484
Brahé, Tycho, 206
Brant, Seb., 321
Bronté, A., 484
Bronté, C., 15, 146, 346, 361, 432
Brooks, C. Shirley, 348
Brougham, 277, 285
Brown, C. B., 208, 273
Brown, Dr. John, 424
Brown, Dr. Thos., 245, 350, 454
Browne, Sir T., 51
Browning, E. Barrett, 72, 73, 243, 355
Browning, Robert, 114
Brownlow, Countess, 197
Bryant, Jacob, 268
Brydges, Sir Eg., 410
Buffon, 187, 210, 289, 418
Burgess, Bp., 105
Burke, E., 144, 286, 326, 339
Burney, Dr., 288, 478
Burns, R., 10, 111, 117, 225, 252
Butler, S., 6, 58, 199, 391, 400, 469
Buxton, Sir T. F., 52
Byron, Lord, 56, 112, 242, 253, 259, 291, 329, 331, 368, 376, 395, 447

C.

Campbell, Dr. G., 207
Campbell, T., 406
Canning, G., 387
Carlyle, T., 8, 124, 156, 161, 212, 220, 236, 260, 265, 273, 330, 351, 368, 373, 452
Carrel, A., 11, 232
Cassius of Parma, 256
Castlereagh, Ld., 25
Cavendish, 472
Cellini, B., 307
Cervantes, 247, 322, 394
Chalmers, Dr. T., 21, 330
Chambers, R., 21, 252

Channing, W. E., 14, 125, 311, 401
Chapelle, 290
Chapone, Mrs., 478
Charrière, Mdme. de, 145
Charron, 54
Chateaubriand, 5, 119, 294, 370, 382, 393, 471
Chatterton, 88
Chaucer, 86, 91, 352
Chesterfield, Ld., 80, 143, 352, 469
Churchill, 64, 164, 379, 427
Cicero, 257
Clusius, 206
Cluverius, 207
Cobbett, W., 262, 280
Cockburn, H., 123, 229, 453
Colbert, 459
Coleridge, Hartley, 2, 11, 82, 100, 113, 233, 337, 443
Coleridge, S. T., 18, 96, 99, 108, 137, 163, 189, 223, 298 sq., 390, 472
Collingwood, Ld., 426
Collins, Wm., 464
Collins, W. W., 203, 452
Collins, W'm., R.A., 25
Combe, Dr. A., 120
Comestor, Peter, 84
Commercial Failures, 221 sq.
Cormontaigne, 22
Corneille, P., 206, 245, 391
Cottle, Joseph, 301
Courier, P. L., 293, 408, 472
Cousin, V., 155, 382
Cowper, W., 21, 28, 73, 124, 151, 215, 217, 266, 283, 328, 371, 475
Crabbe, G., 24, 241, 443
Cromwell, O., 205
Cujas, 4
Cumberland, R., 29, 116
Cunningham, Allan, 397, 411
Cuvillier-Fleury, 386

D.

Dallas, E. S., 252
Dana, R. H., 446
Dancourt, 206

Dante, 445, 469
D'Arcet, 216
D'Argens, 216
Darley, G., 226
Darwin, Er., 3
De Foe, 411
Demogeot, 325
Demosthenes, 277
Dennis, John, 353, 455
Descartes, 475
Dibdin, C., 19
Dickens, C., 358, 360, 403, 447
Diderot, 186, 206, 272
Diodati, 61
Disraeli, B., 64, 185, 192, 219, 239, 433, 437
Disraeli, Isaac, 84, 169, 227, 281, 384
Dorat, 211
Döring, 7
Dowdy Wives, 192
Dryden, 151, 161, 244, 258, 308, 376, 436
Dugdale, 91
Dunbar, W., 374
D'Urfey, 206
Dusting the Study, 453 sq.
Dyer, G., 95, 188

E.

Eagles, Rev. John, 360
Elliot, G., 67, 454, 483
Elliott, Ebenezer, 447
Emerson, R. W., 74, 138, 143
Epictetus, 53
Erasmus, 1, 418
Ercilla, 22
Etty, W., 120
Evelyn, J., 481

F.

Fairfax, 278
Fame, True, 390 sq.
Faria, 271
Fayette, Mdme. de la, 318
Feltham, O., 61
Fenélon, 271
Ferrier, Miss, 348
Feugère, L., 432

Fiction appealing to Facts, 444 sq.
Fiction, Personality in—428 sq.
Fielding, H. 151, 239, 343, 429
Fontenelle, 209
Foote, S., 206
Foster, John, 127, 157, 285, 478, 484
Fox, C. J., 72
Francis, Saint, 221
Francis, Sir P., 287
Franklin, B., 455
Frederick the Great, 156, 374
Fresnoy, 285
Fuller, Margaret, 126
Fuller, Thos., 2

G.

Galiani, 327
Galt, J., 222, 226, 345
Gaskell, Mrs., 68, 171, 186
Gay, J., 230, 327
Gaza, Theodore, 464
George I., 197
George II., 353
George III., 355, 471
German Milton, A very, 364 sq.
Gessner, 327, 470
Gibbon, E., 28, 79, 87—91, 115, 271, 328, 366, 377, 424
Gibbon, John, 378
Giraldus Cambrensis, 468
Glück, 19
Goethe, 18, 29, 72, 190, 194, 254, 261, 337, 342
Gogol, 17
Goldsmith, O., 6, 147, 148, 154, 160, 283, 309, 357, 405, 429
Gongora, 206
Good-bye to One's Books, 480 sq.
Gore, Mrs., 141, 222, 438
Gray, T., 12, 59, 92, 266, 284
Gresset, 72, 246
Grimm, Baron, 243, 325
Guicciardini, 357
Guizot, 79

H.

Haliburton, 63, 169, 355, 366
Hall, Robt., 292

INDEX

Hallam, H., 276, 412
Hamilton, Dr. J., 97, 471
Hamilton, Gerald, 286
Hamilton, Sir Wm., 220, 345
Hamley, Col., 414
Handel, 19
Hard Crust, A, 160 sq.
Harry, 257
Hare, J. C., 191
Hawthorne, N., 61, 107, 121, 314, 484
Haydon, B. R., 30
Hayley, W., 150, 158, 215, 329
Hazlitt, W., 18, 52, 54 sq., 66, 80, 104, 123, 176, 292, 341, 390, 417
Heine, H., 188, 217, 427
Helluo librorum, 84 sq.
Helps, Sir A., 149, 174, 446
Henry, Mat., 207
Henry, Patrick, 476
Herodotus, 426, 466
Hobbes, 2
Hoffmann, 136, 260
Hogarth, 69, 233
Holmes, O. W., 65, 76, 177, 181, 195, 198, 247, 433, 446
Homer, 467
Hood, T., 23, 49, 69, 392
Hook, Theodore, 141
Hooker, Rd., 381, 467, 471
Horace, 25 6, 391, 410
Horsley, Bp., 338
Huet, 207
Hume, D., 210, 230, 285
Hunt, Leigh, 31, 92 sq., 108, 119, 140, 143, 181, 191, 218, 241, 298, 336, 359

I

Imitatione Christi, De, 319 sq.
Immortality, Literary, 368 sq.
Irving, Rev. Ed., 22, 131, 471
Irving, Washington, 13, 23, 120, 126, 147, 161, 173, 218, 310, 336, 337, 405, 456

J

Jacobi, F. H., 231

Jago, 385
James, G. R. P., 442
Jasmin, 187
Jefferson, 98
Jeffrey, F., 146, 229, 477
Jerdan, W., 218, 226
Jerrold, D., 14, 30, 457
Jodelle, 258
Johnson, Dr. S., 6, 64, 81, 85, 143, 150, 156, 180, 251, 268, 284, 309, 339, 349, 357, 367, 369, 408, 480
Jones, Sir W., 308
Jonson, Ben, 203, 278, 289, 301, 355, 410, 425
Joubert, 422
Juvenal, 166

K

Kant, 336, 476
Keightley, 125
Kensington Gardens, 119
King, Wm., 85
Kingsley, C., 60, 77, 415, 419
Kippis, Dr., 57
Kisfaludy, 3
Klopstock, 364, 366

L

La Bruyère, 280, 324, 460
Lacordaire, 208, 330
La Fontaine, Jean, 148, 272, 291
Lalande, 210
Lamartine, 228, 293
Lamb, C., 75, 95, 100, 164, 305, 356, 395, 425, 477, 482
La Mothe, 87, 200
Landon, L. E., 414
Landor, W. S., 49, 70, 119, 191, 259, 267
Lapses in Law, 202 sq.
Larra, 217
Law, Lapses in, 202 sq.
Layard, A. H., 220
Leibnitz, 116, 475
Leighton, Archbp., 101
Le Maître, 19
Lenette, 179, 186
Lermontov, 431

INDEX. 491

Le Sage, 155, 322, 394
Leslie, C., 207
Lessing, 7, 53
Lewes, G. H., 29, 147, 234, 254, 352, 395, 418
Libraries, 459 *sq.*
Library, Circulating, 96
Literary Society, 128 *sq.*
Literature as a Trade, 164
Lloyd, R., 162
Locke, 51, 224
Locker, F., 336
Lockhart, J. G., 331, 396, 440
Longfellow, 186, 244, 315, 465
Lonsdale, Bp., 287
Lope de Vega, 258
Louvet, 228
Lowell, J. R., 53
Luther, 117, 320
Luttrell, H., 50
Lytton, Lord, 25, 49, 57, 76, 106, 121, 166, 176, 190, 193, 194, 198, 221, 240, 242, 326, 359, 375, 380, 405, 412, 445
Lytton, Robert, Hon., 69, 239, 241

M.

Macaulay, Lord, 64, 110, 345, 356, 362, 363, 381, 482
Mackenzie, H., 248
Mackintosh, Sir J., 66
Magliabecchi, 84
Mahony, Rev. F., 391
Malherbe, 265, 279
Mallet, D., 309
Malone, E., 110, 150, 214
Mansfield, Ld., 208
Mansoni, 330
Marcellus, 138
Marginalia, 99 *sq.*
Marivaux, 419
Marmontel, 249
Marot, 14
Marryat, Capt., 178
Marsh, Prof., 422
Martial, 181, 256
Martin, Th., 48, 203
Masks and Faces, 235 *sq.*

Mason, W., 12, 372
Massillon, 208
Masson, D., 67, 278, 363, 403
Mathews, C., 30
Maturin, 23
Maurice, F. D., 419
Mazarin, 482
Melendez, 213
Ménage, 208
Mereweather, 466
Merivale, H., 108, 481
Metaphor, 245
Michelet, 320
Mill, J. S., 180
Miller, J. M., 413
Millevoye, 227
Millingen, 231
Milton, 61, 70, 178, 246, 261, 278, 366
Mitford, M. R., 145, 172, 226, 263, 402, 423, 464
Mitford, W., 215
Moir, G., 248
Molière, 27, 151, 195, 198, 199, 224, 259, 298, 435
Montagu, Lady M. W., 153, 336, 343
Montaigne, 62, 146, 282, 473
Moore, T., 9, 32, 50, 74, 80, 119, 242, 253, 342, 352, 398, 471
More, Hannah, 193, 247
More, Henry, 281

N.

Necker, 325
Niebuhr, 104, 280
Nisard, D., 409
Noctes Ambrosianæ, 11, 25
Nodier, C., 203, 291

O.

Oehlenschläger, 207
O'Keeffe, 37
Oldham, J., 170, 278, 477
Oliphant, Mrs., 75, 483
Overbury, Sir T., 205
Ovid, 203, 244, 251, 371, 383

P.

Pangs in Print, 244 sq.
Paper-sparing, 102 sq.
Parr, Dr., 158
Pascal, 279
Pasquier, E., 279
Patru, 279
Peacock, T. L., 141, 298
Pedant, 55 sq.
Pellisson, 101
Pepys, S., 459 sq.
Personality in Fiction, 428 sq.
Petrarch, 118, 205, 275
Petty Economies, 103
Pinkerton, 215
Piron, 213
Planche, G., 295
Plato, 9, 277, 352, 467
Pliny, 76
Plotinus, 7
Plutarch, 256, 263, 411
Polevoy, 96, 234
Pombal, 210
Ponsard, 185
Poole, J., 380
Pope, A., 51, 57, 74, 102, 149, 202, 283, 290, 353, 358
Porson, 117
Porson, 106
Portraiture, Literary, 437 sq.
Posterity, Appeal to, 376 sq.

Q.

Quillinan, E., 255
Quincey, Thomas de, 13, 78, 128 sq., 137, 156, 189, 219, 305, 319, 323, 382, 421, 464, 466, 476, 477

R.

Rabelais, 348
Rabutin, Bussy, 156
Racine, 194, 238, 323
Radcliffe, Dr., 474
Radcliffe, Mrs., 248
Reade, C., 60, 238, 349, 458
Ready Writers, 256 sq.
Réaumur, 207

Reid, Dr. T., 296
Rémusat, 272
Reynolds, Sir J., 339
Ricardo, D., 306
Richard de Bury, 459
Richardson, S., 345
Richter, Jean Paul, 8, 26, 179, 280, 293
Riddell, Mrs. J. H., 71
Ritchie, L., 234
Rivarol, 63, 241
Robespierre, 293, 470
Robinson, H. C., 96, 99, 165, 481, 483
Robinson, Mrs. A., 157
Rochefoucauld, La, 265, 279, 410, 469
Rogers, Alex., 25
Rogers, S., 72, 158, 171, 264, 291, 355, 483
Roland, Mdme., 24
Romilly, Sir S., 228
Roscoe, W., 385, 484
Roscoe, W. Caldwell, 67, 346, 359, 433
Rousseau, J. J., 4, 5, 19, 105, 118, 135, 144, 183, 186, 259, 289, 325, 336, 341, 343, 430, 464
Rückert, 413
Run upon a Book, 317 sq.
Ruskin, J., 77

S.

Sacy, De, 97, 359
Sainte-Beuve, 67, 225, 251, 265, 270, 272, 299, 376, 411, 428, 431, 435, 474
Sand, G., 25, 313, 438, 453
Sanderson, Bp., 467
Sarpi, P., 4
Sarti, 19
Saturday Review, 99, 154, 182, 361, 376, 413, 438, 444
Savage, M. W., 104
Savage, R., 282
Scaliger, Joseph, 473
Schemings, Literary, 296 sq.
Schiller, 7, 18, 135, 206, 330, 348, 364, 407

INDEX.

Schimmelpenninck, M. A., 3, 112, 127
Schlegel, A. W., 245
Schlegel, F., 231
Schleiermacher, 29, 337, 465
Schyppe of Fooles, 321
Scott, Sir Walter, 15, 17, 24, 70, 85, 122, 140, 149, 233, 238, 240, 260, 330, 331, 341, 345, 347, 358, 395, 435, 436, 440, 455, 469
Scott, Lady, 187
Scribe, E., 206, 270
Scudery, Mdlle. de, 428
Segni, 204
Selden, L., 205
Self-heard in Song, 40 *sq.*
Self-seen in Print, 27 *sq.*
Senior, W. N., 331
Sévigné, Mdme. de, 134, 249, 469
Seward, Miss, 150
Shaftesbury, Lord, (Characteristics,) 27, 280
Shakspeare, 56, 67, 92, 93, 152, 261, 351 *sq.*, 374, 415, 464
Sharp, Archbp., 464
Shelley, P. B., 12, 185, 189
Shenstone, 97
Sheridan, R. B., 286, 288
Sidney, Sir P., 322, 363, 408
Siebenkäs, 179
Simile, 245
Simson, 117
Sismondi, 212
Smeaton, 213
Smith, Adam, 129, 271, 361, 474
Smith, Alex., 423
Smith, Anker, 207
Smith, Charlotte, 132
Smith, Sydney, 58, 270, 273, 334, 426, 479
Smollett, 132, 336, 436
Solis, A. de, 205
Songs, Hearing one's, 40 *sq.*
Soulié, F., 217
Soumet, 474
South, Dr. R., 246
Southey, R., 108, 132, 134, 158, 162, 171, 267, 284, 300, 367, 411, 421, 422, 472, 473, 482

Spedding, 110
Spencer, Herbert, 420
Spenser, E., 93, 363
Staël, Mdme. de, 19, 24, 259, 431
Stephen, Sir J., 18
Sterling, John, 273
Sterne, 180, 470
Stockdale, P., 384
Stowe, Mrs. H. B., 58, 187, 331, 349, 351
Style bespeaks the Man, 417 *sq.*
Surrey, Earl of, 322
Swift, 32, 102, 283, 312, 325, 327, 335

T.

Talfourd, 95, 164, 354
Talk, Bookish, 79 *sq.*
Talleyrand, 197
Tartini, 217
Tasker, Dr., 157
Tasso, 205, 281
Taylor, Jane, 15, 292
Taylor, W., 228
Tennyson, A., 107, 110, 196, 225
Thackeray, W. M., 59, 142, 149, 163, 167, 185, 188, 208, 235, 239, 262, 346, 351, 370, 436, 453
Theobald, L., 215
Thérèse, (Rousseau's,) 183, 186
Thomson, J., 168, 290, 298
Thrale, Mrs., 106, 329, 336
Thurlow, Lord, 379
Tieck, 435
Tocqueville, De, 79, 196, 263, 353
Tollens, 231
Traces and Tokens of True Fame, 390 *sq.*
Transparent Authorship, 405 *sq.*
Trenck, Baron, 329
Trollope, Ant., 222, 242, 358
Trollope, T. Ad., 386, 450
True Fame, 390 *sq.*
Turner, J. M. W., 104, 472
Tytler, P. F., 218, 312

U.

Unread and Unreadable, 350 *sq.*
Urfé, D', 429

V.

Valesius, 208
Varchi, 204
Vaugelas, 279, 282
Vicenti, Gfi, 206
Vico, 209
Vigny, A. de, 295
Villemain, 257, 437
Vinet, Alex., 135
Virgil, 1, 289
Voiture, 155, 279
Voltaire, 105, 156, 206, 212, 267, 270, 352, 478

W.

Walker, T., 13
Waller, E., 266, 291
Walpole, H., 59, 144, 149, 324, 336, 371
Warburton, Bp., 105
Ward, Artemus, 353
Ward, Rev. John, 421
Warton, Dr. J., 310
Watson, Dr., 268
Watt, J., 116
Wellington, Duke of, 22

Werther, 254, 395
West, R., 209
Whitefield, 117, 126
Wilberforce, W., 18, 117
Wilkes and Liberty, 400
Wilson, John, 13, 130, 345, 369
Winkelmann, 97
Wives, Unlettered, 176 *sq*.
Wolcot, 471
Wood, Ant. à, 91 *sq*.
Wordsworth, 18, 68, 72, 73, 78, 151, 296 *sq*., 344, 375, 476, 483

Y.

Young, Arthur, 231
Young, Dr. E., 60, 207, 280
Yriarte, 211

Z.

Zacharie, 213
Zaluski, 472
Zeluco, 112
Zeuxis, 263
Zhukovsky, 413
Zorilla, 218

www.ingramcontent.com/pod-product-compliance
Lightning Source LLC
Chambersburg PA
CBHW051200300426
44116CB00006B/381